Jumping the Queue

Jumping the Queue

An Inquiry into the Legal Treatment of
Students with Learning Disabilities

MARK KELMAN
GILLIAN LESTER

Harvard University Press
Cambridge, Massachusetts
London, England   1997

Library of Congress Cataloging-in-Publication Data

Kelman, Mark.
Jumping the queue : an inquiry into the legal treatment of
students with learning disabilities / Mark Kelman, Gillian Lester.
   p. m.
Includes bibliographical references and index.
ISBN 0-674-48909-8 (alk. paper)
1. Learning disabled children—Legal status, laws, etc.—United
States.   2. Special education—law and legislation—United States.
I. Lester, Gillian.   II. Title.
KF4215.K45   1997
344.73'0791—dc21   97-27488

Designed by Gwen Nefsky Frankfeldt

To Ann, Jake, and Nick

—M.K.

To my parents, and Eric

—G.L.

Contents

Acknowledgments

We began work on this book so long ago that all we can do is hope that the people we need to thank still remember us. Above all, we need to express our appreciation to the special educators and special education administrators we interviewed, for supplying us with both information and a good deal of inspiration.

We are also grateful to our terrific, smart, and energetic research assistants—Marc Bennett, Jennifer DiToro, David Fallas, Ethan Millar, Aaron O'Donnell, Eric Talley, Christine Wade, Shirley Wang, and Lauren Willis—for their help, and to Karen Mathews for secretarial assistance. One of us (MK) has received generous financial research support, over the years, from the Stanford Legal Research Fund, made possible by a bequest from Ira S. Lillick and by gifts from other friends of Stanford Law School; the other (GL) has received generous support from the Laidlaw Foundation, the UCLA Institute of Industrial Relations, the UCLA Academic Senate and Office of the Chancellor, the UCLA Law School Dean's Fund, and the Social Sciences and Humanities Research Council of Canada. In addition, the fieldwork in Louisiana and Mississippi was funded by Stanford's Center for Research on Legal Institutions, and a portion of the statistical research on state disparities in the diagnosis and placement of pupils with learning disabilities was funded by the John M. Olin Program in Law and Economics at Stanford. In that regard, we are especially appreciative of all that Lawrence Friedman and Mitch Polinsky have done generally to facilitate empirical research at Stanford.

Many colleagues have been generous with comments, most particularly Rick Abel, Ian Ayres, Joe Bankman, Craig Becker, John Bogart, George Brown, Evan Caminker, Virginia Flack, Barbara Fried, Robert Goldstein, Bob Gordon, Laura Gómez, Mark Grady, Tom Grey, Janet Halley, Joel Handler, Hank Levin, Martha Matthews, Steve Munzer, Grant Nelson, Rick Sander, Gary Schwartz, Seana Shiffrin, Bill Simon, Clyde Spillenger, Eric Talley, Bernice Wong, and Steve Yeazell. We have benefited from comments made by workshop participants at Harvard, Stanford, UCLA, and Yale law schools and the UCLA Institute of Industrial Relations.

Above all, we thank our families. Mark Kelman is grateful to his parents, Kurt and Sylvia Kelman, his wife, Ann Richman, and his children, Nick and Jake. He loved working on this book, but it's nothing compared with spending time with them. Gillian Lester is grateful for the love and friendship of Eric Talley and of her parents, Richard and Lois Lester.

Originally, fifteen years ago, a learning disabled child had to have a normal IQ and an achievement area that was low . . . Now—and this may be only characteristic of *our* state in an effort to help *our* children—you may have a child that has a 72 IQ and an achievement in the 50s . . . So, in an effort to help more children, you're going to say that this kid has a learning disability so that we can give him some special ed assistance that we normally would not be able to do without the eligibility. When you really look at it, is he really learning disabled? I don't know.

[Sometimes, though, we simply can't find a discrepancy and the kid is just slow, but not mentally retarded . . .] Regular ed is supposed to capture him . . . Are there kids who fall through the cracks? Yeah . . . How often do we evaluate these kids? All the time . . . I think that every year we just keep doing it. We're going to reevaluate to see if we can't fit that discrepancy somewhere. "Did we get it yet? Has he fallen far enough behind in achievement now that we can make him eligible for special ed?" . . .

I think that somehow, someday we're going to all have to say this is our kid, what we need to do is educate this kid. Whether it's the regular ed teacher taking him into a group for a certain subject or whether it's special ed or Chapter One or whomever, it's necessary . . . Mom didn't leave the best one at home. Okay? She sent us all she had . . .

—A Mississippi special educator

ONE

Introduction

A preliminary statement of the problem

Some, but not all, students whose performance in school fails to meet the expectations of their parents or teachers have entitlements that other students do not have. These entitlements are hardly trivial. For instance, some students are legally allowed to receive extra time to complete standardized tests (such as the SAT or ACT) or routine classroom exams, time that might well prove advantageous to substantial numbers of the examinees. Some are entitled to receive educational resources beyond those provided their classmates. Some students who disrupt classrooms can block efforts to discipline them.

This book focuses on one such group of students, those diagnosed as having "learning disabilities" (LD). Over two million elementary, junior high, and high school students in the United States are labeled learning disabled (roughly 5 percent of those school populations). This number has increased dramatically since 1975, the year Congress passed the first significant piece of federal legislation protecting students with disabilities. In 1975–76, before the legislation took effect, only 1.2 percent of the school-age population was diagnosed as having learning disabilities. Moreover, the proportion of students with disabilities classified as learning disabled has risen sharply as well. Only 24.9 percent of students with disabilities were dubbed LD in 1976–77, while just over half were by 1989–90. Only a small portion of that change can be attributed to changes in labeling practices. We estimate that the incremental cost of educating students labeled learning disabled (that is, the cost of educating such students above and beyond the cost of educating such students in the regular classroom) is roughly $9 billion annually.[1] This figure undoubtedly appears small in comparison to the near $5.6 trillion GNP in 1991 (a bit more than 0.1 percent). It undoubtedly appears considerably larger when compared with spending on other discretionary social programs. It is more than eight times the amount spent by the federal government and the states on the JOBS program, designed to reduce long-term welfare dependency through training, and nearly thirty times the amount spent on the At-Risk Child Care Program, which provides child care services for low-income families not receiving income assistance when the custodial parent needs the care in order to work. It is roughly six times the amount spent on Superfund clean-ups of toxic waste sites and four times the budget for both Head Start and the Supplemental Food Program for Women, Infants, and Children, designed to preclude bad health outcomes for pregnant women and children at nutritional risk.

Handicapped students were the subject of federal statutory law as early as 1965, when a one-paragraph amendment to the Elementary and Secondary Education Act (ESEA)[2] expanded eligibility for funds previously available only to low-income communities to include state agencies providing, on a non–school district basis, "free public education for handicapped children."[3] An amendment the following year[4] became the first law specifically to mandate and fund state plans addressing the public education of handicapped children. (This would later become a separate act—the Education of the Handicapped Act.)[5]

These early statutory protections were later expanded, largely in response to the success of litigation efforts by disabilities rights advocates in the early 1970s. Two cornerstone cases, decided in the federal courts, relied on the Equal Protection and Due Process clauses to limit the discretion of school districts to exclude children with disabilities from public school classrooms. In *Pennsylvania*

Association for Retarded Children (PARC) v. Commonwealth of Pennsylvania,[6] plaintiffs brought a class action suit attacking state statutes permitting districts to deny services to mentally retarded children. The court approved a consent decree requiring the state to give every mentally retarded child access to a "free public program of education and training appropriate to his learning capacities"[7] and a stipulation detailing due process protections that the state must provide mentally retarded children and their parents.

The plaintiffs in *Mills v. Board of Education of District of Columbia*[8] sought similar relief, but represented a broader class of students, including children with behavioral problems, emotional disturbance, and hyperactivity. The defendant claimed it was entitled to exclude the plaintiffs from public schooling because it lacked the resources to educate them. The court held that the denial of equal educational opportunity was a violation of both equal protection and due process rights under the Constitution. It decreed that the District of Columbia must provide "to each child of school age a free and suitable publicly-supported education regardless of the degree of the child's mental, physical or emotional disability or impairment,"[9] and that no child could be excluded from such publicly supported education "on the basis of a claim of insufficient resources."[10] As in *PARC,* the decree contained detailed due process protections which included rights to notice, hearings, and representation for pupils and guardians seeking to ensure pedagogically advantageous placements.

These cases and their progeny throughout the states clearly laid the groundwork for Congress's 1975 passage of PL 94-142, the Education of All Handicapped Children Act (EAHCA), which significantly amended the EHA and gave us what is essentially the current federal law. (It has since been renamed the Individuals with Disabilities Education Act, or IDEA.)[11] PL 94-142 dramatically enhanced the pre-1975 protections. It contained a number of core substantive mandates, including the requirement that districts create an individualized educational program (IEP) for each child in special education; the requirement that states affirmatively undertake to identify and locate all unserved children with disabilities; and the obligation to educate children with disabilities with other students to the maximum extent possible, in particular demanding that disabled students be placed in the "least restrictive environment"

(LRE) appropriate to meet their needs. It further required districts to establish extensive procedural safeguards to give parents input in decisions regarding the evaluation and placement of their children; access to records; and rights to participation (with counsel) in due process hearings and judicial review. It also substantially modified the scheme for appropriating federal funds to help states meet the incremental costs of special education.

Students with disabilities also received protections as part of the sweeping civil rights mandate of the Rehabilitation Act of 1973.[12] Section 504 of the Rehabilitation Act precludes any organization receiving federal funds (including public and private primary and secondary schools as well as public and private universities) from discriminating against persons on the basis of disability.[13] Section 504's regulations overlap substantially with those in IDEA, but are less detailed.[14] Special education policy remains dominantly driven by IDEA mandates and regulations, though §504 protects a broader class of persons: all persons (not just students) for whom a physical or mental impairment interferes with one or more "major life activities," such as learning.

Part, though not all, of the impetus behind the movement to secure rights for children with disabilities through litigation efforts such as *PARC* and *Mills* was the desire to fight the exclusion of children of color from the schools. In the years following the landmark school desegregation decision in *Brown v. Board of Education*[15] civil rights activists became concerned that children identified as mentally retarded and placed in special classes or removed from school altogether were disproportionately nonwhite. Indeed, all of the named plaintiffs in *Mills* were African-American. In contrast, the movement to secure rights for children with learning disabilities had its genesis in the grass-roots mobilization of largely white, middle-class parents in the late 1950s and early 1960s to gain resources for what they perceived as their "underachieving" children.[16] This peculiar convergence of parent groups, though, only served to fortify the lobby for entitlements to special education.[17]

Advocates for children with learning disabilities sought to persuade lawmakers that at least some students among those considered "slow" learners were in fact suffering from an organic brain dysfunction, a "specific learning disability," that concealed their true abilities. A number of commentators have attempted to explain why socially privileged parents of poor achievers sought, in the 1960s and 1970s, to argue that their children suffered from specific medical disorders.[18] These advocates lobbied to have their children singled out from other poor achievers both for special resource infusions and for a special label that would be less stigmatic than "slow" or "educably mentally retarded." Advocates proposed that these students not be placed in traditionally dead-end special ed classes, but receive instead supplementary assistance for part of the day in "resource rooms" and help from aides assigned to their regular classrooms. The advocates' claim was that children with specific learning disabilities would be able to manifest their underlying cognitive potential with such appropriate interventions.

This parents' movement led to the formation in 1963 of the Association of Children and Adults with Learning Disabilities (now called the Learning Disabilities Association of America), which successfully lobbied for the passage of thirteen state statutes providing services for children with learning disabilities by 1968.[19] Learning disabilities were not explicitly addressed in federal legislation until the ESEA was amended in 1970, enacting a separate Education of the Handicapped Act (EHA). A special section in that act provided for the appropriation of $63 million to promote research, professional training, and the creation of centers emphasizing the "prevention of specific learning disabilities," which were defined much as they are in current legislation. With the passage of PL 94-142, the federal definition of handicapped children was altered so that children with specific learning disabilities were specifically enumerated among them for the first time. PL 94-142 also formulated, for the first time, a set of substantive mandates to identify and accommodate students with learning disabilities.

IDEA defines children with specific learning disabilities as psychological processing disorders that interfere with one's ability to perform a number of learning tasks; these disorders cannot be the result of physical disabilities or the result of mental retardation, emotional disturbance, or environmental or socioeconomic factors. The accompanying regulations further elaborate that a diagnostic team shall identify as learning disabled students who show a severe *discrepancy* between their *achievement* in one or more subject areas, such as math, reading, or writing, and their *ability* (usually as measured by an IQ test).

We will discuss later, at some length, which procedures are mandated and which forbidden in the context of identifying students with learning disabilities. For now, we want to emphasize two closely related points. First, although federal law is relatively imprecise as regards varieties of learning disability, it clearly conceives of learning disabilities as organic or medical in nature. The key criterion for identification is the existence of an achievement-ability discrepancy that is not explicable in terms of sociocultural causes or other medical problems; the measurement of ability, in turn, is heavily IQ-driven. Second, recipients of federal funds *must* label and categorize students as learning disabled or not. The statute does not allow for judgments that learning disabilities are invariably on a continuum. To put the point another way, federal law does not permit states to allow local districts to decide that there is no class of "students with learning disabilities" who can be neatly distinguished from non-LD students without forfeiting federal funds. A district *could* choose to give benefits to those not called LD that are as extensive as those that *must* be given to pupils labeled LD, but they cannot skimp on the entitlements federally mandated for pupils with LDs in order to "share" resources with students having other needs.

A brief overview of the argument

The basic claim that we will elaborate over the course of the book is straightforward: as a society, we must make decisions about which students deserve resources beyond those devoted to their classmates. We must make decisions about how to measure, reward, and signal the achievement of students. We must make disciplinary decisions, which can be conceived of in essentially punitive/retributivist terms or, alternatively, in social control/incapacitationist terms (that is, as efforts to ensure an appropriate learning environment for the pupils harmed by their classmates' disruptiveness).

Decisions about resource allocation inevitably involve clashes among individuals, each of whom would almost surely benefit (at least to some extent) from a more expensive, personally tailored education. The question of whether students with learning disabilities would benefit *more* from resource infusions than other pupils is, essentially, an empirical question. Current federal law does not permit local districts to engage that empirical question head on. At times, it appears to "answer" it by rhetorical fiat—*defining* students with learning disabilities as that unique group not manifesting its academic potential given "ordinary" pedagogic inputs. At other times, it apparently declares the question irrelevant by deciding that pupils with learning disabilities are entitled to extra resources whether or not the resources would be more effectively employed by competing claimants, because the pupils with LD have some sort of (vaguely defined) antidiscrimination claim to such resources that overrides mere pedagogic claims.

Decisions about how to test pupils turn, fundamentally, on ascertaining which virtues are truly significant. We test reading comprehension or trigonometry skills only if we believe reading or trigonometry significant. The decision to accommodate LD students *should* thus turn on demonstrating that the deficits that require accommodation do not represent deficiencies of genuine academic virtues. Granting a pupil more time to finish an exam because she works slowly is unproblematic only if we don't value speedy responsiveness. Most advocates of accommodation obscure this point, again arguing that antidiscrimination norms preclude using tests that disadvantage a protected group; courts, however, on the other hand, appear to us too deferential to unreflective judgments by test-givers that they have genuinely considered which virtues they want tested.

Similarly, students able to control their misconduct ought to be subject to any reasonable disciplinary code, at least so long as their misbehavior cannot be corrected by shifting the pupil to a more appropriate educational placement. Immunizing students from discipline when we purport to determine that their misconduct is a "manifestation of their disability" is an overbroad method of preventing schools from "using" expulsion to breach obligations to offer disabled pupils a free education.

More generally, we believe that we must make a number of significant decisions about pedagogic policy that will inevitably affect pupils both with and without disabilities, but that we too frequently make them now without regard to the pedagogic issues that are really at stake. Congress has instead protected the interests of pupils with learning disabilities on the supposition that the claims for incremental resources, test accommodations, and discipline immunity are needed to protect the "civil rights" of individuals with LDs (or the group of persons with LDs), although it is hardly clear that a district "discriminates" against individuals (or a group) if it fails to grant them resources, testing accommodations, or discipline immunities that their classmates do not get.

Obviously, antidiscrimination norms need not demand that every individual be treated identically. They may well demand that institutions respond appropriately to distinctions between persons, especially if their failure to do so betrays the fact that they are discounting an outsider group's claims, or is sensible only to those who labor under false stereotypes about the group's members or are aversive to them. We are quite skeptical, though, that it is reasonable to view students with learning disabilities as raising compelling antidiscrimination claims to resources or discipline immunity.[20] The fact that people with learning disabilities may well be victims of some forms of discrimination in social life more generally is hardly dispositive. African-Americans are indisputably victimized by racial discrimination. That does not mean, though, that each decision that adversely affects an African-American or a group of African-Americans is discriminatory: the decision by a school district not to establish an educational program that would funnel incremental resources to blacks need not be racist, nor might a decision to discipline a black student (or even to discipline black students at disproportionate rates) necessarily be a result of discrimination.

We are interested above all in formulating policy toward students with learning disabilities, but we are also, to some considerable degree, interested in advocating a certain form, or model, of policy analysis by lawyers and legal academics. We believe that significant public policy debates must be informed by careful analysis of (a) underlying normative disputes, (b) empirical debates about the nature of the underlying problem and the effectiveness of particular responses, (c) the formal structure of existing policy, and (d) the way in which existing policy is actually implemented. Often, too, we cannot adequately understand many of the underlying normative debates without focusing more carefully on the unstated, deeper theoretical disputes about the precise content of certain general norms that all participants in a debate purport to share.

Thus the most central policy concern of this book is how to allocate scarce educational funds. We must, to elucidate this issue, recognize that there are a number of philosophical perspectives about how to allocate educational opportunities that need to be explored in some depth. Whether children with learning disabilities have compelling claims may depend on whether a child's claims on public funds should be based on, say, prior resource deprivation, the relative prospective benefits of spending more on him than on some other child, or the need to create greater equality of outcome. At the same time, we must recognize that there is a rich empirical literature that will be relevant to resolving debates even among those with a parallel normative framework: to what extent are interventions for students with disabilities more or less successful in improving academic performance than interventions in the lives of other pupils? We must look at formal federal law, too, to determine what districts are nominally ordered to do when they allocate scarce resources, that is, whether (and when) they are allowed to consider cost constraints in establishing appropriate educational plans for pupils with learning disabilities. But we must also look at the slippage between formal law and actual practice to determine whether, in fact, districts invariably allocate funds as federal law suggests they should. In addition, since many advocates for pupils with learning disabilities claim they are simply extending the dictates of antidiscrimination law to a previously unrecognized victim group, and since most citizens who will be involved in the debate over policy toward students with LDs share a commitment to eradicating discrimination, we must explore the multiple meanings of the term "discrimination" to elucidate whether a particular form of resource allocation is mandated by a commitment to end discrimination.

Finally, if we were to confront special education policy as we believe a model "policy analyst" would, we would have to explore one more sort of issue that we simply have never felt capable of confronting: the issue of "second-best" policies. We are ultimately quite critical of IDEA as an "ideal" statute, but offer no real insight into the question of whether a system that would in fact be likely to replace it if it eroded would be preferable to the current system. Our policy analysis, in essence, attempts more to identify an ideal than to identify the best politically feasible alternative, and, in our view, an "ideal" policy analyst would do more than we have endeavored to do to figure out whether existing problems are more likely to be corrected or worsened if we embark on a reform path.

The plan of the book

Before we can discuss how those labeled learning disabled by the local districts either are treated or should be treated, we must first discuss the controversial question of whether there is a distinct class of students with learning disabilities who can be differentiated from classmates with learning difficulties that are either unlabeled or labeled differently. We discuss in Chapter 2 how the two groups might be differentiated, conceptually, and we discuss some of the practical difficulties in implementing any conceptual plan. We briefly examine the proposition that the distinction is not just "real" but biologically based, and we very briefly examine a theme we return to in more detail in Chapter 6: whether (properly) differentiated LD students should be taught differently or whether remedial interventions work better for such students.

The material in Chapter 2 should, though, do more than either provide an elaborate definition of the group we are writing about or an argument about whether the group exists. The fact that the group, even if it exists, is not readily identified is of some importance in evaluating how the program both will and should work. When diagnosis is imprecise, people may receive a diagnostic label for irrelevant or impermissible reasons.[21] Moreover, it may be less justifiable to sharply differentiate the benefits children with and without a certain label are entitled to if the criteria used to categorize a child one way or the other are less exacting.

While we hope that the material in Chapter 2 will permit readers to gain some insight into a series of technical questions that are important *if* we choose to implement a social policy that grants students certain beneficial entitlements because they are deemed learning disabled, we do not think this material especially relevant to the question of *whether* to implement such a policy. It would surely defeat the argument that "those with LDs" deserve special treatment to find out that there are no LDs—in the sense that there is no identifiable subset of students whose learning patterns or biological brain structure make them interestingly distinct from their classmates. Acknowledging that learning disabilities "exist," however, does little to build the case that those who have them deserve special treatment.

In Chapters 3, 4, and 5, we study existing special education practice. In Chapter 3, we look at the formal demands of federal law while we focus in Chapters 4 and 5 on factual variations in local practice, relying on others' studies of district behavior, analysis of publicly available data, and our own fieldwork and phone interviews.

We will address the following basic questions in Chapter 3: how must states go about diagnosing students with LDs; what must they do to ensure that students so diagnosed receive an appropriate education; what rights do parents have to contest what they view as inappropriate diagnosis or services; what limits do districts face in disciplining students with disabilities; and what rights do students with LDs have to accommodations on tests? We will focus particularly on a subset of problems within those broader issues: How should districts diagnose nonwhite children, given the common supposition that IQ tests underestimate the "ability" or potential of such children and the supposition that students with learning disabilities are identified as those whose achievement is far lower than their ability or potential? In developing an appropriate educational plan for a child with a learning disability, to what extent can the district make trade-offs between maximizing that child's performance and other interests? We examine the trade-off issue first in the context of situations in which the district's interests are financial, premised on the desire to free up resources for other uses. We also look at trade-offs when the district's interests are "disciplinary," premised on the idea that removing a child with a disability from the classroom setting which maximizes his achievement might help other pupils (both with and without disabilities), either because the teacher is unduly distracted by the need to attend to him or because his behavior is disruptive. Also, how (and to what extent) does the federal government reimburse districts for the incremental costs of complying with federal mandates?

Because federal law permits a good deal of discretion, we recognized the need to study how a number of local districts implement policy in the area. In Chapter 4, we review some of what we (and others) have learned in examining local diagnostic practice, and in Chapter 5, we look at how the districts deal with issues of mainstreaming disabled pupils, "leakage" (ensuring that special educators do not give their services to non–special ed pupils), and discipline. Although we do not attempt to summarize practice throughout the nation, much less to estimate accurately how prevalent different forms of practice are in local districts throughout the country, we note certain implementation problems and practices that seemed to recur in the districts we studied.

Chapters 4 and 5 are organized around the four basic themes that most dominate our concerns throughout the book: how different districts attempt to identify which students will be classed as LD; how different districts choose the (more and less expensive) settings in which to place children with disabilities (focusing particularly on the differential use of resource rooms and pull-out classes, as well as the occasional use of high-cost private education); the role of testing accommodation in driving the LD diagnosis; and the ways in which the districts have coped with the federal mandate that they not expel students (or suspend them for "long" periods) when the misbehavior that would give rise to the expulsion is a manifestation of a disability.

We then attempt to scrutinize the moral or ethical case for special treatment of students deemed learning disabled by focusing, in Chapters 6 and 7 respectively, on two partly hypothetical problems. In Chapter 6, we will look at how an elementary school teacher, given an offer to receive some extra resources for his classroom, might decide whether to "spend" this entitlement on students diagnosed with learning disabilities. While we focus on this issue using the rather unrealistic metaphor of an individual teacher allocating an educational grant, the discussion clearly applies to the whole range of real decision makers that devise actual policy, from Congress to federal courts to state agencies to school boards to principals. In Chapter 7, we will discuss the arguments that a law school faculty should consider in trying to decide whether to grant at least some students with learning disabilities extra time to finish exams. Once again, most of the arguments will be relevant to *any* decision maker with the partial or complete authority to order test accommodations.

In Chapter 6, we will examine what obligations we have to afford different children normatively appropriate opportunity. We will examine a number of alternative normative conceptions of the steps state actors must take to meet a duty to provide "equality of opportunity." We will also discuss, critically, arguments that students with learning disabilities have claims to educational resources that take significant precedence over the claims of other students under a wide variety of normative conceptions.

In Chapter 7, we deal primarily with a question of pure distributive ethics: is it appropriate that people with learning disabilities receive fewer valuable rewards than otherwise similar people not suffering from the disability? Can the case for accommodation of a student with LDs—and the higher grade likely to result from such accommodation—be adequately distinguished from the claim of another student who could also benefit from extra time? If we accept systems, such as typical grading systems, in which rewards are differentiated, can we justify rejecting outcome inequality based on differential performance that is purportedly a result of a learning disability while accepting the inequalities based on distinctions in performance with other roots?[22] We will also discuss whether testing accommodation is appropriate if the goal of grades is not so much to reward merit as to establish apt incentives to work and/or to provide information to those entities (other schools, employers) to whom one's students later apply.

The questions in Chapters 6 and 7 could be viewed as similar: some might believe that the question in Chapter 7 is whether to accommodate different students' *test-taking* styles, while the question in Chapter 6 is whether to accommodate distinct *learning* styles. We believe, however, that the cases are ultimately more distinct than similar. The question we ask in Chapter 7 assumes that the students we deal with are essentially formed, with whatever set of skills and deficits they've got, and we must evaluate or reward these now-fixed skills. The question is whether to defend or condemn particular inequalities of outcome among adults. The question we raise in Chapter 6 assumes that we believe that students might develop different skills and deficits, depending in part on how we choose to educate them. To put it another way, in Chapter 6 we raise the question what duties we must fulfill to meet obligations to provide adequate (perhaps equal) opportunity. In Chapter 7, though, we raise the question of what principles should govern the distribution of goods to people who are assumed to be different despite prior rectification, through affirmative measures, of unwarranted inequalities in opportunity.

In Chapter 8, we offer speculations on the ideology that lies behind current policy. We note that policy toward students with learning disabilities unites two ordinarily oppositional political ideological camps. The first is a conservative one which radically distinguishes the moral claims of the "deserving poor" from the claims of the "undeserving poor," who must be discouraged from "choosing" poverty by denying their requests for public assistance. The other is what we dub, for lack of a better term, a "left multiculturalist" ideology which radically distinguishes the claims of social groups thought to suffer from irrational devaluation of their capacities from those whose claims are based on either need or solidarity. Students with learning disabilities have been identified by the political right with the physically disabled, uniquely entitled to state largesse. More interestingly, they have been identified by the multiculturalist left with victims of aversive prejudice, wrong-headed stereotypes, or the unjustified imposition by hegemonic groups of their own performance styles as necessary performance norms.

In the course of criticizing the LD advocacy movement's rather ill-founded appropriation—self-consciously or otherwise—of "left multiculturalist" ideology, we present, in detail, our somewhat skeptical view of the transformation of "progressive" American political discourse more generally in disputes over the allocation of scarce resources. In particular, we question the tendency of this discourse to disclaim generally egalitarian arguments in favor of "antidiscrimination" principles that focus on the need to be more tolerant of difference. Thus the claims of students with learning disabilities are treated not as arising from a desire to blunt adult inequality by providing more resources to those with remediable problems in acquiring useful skills, but as flowing from their right to be spared the consequences of prejudice against their disability.

We are perfectly aware that variants of the antidiscrimination principle may seem relatively uncontroversial, while more generally egalitarian ethics are clearly highly politically contested. As a result, we understand why some might think it far easier to build a consensus to aid students with LDs by treating their claims as antidiscrimination claims.[23] Still, we believe advocates for students with LDs are fooling themselves to believe they can ultimately persuade others that the justification for devoting extra resources to educating, and providing test accommodations to, students with LDs is simply to combat "intolerance"; in our view, they rely on highly contestable interpretations of the dictates of the antidiscrimination norm.

It is not ultimately helpfully understood as "intolerant" for a socially disadvantaged child, or his parents, to claim that he both deserves and would benefit more than an LD child from an infusion of incremental public school funds. Opponents of test accommodations will not find it persuasive to "inflate" the grades of the learning disabled unless they are convinced that the initial "deflation" of grades was for an irrelevant reason. It will not do to tell them that we "inflate" the grades of pupils with LDs but not those of "generally poor students," simply because only the former are members of a group that is victimized by bigotry.

It is possible that some readers will agree with our criticisms of existing policy but believe we are simply wrong in our analysis of its mistaken ideological underpinnings. In that sense Chapter 8 is, when all is said and done, a conceptually separable essay about the appropriate reach of the antidiscrimination norm, which uses policy toward students with learning disabilities as a case study in the overuse of the norm.

What we do not try to do in this book

This book is largely prospective and normative, rather than historical and descriptive. Attempting to account for the actual practices that have emerged in this area is a fascinating task, but it is not ours.

There is surely room to expand on the history of legislative action, local district procedures, both isolated and concerted group activity by the parents of disabled children, and the development of special educational ideology and practice at teachers' training institutions.

One could imagine tracing more exactingly the development of congressional coalitions that ensured the rather uncontested passage of the relevant protective legislation.[24] One could envisage, for instance, sorting through competing accounts of the legislative change: was this a "quiet revolution" securing civil rights for the powerless[25] or were special educators simply behaving as an ordinary job-creating, income-enhancing "interest group"?[26]

What motivated the grass-roots movements? Many parents with high expectations for their children may have initially been prone to believe that learning disabilities existed because proof of their existence would reassure them that their children's school failures were a result not of some stigmatized condition—"stupidity," mild retardation, laziness—but of a discrete "disease" which, at best, could be remedied through the application of quasi-medical intervention or appropriate teaching that would tap into the student's existing strengths, or, at worst, be labeled nonstigmatically.[27] At some point, the choice of labels for poor students—particularly LD and ADD ("attention deficit disorder" or, at the time, "hyperactivity") versus EMR ("educably mentally retarded")—closely tracked class and racial hierarchies. The schools' labels may have helped solidify those hierarchies,[28] though the tendency in the past decade has been to avoid stigmatic labeling across the board to the maximum degree possible, or at the very least to reduce or eliminate the correspondence between race and category of disability. Many people may also have been more prone to identify discrete learning disorders as a "medical" problem in an atmosphere in which Americans worried about the "knowledge gap," particularly the perceived gap between Soviet and American scientific education in the late 1950s,[29] and sought to identify the causes of this failure in the biological realm, rather than the social or educational domains.[30]

One could look, as well, to the "sociology of the professions" literature and apply it to the growth of special education. This might help us discern the degree to which legalization and medicalization of discourse in this area helped special educators establish a professional identity and enhance their status, which served not just income-enhancing economic interests, but also interests in prestige and "purposeful" conduct.[31]

One could examine the legalization of special education as a study in the efficacy of bureaucracy: one might be interested in that regard in, among other issues, whether and *which* parents and children are able to exercise their due process rights;[32] the structure of the relationship between the special education bureaucracy and citizens in terms of competing political conceptions of the relationship among the individual, the community, and the state;[33] and the extent to which legalization has enhanced as opposed to dampened local political mobilization and the assertion of rights.[34]

Our goal, though, has been to focus on the considerations that should dominate a discussion of an ideal policy toward pupils with learning disabilities, recognizing that their interests may clash with those of their classmates who do not have disabilities. It is to this task that we now turn.

TWO

Technical Controversies

Overview

The federal definition of learning disabilities implies far more consensus about the concept than actually exists. Among mainstream LD researchers, most agree that there is a sharp line between students who are incapable of performing certain academic tasks because they lack some general cognitive ability, and those who possess such ability but still fail to perform well. Much of the growth in the field over the past thirty years has centered around disputes over how, precisely, to characterize learning disabilities. Most of these debates are "internal" to a body of scholars sharing the consensus that learning disabilities exist, yet also committed to advancing and refining prevailing conceptions of the underlying psychological and biological features of learning disabilities. Other contributions to the literature turn on an "external" critique of the concept of LD, or in other words, skepticism as to whether learning disabilities even exist as distinct from other kinds of learning difficulties.

The claim that learning disabilities exist becomes more persuasive if it can be shown that those with particular behavioral traits share a common, atypical set of biological characteristics, and part of our aim in this chapter is to review and discuss the controversial nature of that contention. We wish to clarify at the outset, though, that while it would certainly bolster the case against special treatment of LD students to show that learning disabilities do not exist, that is not our line of argument. In fact it seems quite plausible to us that a population of individuals exists who possess a biologically unique set of features that interferes with their learning performance despite adequate intelligence. From our vantage point, though, looking at the issue as would-be policymakers, acknowledging the existence of this distinctive subpopulation does not tell us whether its unique traits should have social significance. The latter judgment must occur at the legal and political level. If, for instance, one's goal were to funnel discretionary resources toward those most likely to benefit from them, it would not suffice to show simply that students with LDs exist. In this chapter, we survey—albeit not exhaustively—a number of current controversies about the scope, reliability, and practical utility of the concept of learning disabilities. Ultimately, however, the arguments we advance in the remainder of the book do not depend on whether one is persuaded by the arguments of those skeptical of the existence of learning disabilities, and indeed we make no attempt to advocate on their behalf.

Those skeptical that learning disabilities, most particularly dyslexia (reading deficit), can or should be distinguished from "garden variety" academic difficulties make several distinct arguments. First, some believe there is no real distinction in the cognitive or psychological processes of those with and without learning disabilities; these critics rely, in part, on the controversies in this regard among the nonskeptics themselves as evidence that the conception of LD rests on unduly fragile foundations. Second, and similarly, to the extent that there is disagreement over the biological source of learning disabilities, some skeptics raise questions about the reliability of the category of LD. Third, some critics raise an argument based less on doubt that learning disabilities are "real" than on the concern that they cannot, in practice, be diagnosed with any substantial reliability. Fourth, and finally, some would argue that even if learning disabilities exist and can be diagnosed, the enterprise of distinguishing LD students from other students is ill founded, because there is no set of educational interventions that is uniquely apt to improve the performance of the LD subgroup.

Basic issues in the identification of learning disabilities

We will return in Chapter 3 to discuss in detail how those with learning disabilities are to be identified under federal law and regulations, but we begin with the commonplace legal definition of "learning disabilities" as it appears in IDEA (the Individuals with Disabilities Education Act).[1] Children with specific learning disabilities are

> those children who have a disorder in one or more of the basic psychological processes involved in understanding or in using language, spoken or written, which disorder may manifest itself in imperfect ability to listen, think, speak, read, write, spell, or do mathematical calculations. Such disorders include such conditions as perceptual handicaps, brain injury, minimal brain dysfunction, dyslexia, and developmental aphasia. Such term does not include children who have learning problems which are primarily the result of visual, hearing, or motor disabilities, of mental retardation, of emotional disturbance, or of environmental, cultural, or economic disadvantage.[2]

Federal regulations require that districts create evaluation teams to identify each child whose academic performance is not commensurate with his age and ability,[3] and to treat a student as having a learning disability if the discrepancy between what are thought to be appropriate expectations of performance (the student's "ability" or "potential") and her manifest achievement are not attributable to certain discrete, named sources (most important, limited English proficiency, socioeconomic disadvantage, emotional disorders, and physical handicapping conditions).[4]

Thus the federal definition is essentially "negative," or exclusionary, rather than affirmative. A student is said to have a learning disability not when we observe any particular set of neurological traits, but when we decide that we *cannot* explain poor academic performance on the basis of either low IQ or a set menu of excluded nonneurological factors. Of course, even if excluded "adverse" factors are present (for example, socioeconomic disadvantage, physical handicap), we cannot readily discern whether those forces actually caused the achievement deficiencies.[5]

Initially, some states set "expectations" on the basis simply of age and grade, rather than individual IQ scores, mandating that districts find a discrepancy between achievement and potential when a child's achievement lagged substantially behind age-appropriate levels. Thus if a student were performing, say, two grade levels below the grade he was in, he would meet the discrepancy (inclusionary) aspect of the test for learning disabilities. He might well still have been excluded by the district's observation team if his IQ were low, because the team might have attributed the discrepancy to "mild" mental retardation or because his IQ fell below some explicit eligibility cut-off point.[6] Nonetheless, such systems included low-IQ children and excluded high-IQ children more often than the IQ-achievement discrepancy models more typically employed today.

The use of grade-expectation inclusionary definitions are decidedly on the wane: only two states defined discrepancies in this fashion in 1989–90,[7] while seven states so defined them in 1980.[8] Meanwhile, in 1989–90, thirty-seven states directed that districts should pay attention to the discrepancy between achievement- and IQ-based expectations (federal law prohibits districts from relying exclusively on test scores in identifying pupils with learning disabilities) rather than chronological age-based expectations in making diagnostic judgments, compared with only sixteen in 1981–82.[9]

There are different ways to measure discrepancy between IQ and achievement. The simplest and most prevalent technique is simply to label a child as having a substantial discrepancy between IQ and achievement if her IQ score is more than some number of standard deviations (SD) above her achievement score. Twenty states used such a system in 1990 and another eleven used "expectancy" formulas that had much the same effects and difficulties.[10]

What magnitude of discrepancy[11] will qualify a child for LD diagnosis varies across states.[12] Distinct discrepancy score formulas generate dramatically different numbers of pupils "eligible" to be treated as having a learning disability. In a study by Sinclair and Axelson,[13] the authors sampled 137 children and assessed whether they would be classified as having a learning disability according to distinct formulas used by five researchers: the percentages classed as having an LD were 4, 9, 9, 14, and 28 percent of the same sample.[14] Moreover, growth in the population classified as learning disabled in the late 1980s was lower in states demanding higher discrepancy levels than in those demanding lower discrepancies.[15]

High-IQ children will be overdiagnosed as LD/discrepant in any system which simply compares IQ and achievement scores, given the tendency of all test scores to regress toward the mean. Since the concurrent validity coefficients of achievement and IQ tests are roughly .7, we would expect students with an IQ of 130 to have an achievement score from 121 to 123, not 130, even if achievement and "intelligence" were perfectly correlated, while a student with an IQ of 85 should be expected to have an achievement score of 89. Thus, the hypothetical high IQ child is not truly discrepant unless his achievement score is 1.5 SD below 121–123, while the hypothetical low-IQ student is truly discrepant when his score is less than 1.5 SD below an 89 score. Given that the general correlation between ability and achievement is only .6, the problem worsens; achievement will be substantially lower than "ability" for most high-IQ children and above it for lower-IQ children.[16] To respond to this problem, 12 states (as of 1989–90) required that the student perform less well on achievement tests than would be predicted *given his IQ* (asking, in essence, whether he's done considerably worse than the average child with his IQ has done).[17]

There are also disputes about which form of the Wechsler IQ test that psychometricians generally employ one should use in diagnosing children as having learning disabilities. The basic choice is between using the verbally loaded WISC-R (Verbal), the WISC-R (Performance), or the WISC-R (Full Scale, combining both verbal and performance scores). Once again, the point is not just of theoretical interest: changes in the characteristics of the IQ test used result in the identification of a somewhat different subgroup of "discrepant" children. Different IQ tests not only identify children with distinct sorts of processing deficits,[18] but also identify different proportions of high- and low-IQ pupils, since Performance scores tend to be higher than Verbal scores for students with Full-Scale IQs below 85 and lower when Full-Scale IQs are above 115.[19]

Many have argued that it is important to measure discrepancies between performance-loaded IQ tests and achievement since an LD student's scores on the verbal tests will be unduly suppressed by the presence of the very learning disability that one is trying to diagnose, thus concealing an IQ-performance disparity even when it is present.[20] But the counterargument is powerful as well. If we believe the verbal IQ test score measures verbal potential and not simply current verbal functioning, it *better* predicts the maximum verbal performance we should expect from a particular youngster. We should not, in this view, believe that a child's reading achievement falls below expectations (that is, we should not consider the child "dyslexic") unless her verbal functioning is far inferior to her verbal capacity, nor should we call a child dyslexic simply because her verbal capacity is far inferior to her performance capacity.[21] Still others believe the Full-Scale score (which combines both scores) is most appropriately used, though this position seems to arise less from conviction than from the sense that compromise is appropriate in the presence of irreconcilable controversy.[22]

Strong opponents of defining learning disabilities in terms of disparities between IQ and achievement argue that these problems are insoluble regardless of the sort of IQ test one administers. They believe, among other things we will return to, some combination of the following propositions: (a) the IQ test itself is essentially an achievement test anyway so that most low-achieving students will have suppressed IQs; (b) though the IQ test may measure potential as distinct from current achievement in non-LD students, students with LDs will not be able to cope with the IQ test as generally administered so that *their* IQ scores will be suppressed by their reading deficits;[23] (c) reading itself causes further development in related cognitive abilities so that older dyslexics will have increasingly suppressed IQs as their reading disabilities impair development, even if the IQ test is designed in such a way as to deemphasize direct reading skills.[24] Some opponents believe that attempting to measure "potential" is simply beside the point—that we should seek to remedy students' current deficits, without regard to what will inevitably be imperfect hypotheses about their capacity to overcome them.[25] It is more relevant to the question about "proper" diagnostic method, though, to note that others believe we can identify students with learning disabilities more accurately by measuring potential through non-IQ measurement modes. Stanovich, for instance, argues that students ordinarily score similarly on listening comprehension and reading tests, and that a student who exhibits a substantial discrepancy between scores on these two tests has revealed the particular problem we are trying to diagnose: phonological processing difficulties that give rise to reading deficits.[26]

It is important to recall that the LD diagnosis is not very exacting. Many believe that it is unlikely that the proportion of children who are actually learning disabled in any particular state varies widely,[27] but the proportion of children each state *diagnoses* as having LDs ranges rather substantially. In 1989–90, it varied from a low of 1.69 percent (in Georgia) to a high of 5.8 percent (in Rhode Island); the mean was 3.617, the standard deviation .926. These disparities persist even taking into account the degree to which some states may label children with more severe cognitive disabilities as LD to avoid stigma.

Disputes about the psychological or cognitive processes that characterize learning disabilities

Over the past twenty-five years, researchers have devised a number of theories to try to explain the distinct learning processes characteristic of pupils with learning disabilities. They have focused variously on sensory-motor processes, learning strategies, and the specific encoding techniques used in different kinds of learning.[28] The classic approach has been to postulate the presence of a deficit in one or more areas of psychological "processing" abilities, that is, perceptual-motor skills, attention, memory, cognition, or encoding. The pioneering contributions of Samuel Kirk and others laid the groundwork for psychological processing models.[29] Although early researchers' emphasis on the sensory and motor elements of processing may have fallen out of favor,[30] interest in cognitively oriented processing theories remains robust. Researchers continue to develop models based on such cognitive abilities as decoding (breaking words down into subparts), cognizing phonemes (sound segments), and whole word recognition.[31] We will discuss some examples of controversies that have arisen in this field. While by no means comprehensive, our treatment is intended simply to highlight that some fairly foundational puzzles regarding the cognitive basis of learning disabilities remain to be resolved.

Numerous researchers have conducted studies comparing dyslexic readers and nondyslexic poor readers on a variety of cognitive processing tests. Skeptics have sought to contest the traditional belief that dyslexics will perform less well than other poor readers on certain "phonological tasks" (breaking words down into smaller sound bites), manifest, for example, in a particular inability to read or spell imaginary words.

The skeptics have gathered a good deal of evidence. For example, Shaywitz et al. compared the progress of diagnosed discrepancy-based dyslexics and what are generally referred to as "garden variety" poor readers over time. They found few differences in their performance on any standardized tests.[32] While the dyslexics made more progress in reading between grades two and five, this may well have been an artifact of the diagnostic technique that initially distinguished them in the second grade. Dyslexics are identified in grade two when their reading scores are particularly discrepant from IQ scores. Given two students with roughly equal IQs and roughly similar reading problems, the one who scores especially badly in grade two on reading achievement (and is therefore labeled dyslexic) is also the one more likely to regress toward the mean when he takes another reading test in grade five. Similarly, Siegel found no significant differences on phonological, memory, reading, spelling, and syntactical awareness tests between the groups.[33]

Bruck matched younger nondyslexics with older dyslexics who scored the same on reading achievement tests. She tested the ability of each group to read words versus nonwords, as well as words that followed no phonological rules (for example, "have") versus words that did follow phonological rules (for example, "rust"). Special education traditionalists would expect the dyslexics to be better at reading words than nonwords, and better at reading nonphonological words than phonological words, because they believe dyslexics have unique phonological deficits that compromise their capacity to learn to read by breaking words into sound units. That expectation was not borne out. Bruck's only finding consistent with the traditional picture was that the dyslexics did rely more on context to recognize words than nondyslexics (though this may have been a function of their age differences rather than their disability). While Bruck's dyslexic sample had received eight months of special education training, largely phonologically based instruction, she did not believe the remedial instruction was sufficiently intense to compromise her basic results.[34]

The counterevidence to the skeptics' claim, though, is quite substantial as well. At least when one compares older dyslexics with younger nondyslexic pupils with parallel reading scores (who are generally higher-IQ pupils), a meta-analysis of a large number of existing studies by Olson and colleagues shows that the dyslexics do indeed perform phonological processing tasks more poorly than the younger nondyslexics.[35]

It also appears that some of the studies the skeptics rely upon have serious methodological weaknesses. For instance, the control groups may have been somewhat improperly matched in the Bruck study. She matched groups with equal reading comprehension scores, not groups with equal word recognition scores. Her disabled readers were thus poorer at word recognition than her "matched" group. She showed that the relative gap between word and non-word recognition was the same for disabled and nondisabled readers, but there is no obvious reason to believe that the absence of a larger gap for disabled readers was surprising given their lower levels of word recognition.

The evidence that dyslexics are "different" is far weaker, however, when dyslexics are compared with same-age classmates with equally poor reading scores who have substantially lower IQs: Stanovich's review of these studies notes that while some of the studies have shown some qualitative differences in processing between the groups, others have demonstrated that it is difficult to find any distinctions between dyslexics and "garden variety" poor readers.[36]

Even if performance distinctions between older dyslexics and younger non-dyslexics with an equal capacity to recognize words are demonstrated, it is ultimately difficult to tell whether the distinctions are more a function of age or of dyslexia. It is certainly plausible that all readers, over time, tend to rely increasingly heavily on simple word recognition in order to read, and thus lose some of their skill at breaking words down phonologically. This hypothesis might be tested if studies that compare younger nondyslexics with older dyslexics would also include a group of older nondyslexics for comparison with the younger nondyslexics (presumably matched by IQ). If performance on phonological processing tasks declines with age, we would expect the gap between nonword and word reading to be smaller in the younger readers than in the older readers. We have not located any such studies.

In addition to psychological processing theories, numerous researchers have explored the link between metacognition and learning disabilities.[37] Metacognition is knowledge about one's own cognitive capacities and the ability to regulate cognition. Thus a student who lacks metacognitive skills may have difficulty estimating her own abilities and aptitudes, lack awareness of the tasks and procedures appropriate to solving a particular problem, fail to monitor herself by checking over her procedures and answers, or have some combination of these deficits.[38] Accordingly, an educator will seek to help the student to develop an awareness of her own cognitive processes and implement self-help strategies for acquiring, remembering, and writing information.

Numerous researchers have investigated whether differences in metacognitive ability might explain some of the variance in performance between LD and non-LD children. While several have reported a difference between LD and normal-achieving students on measures of metacognition,[39] others have found no such differences.[40] Interexperimental difference in the tests or batteries used for assessing metacognition might partially explain the inconsistent results. Indeed, some researchers have reported distinctions between LD and non-LD students but only for some subtypes of metacognition. Thus Swanson, Christie, and Rubadeau found that LD and non-LD students differed on only one of a range of metacognitive parameters, in particular metacognitive strategies,[41] and Wong and Wong, when comparing LD and non-LD children on two kinds of metacognitive knowledge, vocabulary difficulty and passage organization, found LD students deficient only on the latter measure.[42]

A puzzle at the core of the studies finding a link between LD and metacognition is whether they can be reconciled with the definition of LD. Stanovich has pointed out that insofar as metacognition is recognized as a component of general intelligence, evidence linking learning disabilities to metacognitive deficits is an "embarrassment" to the assumption that what people with LDs display is a severe processing deficit in a particular area, not a general deficit of intelligence.[43] A rejoinder to this observation might be that we should expect LD students to manifest greater metacognitive problems than other students: early school failure resulting from specific processing deficits may spiral into a web of motivational and self-esteem problems that in turn give rise to the second-order problem of more generalized metacognitive deficiencies.[44] Whether or not this rejoinder deals adequately with Stanovich's conceptual critique, which suggests some blurriness in the boundary between the LD and other poor learners, most researchers in the area now believe there are complex linkages or interactions among cognition, metacognition, motivation, and self-esteem.[45]

Does an inability to determine the biological root of learning disabilities imply they are not genuine?

The medical literature is far from resolute regarding the etiology of LD.[46] Research has focused on a number of interrelated areas, including genetics, neuropsychological assessment of minimal brain dysfunction, metabolic physiology, and environmental influences. Geneticists conducting studies of twins and families are persuaded of a hereditary influence on learning disorders.[47] Although no single mechanism of genetic transmission has been established, several have been implicated. It seems likely that some kinds of learning disorders, notably dyslexia, have a heterogeneous genetic etiology. In addition, certain genetically based but nonhereditary conditions such as Turner's Syndrome and Klinefelter's Syndrome (abnormalities of the X and Y chromosomes) are associated with a higher incidence of learning disorders.

Neuropsychological assessment involves the observation and measurement of responses to a test battery designed to detect aberrations and maturational lag in neurological functioning.[48] Common tests include the electroencephalograph, or EEG, which measures electrical activity on the surface of the brain, basic motor and sensory responses, laterality (left-right dominance/orientation), and coordination. Though the resultant diagnostic labels, such as "minimal brain dysfunction," suggest neurological damage, the "damage" may be quite ill defined, an indirect conclusion based on observed behavior patterns known to be associated with particular kinds of brain dysfunction. It is thought that certain subtle or "soft" clinical signs of abnormality may reveal neurological dysfunction in areas of the brain associated with memory and learning.

Typically, the results of neurological exams are the same in children with and without LDs. For example, Fletcher and colleagues[49] found no significant differences between LD pupils and "garden variety" poor performers on a host of neurological tests designed to measure traits traditionally thought to be associated with learning disabilities. Some studies, though, have found evidence of correlations between particular clinical signs and LD.[50] Results of studies of the relationship between abnormal EEG recordings and LD are inconsistent, though in general there is some skepticism among neuropsychologists about the probativeness of EEG measures.

Clinical signs of lateral dominance or preference (for example, handedness) have also been associated with LD. Early investigators believed that failure to establish left-hemispheric dominance led to difficulties in language and reading acquisition, but more recent research suggests that, although the left hemisphere of the brain indeed specializes in language, problems with either hemisphere can cause deficiencies in learning, and especially language learning. A similar theory—lateral preference theory—is somewhat related to the earlier cerebral dominance theories. According to lateral preference theory, some children show an atypical tendency to perform some basic functions with one side of the body and some functions with the other: such children are more likely to be LD than those with established laterality (that is, those who perform all basic functions on one side of the body). Relatively few researchers, though, are persuaded that laterality and LD are related.

Nonetheless, many researchers continue to believe that there are significant anomalies in the brain structure of diagnosed dyslexics. Post-mortem examinations of diagnosed dyslexics reveal underdevelopment of the language area of the left side of the brain (though not of the hemisphere more generally), and areas of the right hemisphere are often larger and contain a greater number of cells than more statistically typical brains. Some researchers have noted that symmetrical frontal lobe widths are typical of those with poor reading passage comprehension scores, and that reversed frontal symmetry is typical of those with poor word skills.

A considerable amount of medical research has also explored the various environmental factors that might be implicated in learning disabilities,[51] but it is not very definite. Researchers have explored features of the child's environment both before and after birth. A substantial number of studies suggest links between learning problems and aspects of maternal health such as malnutrition, drug and alcohol abuse, infections and disease, maternal and paternal age. Others have focused on postnatal influences. Studies have shown a relationship between nutritional (for example, protein) deficiencies and learning problems, though the results of studies attempting to link food additives or food allergies to learning disabilities are more equivocal. Childhood lead exposure, head injuries, and diseases or infections such as meningitis have also been suggested as potential causes of learning disabilities.

Skepticism about diagnosis

It is plausible that there truly are children with learning disabilities out in the world, but that our diagnostic techniques are so poor that a high proportion of children labeled as having LDs do not "really" have them, while a significant number of those who actually have LDs are not so identified.

Researchers who doubt that students with LDs are accurately identified make use of two basic methods to convince others of the prevalence of misdiagnosis. Some independently review case records of students who are classified either as having an LD or as not having one to assess the accuracy of the identifications. Others run controlled experiments, in which people ordinarily asked to make diagnoses are given the opportunity to diagnose a group of students whose "true" traits are somehow known by the experimenters. There is a good deal of evidence that misclassification is rampant.

Thus, for instance, Ysseldyke, Algozzine, and Epps contrasted a group of fourth graders who had been labeled as having learning disabilities with a group of fourth graders with parallel academic achievement levels who had not been so labeled. They found that there were considerable similarities between the two groups; in fact, an average of 96 percent of the scores were within a common range, and the performance of LD and underachieving children on many subtests was identical. Comparing characteristics of these children with the federal definition showed that as many as 40 percent of the students may have been misclassified.[52] Similarly, Shepard, Smith, and Vojir found that fewer than half of the sample of all children labeled LD in Colorado in the early 1980s "had characteristics that are associated in federal law and professional literature with the definitions of learning disabilities . . . Though most . . . have learning problems, they are incorrectly called learning disabled."[53]

It is possible, though, that some "misdiagnosis" is, in essence, deliberate. Since both students classified as EMR (educable mentally retarded) and those classified as having LDs receive individualized educational programs (IEPs) entitling them to appropriate special educational services in the least restrictive environment, there is no real consequence to mislabeling a child one believes is EMR as LD, so long as one develops an appropriate IEP for the student so mislabeled. The evaluation team members may believe it is a poor idea to use the EMR diagnosis. The child himself may be harmed by the stigmatic label, potential employers may view the label as signaling more extreme inability than is appropriate, or parents may resent or resist the label.

Controlled experiments may be considerably more disheartening to those who believe that we can tailor a workable public policy to help those with genuine LDs without considerable leakage, since such investigations tend to find not only that students with other sorts of learning problems are called LD, but that pupils with no learning difficulties at all are simply "overdiagnosed."

For instance, Algozzine and Ysseldyke assembled a group of 224 professionals from public and private schools in Minnesota, all of whom had previously participated in at least two placement team meetings in which placement decisions were made about real pupils. (Many of the participants, though, were not school psychologists, who are most prone to be making these sorts of placement decisions, and the study seems vulnerable to the accusation that the authors tested too many "nonprofessionals" in the field.) The researchers gave each subject a referral folder in which a student's sex, SES (socioeconomic status), age, grade, parents' occupation, medical history, and physical attractiveness (based on a previously judged photograph of the student) were listed, alongside an explanation of "reasons for the referral." "None of the issues listed under the statement of the referral problem was unusual for a fifth grader." The subjects were then given access to a computer terminal which allowed them to view the results supposedly obtained on forty-nine different assessment devices in seven domains (including intelligence, achievement, perceptual motor abilities, and behavior ratings). Subjects could also request technical information on the available devices as well as "qualitative information" about the child's performance on any device. The key to the experiment was that regardless of the device selected, the subject was always provided with data indicating that the test performance and behavior were within the average range.

Approximately 51 percent of the participants nonetheless identified the child they were asked to assess as eligible for special education services: 8 indicated the child was likely to be mentally retarded, 103 felt the child was likely to be LD, and 48 felt the child was likely to be emotionally disturbed. Our view is that the LD diagnosis is inevitably expectationally driven; that is, a student is viewed as LD when the observer finds it *surprising* that he or she is performing rather poorly. Thus we were not surprised to find that 90 percent of the subjects who reviewed the file of a female student judged physically attractive with a high socioeconomic status felt that special education would be appropriate for her, though of course all the test scores the subjects could examine were in the average range.[54]

In four articles authored or coauthored by Heubner,[55] however, diagnosticians proved more capable of categorizing pupils in the fashion that they were directed to by relevant regulation, at least when presented with data that were more readily manipulable mathematically. Thus Heubner in 1985 re-created Algozzine and Ysseldyke's 1983 study, but provided test scores in "standardized" rather than grade-equivalent form. He presented researchers with a sample, half of whom should have been diagnosed as having an LD and half of whom should not have. Only 4 of 28 non-LD children were diagnosed as having an LD and only 6 of 27 children with LDs were misdiagnosed as non-LD, results which, while hardly a ringing endorsement of diagnostic practices, are less disheartening than those in the Algozzine and Ysseldyke study. Furthermore, while the diagnosticians gave statistically indistinguishable answers to more focused questions (for example, would the student exhibit future difficulties in language development or math?) and only moderately distinct answers on less focused questions (for example, would the student exhibit future reading difficulties?) this failure to differentiate the subject population might reflect a substantive disbelief that students with LDs face distinctive difficulties rather than an inability to recognize those conventionally called LD. In later studies, Huebner found that psychologists made ample use of test data, rather than reaching conclusions based solely on the referral report and that a large (150-person) sample of school psychologists was better able to reach "appropriate" conclusions when given either direct IQ-achievement discrepancy scores or grade equivalent achievement scores than when they were given percentile achievement scores. (On a scale of one to six, they "moderately disagree" with the statement that a non-LD student has a learning disability when given grade equivalents or a discrepancy IQ while they only "mildly disagree" with that diagnosis when the same student's scores are presented in percentile rank form.)

We do not pretend that we can resolve issues about the frequency of "misclassification" according to existing criteria. We want to emphasize a narrower policy point. While we recognize that classification errors inevitably exist in any setting, radical distinctions in the treatment of students ought not to be based on the presence or absence of a diagnostic label in which we have little confidence.

It may well be the case that the number of classification errors is so high as to make the use of the classification system completely counterproductive. But assuming diagnosis remains far better than random, we can make a more tailored inquiry about the propriety of using an imperfect diagnostic system. Presumably, we would feel more comfortable with an inaccurate classification system when the consequences of misdiagnosis are less extreme. A medical diagnostic test with false positives is less acceptable if the proffered treatment is harmful; a medical diagnostic test with false negatives is less tolerable if delay in treatment significantly affects mortality or morbidity.

In the field of special education, we can control how extreme the consequences of mislabeling are. Essentially, every salient increase in the disparity in treatment of labeled and nonlabeled children renders any level of misdiagnosis less tolerable. If getting diagnosed as eligible for special education at one point in time significantly affects the probability of diagnosis at a later point in time *and* diagnosis is non-neutral, either because it is a benefit (entitling the student to extra resources) or a burden (suppressing performance by lowering academic expectations or by placing students in "dead end" school settings), then mislabeling becomes a more serious issue.

Do we teach dyslexics differently or more effectively?

Assume, for illustrative purposes, that there are two pupils, each reading two grades below grade-level expectations. One is classified as having a learning disability since her IQ score is at grade level, while the other, whose IQ is several standard deviations below the mean, is not so classified. If the barriers to reading present among students with learning disabilities are just as recalcitrant, or just as remediable, as the barriers that low-IQ students face, it is not obvious why educators would bother to differentiate the pupils, even if neurobiologists might. Thus two key questions are (a) whether one must use different techniques to attempt to teach the two pupils to read better and/or (b) whether with *some* kind of intervention the student with a learning disability is significantly more likely to achieve reading scores closer to grade level than the low-IQ student.

We discuss at length, in Chapter 6, the issue of whether interventions for children with learning disabilities are especially successful.[56] For now, we simply want to note that it is difficult to make a convincing case that properly diagnosed students with learning disabilities overcome their educational difficulties any better than students whose achievement shortfalls are attributed to other causes. The question is not easily resolved. First, there is a surprising paucity of studies that compare the progress of groups of poor readers with differing IQ test scores. Second, it is possible, given the difficulties we have in identifying pupils with learning disabilities in the first instance, that we have never really been able to study the efficacy of programs directed at a "pure" group of students with LDs, rather than a group of pupils *labeled* as having LDs.[57]

To summarize the material we will review later, though, there is a modicum of evidence that "garden variety" poor readers have a *better* prognosis than LD students with similar "starting-point" achievement levels. There is a great deal of evidence that the prognosis of students with and without LDs who start out with equal reading scores is the same, and that interventions are no more or less efficacious with either group. There is no substantial evidence in longitudinal studies that interventions benefit LD students more.

It is, of course, possible that reading instructors work differently with students with learning disabilities than they do with "slow readers" not diagnosed as having LDs, though the overlaps in teaching techniques might be as pronounced as the differences. Earlier "process-based" attempts to remediate learning disabilities did indeed lead to approaches to teaching the LD population radically different from those used for the non-LD population. (For example, pupils with learning disabilities more typically received training in motor skills that might involve a balance beam or trampoline. Multisensory approaches, such as teaching dyslexic children to write left-handed and blindfolded so that right brain, nonvisual language faculties would be strengthened, were also employed.) The effectiveness of these methods has been criticized, though, and they have given way or at least share the field with other approaches that have greater pedagogical value for all children.[58]

Summary and conclusions

Although it is clear that a class of students can be identified as having learning disabilities, it is less clear that these students can be identified accurately. Unless learning disabilities become directly observable neurologically, diagnosticians will have to rely on inferring that particular students have a learning disability when they exhibit certain behavior traits, behavior traits that doubtless exist in a broader portion of the student population. Learning disabilities are defined *negatively*. Students are dubbed LD when there is a gap between manifest achievement and "ability" that is not otherwise explicable, not when they exhibit some observable neurological trait.

Researchers and diagnosticians will surely disagree about what behavior constitutes a reasonable indicator that the student is likely to have an LD. Some will demand larger levels of discrepancy between manifest achievement and "potential" than others, and diagnosticians will measure discrepancy differently; some will measure potential using one test, some another (for example, different forms of the IQ test; listening comprehension tests; achievement in a subject matter different from the one in which the student is performing poorly). Researchers and diagnosticians will likely disagree even more sharply about which students exhibit this behavior but do so for reasons that would exclude them from classification as LD (for example, social disadvantage, emotional disturbance).

Each of these decisions has *bite.* A seemingly technical decision, for instance, to measure discrepancy between IQ and achievement scores in terms of a constant standard deviation gap rather than to call a student discrepant only if his achievement scores are far lower than those ordinarily attained by pupils with his particular IQ will radically increase the number of high-IQ students labeled LD and diminish the number of low-IQ students called LD, given the tendency of test scores to regress toward the mean.

It is not obvious to us that there is some class of persons with a unique anatomical or physiological brain structure that causes difficulties in phonological functioning that lead them to read less well than one would expect given their general cognitive abilities. "Dyslexia" may not exist. Nonetheless, although it would certainly bolster the case against special treatment of pupils with learning disabilities if we were to show that there is no real class of students with LDs to treat specially, that is, that benefits are given to a completely random group of students with no important commonalities, we do not adopt that line of argument. In truth, we have no strong reasons to doubt the physical uniqueness of the LD population either. People whom we say have learning disabilities may well have physical attributes in common, and these characteristics may well lead them to exhibit similar cognitive difficulties.[59]

What is clear to us, though, is that it simply does not get us very far to recognize that some group of people with learning disabilities exists. Legal entitlement claims do not flow from the possibility of group recognition. Even if we are satisfied that learning disabilities exist, it is questionable whether pupils with LDs have unique educational difficulties. It is plausible, for instance, that all bad readers have phonological difficulties, and if this is the case, it is hardly apparent why we would then organize an entitlement scheme around the learning disabled rather than the phonologically impaired.

But even if those with LDs have unique educational difficulties, it is not clear why that fact alone entitles them to benefits other students lack. In Chapters 6 and 7 we discuss at length the normative cases for allocating incremental resources to students with learning disabilities and for testing accommodations. While we argue that the normative case for benefits is weak, we need not question in so doing that learning disabilities are real, inborn, or practically identifiable. Frequently, real, inborn, and practically identifiable traits exist which are nonetheless "punished" and do not give rise to remedial obligations. Most significantly, those born with mild, nondisabling "deficits" in the sorts of intelligence that are most generally socially prized are not accommodated on tests, immunized from discipline, or entitled by federal law to compensatory education. We argue that remediability is indeed an issue under certain utilitarian conceptions of the just distribution of educational opportunity. But whether or not learning disabilities are a distinctive source of, say, reading problems does not determine whether they are equally, more, or less tractable than other kinds of reading problems.

THREE

The Federal Regulatory Framework

An overview of the relevant statutes

Section 504 and IDEA

Two significant federal statutes govern the education of children with disabilities, including those with learning disabilities. Section 504 of the Rehabilitation Act,[1] enacted in 1973, precludes any organization receiving federal funds (including public and private primary, secondary schools, and universities) from "discriminating" against people with disabilities, including, but not limited to, disabled pupils. Subchapter II of the Individuals with Disabilities Education Act (IDEA)[2] requires that each state receiving federal financial support for its special education programs provide a free education to all children with disabilities, including learning disabilities, which is individualized, appropriate to their specific needs, and in the least restrictive environment possible.[3]

Unlike IDEA, §504 of the Rehabilitation Act does not, on its face, specifically protect people with learning disabilities. Section 504 refers categorically to the need to protect persons with "a physical or mental impairment which substantially limits one or more of such person's major life activities" as well as people who have a "record of such an impairment" and those "regarded as having such an impairment."[4] In the regulations accompanying §504, however, learning disabilities are listed as a "physical or mental impairment."[5] Court cases have also consistently recognized LD as a handicapping condition within the meaning of the act,[6] often assuming as much with little more than a passing comment.[7] In *Puffer v. Raynolds*, the Massachusetts District Court adopted the common formal interpretation of §504: although the plaintiff had passed her courses without special education, had been employed, and had attended college, the court, nonetheless, held that since one of the major life activities listed in the federal regulations is "learning," and plaintiff was impaired in her learning, she was handicapped within the meaning of the act.[8] Not only does §504 seem clearly applicable to all pupils covered by IDEA, but in addition, it appears to be interpreted as more inclusive than IDEA.[9]

Generally speaking, §504 enunciates rather inexact antidiscrimination principles, demanding, in broad terms, that disabled persons not be victimized by either aversive prejudice or wrong-headed stereotypical assumptions about their limitations. The congressional history states a "commitment to the handicapped that, to the maximum extent possible, they shall be fully integrated into the mainstream of life in America,"[10] and the initial regulations enacted to implement the statute state, rather blandly, that the statute "is designed to eliminate discrimination on the basis of handicap in any program or activity receiving Federal financial assistance."[11]

IDEA, in contrast, attempts to implement a more particular conception of what the inevitably contestably broad antidiscrimination norm implies in the context of accommodating disabled students in public schools. It bears emphasis that there is no "fixed" content to general norms prohibiting "discrimination" against persons with disabilities: antidiscrimination norms may simply forbid (generally able-bodied) persons with decision-making authority from acting upon the false presumption, based on irrational prejudice, that persons with disabilities are unable to perform tasks that they are in fact able to perform. Alternatively, antidiscrimination norms may require that disabled persons be accommodated to permit them to participate in activities that they would not be able to participate in, but for the accommodations.[12] An antidiscrimination norm might preclude paying workers with disabilities less than able-bodied workers even when it is more costly to employ them. It might require paying them less, on the grounds that pay decisions must be made without regard to disability status; in this view, paying workers equally when input costs are different would penalize an able-bodied worker or involve illegitimate favoritism toward the disabled worker. An antidiscrimination norm might also be silent on this issue. For example, consider the issue of determining the salary for a blind lawyer at a firm which must employ a full-time reader to accommodate the disability. Should the law mandate that her salary be lower than it would otherwise be, to account for the cost of the reader, should it mandate that it be the same, or should this decision be left unregulated? Antidiscrimination norms in education might require equal or unequal per pupil spending. Such norms might require mainstreaming, without regard to its financial cost or potentially negative pedagogical effects on nondisabled pupils, or they might require only that disabled students attain a particular level of substantive educational achievement, or not be segregated from other children without a weighty reason.

IDEA also provides detailed procedural safeguards to facilitate the implementation of the substantive provisions. In addition, the act appropriates federal financial aid to schools to pay for some portion of the additional costs of meeting the special needs of disabled students at the same time that it mandates minimally acceptable treatment norms.

The basic substantive requirements of the two acts are best summarized in the regulations accompanying §504:[13]

(1) *Handicapped persons, regardless of the nature or severity of their disability, must be provided a free appropriate public education.* We will discuss in some detail how a district meets its obligation to educate a student appropriately under both §504 and the IDEA, which mandates that each child with a disability receive an individualized educational program,[14] but for now, we want to emphasize the following: states and local districts are permitted to pay for or subsidize any educational services that they may believe appropriate that are deemed above and beyond those mandated by the acts,[15] but if they choose not to, parents or guardians must absorb the cost of such services.[16]

(2) *Handicapped students must be educated with nonhandicapped students to the maximum extent appropriate to their needs.* Regulations under §504 refer explicitly to the desirability of integrating disabled

and nondisabled students.[17] The language in IDEA itself is also direct on the integration issue, demanding that students with disabilities be placed in the "least restrictive environment" (LRE) appropriate to meet their needs,[18] and ordering that states ensure that "to the maximum extent appropriate, children with disabilities . . . are educated with children who are not disabled" and that "removal of children with disabilities from the regular educational environment occurs only when the nature or severity of the disability is such that education in regular classes with the use of supplementary aids and services cannot be achieved satisfactorily."[19]

(3) *Educational agencies must undertake to identify and locate all unserved children with handicaps.* There is an affirmative duty to establish standards and procedures to evaluate and place persons believed to be in need of special education.[20] We will discuss, at some length, which identification procedures are mandated and which forbidden in the context of identifying students with learning disabilities. Our point for now though is the simpler one that recipients of federal funds *must* label and categorize students as having or not having learning disabilities. The statute does not allow for judgments that LDs are invariably on a continuum. It also does not allow for more radically different judgments that we have argued are at least plausible given empirical evidence: that poor academic performance derives not from a discrete handicapping condition, but instead from undifferentiable relative academic incapacity, whose roots will doubtless never be adequately specifiable or understood and/or whose roots are of little or no significance to designing an appropriate educational strategy. To put the point another way, states may not permit local districts to adopt the position that there is no class of students with LDs who can be neatly distinguished from students without LDs without forfeiting federal funds.

(4) *Educational agencies must improve evaluation procedures to avoid inappropriate education that results from misclassification of students.* We will defer our discussion of this requirement until we comment more generally on the efforts of federal overseers to shape diagnostic practice.

(5) *Procedural safeguards must be established to give parents input in decisions regarding the evaluation and placement of their children.* The Rehabilitation Act requires that any recipient of federal funds establish certain safeguards for a disabled child's parent or guardian,

including a right to notification, access to records, and rights to participation (with counsel) in hearings relevant to dispositional decisions. Regulations under the act provide that compliance with the procedural safeguards mandated by IDEA is one means of meeting the requirement.[21]

IDEA contains very detailed procedural standards covering notice and consent to the IEP, due process hearings, administrative and judicial review, and the status of the child during proceedings.[22] The parent, guardian, or state-assigned surrogate may examine relevant diagnostic and placement records, and if she disagrees with the agency's evaluation, may, under some circumstances, obtain an independent educational evaluation of the child at public expense.[23] Moreover, she must receive prior written notice in her native language before an educational agency may initiate or change, or refuse to initiate or change, any services a child receives (specifically, identification, evaluation, placement, or access to a free appropriate public education).[24]

Perhaps most important, the parents or guardian may complain about any aspect of the aforementioned services in an impartial due process hearing at the state or local level.[25] At a hearing, parties have a right to counsel, the right to present evidence, and the right to call and cross-examine witnesses; they also have a right to a record of the hearing and the right to written findings of fact and decision.[26] A party dissatisfied with the results of a local due process hearing may appeal to the state educational agency for independent review, the results of which may, in turn, be reviewed judicially by a state or federal district court.[27] During the course of any complaint, a school district may not change the student's placement without the consent of the parents, guardian, or surrogate.[28] The law also provides that attorney's fees may be granted, with certain qualifications, to the prevailing party.[29]

IDEA also provides that the federal government serve as a source of funds for local schools: the expenses covered under IDEA are the costs of programming, related services such as identification and assessment, transportation and room and board where local programs are inadequate, procedural protections, and access to school records. Funds allocated through IDEA are not allocated directly to local districts but rather to states, which must distribute 75 percent of the funds they receive to local educational agencies (LEAs) and intermediate units. Although the federal allocation for each state is based on a "head count" of disabled children, no more than 12 percent of the state's school-age population will be included in the funding formula.[30] Thus even if there were financial incentives to classify more children as disabled to gain more federal funds—an unlikely proposition given the fact that federal contributions do not come close to covering the incremental costs of even the most minimal IEPs—states could not "take advantage" of federal "largesse" by classifying more than 12 percent of the state's pupils as disabled.[31] States, though, are unconditionally obliged to meet the special educational needs of disabled students if they receive federal appropriations to pay for special educational services: the fact that the state claims not to have the money to do so will be no defense.[32]

Local educational agencies and intermediate educational units, in turn, apply to the state educational agencies which deal with the Department of Education's Office of Special Education Programs. The funds the local educational agencies receive are based on the relative number of disabled children within the district.[33] Most typically, this is true regardless of the "composition" of the disabled population or the expenses borne in educating different sorts of disabled students.[34] States, however, provide specific procedures for this application[35] which vary in detail.[36]

A BRIEF NOTE ON CHAPTER ONE PROGRAMS AND "LEAKAGE"

Chapter One of the Elementary and Secondary Education Act of 1965, while primarily designed to provide federal financial assistance to schools serving areas with concentrations of children from low-income families, is relevant to special education as well, albeit more peripherally. Chapter One grants "provide financial assistance to State and local educational agencies to meet the special needs of . . . educationally deprived children at the preschool, elementary and secondary levels."[37] The act recognizes, in this regard, "(1) the special educational needs of children of low-income families and the impact of concentrations of low-income families on the ability of local educational agencies to provide educational programs which meet such needs, and (2) the special educational needs of children of migrant parents, of Indian children, and of handicapped, neglected, and delinquent children."[38] In some sense, then, Chapter One is the statute we will implicitly compare with IDEA in looking at the competition between disabled (including LD) pupils and "socially disadvantaged" children for federal funds and for federal mandates. But Chapter One is also deliberately designed to assist states and localities fiscally in dealing with some students with disabilities, and it may also provide funds that meet otherwise underfunded obligations created by IDEA.

Part A of Chapter One, with a budget in excess of $4 billion a year, deals with the basic programs operated by local educational agencies for children from low-income communities. Although Part A money cannot, as a formal matter, be used to meet an IDEA-eligible student's individualized educational program, some of it may inadvertently "leak" to LD pupils. Part A money is to be spent on poor achievers within high-poverty districts. Some of these poor achievers, though, might be undiagnosed LD students: one might well imagine a district being less aggressive than it might otherwise be in diagnosing LDs because it knows some children who might be diagnosed as having LDs will receive Chapter One funds in any event.

Part D of Chapter One, with a far smaller budget of $150 million per year, covers "State Operated Programs" (SOPs) for migratory, handicapped, neglected, and delinquent children. Some Part D money arguably intended for very seriously handicapped children has almost surely "leaked" to mildly disabled LD pupils. The Chapter One handicapped program was devised with the intention that severely disabled children could be educated in federally subsidized state institutions where they would receive services not available in local districts.[39] In order to encourage transition to mainstream classrooms, though, the legislation provided that students served in SOPs could move into regular schools and continue to receive Chapter One funding. In the late 1970s and early 1980s, many states established state-operated preschools to implement early intervention services for handicapped children, and these schools tended to have a larger proportion (15 percent nationwide) of mildly handicapped children than regular SOPs. These mildly disabled youngsters would get transferred to district schools after preschool, usually taking their Chapter One SOP funds with them. A 1989 General Accounting Office study found, however, that there is considerable variation in the degree to which states count children with mild handicaps under Part D of Chapter One, and the problem persists. The report found that the states dominating the

Chapter One handicapped program (Illinois, Massachusetts, New York, and Pennsylvania) had only 20 percent of the nation's children with disabilities, yet had 47 percent of the total Chapter One–funded handicapped population, largely because these states identified disproportionate numbers of mildly handicapped children as eligible for Chapter One funds.[40]

THE COSTS OF COMPLIANCE WITH IDEA

At the time IDEA's predecessor statute was passed, Congress committed itself to funding, eventually, 40 percent of the incremental costs of special education. However, federal financial aid appropriated through IDEA[41] was, in 1992–93, only $1.94 billion.[42] Although state and local district spending figures are not included in the 1992 or 1993 Annual Reports to Congress, we (conservatively) estimate the "excess costs" of special education as being roughly $26.8 billion by 1991–92.[43]

While roughly half (49.9 percent) of children served under IDEA and Chapter One are learning disabled,[44] one should not attribute half of that $26.8 billion in incremental costs to spending on those with LDs. If we construct a weighted index, in which we assess the relative marginal costs of educating different classes of disabled students, as measured in the most detailed micro-district studies,[45] multiplied by the proportion of students of each disability class served under IDEA and Chapter One, we find it most plausible to estimate that roughly 33 percent of the incremental costs should be attributed to those with learning disabilities.[46] Thus, given these suppositions, the incremental cost of educating students diagnosed by districts as having LDs is roughly $9 billion per year.

As long as a state intends to run *some* special education program, and the federal contribution to such programs exceeds the incremental cost of compliance with IDEA (the costs borne as a result of running an IDEA-compliant program that the state would not otherwise choose to bear), the state will, acting as a simple economic calculator, choose to comply with IDEA. Imagine, for instance, that a hypothetical state's ideal special education program, free of federal influence, would cost $75 million, that the program mandated by IDEA costs $100 million, and that the federal government contributes $30 million to special education if the state chooses to comply with IDEA. The state would then presumably choose to "join" the federal program. It thus seems, at first blush, that IDEA does not establish "unfunded mandates," though it does establish mandates for those states that choose to receive federal funds for special education. We can say, of course, that local spending far exceeds the federal contribution, but we cannot say that local spending exceeds the sum of federal contributions and the amounts that would be spent in the absence of the "regulatory tax" (the requirement to expend funds in a federally mandated fashion). To do so, we would have to be able to assess what states would expend on special education in the absence of IDEA, and this simply cannot be done.

It is possible to argue, though, that the implicit "regulatory" federal tax may be larger than the federal fiscal contribution for two distinct reasons. First, IDEA may well provide not just fiscal leverage but political leverage for local advocates of expanded special education. It might be politically difficult for states to refuse to comply with IDEA, or even more, to drop out of compliance, even if the statute demands federally uncompensated increases in spending above levels that might otherwise be reached in local political contests.

Second, and perhaps more significant, even if a state were to opt out of IDEA, it would still have to comply with the (unambiguously unfunded) federal mandates of §504 of the Rehabilitation Act, and it is not clear that the sum of the legal settlement and substantive costs of complying with §504 would be any lower than the cost of complying with IDEA. It is more plausible, in fact, that the reverse is true. The substantive demands of §504, as currently interpreted, appear no more lenient than those of IDEA, while §504 disputes would engender very high litigation and settlement costs compared with the administrative costs of compliance with IDEA. Once a state chooses to comply with IDEA, parents may well believe they have no entitlements so long as the state has complied with an approved, routinized, and bureaucratized process of identifying and accommodating their children with disabilities. If, though, the state is not IDEA-compliant, not only will parents raise issues that demand procedural responses for which the schools might not be adequately prepared, but they will also raise substantive claims that are colorably reasonable under either statute, but which might seem like more of a "long shot" if a district is already monitored for compliance with a rights-protective statute.

It is conceivable, for instance, that our hypothetical state's ideal special education budget is just $55 million, the IDEA-compliant budget $100 million, and the federal contribution only $30 million, yet the state chooses to comply with IDEA because §504 suits would add more than $15 million to its ideal budget, in some combination of mandated (but federally uncompensated) services and legal defense costs. If this were true, of course, it would be plausible to say that "federal mandates" had forced the state to adopt a budget that was $45 million higher than the budget it would have adopted in the absence of the combination of funded and unfunded federal mandates.

Only one state (New Mexico) chose not to apply for federal funds under IDEA's predecessor statute, the Education of All Handicapped Children Act (EAHCA), when the statute went into full force in 1977. By 1984 New Mexico, too, chose to implement the statute.[47] It is obviously not possible to fully "explain" the ultimate decision to comply, or the initial decision to resist, but it is worth noting that the state clearly faced the prospect of having to comply with most of the law's substantive demands, under §504, without receiving federal funds to help meet the demands. In *New Mexico Association for Retarded Citizens et al. v. State of New Mexico*,[48] the federal District Court upheld the right of the state not to seek federal funds under EAHCA against plaintiff's claims that the court should force participation, but found, nonetheless, that the state was required, under §504, to provide a free appropriate public education for all handicapped children in the state, an education whose contours were defined, essentially, by the EAHCA standards. While the Tenth Circuit reversed the decision,[49] finding that the District Court had, in essence, not adequately considered whether the state's existing special education programs required overhauling to meet the substantive demands of §504, the Tenth Circuit did not deny that the state was obliged to meet these demands, whatever they might prove to be. Since the state decided to comply with EAHCA by 1984, the case became moot before a decision on remand was made that would have enabled us to see how closely §504 and EAHCA demands tracked one another in at least one court's view.

Legal regulation of local districts

While keeping this basic summary of the legal structure in mind, we focus attention on five distinct issues. First, we will look at how federal law regulates district procedures to identify learning disabilities, recalling the discussion in Chapter 2 that pupils with LDs are not uncontroversially or cleanly distinguished from other poor learners. Second, we will look at the nature of the substantive obligations a district has to a child with a learning disability (for example, must the district help him reach his maximum potential? as much of his potential as nondisabled students typically meet? or simply make some academic progress?). Third, we will look at potential limitations on the prima facie obligation to provide services to LD students (including placement in the "least restrictive environment"); we will look, in this regard, at direct "cost defenses" and, more briefly, "disruptiveness" defenses that districts might proffer. Fourth, we will look at discipline issues more generally: under what conditions may the school district suspend or expel disabled students the district believes have violated rules that remain generally enforceable against nondisabled students? Finally, we will discuss federal law on testing accommodations.

FEDERAL EFFORTS TO INFLUENCE DIAGNOSIS

States receiving federal funds for special education have an affirmative duty, under IDEA, to identify those students suffering from a specific learning disability.[50] States *may* choose, in identifying students with LDs, to take account of "aptitude and achievement tests, teacher recommendations, physical condition, social or cultural background, and adaptive behavior," as long as the evaluation is performed by a group of persons including persons knowledgeable about the specific child, and as long as the evaluating team documents its findings.[51]

The goal of the evaluation team is to identify as learning disabled each child who does not "achieve commensurate with his or her age and ability levels in one or more of the areas listed [below] . . . when provided with learning experiences appropriate for the child's age and ability levels, [as long as the team] finds that a child has a severe discrepancy between achievement and intellectual ability in one or more of the following areas: oral expression, listening comprehension, written expression, basic reading skill, reading comprehension, mathematics calculation, or mathematics reasoning."[52] Children are deemed not to have a learning disability, however, whose discrepancies between achievement and ability are "primarily the result of a visual, hearing, or motor handicap, mental retardation, emotional disturbance, or environmental, cultural, or economic disadvantage."[53]

While the federal requirements do not define learning disabilities in much detail, nor give any exacting criteria to distinguish between students with and without LDs, the statutes are not wholly permissive either, at least procedurally. There are limits on the techniques that the local districts may use in diagnosing LDs that are of some importance.

First, although no particular diagnostic procedures are required, both IDEA[54] and the regulations interpreting §504[55] preclude the district from relying *solely* on "objective" tests to identify children as having learning disabilities. In the words of IDEA, "no single procedure shall be the sole criterion for determining an appropriate educational program for a child." We discuss in Chapter 4 the degree to which distinct districts emphasize discrepancies between achievement and intelligence test scores in making LD diagnoses, but federal law bars them from relying exclusively on discrepancy scores in making diagnostic decisions.

Second, both statutes require that the child be identified by a multidisciplinary team at the school site, a team that must include his regular classroom teacher,[56] or, if he does not have a regular classroom teacher, a regular classroom teacher qualified to teach a child of his age. The team must also include at least one person (most commonly a school psychologist) qualified to conduct individual diagnostic tests. At least one team member other than the regular classroom teacher must observe the child's academic performance in his regular classroom setting as well.[57]

Third, federal law attempts to regulate the testing process, both to ensure that districts administer only tests that are generally acceptable measures of the phenomena they purport to measure and to ensure that the tests reasonably measure the traits of students who might be expected to "underachieve" on certain tests for irrelevant reasons (ethnic origin, limited English proficiency, other handicapping conditions). Thus both statutes require that the tests the districts employ have been validated for the specific purpose for which they are being used, and that they be administered by trained personnel in conformance with the instructions provided by the test producers.[58]

Testing should be sensitive both to cultural differences between students and the impact of handicapping conditions on test performance itself. Largely in response to fears that unduly high numbers of minority and "limited English proficiency" (LEP) students were being diagnosed as mentally retarded as a result of tests that purportedly demonstrated their lack of intelligence, §1412(5)(C) of IDEA specifically provides that "testing and evaluation materials and procedures utilized for the purposes of evaluation and placement of handicapped children will be selected and administered so as not to be racially or culturally discriminatory" and that "such materials or procedures shall be provided and administered in the child's native language or mode of communication, unless it clearly is not feasible to do so." Moreover, because of fears that students with a particular disability were wrongly deemed to suffer from disabilities that they did not in fact possess as a result of tests that gave them inadequate opportunity to manifest their actual skills, §504 has been interpreted to require that "[diagnostic] tests are selected and administered so as best to ensure that, when a test is administered to a student with impaired sensory, manual, or speaking skills, the test results accurately reflect the student's aptitude or achievement level or whatever other factor the test purports to measure, rather than reflecting the student's impaired sensory, manual, or speaking skill (except where those skills are the factors that the test purports to measure)."[59]

Provisions designed to protect African-American students against discrimination may be differentially applicable depending on the type of disability the student might arguably have. Presumably, traditional IQ tests are biased against African-Americans in the sense that they understate their actual ability because they contain unduly culturally specific questions, constructed with white test-takers as the unstated "norm." Thus, for diagnosing mental retardation, which requires that the student exhibit "significantly subaverage general intellectual functioning,"[60] one would expect that African-Americans would be overdiagnosed if IQ tests were used exclusively (or even substantially).

In the case of LD diagnosis, though, one would expect the opposite: African-American students would be underdiagnosed as having learning disabilities if IQ/achievement discrepancy testing dominated, unless the achievement tests deflated "true" achievement as much as IQ tests deflate "true" ability.[61] Moreover, if we were to decline to administer IQ tests to African-American children in order to protect them against overdiagnosis as EMR, we might confront the equally troubling problem that they would be under-diagnosed as LD. Problems of underdiagnosis can be managed in two ways. First, we could proscribe excessive reliance on tests, as the aforementioned provisions in IDEA appear at least partly de-signed to do, in order to permit identification of pupils with LDs who would not be identified by test-based methods alone. Second, we could permit the use of IQ tests to diagnose black children as having learning disabilities, but not to diagnose them as mentally retarded.

In *Larry P. v. Riles*,[62] the Ninth Circuit affirmed a district court's finding that IQ tests were not validated for placing black children who scored below a cut-off point in special education classes for the educably mentally retarded.[63] (At the same time, the court affirmed the lower court's finding that the California school system did not use the variety of information required by federal regulations, but instead relied too exclusively on the IQ test in making special edu-cation placement decisions.)[64] In 1986, pursuant to a settlement, the district court expanded its original injunction and banned the use of IQ tests for all special education assessments of African-American children, not just for EMR classes. Not surprisingly, this order was eventually challenged by a group of African-American parents, who recently succeeded in having the modification vacated so that African-American children suspected of having learning disabilities can once more be assessed in the same way that white children in California were always assessed, through the use of an IQ-discrep-ancy method.[65]

As for the requirement that tests and other evaluation methods be provided and administered in the child's native language, this only goes part of the way toward addressing the problem of potential overclassification of students with limited English proficiency. Few cases articulate any standard for ensuring that a child's learning difficulties not be attributed to a disability when caused by limited English proficiency.[66] Naturally, parents (and pupils) also worry (once more) about underinclusion as well as overinclusion in spe-cial education programs resulting from LEP. For example, in *Jose P. v. Ambach*, the court focused on the failure of the defendant district

to identify LEP students as eligible for special education when they
needed special services.[67]

IDEA does not specify the precise claims disabled students are entitled to make to educational resources. As interpreted by the
Supreme Court in the seminal case of Hendrick Hudson District
Board of Education v. Rowley,[68] the act does require that the disabled pupil's IEP be "specially designed to meet the unique needs
of the handicapped child, *supported by such services as are necessary to
permit the child `to benefit' from the instruction.*"[69] Despite this hold-
ing, the Court is quite explicit that the act does not specify any particular level of educational benefit that must be provided. The Court
thus states, "the intent of the Act was more to open the door of public education to handicapped children on appropriate terms than to
guarantee any particular level of education once inside."[70]

It is still, more than a decade after *Rowley* was decided, far easier
to say what districts are *not* required to do to meet the mandate to
provide an education that "benefits" the handicapped child than to
say what they must do.[71] Presumably, an affirmative standard
would inevitably require either explicit "output" goals (each student must gain a particular set of skills, or each student, given a particular diagnosis, must make a particular level of progress); "input"
goals (per pupil spending must be at least $X per year, or must be
$Y per year given a particular handicapping condition); or broader
(albeit vaguer) statements of nondiscriminatory purpose. For example, courts might mandate that handicapped students be
brought to the highest level of functioning that they can attain, so
that resources must be expended till they produce no incremental
benefit. They might order that handicapped students achieve the
same "proportional" level of maximum functioning that nonhandicapped students do, regardless of cost. They might simply declare,
more vaguely still, that resource decisions made about handicapped
students must be made in the same fashion as resource decisions
that would be made about nonhandicapped students, in the sense
that the district cannot choose to deprive a child of resources based
on stereotypes about the limits of her capacity or discounting of the
importance of the quality of her education or life more generally.

Instead, *Rowley* and its progeny simply dismiss certain conceptions of the requirements districts must meet: the law in this area is fundamentally *negative*. *Rowley* itself, for instance, notes that it is not necessary for the district to establish a plan that maximizes the disabled student's achievements (brings her up to her potential),[72] a view that has been echoed in subsequent lower court decisions. Thus, for instance, in *G.D. v. Westmoreland School District*, the First Circuit declared:

> Following *Rowley*, courts have concluded that a FAPE [free appropriate public education] may not be the only appropriate choice, or the choice of certain selected experts, or the child's parents' *first* choice, or even the best choice. . .[A] FAPE is simply one which fulfills the minimum federal statutory requirements.[73]

A district may choose the least expensive among adequate plans,[74] or change a child's placement to a less expensive but still adequate placement in order to save resources.[75] Moreover, the courts are generally rather deferential to district decisions regarding a student's individualized educational program, even in the face of competing experts who claim the district's proposal is inapt. Thus, for instance, one court noted that it would not order a district to implement a plan that a majority of experts at trial testified was necessary, noting that "a head count of clinical experts . . . is not what the Act requires."[76]

State regulations frequently rely on the premise that IDEA requires only a placement meeting the *Rowley* standard, not the best placement. Thus, for instance, state regulations may require that parents and guardians give school districts an opportunity to evaluate and develop an IEP for a child before unilaterally placing the child in a different educational placement, to preclude parties from forcing states to pay for expensive services the district would not be required to provide.[77]

Similarly, the Court noted in *Rowley* that the district need not supply the disabled child with the same opportunities that nondisabled children receive.[78] This aspect of the holding, not surprisingly, has had little influence on subsequent decisions since it is not at all clear what the Court might have meant had it declared that disabled students did deserve the same opportunities as nonhandicapped pupils.[79]

The *Rowley* court rejects yet another outcome-oriented measure, declaring that the local districts need not devote resources to each child with a disability sufficient to ensure that he or she achieves self-sufficiency as an adult, arguing that "[b]ecause many mildly handicapped children will achieve self-sufficiency without state assistance while personal independence for the severely handicapped may be an unreachable goal, `self-sufficiency' as a substantive standard is at once an inadequate protection and an overly demanding requirement."[80]

Rowley also disdains input-oriented measures. Reiterating prior Supreme Court (constitutional) holdings that students were not entitled to demand that states spend equal amounts per pupil[81] and reasoning that Congress, aware of such opinions, would not create a right to equal funding through statute inexplicitly, the Court found that IDEA's predecessor did not demand that districts spend as much on a disabled as a nondisabled child.[82]

Arguably, the only affirmative mandates in *Rowley* are that: (a) The district allocate scarce funds "equitably," that is, that the interests of nonhandicapped children not trump the interests of disabled children, at least if doing so results in disabled children being "excluded" from educational services they need and could benefit from.[83] (b) The district's individualized educational program should be reasonably calculated to permit the disabled child to "achieve passing marks and advance from grade to grade."[84] Lower courts have subsequently clarified and strengthened this second requirement, noting that the schools should not simply declare that a disabled child has passed and move him on to the next grade, but must permit him to make genuine academic progress that merits his promotion,[85] and also noting that IEPs which result in educational regression are presumptively invalid,[86] though even educational regression is not conclusively presumed to demonstrate an inappropriate IEP, given the possibility of "normal regression" (especially associated with shifts in placement).[87] Courts also judge the validity of IEPs "prospectively" (that is, in terms of what seemed appropriate at the time a plan was formed), so that the fact that the pupil has in fact failed to benefit or regressed will not permit the court to infer, without further inquiry, that the district has failed to meet its *Rowley* obligations.[88]

The requirement that students make academic progress has less teeth than it might appear to. For those disabled students whom the school *chooses* to place in mainstreamed classes on a diploma track, the district will indeed be mandated to provide services sufficient to ensure promotion, but there is no real requirement that the child be placed in such a track.[89]

Though deferential to district judgments regarding particular pupils' needs, courts are prone to overturn school district judgments when the districts attempt to establish per se cost-savings rules. In this regard, it is vital to note that a district trying to save money on pupils with learning disabilities would almost certainly act through such per se rules, rather than challenging the cost of each moderately costly IEP.[90] Judges generally believe such per se allocation rules violate the act's procedural requirement that individualized educational determinations be made, in part because they seem to presume that 'general' plans *must* be inadequate for some particular pupils. Thus, for instance, courts have rejected per se rules against providing more than 180 school days per year to handicapped children[91] and rejected general rules capping reimbursement rates for private providers.[92] However, even per se allocation rules have been upheld where the reviewing court found little chance of educational detriment. For instance, a state requirement that placements be made from a preapproved list of service providers was upheld.[93] Where, though, the court believes that none of the preapproved providers will supply an adequate education, such preapproved lists will violate IDEA.[94]

States can, and do, set higher standards than those demanded by *Rowley*. For instance, the Michigan statute[95] proclaims that the disabled child must be educated in a fashion that will allow the child to maximize his or her potential. But courts asked to implement these statutes typically shy away from their facially non-cost-conscious demands: thus in *Barwacz v. Michigan Department of Education*,[96] the federal district court stated:

> [Michigan law] does not define the phrase "maximum potential." We believe that there is some limitation on what kind of program is required. When two competing educational programs which meet the child's requirements are evaluated, the needs of the handicapped child should be balanced with the needs of the state to allocate scarce funds among as many handicapped children as possible.[97]

Similarly, the First Circuit's interpretation of a Massachusetts statute[98] which also nominally requires that special education programs "assure the maximum possible development" of all disabled students was more consistent with the traditionally looser federal standard. The court refused to compare the benefits to the child of a private placement proposed by the parents with the benefits derived from the state placement, though such a comparison would obviously be necessary if the goal were to maximize the child's development.[99] Frankly, we are not surprised (or bothered, normatively) that courts refuse to give much credence to statutes that seemingly demand maximization strategies for one subset of students in a world where the bulk of students do not receive anything close to the sorts of resources that would maximize their potential. To reach this result, though, courts must interpret rather linguistically unambiguous statutes in a very strained way.

LIMITATIONS ON "BALANCING"

Direct cost defenses   The decisions in *Rowley* and its progeny can be seen as efforts to establish prima facie obligations to disabled students. The limits of such prima facie obligations must of course be set with "balancing" concerns in mind. There would be no reason to deny disabled students any resources they requested unless others desired the resources that would be freed up if the disabled student's request were denied. However, these cases do not generally explicitly acknowledge the "competition" among students for scarce resources, or the clashing interests of disabled students who seek inclusion when other students have legitimate, nondiscriminatory reasons to exclude them. Thus we must also ask first, whether a district can deny a pupil a prima facie appropriate and required educational placement because it is too costly, and second, whether a district can deny a prima facie appropriate placement, one more beneficial to the disabled student than more restrictive alternatives, because the presence of the disabled student in the environment most appropriate to her would disrupt the education of other pupils.

We will assume for purposes of this discussion that the district concedes, in the first case, that it would ordinarily be obliged to provide a certain placement to a disabled child, in order to ensure that she has a reasonable chance of making even minimal educational progress. At the same time, the district claims that the cost of meeting even the ordinary minimal obligation is excessive, and that it should be allowed, therefore, to set up a program that would result in the pupil's making less educational progress than most disabled students are entitled to demand. Complainants in this first sort of controversy have typically been seriously physically and emotionally handicapped pupils.

As we noted, districts do limit, to some extent, the cost of educating handicapped pupils because their obligations to ensure more than "some educational progress" are quite limited. Districts have almost no capacity, however, to raise an effective cost defense to a proposed IEP which provides only that the pupil meet those goals that *Rowley* requires the district to meet. Thus, for instance, a district may successfully oppose a request to duplicate scarcely used special education facilities or techniques in different schools in the district because it does not want to bear the costs of duplication, but the formal basis of the defense is that the duplication is not necessary to meet the substantive obligations under *Rowley* to ensure that a child be enabled to make substantial educational progress.[100]

Cost may be raised *directly* as a defense only under certain limited conditions. These conditions, though, are conceptually senseless. The holding in *Greer v. Rome City School District*[101] is typical: "If the cost of educating *a* handicapped child in a regular classroom is so great that it would significantly impact upon the education of other children in the district, then education in the regular classroom is not appropriate."[102] Can the court really mean what it implies—that the district can raise a cost defense only if the marginal cost of educating the particular disabled child is so high that bearing the cost will jeopardize programs for nondisabled children? The court notes, by way of illustration and clarification, that a district needn't provide a full-time one-on-one tutor for each disabled child who might arguably "need" one. But it is difficult to imagine that in any but the smallest districts the cost of even the most lavish full-time services for a single student would have a significant budgetary impact.

Yet courts never explicitly reject this sort of pupil-specific language. No court has said, directly, that a district may resist an otherwise appropriate individualized educational program because if the sought-after IEP were put into place *for all similarly situated stu-*

dents, funds that would provide substantially greater benefits for nondisabled children would be unavailable.[103] Courts frequently note that districts can avoid bearing certain high-cost IEPs in order to ensure that other disabled children can receive adequate IEPs.[104] Even when protecting other IDEA-entitled beneficiaries, though, the courts do not hold that districts are entitled to resist IEPs that while (relatively) affordable in the case at bar, are considerably more burdensome if deemed generally mandatory.

Can the interests of nondisabled pupils trump the interests of students with disabilities in mainstreaming? Cases involving a variety of forms of alleged "disruptiveness" of disabled children in less restrictive "mainstreamed" settings raise the issues of conflicts between disabled and nondisabled students' "rights" more cleanly than do the cases in which the district alleges that otherwise "reasonable" IEPs simply cost more than they are worth. In the disruption cases, the district concedes that the disabled student himself would make the most educational progress in a mainstreamed setting. At the same time, though, the district seeks to place the child in a more segregated setting because he is (a) "disruptive" to education in the sense that his mainstreamed teachers will spend too much time on his needs and/or make undue curricular adjustments to permit him to function in the mainstreamed class, or (b) disruptive in the more traditional "disciplinary" sense, that is, he will seriously impair the capacity of his classmates to learn.

The leading case is *Daniel R.R. v. State Board of Education.*[105] The plaintiffs, parents of Daniel, a six-year-old with Down Syndrome and communication skills slightly below the level of a two-year-old, were unsuccessful in challenging the school district's decision to place Daniel in a segregated special education class. The Fifth Circuit states that one factor in deciding whether a less restrictive placement is appropriate is "what effect the handicapped child's presence has on the regular classroom environment and, thus, on the education that the other students are receiving."[106] The circuit court agreed with the factfinder's conclusion that

> Daniel was disrupting the class—not in the ordinary sense of the term, but in the sense that his needs absorbed most of the teacher's time and diverted most of her attention away from the rest of the class . . .[107]

> [Daniel's presence in a regular classroom was] unfair to the rest of the class. When Daniel is in the pre-Kindergarten classroom, the instructor must devote all or most of her time to Daniel. Yet she has a classroom filled with other, equally deserving students who need her attention. Although regular education instructors must devote extra attention to their handicapped students, we will not require them to do so at the expense of their entire class.[108]

Thus the child with a disability is not entitled to receive the educational placement most beneficial to him because other nondisabled students' interests outweigh his, at least insofar as he compromises such students' interests by taking up the teacher's time.[109]

When it comes to more traditional "disruptiveness" (misbehavior), the court is more ambiguous about whether other students' concerns directly count. Naturally, in discussing the issues that most directly concern us, the treatment of students with mild handicaps, such concerns are likely to be paramount. The *Daniel R.R.* court cites with approval federal regulations that state: "Where a handicapped child is so disruptive in a regular classroom that the education of other students is significantly impaired, *the needs of the handicapped child may not be met in the environment. Therefore regular placement would not be appropriate to his or her needs.*"[110] Thus, at least in theory, the district must find that the disabled child's education is impaired by his behavioral problems in the mainstreamed class. The implicit theory is that a child who misbehaves so badly as to have an adverse impact on the education of nondisabled children will be shunned, stigmatized, or harmed by those resentful children in a fashion that inexorably compromises his own educational achievement, not theirs. This may serve as a polite fiction: districts might simply determine that the disruptive child will do better in a pull-out class, whether they believe it or not, if she disrupts the mainstreamed one. But the nominal substantive decision is that disabled children's interests do indeed inevitably trump nondisabled students' interests.

Other circuits that have ruled on the matter have used a variety of subtle techniques to chip away at the minimal protections *Daniel R.R.* may have provided to the interests of nondisabled students. None has stated explicitly, however, that the interests of nondisabled children are unworthy of formal weight.[111] For instance, in *Oberti v. Board of Education of the Borough of Clementon School*

District,[112] Rafael, a child with Down Syndrome, was placed in a self-contained special education classroom in a neighboring district after a one-year trial of partial mainstreaming in a developmental kindergarten. In the developmental kindergarten, Rafael had exhibited a number of behavioral problems, including temper tantrums, hiding under furniture, toileting accidents, throwing books, disobeying and running away from the teacher, striking out at and hitting the teacher and the teaching assistant, and touching, hitting, and spitting on other children. In the special education classroom, the disruptive behaviors, while still present, were attenuated through a multisensory behavior management plan. While the court acknowledged the possibility that the nondisabled students' interests must be accounted for, it (1) heavily stressed the district's responsibility to provide all appropriate accommodations, and held that the school district had not taken adequate account of the supplemental materials and aids available for integrating Rafael into the regular classroom, including instructing the regular teacher in communication and special education skills, speech and language therapy, providing an itinerant teacher trained in educating the mentally retarded, multisensory behavior management, *and modification of the regular curriculum;* (2) noted that the fact that Rafael needs "more" attention does not mean that he needs "too much" attention; and (3) asserted, essentially as a matter of law, that nondisabled students would benefit from exposure to a child with a disability since it would, in essence, make them more tolerant of those with disabilities.

Obviously, it is an open empirical question whether disruptive students actually impair the educational attainment of their classmates.[113] What is most striking about the educational school literature on this issue is how *little* attention is paid to the question of whether mainstreaming, particularly mainstreaming behavior-disordered children, has impaired nondisabled students' academic performance. There is a great deal of literature, coming to a variety of conclusions, on whether mainstreaming helps the disabled student more than segregated classes do; there is a modicum of literature on the effects of mainstreaming on nondisabled students' attitudes toward disability,[114] but we have been able to find only two studies attempting to measure the academic impact of mainstreaming on the nondisabled student in which a control group of nondisabled nonintegrated students was included in the experimental design, and neither focuses on behaviorally disordered pupils.[115] Both, though, find no ill effects on the nondisabled student population.

There are two distinct issues that arise when one considers disciplining a student with a disability. First, districts must follow appropriate procedures before invoking any of the variety of disciplinary steps that they might be permitted, substantively, to invoke if they follow such procedures. Second, districts might be limited in the substantive decisions they can reach.

The leading case, *Honig v. Doe*,[116] decided by the Supreme Court in 1988, deals, on its face, only with the procedural question. There is nothing in *Honig* that precludes a district from taking any traditional disciplinary step (long-term suspension, expulsion) as long as the appropriate IEP committee recommends that the step be taken, and parents can avail themselves of all the appropriate appeals avenues that they would ordinarily have to challenge any recommended placement. *Honig* simply holds that the school district may not unilaterally impose any discipline more severe than a short (ten-day) suspension, because any discipline more extreme than that would constitute a "change in placement."[117]

Changes in placement may not be unilaterally imposed by the district, but they may occur. First, parents or guardians may choose to accept the district's recommendation that their child be suspended or expelled. Second, the district may go to federal district court, asking such a court to invoke its broad injunctive powers to expel the child (or suspend him for a long period) as long as the child poses a danger to himself or others[118] since the court, unlike the district, is not a local educational agency bound by IDEA's stay-put provisions. If the parents do not accept the disciplinary recommendation and no court will grant the injunction, the child is protected by the stay-put provisions of IDEA that preclude a change in placement without the appropriate IEP committee review, parental notification and participation, and right to appeal.

The substantive limits vary a bit by circuit.[119] All circuits forbid expulsion or long-term suspension of students whose alleged violation of a reasonable disciplinary code is deemed to be at least in part a "manifestation of the disability." The Ninth Circuit, uniquely, demands that the manifestation be "direct" rather than "indirect," though whether that distinction has consequences is open to question. Correlatively, if the behavior is not deemed a manifestation of the disability, the student may be expelled, though some (but not all) circuits require that disabled children who are expelled must still receive educational services (for example, home tutoring) even though other expelled students need not receive such services.[120]

Not surprisingly, there is no interesting substantive guidance regarding how the district ought to make judgments about which acts of misbehavior do and do not arise from the disability. The truth is that the courts appear to have no core cases in mind in which a student labeled disabled could be expelled. Instead, districts are simply admonished, in general terms, to make particularized judgments. Given the general plausibility of determinist explanations within our culture, any behavior could be seen to manifest the child's disability, particularly if the manifestation needn't be either the direct or the sole explanation of the violation. Thus one court ruled that a student's (relatively minor role) in a drug-dealing scheme could not result in his discipline since drug dealing was a manifestation of the child's learning disability, which purportedly impaired his capacity to comprehend or give long-term consideration to the consequences of his action.[121]

Moreover, quite aside from the conceptual problem of making manifestation determinations, lawmakers have responded to political pressure from parents of regular ed students, angered by what they perceive as overly permissive disciplinary rules for students with disabilities. Legislators have introduced bills, at the state and federal levels, to strip students of immunity from discipline for certain offenses, regardless of their disability status (for example, a number of proposed California bills would permit long-term suspension or expulsion of pupils with firearms);[122] and in 1997 Congress acted to weaken IDEA's protection for students possessing deadly weapons or assaulting others with such weapons.

The federal courts ignore a number of rather obvious questions about their partial grant of disciplinary immunity. First, it appears that only *prior* determinations that a child has a disability trigger both procedural and substantive protections against discipline, unless parents actively oppose discipline by asking for a de novo disability assessment. Why isn't every child facing an expulsion hearing entitled to a de novo determination of whether she is disabled and therefore entitled to the protections of IDEA? It is not implausible that every student who violates rules could make at least a colorable claim that he has not been properly identified as seriously emotionally disturbed or learning disabled.

Second, courts seem to assume that when proper procedures are followed, a child with a disability who misbehaves will not be suspended for a long period or expelled, but instead will be "downplaced" into what we call a "more restrictive environment" (MRE). Though it seems quite sensible to curtail expulsion in the name of the child's educational interests, why do the courts assume, so blithely, that the child's discipline problem will be handled if he is placed in a more restrictive environment? While it is facially plausible that misbehavior can be more carefully monitored and contained in smaller pull-out classes, it is at least as plausible that what the courts are doing is tolerating, implicitly, far higher levels of violence and misbehavior in such classes because they devalue the significance of the educational process in the MREs (which will often contain children with serious disabilities who pose no behavior problems).

In our view, both Congress and the courts have been badly confused over what constitute plausible goals in curtailing discipline of those with disabilities. It is perfectly reasonable to believe that schools ought not to expel youngsters at all, that no one should be punished by shortchanging her capacity to learn. But such a position requires that Congress forbid expulsion rather than merely forbid expulsion of a subclass of those who misbehave.

It is plausible, too, that school districts historically tried, and might in the absence of regulation continue to try, to rid themselves of expensive/difficult disabled children by trumping up disciplinary charges against them. If that is the problem, though, the district ought to be required simply to demonstrate that it expels an IDEA-protected child only for violations that have resulted (at some frequency level) in the expulsion of nonprotected children or that districtwide expulsion rates for IDEA-protected students do not exceed such rates for similar offenders who are unprotected.

If, instead, the student's claim is that his misbehavior is a result of inappropriate *placement*, then the district ought to be entitled to expel him if he has violated rules in different placements, or make a case that there is no colorable connection between the misbehavior and the placement.[123] It *is* significant to determine whether misbehavior is a manifestation of an improper placement, in the sense that the child would be less likely to engage in the proscribed conduct if placed in a more apt setting, but it is vacuous to ask whether the behavior is a manifestation of the disability itself. The school is duty bound to increase the chances that each child with a disability will succeed educationally (and part of educational success is not to violate a reasonable discipline code). Thus, if the child is in a setting which does not maximize her chances of obeying the code, it is reasonable to think the district has not appropriately accommodated her special educational needs. But there is no reason to immunize children with disabilities from the discipline code, and requiring only the simple (and utterly ambiguous) showing that their misconduct is a manifestation of their disability is nothing more than a semi-administrable grant of immunity.

TESTING ACCOMMODATION

Section 504 and its implementing regulations mandate that recipients of federal funds make reasonable accommodations for students with disabilities, including pupils with LDs, in their program requirements, including examinations (both those used in making admissions decisions and those used to evaluate pupils). However, both the regulations and the courts that have interpreted §504 permit the use of either a program requirement, a test, or a testing method that factually disadvantages students with disabilities as long as the school can show that modifying the curriculum, test, or testing method will fundamentally alter the nature of the program or lower academic standards.

This general standard, of course, is a bit hollow. The live question is to what extent the courts will defer to a school's judgment that a curricular modification or waiver of a substantive test requirement would undermine or alter the program or defer to the judgment that a particular test format assesses skills that are the very skills the school intends to measure. On balance, courts have been deferential to educational institutions on both questions, but perhaps even more so on the first one.[124]

The starting point in analyzing testing accommodations is that schools may not, under §504, use admissions tests or course-work tests that discriminate against those with disabilities. The Office of Civil Rights of the Department of Education interprets that command to preclude admissions tests with a disproportionate adverse impact on the class of applicants with disabilities unless the test with an adverse impact "has been validated as a predictor of success in the educational program . . . and . . . alternate tests or criteria that have a less disproportionate, adverse effect are not shown by the Assistant Secretary to be available."[125] Schools may validate the tests using first-year grade point average as the criterion, but they are nominally required, periodically, to study whether the tests predict not just first-year grades but overall success in the education program.[126]

Once students are admitted, a school must "make such modifications to its academic requirements as are necessary to ensure that such requirements do not discriminate or have the effect of discriminating, on the basis of handicap, against a qualified handicapped . . . student."[127] Naturally, the key question is whether the student with a disability is qualified if unable to meet the unmodified curricular demands. The regulation specifies that "academic requirements that the recipient [of federal funds] can demonstrate are essential to the program of instruction being pursued by such student . . . will not be regarded as discriminatory." Similarly, examinations (and other evaluation methods) must "best ensure that the results of the evaluation represents [*sic*] the student's achievement in the course rather than reflecting the student's impaired sensory, manual, or speaking skills, (except where such skills are the factors that the test purports to measure)." The courts have been clear in stating that the institutions need not "fundamentally alter" their requirements to guarantee that a pupil with a disability can succeed.[128]

The key operational question for the district courts is whether to defer to the school's purported "expertise" in curriculum design. The plaintiff in the leading case, *Wynne v. Tufts University School of Medicine*,[129] was a dyslexic who was dismissed from Tufts Medical School when he failed a multiple choice biochemistry test three times. The court held that the recipient of funds discharges its duty when it

submits undisputed facts demonstrating that the relevant officials within the institution considered alternative means, their feasibility, cost and effect on the academic program, and came to a rationally justifiable conclusion that the available alternatives would result either in lowering academic standards or requiring substantial program alteration.[130]

On appeal from remand, the First Circuit held that the school had met its burden, by "document[ing] the importance of biochemistry in a medical school curriculum" and explaining why "the multiple choice format provides the fairest way to test the students' mastery of the subject matter of biochemistry."[131] The standard is clearly deferential: "[T]he point is not whether a medical school is 'right' or 'wrong' in making program-related decisions, particularly in a scholastic setting. The point is that Tufts, after undertaking a diligent assessment of the available options, felt itself obliged to [decide] that a reasonable accommodation was simply not available."[132]

It appears unexceptionable to us that the court shows deference on the subject matter that would seemingly be most within the university's competence: whether doctors ought to know biochemistry.[133] But it also is deferential where claims of expertise should be much more suspect: whether a dyslexic student's knowledge of biochemistry is well measured by a speeded, multiple choice exam.

We see little reason why the court gives nearly no weight to the plaintiff's evidence that at least one other medical school and a national testing service occasionally allow oral renderings of multiple choice exams for dyslexic students. The idea that particular university professors, or even departments reflecting on testing methods more collectively, have special expertise in judging whether modifications are needed to permit a student with a disability to demonstrate her knowledge, as the school is required to do,[134] is dubious.

Because schools are permitted to use formats that are especially difficult for pupils with disabilities to handle as long as the pupils' impaired sensory, manual, or speaking skills are "the factors that the test purports to measure,"[135] a deferential court will forever find itself accepting claims that the school meant to test precisely what it tested. In *Wynne*, for instance, the affidavit of the medical school dean stated that multiple choice exams are used because they are expressly designed to measure a student's ability not only to memorize complicated material but also to understand and assimilate it,[136] but the claim seems completely conclusory unless the school is at least willing to state and justify its implicit argument that doctors who cannot assimilate written material quickly are wanting in some meaningful fashion. (Such a claim does not seem facially implausible to us; what we question is the court's deference in the absence of a substantive record.)

The interpretive guidelines of the Equal Employment Opportunity Commission state, in the employment context, that "an employer can require a written test of an applicant with dyslexia if the ability to read is 'the skill the test is designed to measure'"[137] and that "an employer may require an applicant to complete a test within a specified time frame if speed is one of the skills being tested."[138] But the employer must still show that reading skill and/or speed are legitimate job requirements, related to the position in question.[139] We recognize that an educational institution has no clear "goal" (and hence no "criterion" or output measure) that would permit ready "validation" of a job requirement. A business, of course, would ordinarily act as a profit maximizer, attempting to maximize the net productivity of its labor force, and hence could validate a predictor by showing the predictor correlated with productivity. Still, a school must do more than simply state that "reading counts" or "speed counts." It should be forced to articulate a fuller conception of the relationship of the skills it teaches and tests to performance of graduates in relevant adult settings or analogize the faculties to other abilities whose relevance is less disputed.

FOUR

Local Practice I: Diagnosis and Placement

Local practice overview

In this and the following chapter we describe some of the ways in which formal federal law gets translated into local practice. As we have seen, formal federal law is quite open-ended in directing school districts whom to diagnose as having a learning disability, what diagnostic procedures to follow, how to educate those who have been diagnosed, and when it is permissible to discipline those who are or might be considered disabled. For this reason, one cannot truly understand prevailing policy toward pupils with learning disabilities without considering how local districts implement federal law. To this end, we have drawn on a number of sources and methods. First, we have statistically analyzed data collected from public sources. We also conducted a telephone survey of twenty special education coordinators in California and in-depth, semi-structured interviews with special education coordinators in four states. (The methods we employed in conducting the in-depth interviews are described in the appendix.) In addition, we conducted less structured interviews with several special education and classroom teachers, disability resource specialists at the university level, and a lawyer specializing in disability and education issues. Finally, we reviewed secondary materials published on this topic over roughly the past twenty-five years in a variety of disciplines, including education, psychology, medicine, and law.

We present our discussion of local practice in two chapters in order to emphasize two distinct aspects of implementation. This chapter describes our own and others' findings on the social and demographic factors that might influence the diagnosis and placement of students with learning disabilities. Chapter 5 focuses on two of the major local conflicts that typically arise as districts attempt to implement IDEA's mandates—contests over the allocation of classroom resources, and issues of fairness in meting out disciplinary sanctions against children who misbehave. Taken as a whole, though, the materials in these two chapters suggest some general themes that we find quite striking.

In some ways, district practice raises disturbing issues that one would not see if one looked solely at the formal statute. Upper middle-class white boys receive discretionary resources in low-stigma settings that might better be used by other students with learning difficulties. African-Americans get shunted, too often, into dead-end classes. Serving elementary school students in resource room classes for part of the school day may pose severe problems when the pupils attempt to reintegrate. The discipline system we see in the wake of IDEA is troublesome. Irrational distinctions are certainly made between similarly situated pupils, and the school may engage in expensive, educationally pointless warehousing of behaviorally disordered children to comply, formally, with federal restrictions on discipline while avoiding them substantively.

Yet for those of us loath to establish a system in which being labeled "disabled" gives a pupil strong priority to have his educational goals met even when his nondisabled classmates assert powerful competing claims, local practice is *less* troubling than the statute. Many districts deliberately "leak" special ed resources to other poor achievers, and even those that don't do so on purpose can't do a tremendous amount to stop it. Some (generally wealthy) districts do their best to ignore the "medicalized" IDEA model entirely, trying instead to serve all those with performance problems who seem to benefit from aid. Similarly, most districts separate disruptive students from mainstream classes a good deal more readily than the courts, and arguably Congress, suggest that they should, explicitly weighting the concerns of the regular ed pupils just as highly as the educational interests of the disabled pupils.

There is, of course, no way to know what each and every district in the country intends to do, let alone how each classroom teacher, resource room specialist, or testing psychologist is implementing district directives. We do not purport to survey or describe these practices exhaustively. Instead, our goal is to describe existing findings where data have been collected and analyzed systematically; to do our own analysis of reported data in a way that freshly elucidates certain patterns of district conduct; and, finally, to shed some light on relatively undocumented areas of conduct by describing administrators' own accounts of everyday practice.

Diagnosis and initial placement

In this chapter we will discuss several features of the diagnostic and placement process. We will look at diversity in diagnostic rates across states; diversity of diagnostic practices across districts; demographic (racial, class, and gender) patterns in diagnosis and placement, both across and within districts; and the roles that parents/guardians play in inducing or resisting certain diagnoses or placements.

IDEA formally requires that pupils with learning disabilities be identified and served as a discrete class of pupils with distinct neurological traits that cause them to perform considerably below their "potential." We question whether this formal policy is being implemented given persistent, patterned variations in diagnostic rates across states; given professed distinctions in diagnostic goals in socioeconomically distinct districts; and given the overrepresentation of African-Americans and males in the LD category, especially in self-contained classes.

DIVERSITY IN DIAGNOSTIC RATES ACROSS STATES

It is commonplace to note that the federal definition of learning disabilities is so inexact that rates of diagnosis vary dramatically by state.[1] It is, of course, not obvious what we mean when we say rates vary *dramatically*. Presumably, the hypothesis is that underlying population rates of the disability are (nearly) identical across states and that all the dispersion around the "true rate" is therefore a function of inexact diagnosis.[2] If, though, we compare dispersion of diagnosis of learning disabilities with dispersion of diagnosis for more recognizable, cleanly diagnosable physical disabilities (blindness, deafness, deaf-blindness, and orthopedic impairment), we find that dispersion levels are not markedly different. In fact, the standard deviation is roughly 28 percent of the mean for the sum of the physical disabilities, compared with only 22 percent of the mean for learning disabilities.[3]

Even if we assume that rates of LD diagnosis are more dispersed than we could account for without believing that diagnostic practice differs by state, another question remains. Do states with atypically high rates of LD diagnosis identify a higher proportion of substantively indistinguishable pupils as eligible for special education? Or do they simply label a higher proportion of the relatively severely disabled special ed population LD, rather than EMR, presumably to avoid the stigma of the EMR label?[4] In looking at the degree of inclusiveness of procedures to identify mildly disabled LD pupils, who we would expect would have the most diagnostic variability, we thus found it preferable to look at what we call the "soft LD" rate. This is the proportion of the state's school population labeled LD minus the decline in the percentage of the state's population dubbed EMR between 1976 and 1989 (which we believe largely reflects reclassification). We found that the variations in "soft LD" diagnosis are as significant as the variations in LD diagnosis more generally; the range is from 1.09 percent to 5.5 percent, the mean is 3.40 percent; the SD is roughly 27 percent of the mean.

What proved more instructive, both to judge the plausibility of the hypothesis that diagnostic techniques differ across jurisdictions and to investigate what factors might influence these variations, was to regress both the aggregate and "soft" LD rates and the "hard" physical disability rates against a number of variables that are not seemingly connected to pathology prevalence rates (or certainly no more connected to LD rates than to physical disability rates).[5] The results suggest that we can explain a moderate proportion of the variance in soft LD diagnostic rates among states with reference to variables that would not obviously be salient given prevailing biological conceptions of the origin of learning disabilities (adjusted $\bar{R}^2 = .28$; for aggregate LD rates, $\bar{R}^2 = .15$). By contrast, variations in hard disability rates cannot be explained on the basis of these same seemingly biologically irrelevant demographic variables ($\bar{R}^2 = .0$).[6]

VARIATIONS IN (INFORMAL) LOCAL DIAGNOSTIC PRACTICE

On the basis of some of our early in-depth interviews with special education coordinators, it occurred to us that LD diagnostic and placement practice might be influenced by the socioeconomic status (SES) of a district. For our first five in-depth interviews (which we discuss in greater detail later), we chose coordinators from districts with different socioeconomic characteristics. This permitted us to make very informal comparisons of the responses. We were struck by differences in their statements about the degree to which they adhered to statewide regulations requiring that discrepancy scores be given substantial weight in determining whether a pupil had a learning disability. Administrators from two relatively high SES districts in California and New York[7] indicated that they paid little attention to discrepancy scores, but instead sought to serve essentially all children who performed substantially more poorly academically than their peers within the high-achieving districts. Furthermore, unless they were severely disabled, these children were served dominantly in either the mainstream classroom or low-stigma resource room settings.

By contrast, two administrators supervising middle- to working-class districts in California[8] seemed vigilant about their roles as gatekeeper, expressing the view that unless diagnosticians were stringent in demanding an IQ-achievement discrepancy before authorizing services, special education would be overburdened. The one administrator we spoke with early on supervising a largely nonwhite, poor California district[9] told a different story again: in his view, *most* of the children in the district had special needs, and if they were not receiving services through IDEA, they usually received assistance through Chapter One programs. The administrator also told us, though, that many of the LD students were educated in self-contained classes; behavioral problems were a primary concern in the district, and the use of separate classes was an important tool for classroom management.

On the basis of our impressions from these interviews, we devised three hypotheses.

1. *Discrepancy scores as gatekeeping mechanisms* On the one hand, middle-SES districts would rely heavily on discrepancy scores as a way to block demands for services by the moderately high number of poor achievers. On the other hand, there would be low reliance on discrepancies in high- and low-SES districts, but for different reasons. In high-SES districts, districts would tend to give services to all children whose performance dropped significantly below the local norms, regardless of etiology. In low-SES districts, though, it would be true in part because IQ test scores were frequently depressed enough that it would be difficult to find large discrepancies. Also, educational need runs so deep that it cannot be met through special education alone: many of these pupils will receive federal Chapter One funds to provide fairly parallel resource infusions, with or without diagnosis. Thus LD diagnosis in a low-SES district often has relatively little impact on a pupil's access to aides, tutors, or people doing many of the same tasks as resource room teachers do. LD diagnosis may instead be reserved for the very troubled students, and may be driven more by misbehavior than by educational need.

2. *Treatment of high achievers* Middle-SES districts alone would obey federal requirements to identify even a high-achieving student as LD when her high achievement still failed to meet IQ-based "expectations." By contrast, we expect poorer districts would be less likely to provide special services to a high achiever. Wealthy districts, in order to justify widespread intervention in the lives of nearly all poor performers, may have adopted a local ideology/set of practices in which diagnostic work-up is triggered, in the first instance, only by academic or social problems. Moreover, in these wealthier districts, the potential numbers of "good" and "excellent" achievers whose parents still expect more of them will be high, and accommodating demands by all disappointed parents able to find a psychologist to make a claim that their child is underachieving would be difficult. In the moderate SES districts, by contrast, one might be able to accommodate "technically" diagnosed high-achieving LD children without setting off widespread pressure for diagnosis and service-receipt by parents.

3. *Placement* There would be an inverse relationship between district SES and the proportion of LD students placed in self-contained classrooms. In other words, low-SES districts would place

relatively more LD students in self-contained classrooms than mid-dle- or high-SES districts, which would rely more heavily on main-streaming and resource room settings.

We designed a survey of California district coordinators to in-vestigate these hypotheses. We selected twenty-seven districts using the rates of college attendance of local graduates in the previ-ous year as an indicator of SES.[10] In one-third of those districts, the overwhelming majority of pupils (65 percent or more) go on not just to postsecondary education but to four-year colleges; in one-third, fewer than half (30 to 40 percent) of the graduates go on to four-year colleges; and, finally, in one-third, a very low proportion of those who graduate (15 to 25 percent) go on to four-year colleges. One of us (GL) conducted the survey between October 1993 and September 1995. Interviews were in random sequence, by telephone, fifteen to thirty minutes in duration, and consisted of ten questions (which appear in the appendix). Sixty-nine percent (20) of the administra-tors we contacted responded, with roughly equal representation from the three groups. Six of the respondents were from high four-year college attendance districts, and seven each were from the mid-level and low attendance districts.

We are wary in construing the phone survey data. We view it as a pilot study not only because of the small sample size but also be-cause we remain conscious of the limitations of the responses and our ability to interpret these responses. There may well be significant discrepancies between a special education coordinator's view of what is going on in her district and what is actually hap-pening, particularly given (often subtle) irregularities in practice within the same district.

The most suggestive findings of the phone survey were as fol-lows:

a. *Reliance on IQ-achievement discrepancy scores*   The degree of re-liance on an IQ-achievement discrepancy did indeed vary by the four-year college attendance rates in the districts in our sample. A discrepancy was a necessary condition for diagnosis in only one of the six high-attendance districts (and that district had the lowest college attendance of the six), and it was a dominant factor in mak-ing the diagnosis in only one other such district. By contrast, a dis-crepancy was a necessary condition for diagnosis in three of the seven mid-level college attendance districts and the dominant factor in three of the other four. In the districts with the lowest college attendance rates, discrepancy scores were less critical. A discrepancy was a necessary condition for an LD diagnosis in only one of the seven low-SES districts and was dominant in just two of the others. These data were consistent with, though they obviously do not prove, our hypothesis about the patterns in the use of discrepancy scores.

b. *Diagnosis of students in the top third of the class*   There was little distinction across the districts in whether they would give students in the top third of their class aid for learning disabilities: two of the six high college attendance districts did so unhesitatingly, while four, consistent with our expectations that their special ed programs were directed rather single-mindedly at correcting academic failure, did so only when they could not dissuade "high-pressure" parents. But the breakdown was similar in the middle-class districts (two gave IEPs readily to high-achieving students who might be considered LD, one did so only when parents were aggressive, and four did not give them) and low-SES districts (two gave them readily, three wouldn't give them, and practice was more ambiguous in the other two). The finding that many districts may implicitly supplement the formal federal definition of the LD—adding in the requirement that the child have a low achievement level—is an interesting one in our view, regardless of whether this practice varies across districts. It suggests further resistance to the formal federal requirement that "medical condition" rather than academic need should drive delivery of special education services.

c. *Use of self-contained classes*   It appears that the LD category is indeed used for more behaviorally troubled children as districts get poorer and that special ed diagnosis is more often a prelude to separation from mainstreamed students rather than a prelude to the receipt of supplementary educational services in the mainstream class. In only one of six high-SES districts were more than 10 percent of LD pupils put in special day classes, while in only two of seven middle-SES and one of seven low-SES districts were *less* than 10 percent of LD pupils placed in such classes; more than 20 percent of LD pupils were in special day classes in four of the seven lowest-SES districts compared with one each in the high- and middle-SES districts.

DEMOGRAPHIC ISSUES IN DIAGNOSIS AND PLACEMENT

Race and class   Until the early 1970s, it would certainly have been possible to complain that the movement to gain entitlements for students with learning disabilities would divert resources from disadvantaged students—often poorer and disproportionately African-American—to upper middle-class white students. At the 1964 conference of the Council of Exceptional Children, a well-established nationally based research and lobby group for disabled persons, the bulk of the special education categories were explicitly said to correlate with poverty and race: children who were Puerto Rican, Mexican, southern blacks and whites who moved to urban areas, and the poor in rural and urban areas were said to be "unable to keep up" because they were (labeled) slow learners, mentally retarded, emotionally disturbed, or culturally deprived. The other group of students "unable to keep up" were the learning disabled, and they alone were identified without reference to the neighborhoods in which the special educators would find the problem prevalent; instead, they were said to come from "normal family stock."[11] The child with a learning disability would alone be entitled to nonstigmatic supplementary resources ("resource rooms" and instructors who would supplement his instruction in the regular classroom, a form of special ed tutor) while avoiding traditionally dead-end special ed classes.

Because data gathering on the special education population prior to the enactment of EAHCA was very primitive, it is difficult to say with assurance what the demographic profile of the population of pupils diagnosed as learning disabled actually was in the 1960s and early 1970s. However, in published studies on learning disabilities between 1963 and 1973 which reported the race and class composition of the pupils being studied, an astounding 98.5 percent of pupils were white, and 69 percent were middle class or higher in SES.[12] By the mid-1970s, though, the profile of LD students began to shift. Tucker's study of fifty school districts in the Southwest indicated that minority students were overrepresented in the LD category by 1973.[13] Similar data from California in 1981–82 found black and Latino students overrepresented in both LD and EMR programs in California; moreover, students in (predominantly minority-dominated) low-SES districts were twice as likely as students from high-SES districts to be placed in LD classes.[14] At first blush, then, it might appear that the problem of underdiagnosis of minorities with LDs, even if it did exist, has been solved. It looks as though, if anything, we began by the 1980s to witness excessive placement of some minorities, particularly blacks, in special education programs for pupils with learning disabilities.[15]

While there are contradictory findings about shifting racial patterns in the diagnosed LD population in the late 1970s and 1980s,[16] it is clear that today, looking only at gross numbers, "learning disability" is not, by any means, a white pupils' category. The 14th Annual Report on the implementation of PL 92-142 noted that blacks, who represent 12 percent of the youth population, were disproportionately represented in the LD population in 1987 (21.6 percent), though less so than they are overrepresented in the severely emotionally disturbed (SED) (25.1 percent) and EMR (31 percent) populations. Latinos were underrepresented in all three of these categories: they are 13 percent of the relevant youth population, and only 8.4 percent of the LD, 6 percent of the SED, and 5.6 percent of the EMR.[17] The report did not mention any other ethnic or racial groups. Whites are mildly underrepresented in the LD and SED categories—67.2 and 67.1 percent of the LD and SED populations respectively, compared with 70 percent of the youth population, and dramatically underrepresented in the EMR category, where they make up just 61 percent.[18]

We suspect, though, that if one looks in a more detailed way at both diagnostic and, to a greater extent, placement practice, *both* problems persist. It is possible that the IDEA system in practice continues to permit relatively privileged white pupils to capture high-cost or nonstigmatic in-class resources that others with similar educational deficits cannot obtain while, at the same time, allowing disproportionate numbers of African-American and poor pupils to be shunted into self-contained classes. Unfortunately, the federal government does not mandate that states or districts report the proportion of students of color who are placed in less restrictive settings, that is, receive supplementary in-class and resource room aid, as compared with the proportion who are put in self-contained classes or placed out-of-district.[19] Similarly, it does not attempt to measure whether the placement of black special ed students in self-contained classes substantially diminishes black presence in "mainstreamed" classrooms to proportions below what scholars such as

Derrick Bell have referred to as a "tipping point" (the point above which members of the white majority will tend to flee an institution), thus resulting in a form of (incomplete) racial segregation.[20] Nor does it attempt to look at how districts allocate especially expensive private school training to students with mild disabilities who claim that special education in the public schools has failed them.

We were alerted to the possible relationship between race and placement when the coordinator of one California SELPA (Special Education Local Planning Agency, a cooperative arrangement created by districts to handle special education concerns) shared data with us showing that just under 44 percent of the special ed population was Hispanic, just over 44 percent white, and just under 10 percent black. Only 37 percent of the children in self-contained ("special day") classes were white, however, compared with 47 percent of those seen by resource specialists, while 13 percent of the pupils in the special day class were black compared with only 8 percent of those seen in the resource rooms.[21] Meanwhile, thirteen mildly disabled pupils in the SELPA were currently in expensive private school placements. Their parents, claiming that their children's reading disabilities could only be successfully treated in expensive private schools, had successfully contested public school IEPs. Of these thirteen, twelve were white, and all were high-SES pupils.

Statewide figures in California suggest that the public school placement patterns in the above SELPA are not unusual. In 1991–92, 44.5 percent of public school pupils were white, 8.6 percent African-American, 36.3 percent Latino, and 8 percent Asian.[22] In resource rooms across the state, 49.4 percent of the pupils were white and 11.8 percent were African-American. Among children receiving Designated Instructional Services—extremely low-stigma therapeutic interventions, mostly for mild forms of speech pathology— only 9 percent of the pupils were African-American while 51.9 percent were white. In contrast, in special day classes, only 40 percent of the pupils were white and 15.6 percent were African-American. Furthermore, 37.1 percent of African-American children in special education were in special day classes; only 25.4 percent of white special education pupils were. Again, it is noteworthy that—perhaps as a result of the *Larry P.* case—African-American children were not disproportionately placed in special day classes *labeled* as classes for the mentally retarded (only 11.2 percent of the pupils in such classes were black), though disproportionate numbers of African-American children were nonetheless placed in special day classes with other designations (20.2 percent of the children in special day classes who were *not* in classes labeled for the mentally retarded or those with limited English proficiency were African-American).[23]

Disability status, and placement as well, is affected not just by race but also by class status. While only forty percent of students in the general population come from households with an annual income below $25,000, 68 percent of disabled children do. Similarly, 22 percent of the general student population lives in a household headed by a high school dropout while 41 percent of those with disabilities do.[24] The correlation between poverty and disability exists whether one is looking at cognitive/emotional disabilities (severe emotional disturbance, learning disability, or mental retardation) or physical disabilities. This suggests, even if it does not prove, that poverty is associated with a higher incidence of childhood difficulties, rather than that schools use soft disability categories to label poor children as disabled at higher rates than they do wealthier children with similar problems. It is possible, but unlikely, that the physical disability categories are as discretionary or manipulable as the cognitive/emotional categories.

It is plausible, but far more difficult to determine, that the following patterns have become prevalent. IDEA continues to provide white, upper middle-class LD pupils with in-class and resource room services at rates that are at least arguably unfairly high. It is likely that whites receive resource room or in-class aid at rates that are mildly, if not wildly, disproportionate to their population representation. At the same time, the effect of IDEA on mainstreaming is ambiguous. IDEA has clearly resulted in a modest increase in the mainstreaming of physically disabled students. A higher proportion of such students are served in regular classrooms and resource rooms than when the statute was enacted in the mid-1970s,[25] but its effect on the mainstreaming of students with other disabilities is less clear.

One could argue that while IDEA nominally "serves" a disproportionate number of students of color, it "serves" them by shunting them into dead-end special day classes. The growing availability of new, more loosely defined special ed categories, especially LD, but perhaps also SED (serious emotional disturbance), may well have resulted in an overall increase in the proportion of students of color who are removed from the mainstreamed classes.[26]

We performed a regression analysis in an attempt to determine the factors that influence diagnosis and placement of LD students. Our findings suggest that the proportion of a state's LD population that is seen in nonmainstreamed settings is extremely sensitive to demographic and political factors that might have rather little to do with distinctions in the need for more restrictive placements. Using the proportion of the 1989 LD population served outside of regular classes and resource rooms as the dependent variable, we regressed it against the demographic variables we described earlier. The adjusted R^2 was very high (.59) and a number of variables were significant. Most notably, for our purposes now, the proportion of blacks in the state's population was significantly positively associated with the use of nonmainstreamed settings ($p < .01$).[27]

It may be, though, that local practices are sensitive to district demographics in a fashion that makes any across-the-board generalizations about the relationship between race and diagnosis or service provision inapt. Thus, although the picture painted by the federal and state-level statistics we just presented may imply that the typical pattern of diagnosis and placement is that African-Americans are diagnosed and separately educated at disproportionately high rates while white children receive a disproportionate share of resource room and regular class aid, it seems possible that patterns of diagnosis and placement vary from district to district in patterned ways too subtle to show up in macro-level statistics. Our limited interview data permit us to do no more than suggest possible avenues for future research about the relationship between local district demographic patterns and practice, but we do think it worthwhile to present the research hypotheses that we formulated in response to these interviews.

In largely white, nearly racially segregated districts, our interviews suggest that the relatively few black pupils may be placed, at grossly disproportionate rates, into special ed classes in which they will have minimal contact with regular ed students, substantially furthering the degree of actual racial segregation in the district. At the same time, plenty of white pupils are said to have learning disabilities in these districts, but they are put in nonstigmatic settings (thus if one looked at districtwide numbers, there would be a heavy use of resource rooms and in-class aides for the white students). Thus, in one very high SES, heavily white and Asian New York district, the self-contained day classes are disproportionately composed of the (relatively few) low-SES students in the district; most of these students from poor families are Latinos, the primary racially subordinated group in the area.

More interesting, we believe, is the pattern reported to us by the special education director in a Louisiana parish. The elementary schools in this parish are relatively segregated, both by class and by race, as a result of geographical separation and the dominance of neighborhood schools. The junior high into which the elementary schools feed is somewhat integrated by class and race (though it is still predominantly white and middle class). At the elementary school level, the poorer schools (both white and black) diagnose a modest number of children as disabled (no more than the richer white elementary schools). When the schools are integrated in junior high, the administrator told us, a large number of previously undiagnosed black children (and to a lesser extent poor white children) are put into special ed. His account of this phenomenon was as follows:

> What I see here [in this parish] is [elementary] schools that are in the low socioeconomic area, they tend to put up with more misbehavior . . . they will go beyond what's [tolerated] in any other school in order to maintain that child in a regular classroom situation—whereas you take that child and move him to a predominantly white school [in junior high] and they're going to pull him right off the bat . . .
> When these kids head on to junior high on the east side of the river, some of these kids who've been in the regular classroom all along . . . and [the teachers at these schools] call and they say, "Look, we got a problem here, we've got fifteen kids here need to be referred."

Similarly, in a study conducted in Chicago, Rosenbaum, Kulieke, and Rubinowitz found that when a group of African-American youngsters moved from inner-city Chicago to surrounding suburbs under a court order to use housing vouchers to move public housing residents out of concentrated urban poverty settings, there was a dramatic increase in special ed placements. Only 7 percent of the youngsters had been in special ed in the city schools, while 19 percent of them were placed in special ed in the suburbs.[28]

Naturally, it is not possible to say whether the purpose (or, for that matter, even the effect) of these referrals is to resegregate the schools racially (or to drop the number of African-American children regularly interacting with white children below some "tipping point"). It is possible that the Louisiana district's African-American students referred for the first time in junior high should have been specially educated all along, or that their problems worsened over time. Nonetheless, there is evidence that black students who enter white-dominated schools districts get placed into special ed classes at rates far higher than those in segregated settings.

In racially integrated districts, it is obviously not as easy to "use" special education to, in effect, segregate either the special day classes or the mainstream classes. One might therefore expect a far lower proportion of the district's black population to be placed in special day classes than in the heavily white districts. In the most highly racially integrated school district we visited (a district in Mississippi), the schools sustained a very high level of mainstreaming. Even children with severe learning disabilities with very low levels of academic functioning are taught in "paired classrooms" through the sixth grade, where a special ed and regular ed teacher jointly teach classes composed of (roughly) twelve "regular" pupils and (roughly) six or eight severely LD students.[29]

In essentially segregated black districts, two patterns were reported to us. In some districts, "soft" disability diagnoses are commonplace, both SED and LD. One largely African-American Louisiana district diagnosed more than 15 percent of its pupils as eligible for special ed. A very high proportion of these children were termed BD/SED (BD, or behavior disordered, is a specific category in Louisiana). The district administrator attributed this high level of diagnosis partly to parental pressure created by a combination of financial incentives and discipline immunity incentives we will return to, and partly to the district's desire to segregate but not expel children who posed discipline problems. Special ed diagnoses may be attractive for reasons other than their pedagogic consequence, particularly given the availability of the alternative of providing Chapter One teacher/tutors to take care of many of the same learning problems.[30]

In other largely segregated black districts, though, very few students were diagnosed as learning disabled, and even if they were, few were treated as mildly learning disabled and served in resource rooms or in class with aides. The director of a California SELPA, attempting to account for the very low diagnostic rates in an impoverished, heavily African-American district within his SELPA (5 percent of the district's population were given special ed services, compared with roughly 10 percent in every other district in the SELPA) noted:

> There are children walking around in [two upper middle-class predominantly white and Asian districts within the SELPA] who have normal cognition, but have terrible self-esteem. Have emotional problems. Don't have any friends. And fit some of the criteria for SED if you want to push it . . . You take the same guy and you put him in [a very impoverished, dominantly black district within the same SELPA] . . . and he'd be accelerated . . . It has to do with IEP team determination, and the discussion within IEP teams [isn't just about] standard tests.

The SELPA director was not explicit about what he believed to be the cause of the district-specific diagnostic norms he perceived. One potential explanation for low incidence of diagnosis in such districts may be a desire to avoid taking on discretionary expenditures given district poverty. Another hypothesis is that there may be relatively low achievement expectations among many administrators (and perhaps some parents as well) in some very poor, highly segregated districts, so that students who perform "passably" (though they may be doing worse than they might as a result of disability) might go unserved. A Mississippi administrator noted: "[At the higher end, if you're thinking about a student whose IQ suggests he should be getting Bs, but he's getting Cs] most of the time that type of child we don't have in special ed. If they can pass the regular program."

Gender While slightly fewer than half (49.7 percent) of secondary school youth without disabilities are male, more than two-thirds (68.5 percent) of disabled secondary school youth are male. While males are only slightly disproportionately represented among the physically disabled (55.6 percent of those visually impaired, 54.2 percent of the orthopedically impaired, 53.4 percent of those with hearing impairments, and 49.5 percent of the deaf-blind) and moderately disproportionately represented among "hard" mental impairments (58 percent of the mentally retarded), they are dramatically overrepresented in both of the "softer," less clearly defined disability categories. Of those labeled seriously emotionally disturbed, 76.4 percent are male, and 73.4 percent of the population with learning disabilities are male.[31] Interestingly, boys have historically been far more overrepresented in the population of children said to have learning disabilities than in the population of poor readers. In the classic article distinguishing "garden variety" poor readers from those suffering from "specific reading retardation" (a form of LD), Rutter and Yule found that 76.4 percent of those with "specific reading retardation" were male, while only 54.4 percent of children whose poor reading achievement was not attributable to specific reading retardation were male.[32]

Boys may be overrepresented in the labeled LD population for two broad classes of reasons. First, boys may in fact, for fundamentally biological reasons, more frequently suffer from learning disabilities.[33] Alternatively, a far higher proportion of boys may be *diagnosed* as having a learning disability, though underlying population rates are (at least more nearly) the same. Those who believe that the differential diagnostic rates can be attributed in significant part to misdiagnosis believe, essentially, that boys are more frequently labeled LD than girls for three basic reasons.

1. Children are labeled LD not solely because of their learning deficits but because they are disruptive and regular ed teachers want help in managing them. Boys are more frequently disruptive.

2. Children are labeled LD when their teachers or parents are disappointed in their academic performance, and in a sexist world in which it is more common to be concerned about poor performance for boys, girls with identical discrepancies between achievement and potential will be ignored more frequently.

3. Even if special education diagnosticians were not *now* sexist or behavior driven in their diagnostic practices, the residual effects of prior sexism would lead to male overrepresentation. Diagnosticians have learned to identify learning disabilities on the basis of certain psychometric profiles garnered in studying the (dominantly male) population labeled LD of an earlier generation. Females who have

a psychometric profile different from that of the traditional (male) LD profile will thus often fail to be identified.

There is substantial, if not overwhelming, reason to believe, looking at aggregate data, that males are overdiagnosed as having learning disabilities, although we don't think it possible to know what the underlying population rates really are. Shaywitz and colleagues report that rates of reading disabilities among research-identified subjects are not statistically distinguishable by gender, while boys are more than twice as likely as girls to be identified as reading-disabled by schools,[34] but, as already noted, Rutter and Yule, among others, do not share this view.

It appears that girls may not be diagnosed in schools as learning disabled unless they function more poorly than boys who are so diagnosed. Females receiving services for LD have substantially lower IQ scores than males.[35] In the same vein, Chapman identified a sample of girls and boys with learning disabilities using standard accepted research methods for identifying LDs and found that the research-identified sample of girls with LDs read better than boys with LDs,[36] just as "normal-achieving" females generally read better early in life than males and continue to read more as adults.[37] A large number of other studies, though, appear to find that girls with labeled LDs do as well or better than their male counterparts in reading single words, spelling, and writing.[38] Some researchers find that boys with similar discrepancies between achievement and expectations are diagnosed more frequently,[39] while others find no such sex bias.[40]

More striking perhaps is a study in which Mirkin, Marston, and Deno followed seventy male and thirty-seven female elementary school children, looking to see which children were referred as LD by teachers, largely on the basis of behavior difficulties, and compared those referrals with those that are engendered by a continuous (weekly) test-measurement system. Eighty percent of the teacher referrals were of boys, compared with 66 percent through the test-based system. (Moreover, 64 percent of the teacher-based referrals turned out not to be LD by the district's criteria, compared with only 20 percent of the test-driven referrals.)[41]

It appears most plausible that whatever overdiagnosis of boys exists is behavior driven. In her review study, Vogel states (with modest empirical support): "studies indicated that teachers were more likely to refer children for LD evaluation and services if the children had attention deficits and hyperactivity or disruptive behavior, rather than academic underachievement. Since more males than females manifested these behaviors, teachers referred more males, who then received LD services."[42] Other researchers have found that girls with attention deficit disorder (ADD) are likely to be referred only when they are older and exhibit far more severe cognitive and language deficits than boys with ADD, who are perceived as more disruptive.[43]

Some of our interview subjects expressed views consistent with this finding. The director of a northern California SELPA stated:

> [T]he socialization of girls doesn't lead to identification because it doesn't involve as much acting out, it's more indirect displays and quietness. We have search and serve. And [when you're trying to hold diagnostic rates for fiscal reasons to] 9.7 percent, if you're not real loud, in some obvious way, and you're not falling through the floor with the grades, I can really see not being identified.

PATTERNS OF PARENTAL INVOLVEMENT IN DIAGNOSIS

Once a classroom teacher (or some other school staff person) has identified a student as requiring observation to ascertain whether he has special learning needs, the child will most typically be observed by some sort of semi-formal on-site special education committee.[44] If this "observing team" still believes special education services may be appropriate, parents will inevitably become involved: in the first instance, parental consent to diagnostic tests will be required should the district decide to give them.[45]

A theme that came across quite strongly in our interviews was that the process of obtaining consent to a more formal "workup" may depend considerably upon the extent of the district's interest in serving the child and the attitudes of the parents. In one predominantly high-SES New York district, the director told us that special educators will simply back off initial efforts to diagnose and provide services for a child thought to have an LD if the parents resist commencing the process because they fear stigmatizing their child. At the same time, if the child is disruptive as a result of what the special educators suspect may be emotional disturbance or ADD (such children are labeled "other health impaired" in that particular district), special educators will spare no efforts to get parental consent to diagnosis.[46] This reported passivity on the district's part toward parents who don't want their child assessed for behaviorally benign learning disabilities suggests that variance in rates of diagnosis across a district may depend partly upon distinctions in parental attitudes, rather than purely on distinctions in the incidence of the underlying disorders. The director informed us of one elementary school, dominated by a recent immigrant population, which had "almost no labeled LD children," though all the other elementary schools in the district have categorized about 5 percent of the pupils as learning disabled. He said he thinks the reason for this is that many of the parents at this school resist diagnosis because they believe that the LD label is both stigmatic and a "cover" for "laziness."[47]

In that same New York district, there was a battle within the relevant Parent-Teacher Association (PTA). Roughly half the parents of children who would be labeled learning disabled under IDEA wanted the school to go to a "nonclassified" (no formal diagnosis) system, in which resource room services were open to any student who wanted to use them, without having to be "labeled," and the school district experimented with this system in two of its elementary schools for a period. (The experiment was abandoned because of excess demands on expensive resource room services.) The other half of the parents wanted formal diagnosis to continue so that they had the legal right to participate in the formation of an IEP and to demand certain remedial services.

If the school's more formal special education committee believes the child needs special education services, then the child's parents will certainly be entitled to a rather high level of involvement in the initial and ongoing formation of the child's IEP, should they choose to take advantage of the procedural rights granted them by the statute. Special education coordinators we interviewed who had an opinion on the matter uniformly reported that parental participation in conferences to establish or shift IEPs was quite high in elementary grades and started falling off, in an almost linear fashion, from sixth grade through high school graduation. Said one administrator in a middle-class SES California district: "It's a given that parents are more involved at the elementary than at the secondary level," and a New York administrator noted, "[M]ost parents show up in the seventh grade for the annual meeting and almost none show up by the twelfth grade, assuming the IEP's still in place."

Also, several coordinators perceived that lower-SES parents were systematically less likely to participate in conferences, at any given age, than higher-SES parents. Typical of the comments were those made by the director of special education in a low-SES Louisiana parish with high rates of both black and white poverty, where the small middle-class population is largely white: "A very small percentage [of parents is vigorous in advocacy for their child at the IEP hearing]. They tend to be white parents . . . I don't attribute a lack of parent participation as an attitude of not caring . . . [but instead I think it's related to] parent[al] confidence." An earlier study[48] indicated that while as many as 95 percent of parents had participated in their child's last IEP conference in some locations (largely, though by no means exclusively, high-SES districts), participation in most areas was less than 50 percent.

Districts seem to differ in the level of effort they make to ensure parental participation; all must comply with formal notice mandates, but some appear to be more aggressive about ensuring they make genuine contact with parents, that they are flexible in scheduling meetings with parents who might find it difficult to meet during ordinary after-school times, and some are more aggressive still about trying to induce recalcitrant parents to participate.

Most districts we visited had encountered only a handful, if any, challenges to district IEP decisions, but in these cases, our informants generally characterized the parents as middle class. Legal challenges to district conduct were extremely rare in all the districts we visited except one, a California district that could be said to be characterized less by uniformly high SES than a tradition of high levels of political activism, especially disability rights activism. In that district, there had been six legal proceedings in the last quarter preceding our interview. In the other districts of roughly the same size, there had typically been one or two hearings in the past five or six years.

It is clear that most decisions to "work up" a child for more formal diagnosis are, in the first instance, teacher driven. Variations in practice may well be salient at this tier of implementation. An administrator in a high-SES New York district reported the following:

> The referral system is dominantly teacher driven, but sometimes concerned parents are the initiators. There is a tremendous difference

among teachers in referral rates that can't conceivably be explained by differences in the populations they see . . . [T]here are teachers who either disbelieve in LD—they think bad students are stupid and/or lazy—and/or refuse 'extra help' or classroom intrusion. One of the district's best fourth grade teachers simply believes that she can deal with all her pupils . . . no student in her class has ever been classified as disabled.

A pupil, of course, is exposed to many teachers (and other school personnel) over the course of her academic career, though, so that the chances that a student will be diagnosed as having a learning disability at some point might be relatively insensitive to any such distinctions in referral practices. One New York administrator emphasized this point, noting not only that students are likely, simply by chance, to run into some teachers who are at least typically prone to refer a child who might be diagnosed as having a disability, but also that "principals monitor all the kids who are doing badly, and art, music, and library people [who see all the kids in the school] are on the lookout for kids with disabilities."

It is perhaps more interesting, though, to look more closely at the circumstances in which parents rather than teachers initiate identification of their children as eligible for special ed. Most obviously, parents may initiate workups simply because they believe that their child can be helped by special education services. Administrators often perceived that what motivated parents to seek services was disappointed expectations of high achievement; not surprisingly, these high expectations were more frequently dashed among higher-SES parents. A special education administrator in a high-SES New York district contrasted his experience with the experience of a close professional colleague, working in a district, which, while geographically rather proximate, was one of the lowest-SES districts in the region: "The LD diagnosis depends on *disappointed expectations;* in [the low-SES district] there's nearly no parent pressure and little demand for services. [In my district] there is little toleration for nonperformance." The special education director in a very poor Mississippi district in which most of the (very few) middle-class children were sent to a local private school responded as follows when we asked her whether parents ever requested assessments: "[M]ost of our parents don't come asking for us to test their children, unless the child fails. Now in the private schools, we've had a few requests for us to get a test for two or three children in the private school. But most parents that come, it's because their child's failing."

High SES parents may also be more likely to be able to pressure districts to take action when they want their child assessed or want him to receive services, in the face of bureaucratic inertia and queuing caused by shortages of funds. Thus in a moderately class-integrated elementary school within a generally high SES California district, there was (in 1993–94) a four- to six-month wait to receive full psychological testing for disabilities when a student was simply referred by a classroom teacher, unless the student had a behavioral problem.[49] We were told, though, by the school principal that the most aggressive parents, all of them from the highest SES group within the school, frequently were able to have their children tested immediately, both by making personal contacts with relevant administrators and by being aware of their legal rights to diagnosis.

What is more interesting is that parents may seek to have their child classified as disabled in order to gain some benefit other than educational services in the school district itself. Parents may seek diagnosis so that their child will be eligible for testing accommodation, face easier high school graduation requirements, or be eligible for disability support payments.

For example, some parents, particularly high-SES parents, may initiate "workups" not so much to get educational services as to get testing accommodations, especially on standardized college entrance exams like the SAT, believing that their child will have an easier time getting accommodations on college entrance exams and on college exams if identified as having a learning disability by the public school.[50] While the LD category may no longer have been dominated by upper middle-class white males by the mid-1970s, demands for testing accommodation remained, it seems, the strong if not exclusive province of the well-off, and might well still remain so. The median income of the parents of college-bound seniors taking the SAT from 1979 to 1983 was $25,525 (and the median family incomes of "hard" disabled pupils—the hearing impaired, the physically handicapped, and the visually impaired— was essentially no different, ranging from $24,085 to $26,900). The median parental income of LD students who took nonstandard administrations of the SAT, though, was $37,736, nearly 50 percent higher. While 18.3 percent of college-bound seniors taking the SAT between 1980 and 1983 were minority pupils, only 8.1 percent of the LD pupils taking nonstandard administrations of the test were.[51]

One high-SES New York district receives (and automatically refuses) a large number of requests each year for what the special education coordinator refers to as "naked diagnoses" (a label without any educational services). Parents frequently get their child assessed at a nearby hospital by psychologists and ask the district to confirm the diagnosis.[52] In yet another New York district, the special education coordinator noted not only that parents of high school students frequently came in with outside private diagnoses of learning disabilities ("which we either fight or ignore"), but also that many of the disputes he'd had with parents involved declassification of high school seniors, who, in his view, no longer needed services. Since senior year status often drives both admissions decisions at colleges and decisions about the accommodations (of curriculum and testing) that the student will be offered at college, one might predict that parents would be far more likely not only not to resist classification, but to seek it, at that point.[53]

Other parents apparently seek to have their children diagnosed as eligible for special education in the sometimes incorrect belief that a "borderline" student will receive a high school diploma more readily if he is in special ed, not because the special ed program will improve his academic performance but because graduation requirements will diminish. Particularly in states (like Louisiana) that have statewide uniform graduation requirements (including passing an exit exam), special ed students do not receive a high school diploma simply because they perform satisfactorily in special ed classes. In other states (like Mississippi), curricular modifications for special ed pupils, permitting them to receive a modified diploma, are more commonplace. Nonetheless, as the director of special ed in one Louisiana parish noted:

> [Parents may want their child in special ed because] the child's grades are so far behind, and they think—I don't know why they think this— but they think that just because the child is in special ed, he's going to graduate. I have parents call me up . . . they want me to do something [when their children are failing], and my response is I'm sorry, that's the school, you need to talk to the school. I do not promote or retain

students. But they think, the majority of them think, that if you get the child in special ed, he is going to pass and get a high school diploma.

A similar pressure was noted by one Mississippi administrator:

> I was faced with a situation . . . with the coach of a football player . . . [who wanted to] use special ed so the kid [could pass from grade to grade and thus] be eligible [to play football] . . . He thought he could be labeled special ed, come in there—or not come in there—he was skipping classes, too cool to be in special ed—but he thought it was a free ride to the football field [since special ed children are graded on attainment of IEP goals which he expected would be made more and more limited]."

Another pattern of initiation may have existed prior to federal legal changes in 1996[54] among some very poor parents financially dependent upon public assistance. Supplemental Social Security Income (SSI) benefits were available to families supporting disabled children. The financial incentive to seek a disability diagnosis to obtain these benefits was particularly powerful if, as in Mississippi and Louisiana, AFDC benefits were set at levels low enough that SSI receipts could increase family income even for households already dependent on welfare. Moreover, even when parents did not seek a disability diagnosis, some may have resisted declassification of older children, or sought to keep disabled children in school well past normal graduation dates, to retain SSI eligibility. Our point, in this regard, is not to investigate something that might be thought of as a form of prereform "welfare fraud." If it were, it would have been necessary to get far more accurate information than we could possibly have obtained in questioning a handful of school administrators who neither checked their own files to ascertain the frequency of these requests nor had any reason to know how these requests were subsequently processed by Social Security officials. We simply note, once more, that in looking at parental participation in the IEP-formation process, one must always recall that the receipt of appropriate educational services might not be the only, or even the most pressing, issue.

One Mississippi administrator in a mid-sized (7,000 students) district, 41 percent of whom are poor enough to be eligible to receive federally provided free or reduced-price lunch according to data the administrator supplied us in responding to a written questionnaire, gave the following account of this practice:

> What happens is if a child is eligible for special education a parent can apply through the Social Security office for disability on this student for Social Security supplemental income because they're a special ed student... [The parents may not be] as concerned about educational issues and what he's going to do in school [but rather may be eager that he be diagnosed as disabled because the family] might get $100 a month because he's disabled ... We usually [get anywhere between] five and ten [requests] a month [to certify to the Social Security office that a child has been diagnosed as disabled, though ascertaining how many of the parents *sought* the diagnosis for this purpose is obviously not possible]."[55]

Conclusion

Secondary sources of empirical data, as well as data we collected ourselves on the diagnosis and placement of students with learning disabilities reveal a number of troubling discontinuities between local practice and the formal provisions of IDEA. For example, a district's decision on how heavily to rely on discrepancy scores to identify LD children may depend both on the number of children in that district likely to qualify and on the capacity of the district to serve those children once diagnosed. In this sense, local diagnostic practice may serve a "gatekeeper" function. Race, gender, and class certainly correlate with, and may well powerfully influence, LD diagnosis, or if not diagnosis, the choice of settings—mainstream or self-contained—in which diagnosed students are educated. Parental involvement may also have a significant influence on the likelihood that a child will be "worked up" for a diagnosis.

That sociopolitical factors should influence everyday bureaucratic practice is not surprising in itself. What is striking in the case we are studying, though, is that these factors have so powerful a force despite how exacting IDEA is about the requirement that learning disabilities are organically based disorders and *not* either the educational shortfalls that result from environmental, cultural, or economic disadvantage or a label to be granted those with the political power to claim certain kinds of extra resources from the local districts.

FIVE

Local Practice II:
Resource Management and Discipline

Introduction

Here we turn our attention to a number of the decisions that districts must face in managing the education of students they have labeled learning disabled: most particularly, whether to place these children in mainstream classes, special day classes, or pull them out of mainstream classes part of the day for resource room help; how to stop (or facilitate) the instruction of regular ed pupils by instructors formally assigned to educate disabled pupils ("leakage"); and when to discipline students with disabilities who have violated behavior codes.

Two powerful themes emerge in these discussions: first, districts must often manage conflicts between the perceived interests of (at least some of) the parents of regular education pupils and the parents of pupils with disabilities. Conflicts may occur over which group of pupils should get certain educational resources (whether it is the attention of a special educator or the attention of a regular classroom teacher who might devote atypically high amounts of time to disabled pupils in her class); they may occur when parents of regular ed pupils believe their children's education is "disrupted" (in a variety of distinct senses) by the presence of special ed pupils who might nonetheless be better served themselves in the mainstream setting; they may occur when parents of regular ed pupils believe it is unfair for their children to be suspended or expelled when they've engaged in behavior that is no more problematic than the behavior of a disabled child who is not disciplined in this severe fashion. Second, in looking at district management practices, one recognizes that IDEA is often seen as a rather trivial barrier to tailoring local practices to the districts' actual pedagogical goals. At the same time, IDEA can serve as a useful instrument—not necessarily by statutory design—for local authorities to meet their own ends. We discuss in this regard the possibility that local officials use IDEA to *limit* the obligations they might face if confronted with potentially more open-ended demands that claimants might make under §504 of the Rehabilitation Act.

We first discuss issues surrounding a district's decision about which students to "mainstream" fully, which to serve in resource rooms, and which to serve in wholly separate classes or facilities. We also examine decisions about how to manage the educational functions in each of these settings.

We consider discipline issues as well. We ask whether districts succeed in following, or even attempt to follow, formal federal guidelines that generally forbid subjecting disabled students to serious discipline when the behavior for which they might otherwise be disciplined is a manifestation of their disability. We also discuss the degree to which districts move students to more restrictive environments when they violate behavior codes, despite formal mandates that forbid districts from doing so unless the move is educationally beneficial to the special ed pupil, in order to meet the classic aims of disciplinary punishment.

Finally, we focus briefly on a widespread fear articulated by many special education coordinators, the fear of open-ended §504 liability, particularly in relation to ADD pupils. We do so in large part to explore the possibility that IDEA has created both a floor and a practically enforceable ceiling on districts' special ed obligations, transforming open-ended claims of need into more limited claims that certain local bureaucratic procedures must be followed.

Classroom management

INITIAL PLACEMENT: MAINSTREAMING VERSUS SPECIAL CLASSES
As we discussed at length in Chapter 3, formal federal law requires

that students with disabilities be placed in the "least restrictive environment" appropriate to their needs, and be educated with nondisabled students to the maximum degree possible. The courts have generally interpreted this standard to require that placement decisions shall be made according to the interests of the disabled student, but should not (at least not explicitly) take into account the competing interests of regular ed students in any form of balancing process.

It is fairly clear that most pupils who have learning disabilities are served in mainstreamed classes, unless the learning disability is accompanied by a serious behavior problem.[1] Nationally, more than three-quarters of pupils labeled LD are served either in the resource room (56.1 percent) or exclusively in the regular classroom (20.7 percent). It is an open question how many of those served in self-contained classes (21.7 percent) or separate schools, residential facilities, or hospitals (1.5 percent)[2] are "true" LD pupils as opposed to deliberately or inadvertently misclassified students with other problems.

Several of our informants stated with confidence that students are frequently pulled out of ordinary classes[3] and served in special day classes or given long stints in the resource room because they are considered disruptive, even though as a pedagogic matter, they could be served in the regular classroom.[4] In the words of one California administrator: "Special ed is only designed to help 10 percent of the student population, but we become the primary solution for every kid who's got a problem . . . All [general educators] know is, the child is disruptive and they want help, or just want somebody to do something." Another California administrator was even more pointed: "The existence of ADD is the single most unifying characteristic of kids in special day classes. The big mainstreaming issue for classroom teachers, whatever the disability, is behavior. Thus, a classroom teacher [will be more than willing to mainstream] a very slow, well-behaved child, but [will] refer the mildly disabled, poorly behaved child to [a special day class]." In a Mississippi district in which resource rooms were used for all special ed elementary school pupils except for those with severe-profound mental retardation, we asked the director what she thought was the most powerful predictor of how much time a child spent in the resource room. She replied:

> In the lower elementary level, behavior. Behavior in the lower elementary as to whether they even get . . . [diagnosed as disabled] . . .

Or get referred. You can be a *real nice child,* never say "boo," and never get referred. He may flunk first grade. He may flunk second grade. But if you're a real nice kid, you won't get referred. You may be a horrible acting child and make really good grades, but you might get referred . . . The squeaky wheel gets the grease.

As we note below, placing a disruptive student in a "more restrictive environment" may (at least on occasion) be in the interests of the student herself, but we have little doubt that administrators in every district in which we interviewed paid serious attention to the concerns of non–special ed pupils. This practice appears ethically defensible if one believes, as we do, that administrators have no substantive reason (like a maxi-min ethical principle which assumes the disabled are the worst-off group whose welfare must be maximized) to weigh the welfare of disabled children more highly than the welfare of regular ed children. Nonetheless, it appears to be impermissible under any plausible interpretation of current formal federal law.

Administrators who believe such balancing to be formally permissible may argue that it is impossible to say whether removal of children from the least restrictive environment (LRE) is genuinely in the educational interests of disruptive children, or involves de facto balancing of the interests of nondisabled children with those of pupils with disabilities. It is perfectly plausible to argue that a disruptive child needs the lower staff-student ratios prevalent in the resource rooms or self-contained classes, that his misbehavior leads to ostracism that damages both his self-esteem and his capacity to learn, or that IEPs designed to work on the behavior problems that preclude the child from focusing on intellectual and social growth are best applied in highly structured and monitored settings. The following comment by a New York special educator was typical of remarks expressing this view: "I do explicitly account for the interests of other students in making a placement decision, but I really don't think a kid who's really disruptive would do himself any good being mainstreamed." However, a Mississippi administrator deliberately tried to avoid pulling out behaviorally disordered children and placing them in small self-contained classes, believing that this badly misserved children whose behavior was unacceptable: "When you . . . throw them all in self-contained . . . they just feed off each other, they get worse. You need to put them out where there are some good behavioral models all the time."

It is also possible to argue that the *political* (and ultimate *fiscal*) stability of special education depends on special educators' not making undue demands on mainstreamed teachers and/or the parents of nondisabled children.[5] One New York administrator noted, explaining why disruptive ADD pupils who prove unresponsive to medication are often separated from their classmates early on: "The special education program will not remain effective if it is perceived as oppositional to 'ordinary' teachers and students."[6]

Special educators, as a group, are probably atypically prone to look critically at disciplinary norms in the regular ed program, worrying that general education teachers often proscribe unfamiliar behavior that disabled children more frequently exhibit whether it is actually "truly" disruptive or not.[7] Thus, for instance, one New York administrator commented:

> Many times, when a student's "mildly disruptive," I think that regular ed teachers are looking for us to help them get rid of someone when the problem isn't that other students are getting hurt, but just that the teacher's intolerant or rigid about some rules in his head . . . For instance, I just got a complaint about a kid who gets up and walks around, who needs to leave the room every fifteen minutes or so. I don't think the other students really care.

We did not, though, consistently encounter this attitude among our informants. Some believe, instead, that administrators and regular educators are tolerant of the disabled and the "unusual" manifestations of disability, while refusing to accept disruption. An administrator in a Louisiana parish put it as follows: "Principals would like their schools to run in a very smooth fashion . . . But that's not an unreasonable thing for a principal to want . . . They don't mind the severe/profound [disabled] . . . they don't mind any disability except behavior disorders."

"LEAKAGE" IN MAINSTREAM CLASSES VERSUS EDUCATIONAL DISRUPTION THROUGH PULL-OUTS

At the elementary school level, "mainstreamed" special ed (including LD) children generally receive special services in two ways. First, they may leave the classroom for some portion of the day and

spend time in a "resource room" receiving services. Second, resource specialists may enter the regular classroom and help the student with the routine work all students are assigned, or adjust assignments during the ample open-ended periods of time in which
students work "on their own" or in small groups, rather than being
instructed en masse.[8]

Each of these methods poses a characteristic "difficulty," though
whether these problems are "genuine" or "pseudo-problems" depends upon one's pedagogic philosophy. "Pulling students out" is
arguably troublesome for three sorts of reasons. First, it disrupts
students' capacity to keep up with their classmates, especially since
the teacher in the regular class may cover subjects that the child
with a disability misses while away from class. For instance, the student may attend math in the regular class, then receive remedial instruction in the resource room on that day's math lesson, but in the
meantime miss the social studies lesson in the regular class. Second,
it arguably stigmatizes students with disabilities by highlighting
their differences from other pupils. Third, it decreases the capacity
of the special educator to focus the student's attention on how to use
her particular strengths to cope as well as possible with routine educational demands.

Pulling students out does, however, preclude "leakage" of services to ineligible students (assuming for the moment that preventing leakage is desirable). It also allows special educators to work on
the particular student's deficits, without requiring regular ed teachers to modify their curriculum for the whole class. It also permits
special educators to pay concentrated attention in low-distraction
settings to the development of significant skills (especially reading
skills for children with dyslexia) and permits scale economies in
dealing with recurring deficits that are common among disabled
pupils. One New York special educator we spoke with thought the
best solution was simply to elongate the school day for many disabled students, "pulling out" only after the school day was done (so
that the disabled students wouldn't miss regular lessons but could
still focus attention on their more systematic special needs), but he
recognized this might be (a) fiscally unfeasible, (b) difficult for children in terms of schedules and social lives, and (c) especially
difficult for special ed pupils, many of whom find it difficult to sustain attention throughout the regular school day.

"Pulling resources in" to classes is hardly unproblematic either. The most common objection is that it results in service leakage to nondisabled children. Even in a California district in which the special education coordinator was personally quite unambivalent about trying to enforce the formal norm that special education aides in the regular classroom attend only to special education eligible children, the coordinator noted, "It is virtually impossible to ensure that the RSP [resource specialist] will attend *only* to the children with special needs." Another California administrator put it as follows: "In our SELPA . . . from an accounting point of view, it's tight . . . [Special educators serve IDEA-eligible children only.] But if it's a collaborative program and someone is working in the classroom and a general ed kid says, 'hey, show me how to do this,' the [special ed] teacher's not going to say, 'I'm sorry, I can't help you.'" In other districts, special educators are far less apologetic about leakage. For instance, an administrator in one largely middle-class Louisiana parish remarked: "The resource specialist in the regular classroom gives help to all kids in the class. We urge them to do that."

Whether "leakage" is a problem or a virtue of the "pull-in" method turns on three related questions. First, is there a clean diagnostic distinction between the disabled and nondisabled population? Second, is the diagnosed "soft disability" population uniquely assisted by the services the resource specialists supply? Third, is the diagnosed "soft disability" population more entitled to these services than other poor learners? A substantial minority of the special educators we spoke with clearly disbelieve in drawing an overly bright line between the "soft disabled" population and other poor learners, and (therefore) encourage aides who go into the classroom to help all students who need help.

One California administrator who views leakage as affirmatively desirable explained his position in part by noting: "When the classroom RSP provides assistance to the slow learners and LD students alike, it's a compromise solution to the over- and underinclusiveness debate surrounding categorization. This way, the sharp categories formally exist, but all students who need assistance, for whatever reason, get it." Similarly, in a Mississippi district in which 70 percent of the pupils receive Chapter One aid, special ed teachers sent into inclusionary classes are instructed to work with small groups which contain IDEA-eligible children, but are never composed exclusively of such children. The special education coordinator in that district noted pointedly that many of those non-IDEA Chapter One children could be labeled LD, if testing were more widespread.

In some districts, administrators worry about over- and underinclusive diagnosis but nonetheless report that they try to block leakage, generally because levels of underlying need are so high that some portion of poor learners simply cannot be served. But they remain quite bothered by the fact that "LD" children may be no more needy (or well served by special services) than other poor performers. A number of our informants told stories of special ed personnel testing a poor student year after year, hoping to find a discrepancy that will make the student eligible for services.[9] In the words of one Mississippi administrator who worries a great deal about this issue:

> Originally, fifteen years ago, a learning disabled child had to have a normal IQ and an achievement area that was low . . . Now—and this may be only characteristic of *our* state in an effort to help *our* children—you may have a child that has a 72 IQ and an achievement in the 50s . . . So, in an effort to help more children, you're going to say that this kid has a learning disability so that we can give him some special ed assistance that we normally would not be able to do without the eligibility. When you really look at it, is he really learning disabled? I don't know.
>
> [Sometimes, though, we simply can't find a discrepancy and the kid is just slow, but not mentally retarded . . .] Regular ed is supposed to capture him . . . Are there kids who fall through the cracks? Yeah . . . How often do we evaluate these kids? All the time . . . We're going to reevaluate to see if we can't fit that discrepancy somewhere. "Did we get it yet? Has he fallen far enough behind in achievement now that we can make him eligible for special ed?" . . .
>
> I think that somehow, someday we're going to all have to say this is *our* kid, what we need to do is educate this kid. Whether it's the regular ed teacher taking him into a group for a certain subject or whether it's special ed or Chapter One or whomever, it's necessary . . . Mom didn't leave the best one at home. Okay? She sent us all she had.

Other special educators who favored leakage also felt that distinctions between the needs (and capacity to benefit from intervention) of disabled and nondisabled pupils were exaggerated. A New

York administrator in a high-SES district in which most students with academic difficulties receive some aid confessed: "If we're treating people successfully who are not 'formally' LD in some sense, that's fine with me . . . IDEA gives me political clout with the school board to get them to fund all successful remedial programs for all students in the district who can use them, in situations where ordinary requests might get turned down for fiscal reasons."[10] The director of a California SELPA covering a fairly wide SES range of districts explained why he had no objection to serving pupils without "real" disabilities:

> There probably is, at core, such a thing as LD and maybe half the people we label are "really" LD. The problem is that the truly LD kids are irremediable. The 25 percent [of special ed pupils] who eventually show significant changes were probably misdiagnosed. In theory, the LD kids have alternative coping mechanisms, and the educator should try to help the kids tap into these alternatives, [but] slow learners may also have untapped abilities . . . The difference between the two is merely a matter of degree.
>
> Good teaching, simply, is what makes it work . . . For the LD kids or for anyone else, good teaching is good teaching . . . If there's magic out there, some "trick" for LD kids, then wonderful. But there *isn't* anything out there . . . Just good teaching.

Generally, these educators also believe that leakage helps the disabled children themselves by reducing the stigma of being singled out, though the beliefs are obviously not logically related. One Louisiana special educator noted that the state now specifically authorizes special education teachers to address the problems of other "at-risk" pupils when they are in the mainstreamed classroom: "[Her] first obligation [is] to the special education students. [But] that obligation we're now interpreting as meaning that one of the greatest things you can do for the special education students is to offer an opportunity . . . to see that they're not alone in their learning difficulties."

Only a minority of our informants, though, expressed such skepticism about the practical distinction between children identified as LD and other poor learners. Those educators we interviewed who most worried about leakage, and tried to direct aides to avoid it as much as possible, tended to believe that the interventions that were effective for LD pupils and slow learners were quite distinct. Thus a California administrator who worried a great deal about leakage in her district stated:

> There is a genuine distinction between a learning disabled student and a slow learner, and they require different kinds of interventions . . . Whereas the slow learner needs more time (repetitions, instruction, etc.), the LD student may merely need a different strategy. The LD student may also have picked up affective disorders and thus require appropriate counseling.

She did add, however, that lower-IQ LD pupils (those with IQs of 85–90) will be less distinguishable from non-LD "slow learners," and that the higher-IQ LD pupils may be far more able to pick up the coping strategies uniquely directed at the LD. Yet another special educator in a New York district, while believing far more strongly than some others we spoke to in the conceptual distinction between the learning problems of LD and non-LD pupils, nonetheless acknowledged that he believed that "the strategies we use to work with identified pupils work as well or better with the non-identified children who make use of the same resources."

Discipline

When we first examined the formal federal law governing the treatment of the disabled, it struck us that federal rules governing discipline were (a) close to uninterpretable, but (b) probably of little practical moment. Formal federal standards forbid severe discipline (expulsion or suspension for more than ten days during the school year) for disabled students when their misconduct is a "manifestation of the disability." When a disabled student engages in misconduct that would normally trigger severe discipline, the IEP committee must hold a "manifestation" (or "determination") hearing, to ascertain whether there is a causal connection between the disability and the misconduct. The hearing requires a philosophical and empirical determination (what is the cause of some particular instance of human behavior?) that very few special educators we interviewed believe is possible.

If we were right in believing that districts would find formal discipline law incoherent and uninterpretable, we were wrong in thinking it would have little practical impact. Time and time again, our informants identified the intersection of special education and district discipline policy as a locus of overwhelming uncertainty and anxiety. We underestimated the degree to which some districts would still, in the absence of federal disability law, use severe discipline frequently enough that federal law could be said to "interfere" with spontaneous local ordering practices.

Disciplinary restrictions are obviously a more serious issue in districts in which long-term expulsions and suspensions are reasonably commonplace. In a number of the districts we visited, especially in Louisiana and Mississippi, informants reported that IEP committees were asked to make manifestation determinations quite frequently, given the proclivity of the districts to use long-term suspensions and expulsions as a response to a wide range of breaches (from "disrespect for authority"—the leading cause of expulsion for students in Louisiana from 1990 to 1992—to "creating disturbances," to "physical conflicts with others," to drug and weapon possession).

We were unable to locate any national data on either the number or treatment of special education pupils subject to manifestation hearings or on the use of severe discipline for regular ed pupils. It appears, though, that in the Louisiana and Mississippi towns and parishes which we visited, between one in thirty and one in fifty special education pupils engaged in misconduct each year that, but for the legal protections against discipline, would lead to their expulsion or long-term suspension. Thus our informant in one Louisiana parish in which the nongifted special education population is roughly 4,400 (many of whom are younger elementary school children, unlikely to have the capacity to violate most of the rules that lead to expulsion or suspension) reported that school administrators recommend that at least 100 special ed pupils *per year* be expelled or suspended for more than ten days, pending a determination that the misconduct is not a manifestation of the disability. In another, smaller (but markedly poorer) parish with 2,750 disabled elementary and secondary school pupils, the administrator related that "we run in the hundreds of determination proceedings or determination decisions per year." A Mississippi administrator in a town with a special education population of roughly 800 said that there are between twenty and twenty-five cases per year in which special educators must review a recommendation for severe discipline to determine whether the discipline is legally acceptable given the child's disability.

Local practice differs from district to district not only because formal federal law is ambiguous, directing districts to determine causal connections between behavior and disease they are not competent to determine. It seems also to reflect local attitudes regarding the appropriateness of the restrictions on discipline. Given the fact that many administrators with whom we spoke have little respect for the formal legal regime, they may often ignore its rather clear implications: thus, for instance, it is *formally* clear that a disabled student ought not to be disciplined when her misbehavior is a manifestation of her disability *whether or not* she already had an IEP when she engaged in proscribed conduct, but most districts will not "work up" previously undiagnosed students pending disciplinary action. It was equally clear until 1995 that, as a formal matter, a disabled student should be free from punishment regardless of how severe his offense was if the offense was a manifestation of his disability,[11] but that disabled students were not to be deemed categorically immune from punishment. If they commit a more minor offense, but still one severe enough to merit serious punishment, they should be punished if the misdeeds are deemed causally unconnected to the disability. Many districts, though, pay a good deal of attention to the severity of offenses. Finally, many districts use alternative placement decisions which might serve many of the same ends that expulsion or long-term suspension would serve but which remain outside the purview of federal "discipline law."

ATTITUDES TOWARD LIMITS ON DISCIPLINE

Our interviews revealed distinct attitudes among administrators about whether there should be legal limits on disciplining students with disabilities. Several administrators expressed the belief that there is no coherent justification for forbidding districts from disciplining special ed pupils, regardless of the relationship between the disability and the conduct. The words of one Mississippi administrator were typical:

> How do I explain to a principal when there are two kids who have gotten into a really severe fight before school. One of them is a special ed kid and the other one isn't . . . How do I say that, you know, this kid can

be expelled and this kid cannot when they are both equally responsible for the fight? How can I *say* that? ... Is there a double standard for [disciplining regular and] special ed students? You bet your bottom dollar there's a double standard. [At the diagnostic stage] I can't say that this LD's problems are related to their culture, their economic status, or their environment. But then I have to say ... [that their misbehavior is caused by their disability]? ... We have to play God sometimes to determine if it's related ... Because there are so many factors ... Is self-esteem a problem? Is self-esteem a problem because of the handicap?

As a normative matter, we have grave doubts that schools ought to expel or suspend students for a long period of time when they violate behavioral rules. We are not certain, though, that the federal government ought to impose an antiexpulsion policy on all local districts. Moreover, if the federal government wishes to ban "severe discipline," it ought to do so outright, without any regard to "disability."

Even administrators less skeptical of legal limits on disciplining the disabled concede that the policy is politically vulnerable. This is especially true in Louisiana, which has a category of disability, "behavior disordered," that is *defined* in large part by reference to the frequency with which a student has misbehaved. Thus if two students get into a fight, one of whom has been in many fights and one of whom is a "first timer," the "first timer" is far more likely to be disciplined severely; recidivists are much more likely to be exculpated because they will be considered "behavior disordered." In the words of one Louisiana special education coordinator who believes this differential treatment is morally proper:

[What happens when a special ed child and a general ed child have had a fight? We don't do an assessment of the general ed pupil just to make sure we're not giving unequal treatment to two students who are in fact both disabled, just because one's previously been diagnosed.] It might be an isolated incident for the regular ed child ... [But parents of the nondisabled child complain all the time.] It's common.

Administrators skeptical about the wisdom of limiting discipline may adopt quite distinct strategies, though. One strategy they seem to share is that they do not proactively seek to ascertain whether a student who is threatened with discipline might, if worked up, be diagnosed as having a disability. In the words of one California administrator:

> Not every kid who is suspended or expelled is put through an as-
> sessment battery to make sure they're disabled . . . We had a kid this
> year, a transfer . . . and in the first week [he] got into a verbal alterca-
> tion . . . [and] subsequently brought a gun to school . . . in reaction to
> [the kid with whom he fought], whom he heard also had a gun. Both
> kids were expelled. Subsequently, [the transfer student, who was pre-
> viously undiagnosed] obtained an attorney, successfully argued that
> there was eligibility for special education in SED. And at this point the
> expulsion has been rescinded.

Similarly, an administrator in one Louisiana parish reported that
the district had recommended expelling roughly twenty students
without IEPs in the previous year, and that only three or four of
these pupils requested, prior to expulsion, that they be assessed to
see whether they were eligible for special education. The district
made such assessments only in these cases. (Typically, she reported,
the request was made by a social worker who has some other contact with the child, though it might be made by a parent as well.)[12]

Most districts in which administrators are skeptical of limits on
the local authority to discipline will try to subject students who
commit the most serious offenses to serious discipline, regardless of
the relationship between the disability and the conduct. This was
even true at a time when their formal authority to discipline those
who had brought weapons to school was more limited than it is
today. (Severe offenses were typically defined as assaults on teachers, weapons possession, the sale of drugs, and sexual violence.)[13]
Such districts may pressure manifestation committees to find such
conduct not to be a manifestation of the disability. Alternatively,
there simply may be a local culture in which those who serve on
manifestation committees come to believe that finding that the
pupil is immune from discipline in such cases is at least impolitic
and at worst, wrong.

At the same time, these districts might immunize disabled students when they commit less serious offenses, even if the offense
is serious enough to result in severe discipline for nondisabled
students. The immunity would function more like diplomatic immunity—in which a person with a particular status (in this case,
"having an IEP") is freed from punishment—rather than an ex-
cuse that purportedly diminishes culpability (conduct is caused
by disability).[14]

Other administrators skeptical of the ethical validity of manifestation hearings nonetheless have decided it is fiscally irresponsible either to discipline or to place in expensive residential settings any students with IEPs, regardless of the offense they have committed or the danger they believe they pose to other pupils in the regular or self-contained class setting. A Mississippi administrator recounted the following story:

> Several years ago . . . [we had a kid who was] dealing drugs on campus . . . a mildly disabled kid, a mild LD, but regular diploma . . . only going to special ed for study strategies . . . and the parents brought [a suit] . . . We won this one, [but it was very costly. So now, what we really say is everything a disabled kid does is] okay. It's okay to shoot your mama on the weekend . . . Shoot her and kill her. And I'm fifteen years old and I have a learning disability. One week from Monday you got to have me back in the school . . . because I'm a special ed student . . . Is it okay to put [him] in the school . . . If we don't keep him then he has a right to a free appropriate public education . . . [If] I send him to an institution at the tune of $250,000 [*sic*] a year, at whose expense?

Some district coordinators, in contrast, indisputably believe that the manifestation hearings are in fact meaningful, and that those who would subject disabled children to the same disciplinary norms as regular ed pupils' regardless of whether misbehavior is caused by the disability, in some sense, simply "don't get it." These administrators adopt an exclusively retributive (blame-oriented) perspective toward punishment, and believe that the special ed pupils (like the traditionally legally insane) are simply less culpable, less able to control their misbehavior. A Louisiana administrator held this position strongly: "I don't have a problem with the restrictions on the punishment of disabled kids. General ed types and the general world don't understand, of course. They don't understand differential treatment." In her district, there is almost total immunity from serious discipline for SED/BD children: "We have a fairly large number of behaviorally disordered kids, and there it's almost impossible to say that the behavior is not related to the handicap." Moreover, she reports that the *majority* of misbehavior by pupils with LDs is also found to be related to their disability.

Since the district will rarely engage in what we are calling "serious discipline," actual "discipline" consists of moving special ed children to more restrictive environments. This way, they can harm only others who have caused harm. Thus the behaviorally disturbed children in the district have a self-contained class that consists only of BD children.

OFFENSE SEVERITY AND QUALIFIED IMMUNITY

Whether there is a causal connection between disability and an episode of misconduct should not depend, in theory, on the severity of the misconduct. At the time we conducted our interviews only this causal connection was legally relevant. Despite this, several of our informants conceded that district practice blurred the conceptual distinction. One Louisiana administrator claimed that her district takes manifestation hearings quite seriously, though she personally opposes severe discipline for all children. She believes that special ed students might well be served by more restrictive environments when their behavior is especially troublesome, but worries that principals put pressure on committees to "ignore" the genuine connection between the disability and misbehavior in order to get rid of troublesome students: "[It's fine] to ask the question, is the child benefiting from the educational program that he's in . . . If he's not . . . then you challenge the [placement in a less restrictive environment] . . . But leave the determination hearing and the determination process alone . . . It's there for a purpose." When pressed, though, the informant spoke of practices that appeared to be inconsistent with federal law: offense severity had a big influence on the conceptually unrelated question of whether the misconduct was a manifestation of the disability. Asked when students were disciplined, she replied:

> Drugs, of course, drugs and alcohol, in possession of or being under the influence of [would guarantee a suspension for more than ten days or expulsion] . . . Extortion, which is not that common. I would say very serious fighting that maybe reoccurred where someone's hurt . . . Weapons [too, though that's] not as prevalent.

That same concern with offense level was evident as well in the remarks of another Louisiana informant. Asked whether the disability or the severity of the misconduct would be more determinative of the ultimate placement decisions (whether "serious discipline" or movement to a more restrictive environment), the administrator replied:

It would be what they've done. . .[If the pupil were not yet in a self-contained class when he engaged in behavior that would result in the suspension of a regular ed pupil] we'd [typically] go to self-contained. If they were in a self-contained, sometimes depending on the severity—if you have the cussing, the fighting, but you know, no damage other than scrapes and maybe a black eye—you could look at reducing the schedule . . . [This might serve some of the same purposes as suspension but isn't quite the same, because if the IEP committee, which includes the parent, says the kid can't be in school for educational reasons] it's not a suspension. If you said to a student you can't come back for four days, you have been suspended, that's different from saying your IEP committee has determined—with you a part of it—that your state of mind now is such that . . . it reduces the explosions if you [just] come to school Monday, Wednesday, and Friday. [Only where the misconduct is extremely severe—] weapons at the school . . . drug-related things . . . [—would we consider doing more than offering more in-school services].

One California administrator, though he personally believes more emotionally disturbed children ought to be excused from discipline entirely, recognized that the committees, despite the lack of formal legal permission, were sensitive to the level of offense in making manifestation determinations: "IEP teams generally will give less slack . . . to things like guns and drugs. They would have a really hard time saying, because this kid is LD, they sold drugs, or [even] because they're SED, they took a shot at a kid walking down the hall."

DO DISCIPLINARY RULES INFLUENCE SPECIAL EDUCATION ASSESSMENT AND DIAGNOSIS?

As we noted above, districts would, consistent with the spirit and letter of federal law, try to ascertain whether any misconduct that might ordinarily warrant severe discipline arose from a disability, whether or not the disability had previously been diagnosed. We noted that our informants indicated that it was unusual to evaluate a child proactively who was about to be expelled to ascertain whether she was disabled. It is surely the case that some number of students who deserve special education services do not receive them because districts do not perform diagnostic tests on them when discipline is pending.

Diagnostic and pedagogic practice may be affected in irrational ways by the fear of immunizing special ed pupils, far before the time a child engages in serious misconduct. Anticipating that a child may ultimately be someone the district might want to expel, the district may be loath to place him in special ed, especially when it is a close question whether he is disabled or would benefit from services ordinarily given disabled children. The special education coordinator of a California district, who was otherwise generally more supportive of the formal IDEA framework than anyone else we spoke to, nonetheless noted:

> Once a [pupil] is diagnosed as disabled, under IDEA or 504, they are protected from [severe] discipline. The result is I'm] eager to keep [behavior disordered] kids *out* of IDEA and 504 unless they clearly have a disability. [It's also why] there are no purely [attention deficit disordered] kids diagnosed in [this district].

A Mississippi special educator made a nearly identical point: "We try to steer clear of . . . assessment [of children whose behavior disorders might plausibly lead to diagnosis as [seriously emotionally disturbed or other health impaired] because of the restrictions on discipline."

Discipline immunity is also an important issue because awareness of immunity may alter the behavior of children. When we asked one Louisiana administrator whether parents of disabled children complain when the school threatens to discipline their child, knowing that federal law might preclude that, she replied:

> *Children* say that to the counselors. It's not just the parents. We hear it from parents, but the principals are more frustrated because they hear it from the children. "You can't suspend me . . . You can't do anything to me. I'm behavior disordered. You tried to put me out three or four times last year and I'm still here." So it becomes a crutch for the student in the regard that they interpret their rights under IDEA as a victory issue in reference to whether or not they can be kicked out of school.

THE "MORE RESTRICTIVE ENVIRONMENT" ALTERNATIVE

It is vital to note that while districts might be restricted in their use of long-term suspensions and expulsions, many districts meet the "incapacitationist" ends of these measures by moving disabled pupils who "act out" to more restrictive environments. These students might well disrupt the education of other special ed pupils, since the more restrictive environment does not inevitably remediate the behavioral problem, but they will have less capacity to disrupt the educations of regular ed pupils, especially if they are moved to self-contained classes that are not housed in the same school buildings. Not surprisingly, few administrators we spoke to explicitly acknowledged the possibility that the interests of other special ed children were being given less weight than the interests of regular ed pupils when this sort of more restrictive environment (MRE) placement was used in lieu of expulsion or suspension. However, few said that they believed that the move to the MREs typically alleviated the behavior problems either.

The dominant reason we believe that moving children to MREs undervalues the interests of other special ed pupils is that we are persuaded by a California administrator who notes that a classroom filled entirely with BD children cannot possibly be functional: "[It is latently if not patently obvious] to every educator and administrator that referring a kid to an SDC [special day class] is tantamount to calling him 'an acceptable loss.' SDC's are overwhelmingly dead-end, and the best indicator of whether a child will be put back in the SDC is how long he's already been in the SDC." Data from his SELPA that he reported to us support his pessimism: only 10 percent of pupils placed into special day classes ever return to resource room placements in high school (in which they spend at least part of the day in mainstream classes).

A Mississippi administrator made a similar point, noting that while unwilling to "expel" in a formal sense, the school could not tolerate having students on campus who had engaged in violent criminal behavior:

> [If the student's coming out of jail for a serious crime, like a rape] we're not going to put him back into school . . . We're going to provide . . . homebound services where the teacher goes into the home or into the youth court facility . . . and teaches him there. Anything that is done . . . that is so severe as to cause an expulsion [rather than just long-term suspension] from a school, we're going to provide an alternative means of education for the protection of our other children in the school . . . [This] doesn't happen a lot [though]. [Just under 1 percent of the town's special ed population is served like this at a time.]

Fears of §504

Many of the administrators with whom we spoke expressed the fear that districts faced real threats from a potential explosion of §504 claims, even though the IDEA system was working, on the whole, reasonably well. The fears were just that—fears—at that point. None of the districts had received more than a handful of §504 claims, either informally, formally through the Office of Civil Rights, or formally through civil suit. Nonetheless, the concern was extremely widespread.[15]

The pervasiveness of the fear was striking, particularly because it is not clear to us that all of the fears the administrators most explicitly expressed are well grounded from a legal standpoint. From our informants' comments, we were left with the impression that IDEA is perceived by administrators as playing a particular role in managing special education and the demands of pupils with disabilities. IDEA not only is perceived to establish a set of minimum substantive and procedural standards for students with disabilities, it also appears to be seen as serving both to limit the claims that can be made and to leave more control over the administration of special education programs in the hands of local directors. Section 504 is perceived as threatening both local bureaucratic control and routinized limitations on open-ended claims of need.

Our informants offered several explanations to justify their "§504 anxiety." First, many of the administrators pointed out that the federal government did not provide the district with any funds for children identified as eligible for §504 services, so that the local districts would bear the entire cost of the services.[16] One California administrator said: "[I and many of my special education colleagues] are increasingly anxious about the prospect of 504 actions by ADD parents [since 504] offers civil rights protections, but it doesn't mandate any additional federal or state funding for protected individuals . . . Successful 504 actions could really bankrupt the districts." Another California administrator, noting that he preferred to classify ADD pupils as LD, rather than wait for them to be classified under §504, explained: "[My] fear is the budgetary consequences of a successful 504 claim. Rather than being largely covered by state and federal assistance, as with IDEA, the cost of compliance with a 504 accommodation is entirely the district's responsibility."

Second, several of our informants articulated a fear of having to serve more pupils under §504 than they were obligated to serve under IDEA. Here the notion is that the formal criterion for §504 eligibility (does the child have a disability that "interferes with a major life activity"?) encompasses a broader range of disabilities than IDEA's fixed set of disability categories and more formal eligibility criterion (does the disability "impair educational functioning?"). Once more, this does not appear a genuine concern to us.[17]

The "related services" provision of §504 is another mechanism that administrators fear may make the districts responsible for certain costly services that they do not have to bear under IDEA. A disability rights attorney from Northern California told us:

> [Districts worry about higher obligations under §504] because IDEA requires that the child need special education *and* related services whereas 504 requires that the child need special education *or* related services. Thus, for example, a diabetic child might not meet the IDEA eligibility requirement because all she needs is insulin each morning, not special education, but she will be eligible under 504 for services to accommodate her need.

A number of our informants expressed a fear of being forced by §504 to care for severely disabled children at great cost, in situations in which the educational aspects of the care are minimal. The only specific account of a child currently receiving such services in any of the districts we visited, however, came from an attorney for a large California municipality:

> [We're] "educating" a kid who's brain dead . . . His IEP goal is to learn to say 'yes' and 'no,' he requires a full specialized teacher and a full aide, totalling $75,000 per year in salaries alone, plus partial services of a physical therapist and occupational therapist, services to facilitate operation of his life support system, and special computer equipment for his program of "facilitated communication."

What the educators who fear these §504 claims overlook is that, though there are clearly some exceptions, most of the pupils with serious and expensive medical problems that special educators resent paying for out of school funds are already covered under IDEA. We were repeatedly struck by the fact that many special educators seem to most vociferously resist high-cost accommodations for the pupils who seem, in our view, most clearly protected by IDEA, severely physically disabled students who simply cannot be educated unless the school districts set aside ordinary fiscal concerns and accommodate them, even at great cost.[18]

A third, related worry is that certain conditions that have been covered under §504 (most especially ADD) have especially vague diagnostic criteria so that the schools will be less able to draw bright lines between students who do and don't merit special services. One Louisiana administrator stated: "There's a lot of insecurity with respect to what's going on with 504 . . . I'm very much concerned, as are many educators, that the ADD/ADHD diagnosis does not have to be a very technical one for a child to be identified under 504." A Mississippi administrator put the problem even more starkly: "In my opinion the IDEA is much more precise, much more specific . . . 504 is the same as saying, 'you have a problem here.' [Anybody can say some problem] 'substantially limits' [a life activity and even though] it's not my opinion [that it does] what's the line there? So you're wide open."

A number of our informants expressed the view that demands for special services will rise as a result of §504 because parents who are reluctant to accept stigmatic special ed diagnoses will willingly demand services within the regular education context through §504. In the words of one Mississippi special education administrator:

> What we're seeing more with ADD kids now are kids who have a diagnosis from a doctor that this child has an attention deficit disorder. And we have parents who are saying I don't want special education. But under Section 504 we're supposed to give them everything they need under regular ed without labeling them special ed. This is what I've been looking for . . . I've got this "B" and "C" student who I really want to be an "A" student . . . And usually these parents go to an outside agency. They don't go through the process at school . . . [and they] get the outside [agency] evaluation to say the child has a mild ADHD problem. Then they yell Section 504. "I want you to give this child what's necessary in the regular education program. I don't want him labeled special ed and I don't want him taken out and I don't want him part of special ed." . . .
>
> [The problem is growing rapidly. I'm] seeing more and more of your literate, high average, two-parent families [in a district in which 41 percent of the school population is eligible for federally subsidized or free lunches]."[19]

Finally, a recurrent theme in our interviews was the concern that obligations under §504 are open-ended and unsettled while obligations under IDEA have become routinized. Troubled students are tested and diagnostic exclusionary criteria are well-enough established that students *can* be rejected without fear of review. If a student can describe herself as disabled whenever her ability to perform a "major life activity" is compromised, there is no obvious limit on who can make claims: every weakness can be described as a handicap. One Louisiana administrator noted:

> There's a feeling that eventually there'll be no regular ed kids, and everybody will be special ed or 504 . . . Perhaps that's what it should be—that education should be individualized where everybody can succeed. But there is a debate or a discussion of how many kids will get modifications, how many modifications can you give and still teach what's supposed to be taught.

Moreover, while IDEA seemingly establishes few formal limits on the resources an identified pupil can demand, a well-established bureaucratic structure has emerged, and, significantly, it is supervised by local special education bureaucracies and those accustomed to monitoring these bureaucracies. In essence, disabled students are mainstreamed with aids, given resource room help with established student/teacher ratios, put into self-contained classes, or, very occasionally, put in special hospitals or schools. Section 504 demands, in contrast, can ultimately be enforced by federal judges. This may well create discomfort among local special education administrators because it allows parents to "go over their heads," and also because the federal judiciary may be willing to entertain specific claims that a child is simply not flourishing adequately given prevailing practices, and that the district must do something different, something more, to ensure educational progress. One lawyer for a California district specializing in disability law explained:

> [Even if a parent appeals an adverse judgment under IDEA to the State Department of Education], the department primarily reviews whether the IEP was appropriately determined and followed, [rather than making a de novo judgment about whether that constitutes] discrimination . . . [An] OCR [Office of Civil Rights] hearing [under §504] focuses on whether there has been discrimination.

Summary and conclusions

We cannot say that we now fully comprehend how IDEA is implemented in any particular district, let alone how prevalent each practice is among the vast number of service providers across the country. In many ways, our goal in these past two chapters has been to present research hypotheses rather than conclusions. This is especially true when we are relying on our interview informants, but is even true when we have analyzed more systematic data.

We do believe, though, that when one thinks about the normative justifications for what we see as the three key aspects of federal disability education law—the priority that children with disabilities have in making claims for resources, the power of children with disabilities to demand test accommodations, and the capacity of pupils with disabilities to be protected from discipline in certain cases—it is important to recall some of what we have learned in looking at local practice. One must remember, for instance, that studies of variation in state practices demonstrate rather convincingly that special education diagnosis is imprecise, but we certainly do not use this fact to imply, as some might, that one cannot justify resource claims made by the "disabled" because *some* labeled "disabled" will not actually be differentiable from some not so labeled. Imprecision in diagnosis, though, may nonetheless be relevant in designing policy: for instance, when we discuss testing accommodations in Chapter 7, we note that one reason it might make more sense to abolish "speeded" exams altogether, rather than to give pupils with disabilities more time, is that if we abolish speeded exams, we need not diagnose so accurately in the first instance. The fact that IDEA's "loose" disability categories may have facilitated increasing use of self-contained classes to segregate African-American pupils may not imply that we should attack IDEA, but rather imply that we must work harder to ensure that local districts don't administer special ed (or other) programs in a racist fashion.

This is not a "gap study," attempting to show the discrepancy between the commands of formal law and "life on the streets," but we are interested to find that formal law is both difficult to administer and, more significantly, actively resisted. In working through the normative material, which is in many ways quite critical of the current legal regime, we were often inspired by the local resistors that we encountered. The failure, for instance, of some administrators to block "leakage" of resources from IDEA-eligible pupils to other troubled students and the widespread refusal to pay a great deal of heed to federal discipline law were grounded in a practical understanding of the need to treat the interests of all students, whether called disabled or not, with equal respect. This practical understanding certainly inspired our more theoretical inquiries.

SIX

Extra Resources for the Classroom Teacher

The context

In this and the remaining chapters, we turn to the normative issues underlying a system of legal entitlements designed to respond to the claims of people with disabilities. The present chapter addresses the distribution of resources in a local school district. To assist the discussion, we will use a stylized hypothetical problem. In doing so, we hope to gain insight into a larger issue—how to allocate scarce educational resources to students with different capabilities and limitations—by examining a complex "micro" setting.

Suppose an elementary school teacher, acting without the legal constraints we detailed in Chapter 3, is told that he is entitled to receive some extra resources and that he must decide how to use them. First, what are the basic options such a teacher might face? Second, what kinds of normative decision-making rules might he use to evaluate the options? We will address each question in turn, although we will not explicitly evaluate each of the options in terms of each of the normative schema. Instead, we hope that by presenting the argument this way, readers can most readily discern how difficult the empirical issues that the teacher faces really are and also recognize how ambiguous our normative conceptions of "fair opportunity" are.

The options

First, the teacher could use the resources to try to improve the performance of his dyslexic students, employing the variety of strategies that we discussed in Chapters 2 through 5 (for example, resource room reading aides focusing on phonological tasks).

Second, he could get an aide both to educate and help to manage students who might suffer from "attention deficit disorder" (ADD). The teacher believes that an aide more sensitive to the special needs of ADD students will simultaneously increase their academic performance and reduce their disruptiveness, thus improving the performance of non-ADD students as well.

Third, he could employ an aide to increase the academic challenges that a small group of very gifted students faces,[1] challenges he has not provided both because he feels he cannot justify spending the time necessary to develop a tailored curriculum for such a small number of students (particularly ones doing "fine" already) and because he is not particularly good at math and the hard sciences, the fields in which he believes the gifted students need the most stimulation. The teacher might believe that in the absence of such interventions, there is a high probability that at least one of the gifted students will become bored and resentful and, as a result, will eventually do dramatically worse, both academically and socially, perhaps performing below grade-level expectations. Such a student would thus have one of the key traits associated with students with learning disabilities—a substantial discrepancy between IQ and achievement—but it would not be attributable to a specific learning disorder. Our hypothetical teacher also believes that he has no way of identifying which of the gifted students is liable to regress in that fashion, so that he would have to provide "extra" services for all the gifted students to prevent just one from backsliding over the long haul.

Fourth, he could hire an aide to work with the group of students, most of whom are socioeconomically disadvantaged, who have received the least educationally enabling support outside of school.[2] The majority of these students are now performing below grade level academically. In addition, a smaller subset of them are having social difficulties that, in the teacher's view, are subjectively painful for the students themselves, disrupt the class so as to dampen the academic performance of all students to a limited extent, and, finally, contribute to the fairly widespread, but troublesome, belief that more "privileged" students are intrinsically more academically capable.

Some of the less-privileged students would be helped if he chooses one of the other plans he is considering. One is "gifted," a substantial number are dyslexic, and a number suffer from "attention deficit disorder." He surmises that none is working up to potential, though, given his belief that resource deprivation always has *some* negative consequences. The teacher knows that he may well subjectively overestimate the distinctions in performance between socially advantaged and disadvantaged pupils. On balance, though, the evidence that at least some forms of material deprivation in the home are correlated with poor school performance[3] and that poor performance on tests of academic skills in turn depresses earnings[4] strongly suggests that some distinctions are likely to exist. At the same time, the teacher realizes that whatever the performance gap, at least some of it might be attributed to his own problems as a teacher: his expectations of relatively disadvantaged students may be lower, and he thus may both misperceive their performance and worsen it, over time, by demanding less of them.[5]

Fifth, the teacher could devote all the additional resources to one student who has a number of very severe physical and learning disabilities. While the student comes from a socioeconomically disadvantaged background, the teacher does not believe that he has been educationally understimulated at home; on the contrary, inputs in his home seem to have been far superior to inputs for any of his other students. He believes the student will be able to function independently as an adult only with very high levels of intervention.

Sixth, and finally, he could add aides and physical materials in such a way that each of the students in his class gets a bit more attention and a bit more material to work with, but none gets more than any other student. To the degree possible, the teacher remains committed to an ideal that students should receive the same inputs from the school (the same amount of attention from teachers and aides, the same dollar value of physical materials, and so on).

It is important to recognize, when considering the difficulty of the teacher's task, that he must not only attempt to resolve enormously complex normative quandaries, but must also resolve a host of thorny empirical questions. To illustrate how tricky it would be to ascertain the impact of each intervention, we highlight some of the "program evaluation" problems we imagine the teacher would face.

Assume, first, that the teacher simply wanted to maximize the aggregate standardized test scores of his class. He would have to figure out whether the aggregate gains would be higher if an aide were assigned to dyslexic students than if the aide were assigned to ADD students, taking into account the indirect gains to non-ADD students under the second scenario owing to the decrease in classroom disruption. He would have to figure out both the degree to which improved educational inputs improved the test scores of gifted students and whether such improvements represented a boost in lifetime performance or simply accelerated gains that would occur later in any case. If the teacher simply provided identical but modest additional inputs for all students, he would have to know who is likely to benefit from such small changes: one can imagine that such a program might have very uneven impacts. For example, an aide brought in to work a bit more with each student might have only enough time to instruct parents on how to work with their child at home, but this might prove useful only where the parents were able (in terms of the time they had available and their own educational skills) to do the follow-up work.

Assume, instead, that the teacher was concerned with maximizing the lifetime social and economic impact of his interventions. In this event, he would need to know a lot about the effect of distinct improvements in academic performance. It might be the case, for instance, that a 10 percent improvement in reading test scores matters very differently depending upon one's base reading score: a 10 percent gain in scores which represents a move from borderline literacy to comfortable literacy may matter a good deal more than 10 percent test score improvements among students in the middle ranges. The value of the gains to society from boosting a gifted student from being "very successful" to "likely to make significant innovative contributions" might or might not be greater than the social welfare gains to society from boosting other students from being "successful" to "very successful." The teacher might believe that the distinction between a severely disabled child's having the capacity to live independently and not being able to do so has far greater consequences in his and others' lives than more marginal changes in economic status associated with improvements in reading scores across a broader segment of the class.

Normative frameworks

Not only will the teacher doubt that he has accurately assessed the factual effects of each of the interventions that he has considered, but he will also wonder whether there is any principle or set of principles to help him decide whether he has chosen among alternative outcomes correctly. Inspired by a reinterpretation of Christopher Jencks's edifying work on equality of opportunity,[6] our imaginary teacher believes he must choose among seven fundamentally distinct views of how educational inputs *should* be applied.

He may believe, first, that each student should receive equal resource inputs from the school (in terms of both physical resources and the teacher's attention). Jencks dubs this an ideal of "democratic equality"[7]—demanding that the state grant each pupil equal resources just as the state grants each citizen an equal number of votes in a democracy. Jencks believes, erroneously in our view, that "democratic equality" is best justified as a fallback principle, a principle that one adopts not because it is intrinsically compelling but because efforts to justify more complex views of the dictates of equal opportunity are too flawed to accept.

Second, the teacher may believe instead that each student should receive extra resources only to the extent that she tries harder. In this view, which Jencks describes as "moralistic justice,"[8] resources are a reward for morally admirable behavior (as distinct from "talent," which is outside of the student's control). We share Jencks's view that moralistic justice is hard to defend, largely because it is not always possible to distinguish between effort and talent on the basis of the degree of control the student exercises: students may not have much control over the degree to which they try harder.

Third, the teacher may believe that each student should receive compensation for environmental, but not genetic, deprivations, thus rendering these environmental deprivations inconsequential. We think a more pragmatic formulation of this view, which Jencks calls "weak humane justice," is that each student should receive enough public, in-school resources to equalize the sum of the educational resources each student receives from both "private" (out-of-school) and public sources.[9]

Fourth, the teacher may believe in what Jencks calls "strong humane justice": the tenet that the school is obliged to compensate a student for any disadvantage he suffers, whether the root is genetic or environmental.[10] Thus Jencks's advocate of strong humane justice demands that all students end up equally skilled, while the advocate of weak humane justice can live with substantively unequal outcomes provided they arise from genetic differences. Jencks does not believe it is possible to give rational arguments for advocating weak, but not strong, humane justice.[11] We disagree, for reasons we will return to.

Fifth, the teacher may believe that the proper goal is to maximize the aggregate value of the educational experiences for the group, that is, to maximize some utilitarian social welfare function. Jencks has a narrow conception of the dictates of what he calls utilitarianism which we will call into question. In essence, he believes that the utilitarian distributes resources either as a reward that would serve as an incentive for students to learn more (a criterion that has the same effect, though not the same rationale, as the moralists' position) or as an investment to maximize the amount of prospective learning.[12] Jencks views the utilitarian program as essentially indeterminate because these two strands of utilitarianism may, in his view, conflict with each other (rewarding those who have tried in the past in order to induce effort generally may be ill advised if resources are devoted to those who have worked hard in the past but will prospectively benefit little from current input).[13] We think it is easier to understand the utilitarian perspective by dealing with it more directly and generally: the utilitarian simply seeks to distribute resources so as to maximize some stipulated social welfare function. If, for instance, welfare is simply a function of academic performance, then she will attempt to maximize such performance.

The utilitarian may be indifferent to the identity of people benefited by a particular resource allocation (for example, of academic performance). She will be indifferent if and only if she believes (a) increasing "knowledge"/academic skill does not have diminishing marginal utility (so that an increase in performance by the already-skilled has as much impact on human happiness as an increase in the performance of the relatively less adept); (b) there are no distinct "external" effects when certain people learn more (that is, for instance, she does not believe that an increase in the academic performance of either the most capable or the least capable matters more than increases in the middle and she does not believe that the *identity* of those with more and less academic proficiency has any utility impact on others). If she is indifferent to the identity of learners, she will take steps simply to maximize the aggregate educational achievement of the group and will remain uninterested in its distribution. Obviously, her utility/social welfare function will be different if she is distributively sensitive: she may choose to trade off larger gains in academic performance by one group for smaller gains by another group if she believes more utility will be gained if members of certain groups are benefited.

Jencks's list is not exhaustive. It is possible, for instance, that our teacher should choose, sixth, to ensure a minimally decent life for all students who can possibly achieve it, but then distribute the remaining resources by some other criterion. He may believe that the duty to ensure a minimally decent life for everyone is absolute, or he may believe that he has met the relevant duty as long as he has invested resources in the least competent students to the point at which the return to additional resources either approaches or reaches zero. Obviously, his standards for resolving what constitutes a "minimally decent life" will be inexact, but we will assume, for argument's sake, that the teacher following this conception puts a very high premium on ensuring the capacity to live as independently as possible as an adult.

Seventh, the teacher may believe that resources should be expended to ensure that students with moderate or high scores on IQ-type tests who perform more poorly than we'd anticipate come closer to meeting the potential they supposedly demonstrate on these tests. Such a claim could simply be a (controversial) factual application of the utilitarian normative scheme if one posits that investments are most likely to pay back significantly when a student is currently performing below (moderate or high) IQ potential. But there may be an alternative normative claim instantiated in this choice, holding, in essence, that "high"-IQ children's failure to maximize their educational performance, or to meet social expectations generally consistent with children of their IQ, is more tragic than lower-IQ children's similar failures.

Comments on some of the alternative normative frameworks

DEMOCRATIC EQUALITY VERSUS COMPENSATORY OBLIGATIONS
(WEAK AND STRONG HUMANE JUSTICE)

Debates between those who believe the state satisfies its duty to equalize opportunity so long as it provides equal inputs to different students (proponents of "democratic equality") and those who believe the state satisfies this duty only so long as it compensates them for some or all disadvantages they bring to the school setting fundamentally recapitulate a number of traditional controversies in legal and political thought.

Jencks argues that the proponents of the democratic equality ideal adopt the posture only as a default position, the principle they return to when they recognize that they cannot implement any of the more complex (but normatively more appealing) visions of what it would mean to provide equal opportunity to all students.[14] Although we do not find the case for democratic equality compelling, we believe Jencks seriously underestimates the affirmative argument for the principle, an argument with strong resonance in belief systems which maintain the classic division between the public and private spheres.

In the view associated most strongly with pre-Realist classical legal thought, the state does not act when it simply permits private citizens to exercise unfettered legal privileges to act in a certain area.[15] Thus, for instance, though the state might, in theory, preclude wealthier parents from showering their children with educationally stimulating gifts, gift giving remains private conduct in this view. The state's obligation to treat citizens equally extends only to its own direct conduct: it cannot directly distribute resources unevenly, but it is not deemed to be distributing resources unevenly when it simply *permits* them to be distributed unevenly, by private parties privileged to make whatever distributions they choose.

It may well be the case that this pre-Realist position has lost much of its analytical vitality for reasonably sophisticated late twentieth-century legal thinkers. Nonetheless, the precise impact of the Realist recognition that the state is active, not passive, in making a decision to remit certain discretionary decision-making authority to actors in what is then denominated the private sphere is hardly lucid.

Thus, for instance, in one view, the fact that state authorities stand behind a private property owner's decision to eject a trespasser, that his discretion to choose occupants was not just authorized by the state but ultimately enforced by the state, makes the ejection state action.[16] The implication of this view is that the owner cannot eject people for any reasons that state officials would be unable to use to bar persons from public property. In another view, the relevant state action to assess is simply the decision to allow private owners to eject, and it is that decision alone whose propriety must be evaluated.[17]

In the educational context, the second view implies that the fact that parents may distribute quasi-educational goods to their children because permitted to do so by the state need not suggest that the parents must operate under the same constraints as the state. This is clearly the prevailing view in some regards. For instance, the state cannot directly officially support the religious education of the young,[18] but parents clearly may (that is, the state not only *may* clearly permit them to do so, it almost certainly *must*).[19] In the compensatory educational context, this view suggests that the sum of parental and state contributions need not be equalized on the grounds that it is this sum that represents the true total state input: the sums the state "permits" to be expended simply do not count as state expenditures. In this second, more prevalent view, we must simply judge whether the state has violated some legal/ethical obligation in bestowing parental discretion. It would, for instance, almost surely violate the equality principle if some, but not all, parents had formal discretion to distribute goods as they wished to their children. It need not violate that principle, though, that the value of the state's grant of discretion differs for different parents.

We certainly do not mean to advocate resting on what strikes us as the quite wrong-headed traditional public/private distinction. What we do mean to note is that the tradition is hardly without normative force. Instead, it rests on the conception that the state is (at least relatively) uniquely capable of monolithic, antipluralistic spending patterns, which shut off distinct social development paths[20] and (at least relatively) uniquely subject to capture by factions that expropriate political outsiders for their own benefit.[21] In this view, then, the state must spend the same sum on all children to preclude politically ascendant groups from funneling grossly disproportionate resources into their own communities. At the same time, it may not bar private educational or quasi-educational spending, even in order to ensure equal access to resources, for fear that in doing so, it would squelch diversity of child-rearing methods.

INPUT EQUALITY (WEAK HUMANE JUSTICE) VERSUS OUTCOME EQUALITY
(STRONG HUMANE JUSTICE)

It is surely possible to believe that the state should allow uneven distribution of educational resources in the "private" sphere, particularly because the effort to equalize "private" spending would not permit families an adequate level of autonomy and freedom from intrusion into internal spending patterns.[22] Nonetheless, one might believe that the state retains residual obligations to ensure that children are treated more "equally" than they are in "private." Remedialists will divide into two quite distinct camps: proponents of "weak humane justice" and proponents of "strong humane justice." Backers of our variant of "weak humane justice"—that is, those who believe the state must try to fill the gap between the resources available to environmentally privileged and environmentally deprived children—will not urge that the state ensure that all children have the same probability of success, but will simply demand that they be given the same external, tangible inputs to try to make what they can of themselves. Those who adopt this position do not suggest that the state is obliged to correct environmental but not natural handicaps because the genetically "handicapped" child is somehow more to blame for her failures than the environmentally "handicapped" child would be, but because they believe that outsiders are obliged only to provide input materials.

Some advocates of weak humane justice imply, however, that we owe special duties to help children overcome environmental handicaps because they can invariably more readily be corrected or compensated for than genetic ones. Jencks persuasively notes that this argument is, on close inspection, decidedly flimsy. For instance, it would hardly matter if one were looking to accommodate a hearing impaired student whether she had been born deaf or became deaf early in life because of a disease that might have been prevented by better medical care.[23]

The second argument Jencks makes, though, that the justifications for weak and strong humane justice are ultimately indistinguishable, seems considerably less telling. He contends that if we
deem the state responsible for the presence of distinctions in up-
bringing because it chooses to permit "family privacy," it must be
held equally responsible for genetic disparities because it chooses
not to engage in eugenics programs that would limit births of those
deemed genetically disadvantaged.[24] The cases are hardly indistinguishable. One could maintain, for instance, that individuals who
seek compensation for environmental shortfalls would prefer that
the state had intervened, ex ante, to collectivize child care and had
thus prevented the conditions that caused them harm, while those
who seek compensation for genetic shortfalls would still elect that
the state not have chosen to prevent their births.

More significantly, though, Jencks simply fails to explore a number of weighty distinctions between the cases. The backer of (our
variant of) weak humane justice, on the one hand, may believe that
her goal is fully realizable without harming the absolute performance of the relatively privileged (as opposed to harming them
merely in relative positional terms, which any egalitarian reform
will do). She knows that she has compensated disadvantaged students as soon as such students have received a certain level of inputs—a level of "public" inputs that ensures that the sum of "private" and "public" inputs received by each child is equal. Once she
has done this, her duty is realized; whether in fact this equalizes
achievement given unequal "natural" talent remains open to question.

The backer of strong humane justice, on the other hand, has no
obvious input goals. If one is being fully deterministic about char-
acter formation,[25] every distinction in achievement can be traced to
differences in innate and environmentally created structure. Thus
one hasn't "compensated" for "shortfalls" in innate talent and environmental input until people are identically successful. Moreover,
to the degree that additional inputs for the disadvantaged seem, at
some point, to lack effect, backers of strong humane justice may believe they have no choice but to "level down," to try to destroy the
capacity of the relatively genetically or environmentally privileged
to succeed. While the backer of weak humane justice *could* meet her
stated goal—equalizing total resource access for all children—by

depriving relatively advantaged children of some of their privileges, there is nothing intrinsic to the goal that demands that. If, instead, one's goal can only be realized if one equalizes outcomes, and additional inputs for the disadvantaged stop having positive effects, the advocate of strong humane justice seems duty bound to "level down."

It is important to note, of course, that *any* advocate of compensatory obligations—whether an obligation to remedy environmental or "innate" barriers to success—might qualify or limit his commitment by urging that no inputs be provided which are either utterly without impact or fall below some minimum threshold of impact. It would surely be possible, then, to argue that the commitment to strong humane justice should be understood not to demand outcome equality, but to require continuing compensatory efforts for those disadvantaged by innate or environmental factors only until those efforts proved worthless or close to worthless. In a similar fashion, it would surely be possible to understand proponents of this qualified version of weak humane justice as demanding not equal total inputs, but an increase in public inputs for environmentally shortchanged children until any further marginal increases in inputs either would not help at all or would not help adequately significantly. Adopting this sort of qualification, though, is not the same as adopting something like a general utilitarian framework— one in which the educators seek to maximize the return to any marginal investment of resources—since the obligation to equalize has priority over higher-return investments in the privileged *until* these investments become worthless or "nearly" so.

One might explain the distinctions between the programs in yet another, more conceptual way. Proponents of weak humane justice remain wedded to the idea that there is a core of nonsocially determined ineluctable individuality. They may believe that the core is genetic (distinctions in innate capacity) or that it is a matter of some moral will (distinctions in application that cannot be traced to factors that "determine" how hard one tries). They believe the state is responsible to ensure that ineluctably distinct individuals receive the same tools to work with, the same inputs, but they expect diversity of outcome given diversity of persons. Proponents of strong humane justice believe that distinctions between individuals are a result of determined, external forces that remain subject to our conscious manipulation. Thus the decision not to alter the determining forces represents a decision to tolerate outcome inequality. Moreover, even though the backers of strong humane justice believe that there are two forms of determining forces—biological and social—they remain wedded to the belief that conscious decisions to manipulate socially determining forces (like educational resources) are sufficiently potent to create equally successful individuals. Once more, our point is not to advocate one or the other of these positions, but simply to note that Jencks radically understates the rationality of *distinguishing* the case for our variant of weak humane justice and strong humane justice.[26]

UNTANGLING UTILITY-BASED PRINCIPLES

The basic injunction that utilitarians considering alternative social investments follow is seemingly straightforward. Educational resources should be expended so that total utility is maximized. Presumably, the decision maker sees herself trading off among alternative spending/investment opportunities, at the margin. She must first ascertain what effects the incremental spending/investment dollar will have on outcomes (educational attainment for all affected students, social adjustment for each student, social attitudes about social mobility, and so on), and she must then evaluate each alternative end state. Some of the problems of implementing the utilitarian program will be empirical: the impact of spending additional resources in alternative ways even on relatively measurable outcome variables (like reading scores) is, in essence, never really known.

The teacher's task is far and away most tractable if he assumes that he is trying simply to evaluate the joint output of his class (for example, the total number of reading test questions answered correctly on some set of standardized tests, without regard to which student or students give more correct answers). If, however, he believes that the level of utility obtained from any given quantity of achievement is distribution-dependent, his task is still more complex. If, for instance, it may "produce more utility" for one student to increase his reading score by ten correct answers than for some other student or group of students to increase total scores by fifteen correct answers, then the judgment he must make is especially difficult.[27]

As we indicated earlier, an educator may make two quite distinct sorts of assumptions that would make her suspect that she should be distribution-sensitive in evaluating outcomes, that is, that she should care not only how many test items the class got right but who in the class improved. First, utilitarians have traditionally tended to believe that *income* (like particular consumption goods) was generally of declining marginal utility: that an additional dollar in the hands of a poorer person typically gave him greater happiness than that additional dollar would give a richer person.[28] While it may not be the case that we would think it worthwhile, even as a rough approximation, to imagine that the utility returns to incremental knowledge/cognitive capacity steadily declined as cognition/knowledge increased in quite the same fashion, it seems important to recognize that utility gains from scholastic improvements may not be constant. There may, for instance, be radical discontinuities between basic illiteracy and literacy that do not occur when parallel gains in reading comprehension scores are made at higher ends of the spectrum. Similarly, gains that permit students to pursue post–high school education might be more significant than parallel gains for students who are either poorer or better readers.[29]

Second, utilitarians might also be distribution-sensitive because, given a choice between improving the scores of one student or another whose selfish gains would be equal, we should improve the performance of the student who would provide more benefit to others when she makes those gains. It strikes us that there are at least four forms of "externalities" of this sort that the educator is likely to focus upon.

a. Educators especially interested in "gifted" students will be prone to argue that improvements for first-rate students may induce them to do quite significant work, of great social benefit, not readily duplicated by other members of the labor force. Enhancing the skills of those with the potential to make relatively unique contributions (whether to culture or technology) will redound to the benefit of others, even assuming the gains to the gifted pupil herself are no more considerable than the gains to students with more replicable labor market skills.

b. Educators especially interested in highly challenged students will tend to note that gains in their functioning may relieve others of the difficult duty of dealing with their dependency. While many focusing on the utility gains from helping to nurture the possibility of independence could better be translated as making our first argument, that is, that the marginal utility of cognitive gain is especially high when it permits a move from dependence to independence but declines thereafter, some would clearly choose to emphasize third-party effects, whether the removal of expensive support obligations from the polity or the extended family.

c. To the degree that we believe that utility functions may be group interdependent—that is, that most African-American individuals, for example, gain far more from the increased success of other African-Americans than from the increased success of non-group members[30]—then the identity of those who gain from our programs matter. Success by members of groups that are socially recognized as subordinated—whether by class background, race, gender, physical disability, or, at least arguably, certain forms of cognitive disability—may redound to the benefit of others in their social groups in a fashion that success by one member of a relatively privileged group does not.[31]

d. There is another distribution-sensitive utility effect worth considering. Analytically, the effect resembles distribution-sensitivity arising from group consciousness. In both cases, people "gain utility" by knowing that certain people succeed, while they are indifferent to the success of those outside the identified "preferred" groups. It is worth precipitating out this explanation for distribution-sensitivity, though, since it resonates not so much in sensitivity to group identity as in sensitivity to "individualistic" justice; the "preferred" beneficiaries in this scenario are not identified by their membership in a social group, but by the justice of their particular claims.

In the context of analyzing takings doctrine, Michelman argued that utilitarians must frequently account for citizens' sense of justice: one "utility" cost we must consider then—whether we are talking about the cost of "uncompensated" takings or the cost of improving the achievement of the "undeserving" rather than the "deserving"—is that, all else being equal, we should ensure that the improvements in academic success are distributed as much as possible to those whose claims to make such gains are considered most morally compelling.[32] In this sense, even the strictest utilitarian will have to know whether substantial numbers of citizens feel worse if ideals of, say, weak humane justice are breached (for example, if we expend marginal resources to improve reading scores for the socially advantaged more than we do for the relatively deprived).

ARGUMENTS FOR MINIMALISM

Our hypothetical teacher might believe that his primary responsibility is to ensure that each student become minimally functional,[33] but that once he has met that duty, he can use other principles to allocate any leftover resources. (This duty is most likely to be germane in dealing with the most severely disabled children. It may well partly underlie the obligations under the portions of IDEA that are not our primary focus in this book, obligations to spend quite large sums of money on severely disabled pupils.) There is, though, no general demand that poorer performers inevitably have priority over better performers.

People advocate variants of this sort of minimalism for at least three reasons. For some, it derives from their basic utilitarianism. Minimalism, in this view, is premised on the supposition that utility gains when people move from subminimal to minimal levels of functioning are especially pronounced. For others, minimalism may derive from something resembling (but distinct from) Rawlsian "maximin" ethics,[34] the belief that those selecting justice principles "properly," that is, without knowledge of their particular self-interest,[35] would select principles that protected the least well off against calamitous results, averse to the risk that they themselves would turn out to be among the least well-off.[36]

For still others, minimalism is the most reasonable approach to solving otherwise insoluble problems of reconciling competing commitments to equal opportunity and family autonomy. In this view, the state must recognize that it cannot really guarantee equality of inputs (let alone an equal probability of success, given distinct innate endowments) as long as it allows children to be raised in different households. Yet the state remains committed to allowing particular households to form, each conveying distinct physical, cognitive, and emotional resources.

Once the state acknowledges that it has no real capacity to equalize exposure to inputs, it must rethink its goals. It may well decide that families must only be precluded from preventing children from developing the capacity to function at some minimal level; thus we prescribe no canon of developmentally appropriate stimuli, but instead simply forbid child abuse and neglect, limiting family autonomy only when it threatens certain ideals of minimal functioning.[37] When young people require atypically high levels of resources to function minimally, we will not allow their access to these resources to turn on the accident of the family in which they happen to be placed; we do not, in this view, want our commitment to family diversity and autonomy to cost children "too much." But just as we don't demand that parents do an especially "good" job of nurturing their children, so we don't demand that all youngsters get as many resources as the best-off get. We simply ensure that no child be denied (socially available) resources to become functional merely because of the accident of family circumstances.

This third argument appears somewhat strained, though. On its face, it appears to apply better to explaining why we have developed abuse/neglect laws designed to guarantee minimal functioning than to explaining a decision to provide especially needy children with more resources than even typical families would be able to muster to ensure their independence. Minimalists making this argument perhaps believe that the recognition of the significance of family autonomy was simply a first step in developing a refined view of what sorts of opportunities must be guaranteed. If, in an effort to balance competing interests in autonomy and opportunity we "discover" what sorts of opportunities we are unwilling to sacrifice, the lesson may be germane. Just as we won't trade off the child's claim to an opportunity to lead a minimally decent life for more family autonomy, so might we not trade off that same opportunity for other sorts of important social gains (for example, general utility improvements; assurance that the sum of inputs for all youngsters, private and public, is essentially equal).

THE "TRAGEDY" OF THE DISAPPOINTING HIGH-IQ STUDENT

The positions that we have analyzed up to this point are self-consciously held, analytical positions. In this section, we attempt instead to identify an unself-conscious attitude, recognizing that it would almost surely fail to survive even the most minimal scrutiny: the view that society's primary goal should be to do all we can to protect high-IQ students against relative failure.

The argument for putting the claims of high-IQ students ahead of competing claimants' demands may be, for some people, simply an application of a more general utilitarian framework. Some, postulating that incremental investments can be effective only if students are not yet performing up to their capabilities, might believe that the utilitarian's task is to identify students performing below potential. In this view, then, high IQ is simply a measure of potential, and the presence of a gap between manifest performance and IQ simply a sign that additional resource inputs will have a particularly significant payback. As we have noted and will soon discuss in more detail, the empirical claim that the returns to investment in high-IQ/low-achievement students with learning disabilities are systematically high proves to be quite difficult to sustain. But even as a purely analytical matter, we would have little reason to precipitate out a concern for "high-IQ" students as a normative "principle" if it were nothing more than an effort to identify those who would most benefit from social investments. The interesting question, in a sense, is why the advocate for focusing incremental resources on pupils with learning disabilities has asked us to perform just one thought experiment—how would high-IQ/low-achieving children perform in a different world, one in which we focused resources to try to overcome their deficits?—rather than a host of seemingly parallel ones. How would the socially disadvantaged child perform in a world in which we used resources to minimize her disadvantage? How would "Black English" speakers perform if math and science texts were written in language that tapped into their special linguistic competence?

When we worry that advocates on behalf of pupils with learning disabilities "fetishize" high IQ, though, we believe that they are not employing the concept of "potential" in its conventional sense, that is, they are not referring to the capacity to develop. The fetishist need not believe that high-IQ LD children can actually be taught to manifest the performance generally associated with equally high IQ youngsters; their IQ is not their potential in the ordinary sense of a capacity that can be realized in fact. Rather, the metaphor that animates the IQ fetishist is the (unself-consciously paradoxical) idea of "unrealizable potential," a core of essential personal identity that transcends behavior revealed in any actual setting. Thus, in a mid-1960s book advocating increased attention to "bright underachievers" (students who rank in the top decile in IQ tests but perform at or below the mean in academic achievement), Raph, Goldberg, and Passow showed particular concern for wasted "genius": "However one focuses the problem of loss to society of high-level ability, there are sufficient wasted human resources of an exceptional type to point to a critical need for making better use of our talented generation of young persons."[38] While the authors frequently justified their concern for "bright underachievers" in just the sort of utilitarian terms we have outlined, they acknowledged that they did so recognizing that they had no solid empirical evidence that remediation of bright low achievers would produce greater gains to society than the attempted remediation of other low achievers. In fact, they acknowledged that "bright underachievers" had done poorly in special classes.[39] (They attributed this failure to mutually reinforcing discipline breakdowns among students we would now call LD and ADD, which suggested the need to separate them from one another.) At the same time, they assumed, without data, that "other low achievers" might just as well be left with one another. We believe this casualness about empirical support for a utilitarian rationale for concentrating resources on "bright underachievers" reflected the fact that, for many, the real rationale for focusing on the learning disabled in the first place was *not* utilitarian, but based on some poorly specified claim of "merit."

If IQ tests can be said to measure some "core" aspect of identity, people whose core identity is "successful" (even if their scholastic behavioral manifestations are those of someone relatively "unsuccessful") are thought to have entitlements to rewards and opportunities. If "fetishists" are especially disturbed that students who are "like" successful students perform poorly, they may be prone to overstate their achievements (this is, of course, one unsympathetic view of what accommodation on tests accomplishes) or to focus resources upon them to ensure that they achieve a bit more like "similar" students even if their performance improves only marginally. If "fetishists" think it tragic that someone so much "like" successful people should fail—someone so close to success that it is hard to believe she can't grasp it—then the task is simply to identify the dimensions along which "likeness" ought to be measured.

We doubt that anyone would acknowledge that he fetishizes IQ in precisely this fashion: brought out in the open, the argument may seem to self-destruct almost instantaneously. Even if one had some principle that "similar" people ought to end up in similar social positions, it is difficult to defend the proposition that similarity along this dimension (high IQ) is especially significant, even if scoring high on IQ tests were in fact the single trait that most successful people had in common. But, of course, it *is* more socially plausible to say that people are "alike at the core" when they are equally "intelligent" (in whatever sense might be revealed in tests) than when they are equal along a host of alternative dimensions: hair color, size, schizoid tendencies revealed on projective tests, kindness, and so forth.

Indeed, the early advocates for children with learning disabilities displayed just this sort of belief in the superiority of high-IQ children to "slow" children of similar achievement, this sense of the "tragedy" of "confusing" the "bright" with the slow. (There is no parallel implication that confusing the "disadvantaged" with the slow or the academically "slow" with people without developable capacities is problematic.) In the first volume of the *Journal of Learning Disabilities*, Pat Green, the mother of an LD child, writes:

> When we worked with [Jaye, a learning disabled youngster] for several nights on the assignment, but failed to make much progress, all of us—Jaye, Jim, and I—became completely discouraged. This was the first time that Jim decided Jaye was simply "slow". I did not know what to think, but in tears I said, "No, I don't think you're right." . . .[40]
>
> "Slow" meant dull, uninteresting, and also uninterested. These "cliches" simply did not describe Jaye, for she was none of them! "Exuberant" would better describe her than "dull" and "full of life," "eager to know" have been a part of her since birth. So, I was not willing to accept the "slow" theory . . .[41]
>
> "The standard IQ test score would never show this," Dr. Austin stated, "but, the interpretation tests we give enable us to determine what a child's potential is. Jaye has a greater potential than you would imagine . . . We must have the opportunity to help *this bright child!*" (emphasis in original)[42]

The implicit argument is not always the straightforward one that we are especially disappointed whenever someone possessing traits successful people typically possess fails. It would appear quite socially unacceptable to acknowledge the notion that it is particularly bothersome if a socially privileged child fails (though like the high-IQ children, he is also *like* those who typically succeed). But there is little doubt that advocating the idea that high-IQ children are especially meritorious is not only difficult to defend on its own terms, but also has disturbing political overtones of class bias. That straightforward bias was evident in crude form in the literature of the early LD advocacy movement. For instance, Barsch, in the very first article published in the *Journal of Learning Disabilities,* wrote:

> [The learning disabled child] is the child who measures near, at, or above the range of normal intelligence. He lives with parents who are no more or less confused than the average; he has enjoyed a reasonable amount of social advantages; he is not sufficiently emotionally disturbed to warrant treatment . . . [H]e has returned from the neurologist without diagnosis and is genuinely and sincerely regarded by most people who encounter him as a "fine young boy possessing good capability." Yet his day-by-day travels on academic terrain are marred by persisting inabilities. He is not alone. He is legion—and he belongs.[43]

Notwithstanding such occasional expressions of straightforward class bias, we do not believe that most IQ fetishists are simply masking their socially unacceptable concern that high-status children oughtn't to fail by showing ostensible concern for those with high IQ, which actually, of course, correlates closely enough with social class that those most benefited by a concern with low-achieving, high-IQ students will be more socioeconomically privileged.

Rather, we believe their class bias takes a more subtle form, in which IQ fetishists, consciously or not, seek initially to legitimate social inequality by noting the correlation between IQ and class. Social inequality, then, is initially explained and justified by its correspondence with a root, or core, inequality. Having put so much pressure on IQ to do the serious work of social legitimation, fetishists come to believe that differences in IQ are the fundamental, socially pivotal differences among people. At that point, one's IQ becomes synonymous with one's basic nature, and a disparity between IQ and performance comes to indicate a breach in the natural order, a failure of one's true nature to be manifest in practice. Thus Ames, once more writing in the first volume of the *Journal of Learning Disabilities,* urging that schools administer intelligence tests to avoid misclassifying students as having an LD whose learning problems are attributable to low intelligence, was typical:

> Those dealing with the general subject of learning disability should, perhaps, be as fully informed about what problems need not be considered as learning disabilities in the usual sense as about those which should. There is a large percentage of the school population in this country (it might run as high as 15 percent) who will have difficulty in school simply because of their low intelligence . . .[44]
>
> Intelligence, operationally defined, is the aggregate capacity of the individual to act purposefully, to think rationally, and to deal effectively with his environment . . . National and racial differences do exist—probably of both genetic and environmental origins, in varying degrees. But the fact is that these differences are not large or relevant in the individual case. An IQ is merely a measure of relative brightness . . . *When it is asserted that intelligence tests are unfair to the disadvantaged and minorities, one must be mindful that they are simply recording the unfairness of life.* (emphasis added)[45]

Efficacy of educational interventions

As we have noted, those who advocate devoting available incremental resources to students with learning disabilities do not explicitly reduce their normative distributive claim to any of the propositions described above. The proposition that children with LDs are the preferred recipients of discretionary funds, though, certainly demands closer scrutiny. Surely, the claim is untenable that spending on children with LDs is the *only* effective use of discretionary funds—that is, that students with LDs are uniquely situated to improve their cognitive and coping skills if given additional inputs.[46]

At times, advocates for the learning disabled may make this point simply by defining the group they defend as that (unique) group demonstrating a gap between performance and potential. We suspect, though, that the advocates of devoting "incremental" resources to those with learning disabilities most typically share the commonplace assumption that resources devoted to nondisabled students *do* help the performance of these nondisabled students.[47] It would be hard to make the case that school was worthwhile for the learning disabled alone if schooling provided no human capital for the non–learning disabled.[48]

Assuming that advocates for devoting incremental funds to children with learning disabilities do typically treat schooling as worthwhile, there are two distinct empirical issues to consider. First, we must ascertain how substantial the returns to typical discretionary educational programs directed at non-LD students are, and second, we must investigate the possibility that the returns to incremental expenditures on LD pupils are not always clearly substantial or even positive.

Questions about the efficacy of increasing educational expenditures remain among the most hotly debated in education economics, and we do not purport to "resolve" controversies that have raged for decades. Nonetheless, it is worth noting why it appears to us that those who make the case for focusing all "discretionary" funds on LD students by relying on the inefficacy of alternative spending plans will have difficulty sustaining this line of argument.

It is helpful to treat general questions about the efficacy of increased spending as conceptually comprising a series of related subquestions:

a. Given typical educational system practices, will an increase in spending improve students' academic achievement, measured in terms of test score performance?

Generally speaking, this question has been answered in the negative, though the negative findings are hardly unproblematic. The "classic" work answering the question is the Coleman Report,[49] which remains the basis for the "common wisdom" that educational spending is of no moment, that children are influenced by their peers and home background but are not aided by boosting school inputs. This "common wisdom" received considerable support when standardized test performance dropped markedly in the 1970s at the same time that real expenditures per pupil rose dramatically.[50] While, for reasons we are about to explore, Coleman's research is not especially persuasive, some of the conclusions of the report still appear, to most observers, correct. School districts typically spend more money per pupil when they (a) lower class size; (b) increase teacher pay, particularly by giving bonuses to teachers who receive post-bachelor's degrees and encouraging a higher proportion of the instructional staff to obtain advanced degrees; and (c) improve physical plant. In his careful review essay, Hanushek summarized 147 prior studies and concluded that none of these interventions is typically effective in improving students' test scores.[51]

Supporters of the position that it is pointless to increase educational expenditures (or supporters of the narrower corollary that increased spending on LD pupils does not compete with other worthwhile goals) have neither dealt effectively with criticisms of the studies nor responded adequately to the other conceptual subquestions, though.

The Coleman Report itself purported to find that increases in educational inputs do not help students, but it is unlikely it will persuade a skeptical reader. First, it measured the inputs that are in fact available to students on a districtwide basis, ignoring substantial heterogeneity in the inputs made available to different students within the same district. In fact, within districts, the schools the Coleman Report studied had quite different student-teacher ratios. Moreover, teachers in schools dominated by minority and poor children were typically less educated, less experienced, and poorer performers on National Teacher examinations[52] and were probably paid less well as a result, since differences in teacher characteristics explained three-quarters of the variance in teacher salaries that Coleman found.[53] Second, equating a student's exposure to "high spending" with her exposure to more educational resources is problematic. Imagine, for example, that teachers are paid a salary bonus for working in a more violent atmosphere. Expenditures per pupil will be higher in violence-prone districts, all else equal, but there is no reason at all to believe that that particular form of increased expenditure will improve pupil test performance, nor, more important for our purposes, is there any reason to believe that if the district received still more resources (for example, more computers, a music teacher), that these would *not* improve student performance. Third, the report assumed, quite incorrectly, that one can readily control for differences in either the "innate ability" or the socially acquired skills of students, so that we can be assured that those receiving similar test scores in districts with different spending levels are in fact equally capable.[54] Fourth, and quite significantly, the Coleman Report systematically underestimated the proportion of variance explained by differences in resources invested in schools by determining first the proportion of variance explained by distinctions in student characteristics (for example, family background). While it would not matter whether one estimated the additional variance explained by student background or school investments first if these two variables were orthogonal to each other, these variables are almost surely highly correlated, leading Coleman to understate the contribution of school spending to the extent that some of the effects of school spending would have already been accounted for when he measured the proportion of variance explained by student background characteristics.[55] Last, though least significantly in our view, the report ignored the fact that education is cumulative. Current test scores were compared with current spending levels in Coleman's work, without any regard for the inputs that had been made available to different students in the past.[56]

These conceptual problems can be significantly reduced by altering the focus of input effectiveness studies. Instead of trying to account for aggregate test scores as the dependent variable, and assuming that "district spending level" is just one of many independent variables that might or might not influence the dependent variable, it appears far more reasonable to look at the impact of alternative expenditure levels on *changes* in academic performance in a discrete period. Thus, rather than assume that we will be able to hold all other factors other than spending truly constant when we try to explain, for instance, why one group of sixth graders has a score of X on the reading test and another $1.2X$, we should look, for instance, at numbers of groups of students with score Y in the third grade, and follow them through to the sixth grade, attempting to explain *differential* changes in performance on the basis of distinctions in school and nonschool inputs.[57]

b. Will an increase in educational spending improve adult earnings?

Even if increased district spending typically does not improve test scores, we must still ascertain whether augmented spending typically helps students in ways that are not captured by shifts in achievement test scores. Most significantly, we look to adult earnings. There is, not surprisingly, nothing resembling consensus on the answer to this question, but it appears most plausible that educational expenditures *do* affect earnings.

Earlier studies tended to find no significant relationship between adult earnings and general district spending levels or more specific high school attributes that the adult worker had been exposed to.[58] A number of recent studies, however, have found that workers' earnings increase more for each additional year of schooling they have received when they have been educated in districts that spend more for "traditional" reasons (lower pupil/teacher ratios, longer terms, and higher teacher pay).[59]

An interesting issue is whether it would be possible to reconcile (convincing) factual findings that school spending affects earnings but not test scores. Most people would tend to believe that the *mechanism* by which schools influence earnings is to improve cognitive skills, as measured by tests. It is possible, though, that schools influence earnings by influencing the propensity to continue in school.[60] It is also conceivable that low-spending districts focus unduly on standardized test performance. They believe they can most readily satisfy parents by ensuring that children don't lag on the most visible measures of academic progress, while they fail to educate students in the broad array of skills actually useful to adult success. It is also possible that achievement test–taking skills are both essentially irrelevant to adult performance and insensitive to school district interventions, but that more relevant problem-solving skills are indeed taught better in higher-spending districts. Whatever the reason for the stronger impact of school spending on earnings than on test scores, though, the studies of adult pay levels lend support to the proponents of the position that all students, not just learning disabled students, will benefit if given incremental funds.

c. Do distinct types of educational inputs differentially affect performance?

The problem with concluding that school spending doesn't matter from studies that show insignificant correlations between spending levels and performance (whether measured in terms of achievement scores *or* earnings) is that inputs are excessively aggregated in the studies; effective inputs are mixed with costly and ineffective ones in the same district. Thus it is important to ask whether discretionary funds might be expended on programs that have proved effective.

Some of the inputs may simply be misspent; that is to say, districts with "surplus" budgets beyond the ordinary budget misallocate their incremental funds, choosing (relatively) worthless over worthwhile discretionary programs. But the higher-spending districts may also simply confront greater "needs" and have no additional "discretionary" money to spend.[61] Imagine, hypothetically, that each local district spends one dollar per day per pupil eligible for hot meal support; a district with more eligible students would spend more per pupil, though both districts would be meeting the same end by ensuring that all children in the district received a certain amount of nutrition during the day. There is, obviously, no reason to hope that the increase in expenditures required to meet an end that is met "off-budget" in other districts would improve student academic performance.

It is often helpful, though, given the difficulty of interpreting districtwide data, to look at studies of more particularized interventions. Thus, for instance, while it may well be true that smaller class sizes, districtwide, are irrelevant to the success of district students, more disaggregated studies by Wolfe and Summers show that smaller class size is valuable for students whose achievement test scores are low though it is mildly counterproductive for the highest achieving students.[62] Similarly, Summers and Wolfe find that experienced teachers, who typically cost more, appear to be *less* effective for poorer students (perhaps because they have become more cynical in their expectations than new teachers, who might be more willing to give poorer students a chance to prove they can improve), though they are more effective for better students.[63] A district might spend more if it pursued optimal matching policies (because of the administrative costs of ensuring effective matches), but such policies might be helpful. Similarly, Winkler found that teachers from more traditionally prestigious colleges improve their pupils' performance more than other teachers.[64] While such teachers, dispersed through a district, might be no more expensive than other teachers, recruiting and retaining *more* of them might well be more costly. Districts typically spend more on teachers with advanced degrees, and encourage teachers to get more training, though this appears ineffective;[65] paying more initially for teachers from "better" colleges may, however, be an effective strategy.

d. Do narrow discretionary programs directed at non-LD pupils produce significant educational benefits?

When we are imagining our teacher seeking extra resources for his classroom, we frequently envision him as choosing between *discrete* marginal programs. We see him as choosing, for instance, between a reading specialist for his kids with learning disabilities and a computer, or an art teacher, or a language teacher; we do not believe that he is contemplating more general reform (for example, shifts in class size, recruitment, and placement policies).

Once more, there is considerable evidence that specific incremental spending plans may be worthwhile. A number of studies find that certain sorts of intensive preschool interventions have proved beneficial over time, though not surprisingly, the results finding favorable effects are not uncontroversial. Thus, for instance, in Barnett's well-publicized long-term longitudinal study following students at the Perry Preschool in Ypsilanti, Michigan, till the age of nineteen, the author found that students in the program fared better than the control group in terms of school achievement, employment, and educational placement and attainment.[66] Significantly, too, the decision whether to spend the money to expose students to computers appears, in several different studies, to be an important one: increased computer education appears to affect both achievement test performance and earnings.[67] Similarly, some authors critical of traditional strategies for improving performance are nonetheless enthusiastic about certain alternative interventions: thus, for example, Levin, Glass, and Meister find that a peer tutoring program was nine times as cost effective in raising math achievement as an extension of instructional time in math, four times as cost effective as an equal cost reduction in class size, and four and a half times as effective as the use of computer-assisted instruction, though computer-assisted instruction was more cost effective than any intervention other than peer tutoring for improving reading.[68] If one disregards the costs of the interventions, one still sees considerable distinctions in the "effect size" of interventions (that is, the differences in after-intervention scores between the experimental and control group, expressed in terms of the number of standard deviations of the effect where the standard deviation is the standard deviation of the control group scores). Tutoring (by either peers or adults) had dramatic effect sizes (.79 for math, .42 for reading), while changes in instructional time and reducing class size by modest amounts had very small impacts.

There are similar "success" stories painted for a variety of programs which featured, among other attributes, quite intensive tutoring, for example, the Reading Recovery Program and the Success for All program. The thirty to forty hours of Reading Recovery tutoring in Columbus, Ohio, brought 90 percent of a group whose pretest scores were in the lowest 20 percent of the class up to or above the class mean, a position they appear able to sustain; this result far exceeds regression-to-the-mean expectations.[69] Similarly, inner-city African-American Baltimore students at high risk of educational failure educated under the Success for All program achieved far better scores than control group students; after first grade, the group enrolled in the program scored at grade level compared with a 28th percentile score for the control group, and special education referrals for graduates dropped dramatically. The effects were less dramatic after two years of school, but more dramatic after three (effect sizes are .67 after first grade, .28 after second, and .95 after third).[70] More generally, Slavin and Madden, while deeply committed to the proposition that incremental educational resources are extremely efficacious, also believe that many interventions, especially remedial interventions for mildly handicapped and socially disadvantaged students alike, fail to do much, and that prevention of academic lags and immediate responsiveness to lagging students is therefore critical. While they laud programs in which small groups matched not by age but by ability work in teams to meet carefully sequenced challenges, and also strongly support one-on-one tutoring to prevent students from developing deficits, they are rather skeptical of, among other things, the impact of preschools on long-term cognitive achievement, smaller class size (other than individual tutoring), the use of either resource room specialists or classroom aides for mildly disabled (IDEA) or socially disadvantaged (Chapter One) pupils.[71]

Our point, for now, is not that these studies are either convincing or deficient demonstrations that certain educational interventions work; it is simply that there is sufficiently credible evidence that particular interventions improve the performance of non-LD children to make it unacceptable to dismiss the possibility that expenditures for LD children *compete* with expenditures for non-LD pupils.

e. Do existing programs directed at students with learning disabilities appear to be effective in improving their performance?

It is not at all obvious that interventions to improve the academic performance of children with learning disabilities have proved especially helpful: it is certainly not theoretically implausible that LD students have neurological deficits that can neither be reversed, through medical procedures, nor compensated for, by alternative means of education. It is actually extremely difficult to judge whether educational interventions aid learning disabled students, not just because there have been so few well-designed long-term longitudinal studies, but because there is little reason to believe that *any* study has focused on a group of "genuinely" LD children, rather than the more random group of children diagnosed as learning disabled by either the districts or the researcher performing the longitudinal study.

It is hardly obvious how the policy analyst should react to the presence of misdiagnosis. Advocates for children with learning disabilities are prone to argue that if diagnosis were more accurate, we would see larger improvements in the performance of the group labeled as having LDs because the group would then only contain those capable of making such gains. The opposite claim is just as plausible, a priori, though: that is, the children who currently improve with additional teaching are misdiagnosed, so that special education interventions appear to succeed with some portion of LD children because they succeed with some who are not truly LD.[72] Our own view is that misdiagnosis, though surely present, should not compromise a policymaker's use of efficacy studies for two reasons. First, the weight of the efficacy studies is that troubled learners, whether LD or non-LD, rarely improve performance dramatically with interventions. Second, and more important, we must, in evaluating IDEA, assume that resources will be channeled to whatever population districts are actually capable of identifying: thus, even if we granted for argument's sake the proposition that interventions focused on a more accurately identified class of truly learning disabled students would be more efficacious, we must evaluate the relative success of interventions directed at those students who will actually receive resources because they are identified as learning disabled and those directed at nonlabeled pupils.

If interventions in the lives of children with learning disabilities were successful, we would expect them to perform at least substantially closer to the levels commensurate with their supposed potential rather than at levels more typical of students with their low levels of early achievement. Children with learning disabilities, like other poor readers, do not catch up *as readers* with their classmates, regardless of interventions, though. With respect to poor readers generally, Simmons notes that the probability that nondyslexic poor readers who read below grade level in grade one will be below grade level in grade four is .88 (and presumably many of the 12 percent who "escape" are closer to grade level when they begin).[73] Similarly, in Short and colleagues' analysis of the same Carolina Longitudinal Learning Disabilities Project data, "learning-disabled students" became *more disabled* with age, despite special education services, in the sense that their IQ-achievement discrepancies grew.[74]

Longitudinal studies are perhaps more useful than short-term studies in determining the effectiveness of educational interventions for various troubled learners. Unfortunately, there are simply no good longitudinal studies matching LD students with an IQ of X and achievement scores of Y in early grades with non-LD children with similar IQs and similar achievement scores, respectively, exposing each low-achieving group to special instruction or each group to ordinary instruction. If intervention were uniquely successful for students with learning disabilities, we would expect them, after intervention, to perform (at least substantially more) like the students matched by IQ than those matched by (low) achievement.

There are numerous studies, though, that attempt to compare the progress of what are usually called "garden variety" poor readers—low reading achievers with low IQs—with the progress of students with learning disabilities. Stanovich's review essay[75] may be thought by some traditional special educators to be unduly hostile to the usual pattern of intervention, but his finding appears unexceptionable: "[T]here are . . . no good data indicating that discrepancy-defined dyslexics respond differently to various educational treatments than do garden-variety readers of the same age."[76]

This finding appears true both for those researchers who find interventions efficacious for both groups and for those who find nothing works especially well for anyone. Thus, for instance, Pressley and Levin find that all categories of poor students, including those with LDs, respond (equally) affirmatively to a variety of techniques to increase "learning efficiency" (including learning particular strategies, for example, rehearsal and semantic organizational strategies; thinking more effectively about what strategies might be useful; and learning to monitor one's academic progress more carefully).[77] Lytton found that children given remedial education made significant gains from remediation even when they had low IQ scores: in fact, students with relatively low IQs (85–99) made more progress than those with higher IQs in math, and trivially less in reading. However, both groups made considerably more progress than did very low IQ pupils (IQs 63–84).[78] More pessimistic researchers like McKinney found that both nondiscrepant and discrepant North Carolina children placed in special education programs at a time when the state's selection system focused less on discrepancy than absolute achievement shortfalls continued to perform well below the level of "normal achievers," and that "status as discrepant or nondiscrepant was not a significant variable."[79]

In one of the most extensive studies of the prognosis of LD and "garden variety" poor readers, following seventy-one learning disabled and seventy-three "garden variety" poor readers with matched achievement scores on the Isle of Wight, Yule found that the garden variety poor readers fared somewhat *better* than the poor readers with LDs over time.[80] This result, however, has typically not been replicated: the reading skills of "garden variety poor readers" do not appear to become stronger than those of LD students over time, though they do not appear to become weaker either.[81]

Review articles from the early 1980s summarizing existing longitudinal studies of special education interventions reach different conclusions, but even the articles most favorable to special education practice give us little reason to believe that students with learning disabilities are *uniquely* benefited by intervention. Spreen was extremely pessimistic, concluding that "most children who are referred to a clinic for a learning or reading disability do not catch up. In fact, their disability is likely to become worse with time. In addition, remedial instruction has in general not been shown to improve the prognosis for these children."[82] Schonhaut and Satz are only a bit more optimistic in their review of the literature, classifying only four of eighteen studies as showing favorable results and two as showing mixed results: if we look only at what they view as the most methodologically rigorous studies, four of five showed that the prognosis for improving the performance of LD children was poor, even with remediation.[83] Finucci, recognizing how few studies adequately differentiate poor readers from LD poor readers, seems to concede that most poor readers continue to read poorly, but believes that the LD (poor readers with higher IQs) have a greater chance of success, as do poor readers with a higher socioeconomic status.[84]

Horn, O'Donnell, and Vitulano found far more variability in results in their review of longitudinal studies, and much more reason to consider significant questions open, since "methodological shortcomings of available follow-up studies make inferences regarding the efficacy of treatment premature."[85] They are, though, on balance, optimistic that the long-term prognosis for treated pupils with LDs is favorable, especially if one measures their vocational and educational attainment[86] rather than their performance on academic skills tests,[87] a fact that may reflect either the success of remedial programs in training pupils with LDs to compensate for deficits that cannot be directly overcome or may simply reflect the generally attenuated relationship between academic skills and adult success. However, as they note, no study published prior to their review, other than the Yule study which found that "garden variety" poor readers fared *better* than the learning disabled, even attempted to distinguish between learning disabled and other poor reading students.[88]

In the absence of careful matched long-term longitudinal studies, we must rely to some extent, instead, upon gross measures of the adolescent and adult achievement of children with LDs who have received special education. As it turns out, these sorts of studies provide little more basis for optimism than existing cross-sectional and longitudinal studies do that interventions in the lives of children with LDs are efficacious. Horn and colleagues' statement that adult outcomes for LD pupils are relatively favorable appears an outlier in the literature.

The 1992 SRI International study of the long-term "transition" of special education students[89] hardly constitutes a ringing endorsement for the efficacy of special education of students with "soft disabilities" (LD and SED pupils), at least as it is presently constituted. The results for physically disabled children are more encouraging, a finding that should, at least, give us pause in accepting the contention that the dominant factor inhibiting the disabled educationally is the prejudice of school officials and teachers against those who are "different," a prejudice that one would think would be more likely to be manifest against those *visibly* different. Students with disabilities in regular schools had a GPA of 2.3 (compared with 2.6 for nondisabled students) and more than two-thirds of disabled students failed at least one course during high school.[90] Students who performed poorly were disproportionately SED and LD pupils. A 1993 SRI study found that 28.5 percent of children labeled LD dropped out of high school; less than 15 percent of pupils with physical disabilities dropped out.[91] While students with sensory/physical disabilities enrolled in colleges at rates similar to those of their nondisabled classmates,[92] only 27 percent of disabled youth in general had enrolled in postsecondary school within five years of leaving high school, compared with 68 percent of the general youth population.[93]

Adult outcomes for LD children who have been specially educated are certainly poor, compared with outcomes for the population at large, but whether they are (a) better than they would have been without the interventions, (b) better than would be expected on the basis of early achievement scores, or (c) worse than would be expected on the basis of other predictors of adult achievement (most particularly IQ, parents' SES, race, gender) is impossible to discern from the existing studies. In a 1992 review article of the literature on the adult status of those with learning disabilities, White and colleagues find that adults who have suffered from learning disabilities continue to perform poorly on quasi-academic tasks (reading, spelling, and arithmetic), fare poorly in the labor market (studies find unemployment rates ranging from 13 to 64 percent, with the average in the surveyed studies around 50 percent; average wages are roughly $4.40/hour; only 50 percent live independently and even fewer are self-supporting). The only encouraging sign is that adults with learning disabilities do not manifest atypical adjustment or behavior problems.[94] It is difficult to ascertain, though, whether all the sampled adults received any special school interventions, let alone the sort of interventions that would be deemed appropriate by special educators.[95] The afore-mentioned SRI study finds that employment rates for LD and SED adults have improved, though they are still substantially lower than for the general population; wage rates remain quite low (the median hourly wage for those out of school three to five years was $5.72 per hour).[96]

Even those studies which find relatively favorable outcomes for dyslexics must be interpreted cautiously. Thus, for instance, while it may appear heartening to find that 50 percent of the sample in Finucci, Gottfredson, and Childs's long-term follow-up study of 965 graduates of the Gow School, which specializes in treating developmental dyslexics, had finished college and that 50 percent held managerial jobs as adults, "the men did not do as well as might be predicted . . . considering only the socioeconomic status of their families and their own intelligence."[97] For instance, 95 percent of the control group—from the Gilman School, a boys' school serving socioeconomically similar nondyslexics—graduated from college.[98] Moreover, the IQ test did not appear to measure the actual realizable potential of the dyslexic group: while father's educational attainment and subject's own IQ typically predict academic attainment, they did not do so for the Gow group;[99] instead, the severity of the dyslexia at the time of entry into the school, coupled with higher relative improvements in reading scores following exposure to the school's Reconstructive Language course (which might most profitably be seen as an ex post measure of otherwise undetectable ex ante "remediability") proved far more predictive of every variety of adult success.[100]

In much the same way, Vogel and Adelman may well be unduly heartened to find that while students with learning disabilities perform more poorly on the ACT test and in high school than a control group at Barat College, they graduated from school at the same rate and in the same time frame.[101] Their optimism seems heroic, though, given that the LD students' grades were significantly lower and they received substantially more D grades.[102] Although the authors attributed high graduation rates to the success of the students and the institutional support system, they could be explained at least as plausibly by the unwillingness of the school to fail students generally, or students construed as disabled in particular, whether as a result of legal pressure, economic self-interest, or self-imposed ideology.

Purely educational outcomes are hardly encouraging. Nationally, while roughly 5 percent of elementary and secondary students aged six to seventeen are served by the schools as LD,[103] only about 1 percent of college students are:[104] thus, youngsters with learning disabilities who have received special services seemingly go on and stay in college at little more than 20 percent of the rate of non-LD youngsters (though recorded incidence of LDs may decline in college because of reliance on self-reporting).[105] Only 52 percent of children with learning disabilities graduated from high school with a diploma (and another 10 percent graduate with a certificate);[106] nationally, 83 percent of white students and 75 percent of African-American students graduated from high school in 1993.[107]

Applying nonutilitarian normative frameworks to the policy options

If one accepts the supposition that students with learning disabilities are uniquely educable, they may also be uniquely entitled to the sorts of inputs that can be claimed under the dictates of "humane justice." They are, in this view, people who are blameless for their poor performance, people who have been disadvantaged by some biological lottery (for those who assume that learning disabilities are genetically hard-wired) or disadvantaged by receiving inadequate quasi-educational input (for those who link learning disabilities to inadequate nurturance). Obviously, the claims of the students with learning disabilities are particularly strong for believers in strong humane justice (committed to undoing the impact of bad "biological" breaks), if they believe that among the "biologically disadvantaged," those with learning disabilities are atypically prone to benefit from resources directed to them.

While it might not appear that the backer of weak humane justice would be especially moved by the pleas of those with learning disabilities compared with the pleas of the generally socially disadvantaged, there are certainly those who believe that the learning disabled can be described as a group which is environmentally disadvantaged by the failure of the schools and the society more generally to "bring out" their skills as a result of unduly narrow teaching and workplace styles.[108] Although students with learning disabilities may or may not be generally socially disadvantaged, they are, in this view, (almost definitionally) disadvantaged environmentally because they live in an environment "hostile" to their cognitive styles. In this view, though many non-LD students may be deprived of the obvious "private" inputs—being read to, helped with homework, and so on—all receive a "private institutional" one, an environment in which their cognitive styles "pay off." The educator committed to using the schools to bridge the gap between the inputs different students receive will inevitably note that the student with a learning disability lacks the "private" privilege of living in a world ready to appreciate her as she is, ready to use the skills she'd have regardless of whether we "specially" educated her or not.

This view of environmental deprivation is not untenable: while it is easiest to conceive of "private" opportunity enhancing structures as simple quasi-educational inputs, designed to create "output" whose valuation is a wholly separate concern, it is clear that our "private opportunities" are expanded as much by private appreciation of our skills as by their development. If a child is "by nature" a gifted zeppelin craftsman, his opportunity set is enhanced in a world in which that skill is valued, and we could view him as environmentally deprived to the degree that his skills were less appreciated than, say, his sister's computer skills. This view is troublesome, though, both because it is not held especially consistently, and because it is not uniquely applicable to the learning disabled, or even the disabled more generally.

The inconsistency, in essence, is the failure of those who believe the LD population's claims take priority to acknowledge forthrightly whether to treat the capacities they hope to develop in the child with a learning disability, if she's specially educated, as genuinely valuable capacities or simply to treat them as capacities she's *prudent* to develop because she will live in an unjust and irrational world. The claim of "environmental deprivation" we're unpacking is, at bottom, a claim about social inequity and irrationality: the LD child's cognitive style is just *different,* and it is *disabling* only because the (inequitable and irrational) environment renders it disadvantageous. If we treat the (inequitable and irrational) environment as given, though, we might, as weak humane justice advocates, have to give more resources to the children disadvantaged by that irrationality, to permit them to overcome it; ideally, however, it would appear better to change the world in which the LD "style" disadvantaged LD adults.

This position appears sentimentally attractive—resonating in general ideals of accepting, rather than trying to overcome difference—but it also appears to us to rest on a wholly disingenuous description of the educators' preferred practices. While most advocates of increased educational spending on students with learning disabilities indeed would prefer it if employers were asked to accommodate to *some* extent, for instance, those who have trouble reading, they attempt to teach students with learning disabilities to read as much like non-LD students as the LD students can. The educators hardly seem to have disclaimed the importance of reading (or memory, or reasoning, or numeracy): we needn't *blame* the victim to believe that he is the dominant *locus* of the problem. The inability to read may not be the LD student's *fault,* but the social interest in the capacity to read may not be anyone else's fault either.[109]

Even if one wanted to adopt the position that we should devote atypically high levels of school resources to some students because the social environment generally poses barriers to their success, it is certainly not clear that we'd single out learning disabled—or even other disabled—students if we chose to implement such a plan. We could readily redescribe all students lacking academic skills, for whatever reason, as people unfairly victimized by the overvaluation of certain forms of academic skills. Whether the judgment that society irrationally misevaluates skills is an accurate one or not is not really the point for now: the point is that there is little compelling reason to believe that the skills of those with learning disabilities are more unfairly belittled than the skills of others with "traditional" academic deficits. If there is some claim, parallel to a claim frequently made quite plausibly on behalf of physically challenged workers, that workplaces irrationally organize in such a way that they fail to take advantage of the contributions of this particular group of workers, we have not seen it articulated in a form that would appear credible.

Advocates for the position that the claims of students with LDs will generally trump those of competing claimants might also describe students with LDs as particularly vulnerable to adult dependency in the absence of special educational accommodations in order to appeal to advocates of "minimalism." To sustain this claim, one must convince the minimalists that the vulnerability arises more from the disability than from poor academic performance. If *all* students who perform very badly academically are at pronounced risk of leading lives that don't meet whatever standards the minimalist demands, then *any* student whose academic performance is very bad deserves special remedial attention. Conversely, if (at least some identifiable subset of) students with learning disabilities frequently do reasonably well despite their disabilities—

even if they do worse than they might do if more resources were devoted to them—then the minimalist would be unmoved by their pleas.

In the final analysis, "disability rights" advocates urging that the claims made by learning disabled pupils should have significant priority appeal most directly to "IQ-test fetishists." In a sense, those with LDs are identified as that group with the biggest gap between academic performance and potential (however defined), and if we view people with either realizable or nonrealizable "potential" as particularly strong claimants, then those with LDs are specially entitled. As we noted, the views of "potential" that are being constructed here are not enormously rationally sustainable—they ultimately focus not so much on the actual capacity of the student to perform as they focus on the ways in which she resembles others who are high performers. Moreover, the moral claim—that those most "like" others capable of high performance are more entitled to both rewards and inputs than others who perform poorly but don't resemble high performers as much—is highly suspect as well.

Proponents of increasing spending on the gifted may well share something with advocates for the learning disabled in this regard: a belief that there is something particularly galling in permitting students to perform at levels lower than their IQ scores would predict. What is most interesting for us, though, is to sort out why advocates for the learning disabled would typically oppose incremental spending on the "gifted," even if they believed gifted students don't reach IQ potential in "understimulating" classes.

There is one explanation which we would find quite benign: that the advocates of spending on those with learning disabilities rather than the gifted simply treat the shortfalls in performance faced by LD students as more consequential in terms of their lived-out experience. There is a less benevolent explanation as well, though, that those who advocate spending on the learning disabled (unconsciously) have adopted the potential-development position to stand in for a publicly unarticulable fear that students, generally from certain socially privileged positions, with certain "virtues" generally held in esteem in middle-class culture, ought not to face status degradation. If this is the explanation, they naturally will feel less anxiety when confronted by the gifted student who does well, but not nearly as well as she'd do if she were adequately stimulated in class. In this view, the advocates for those with learning disabilities fetishize not so much the realization of potential as the avoidance of socially discordant status attainment.

Summary and conclusions

In a world of limited resources, it is not enough to say that children with learning disabilities "deserve" resources: their claims inevitably compete with claims that could be made by other "deserving" pupils who can be described in a wide variety of ways (poor achievers, socioeconomically disadvantaged, gifted but understimulated, and so forth). Students' claims can also be "adjudicated" using a number of distinct "principles" that might be used to allocate scarce educational resources. We are probably most favorable toward some variant of a distribution-dependent utilitarian principle (in which we allocate educational resources so as to maximize the "value" of educational performance, personal adjustment, and social attitudes, aware that shifts in the performance of certain individuals—both as individuals and as group members—may have greater impact than parallel shifts in the achievement of other students). At the same time, we acknowledge the considerable power of other competing principles (for example, principles that demand that we compensate for environmental or both environmental and genetic disadvantages even when the gains from so doing, measured in certain ways, are lower than the gains that would accrue if we followed some nonrectification precept; principles that require equal per pupil spending; principles that those who make claims to resources to ensure "minimal" functioning trump all other claimants). We have little sympathy, though, for the position most clearly compatible with IDEA's treatment of those with learning disabilities: a position that fetishizes the IQ test and demands that resources be applied in such a way as to ensure that educational performance correlates as closely with IQ as possible.

IDEA gives legal force to the position that claims by students with learning disabilities to receive incremental resources should have some significant priority over claims made by other students not diagnosed as having a disability. This is often justified by using the arguments that among those with learning difficulties, only those with LDs manifest a gap between "potential" and achievement and are therefore uniquely capable of benefiting from discretionary interventions. This is an empirical proposition, though, a fact which has too often been obscured by fiat. Learning disabilities are *defined*, in abstract theory, as an otherwise unexplained performance-potential gap; the logical conclusion is therefore inescapable that, assuming accurate identification techniques, those who are in fact diagnosed as LD must suffer from remediable performance deficits. Once one treats the proposition that those with learning disabilities are uniquely able to benefit from interventions as an empirical question rather than as the logical conclusion derived from the definition of LDs, the assertion becomes extremely weak. There is considerable evidence that non-LD pupils would benefit from higher levels of educational inputs, and even stronger evidence that *as a group*, if not in each individual case, those with diagnosed LDs have been remarkably unresponsive to the costly special education that has been provided to them. There is very scant evidence that dyslexics, for instance, benefit more from the interventions of reading specialists than do garden variety poor readers, either in helping them read or in compensating for their ineradicable reading problems.

We would not suggest that IDEA's most basic mandate—that those diagnosed with certain quasi-medical conditions must receive an appropriate, individualized education—must be scrapped. Nor would we suggest that schools stop doing diagnostic work-ups to identify what learning problems a student faces—to the extent that the diagnostic work aids them in ascertaining what services are beneficial in remediating the pupil's difficulties. But we would suggest thinking about two very different sorts of reforms in special educational practice: the first assumes (too optimistically) that considerably *more* resources will become available to public schools, and the second, more realistically perhaps, assumes that existing resource constraints will persist or worsen.

Should markedly higher levels of resources be available, we would recommend the individualization of educational plans and intervention packages for all low-achieving pupils, regardless of disability status, as well as for all pupils where there is reason to believe they are performing below potential in the only sense that ultimately matters—that is, that they are performing markedly less well than they would if the interventions were put into place. Severe socioeconomic deprivation would, we believe, presumptively mark students as eligible for tailored services, just as "discrepancy scores" now do.[110] In addition, even students whose achievement levels were average or better would be entitled to diagnostic testing and/or experimental remedial teaching to ascertain whether more individualized services than those provided in the regular classroom would be appropriate, at least as long as there were reasons to believe that tailoring a plan would prove atypically beneficial. Thus such interventions might be appropriate, for example, if teachers observed atypical disparities in performance across academic subjects, if achievement fluctuated atypically over time, or if students complained of difficulties in studying that are atypically prevalent in students who have been helped by particular forms of remedial intervention. Many of the richer districts we visited followed a model fairly close to this one; either explicit special education services, or very similar educational supplements, were offered to all students exhibiting academic and behavior problems, at least on a "trial and error" basis. Some of these districts discouraged parents from entering the formal IDEA system to the degree possible (for example, by allowing long queues to develop for diagnostic testing) while offering the sorts of services that students who were more likely to be certified IDEA-eligible would get in any case.

Assuming, though, more pessimistically, that there will not be a radical expansion in the number of costly individualized educational plans that districts can make available, so that the schools will fundamentally have no choice but to allocate such plans among competing claimants, we would recommend that the current system be modified in significant ways.

First, while disability diagnosis would still generally trigger an IEP determination, and the receipt of a set of presumptively beneficial interventions, districts would ultimately be allowed to withdraw special services even from properly diagnosed students when the services proved inefficacious over some substantial period for the individual. Naturally, to avoid giving districts perverse incentives to offer inefficacious services (so as to be able to withdraw them), state administrative bodies and courts would have to supervise claims that services of reasonable quality had been provided without marked effect. Moreover, over time, districts should be more explicitly entitled to litigate the question of intervention efficacy for categories of services and problems, even when they concede the existence of a disability: the existing practical presumption that IEPs should invariably involve resource provision, while not formally guaranteed by the statute, should disappear.

Second, districts with low per pupil spending levels ought to be allowed to temper IEPs to account for district poverty. For the federal government to mandate that districts unable to serve the bulk of their student population adequately serve some subset according to "best prevailing national practice" without funding that requirement is to impose intolerable burdens on nondisabled students in these districts. While we would clearly prefer that poor districts have adequate resources, we see no reason to believe that squeezing the nondisabled students has increased political pressure to obtain sufficient funding rather than simply further compromising inadequate educational systems.

There are a number of "rule-like" administrative mechanisms that might be used to accomplish this goal if the political will to accomplish it were present: mandatory maximum resource room student-teacher ratios, for instance, could be stated in relationship to such ratios in the district generally rather than in absolute terms. Limits on the requirement for "neighborhood school placements" that interfere with achieving scale economies in the provision of special education could become routine for districts whose per pupil spending levels for nondisabled students are below certain thresholds. Parents might have to elect between resource room placement and full inclusion more frequently when districts "plead poverty" in supplying one-on-one classroom aides if the district is unable to supply certain core services to nondisabled students, or when its per pupil expenditures fall below some threshold. One could also imagine less administrable systems working off of a "general" §504 antidiscrimination model rather than the more bureaucratized IDEA model: in such systems, districts would be entitled to defend "less than best prevailing national practice" treatment of the disabled population by attempting to prove such treatment was nondiscriminatory, in the sense that the interests of the disabled were as adequately represented as those of the nondisabled population.

Third, we would encourage districts to establish (or maintain) programs of the sort described in Chapter 5, in which there is a high degree of leakage of resources from special education students to other needy students. Thus aides who enter mainstreamed classes should give help not just to the IDEA-eligible students formally in their charge but also to other students exhibiting academic problems. Such a policy is justified not only because it puts far less pressure on districts to be "accurate" in making inevitably contested diagnoses of eligibility, but because the substantive claims that even accurately diagnosed students with learning disabilities must receive extra attention are, in our view, extremely attenuated.

In our view, IDEA imposes a conceptually unsound model: the assumption is that we work forward from quasi-medical diagnosis to a legal right to treatment that, if not wholly unlimited, is limited only by whatever limits are inherent in "ordinary prevailing professional practice," regardless of the cost of such practice. We have serious doubts about whether "rights" to treatment even of indisputable diseases ought to be framed in that "absolutist" way—all services are, in some sense, rationed whether the balancing process is explicit or not.[111] In this field, though, the "right to treatment" model is even more inappropriate: diagnosis is useful in our view only insofar as it proves helpful in identifying presumptively appropriate services. But we should fundamentally work *backwards* in providing special services for pupils: we should experiment with different service delivery packages to particular individuals (and groups identified in terms of having markers that indicate they are likely to benefit from services) and continue to provide those services that are efficacious, experiment with new services when the first efforts fail, and be willing, at some point, to call it quits. When two students—one of whom is "disabled" and one of whom is "deprived"—prove to benefit equally from the same set of interventions, they should be equally entitled to those interventions. IDEA would be acceptable only if it resulted in the identification of pupils who are systematically markedly more likely to benefit from intervention than their classmates, and if the ongoing entitlement to interventions depended upon those interventions proving substantially helpful. Unfortunately, it fails on both scores.

SEVEN

Accommodation on Law School Exams

The context

Should a law school faculty grant extra time on exams for students classified as "learning disabled"? We will assume, for argument's sake only, that the question can be addressed in an authoritative vacuum, that is, that the faculty is legally privileged to make whatever decision on the matter it chooses. (Thus issues raised, for instance, about the requirements imposed by §504 of the Rehabilitation Act, which we addressed in Chapter 3, are wholly beside the point for now.)

Although we do not know of any law school faculty that has directly debated this question, we are by no means confronting a fatuous hypothetical. Students with learning disabilities *are* frequently accommodated on exams. In fact, the number of students allowed extra time on the most critical college entrance examination, the Scholastic Aptitude Test (SAT), administered by the Educational Testing Service (ETS), rose dramatically in the early 1980s, increasing by over 80 percent from 1980 to 1983. Most of this change was due to an increase in the number of learning disabled students who registered for special administrations: the proportion of accommodated students who were learning disabled rose from 57 to 71 percent in that short four-year period.[1] Nonstandard administrations continue to rise rapidly. Between 1987 and 1993, the number of nonstandard administrations rose by 87 percent (to 12,259 out of 1.045 million students) even though the number of test takers declined by nearly 3 percent.[2] It would appear that almost all of the increase can be accounted for by pupils with learning disabilities. In 1989, 0.8 percent of respondents to ETS questionnaires indicated that they were LD (2 percent had other disabilities); by 1993 1.3 percent said that they were LD (an increase of 4,800 pupils), while the number of deaf, blind, paraplegic, orthopedically impaired, and multiply disabled students all declined incrementally.[3]

Similarly, the number of persons requesting special accommodations to take the California Bar exam rose from 107 in July 1988/February 1989 to 410 in July 1993/February 1994. Although candidates requesting accommodations did not identify themselves as having learning disabilities until the February 1990 administration, the number of applicants with learning disabilities nearly tripled (from 33 to 90) between the July 1990/February 1991 testing cycle and the July 1992/February 1993 cycle, and the number identified as having a learning disability rose 17 percent further in the next testing cycle.[4]

We will assume, for purposes of this discussion, that exams serve only one of the many functions they might arguably be designed to serve. We will examine graded tests on the supposition that grades reward or punish performance (though rewards and punishments themselves conceivably serve a number of distinct ends). We are aware that by ignoring a number of functions that exams might serve, we also ignore functions that accommodation might serve. For instance, one might believe that exams are learning experiences and that accommodation facilitates that learning experience. More significantly, some might assume that law school exams help employers identify students who will be the most competent or productive employees.[5]

Giving some students better grades than others may reward performance on the particular tasks the students have been asked to master, without regard to whether the students' performance on these assignments predicts their performance on some future set of tasks. In this regard, better grades are an intrinsically desired good (that is, a higher grade is like a material consumption good that we presume all students would desire). As long as grades are unequal, then, the task is to defend the (local) social inequality arising from the unequal distribution of this desired good.[6]

In examining justifications for giving some people higher grades than others, we will look at the typical arguments invoked to rationalize differential material rewards. We will look predominantly at desert arguments (those who are more "meritorious" along relevant dimensions "deserve" greater rewards). We will also, to a limited extent, look at incentive-based arguments (the promise of receiving higher rewards for certain forms of "valued" behavior will induce that behavior).

We will assume, too, that the accommodated learning disabled student will receive a higher grade than she would have without accommodation; otherwise, of course, the accommodation would be essentially pointless. Surprisingly, perhaps, there has been no systematic, empirical study of this issue in the law school (or college) context so one cannot rule out the possibility that accommodations are unhelpful.[7] But there is substantial evidence that accommodation helps students on standardized tests. For instance, Centra found that LD students score .5 SD below the norm when they take the nonaccommodated version of the SAT, and rise to .3 SD below the norm when given special administrations of the test.[8] Thus the relevant question for us is whether the student with a learning disability "deserves" the lower, nonaccommodated grade or the higher, accommodated grade. We will return at considerable length to a vital question about which we make no preliminary assumptions: would non-LD students benefit if they received the accommodations that students with LDs receive?

In investigating the social practice of grading, we will ultimately take it as given that merit is a legitimate criterion for distributing grades. We do so fully aware of attacks, from both the political right[9] and the political left,[10] on the idea that we should evaluate an existing distribution of social benefits by ascertaining whether it corresponds to the distribution of merit. We proceed on the assumption that schools have resolved the issue in favor of distributing grades in accord with some notion of merit when they decide to give unequal grades. Thus we ultimately focus instead on how, *within* a merit-based system, a school should decide whether to assign a student with a learning disability her lower (nonaccommodated) grade or her (presumptively higher) accommodated grade.

Are exam accommodations for learning disabled students justified?

WOULD THE ACCOMMODATIONS STUDENTS WITH DISABILITIES RECEIVE SIGNIFICANTLY AID STUDENTS WITHOUT DISABILITIES?

It may well be the case that some significant proportion of students diagnosed as having learning disabilities work more slowly than other students; if this is the case, one would naturally expect them to benefit from extra time. Dyslexic students, for instance, may take longer to read complex fact patterns. Indeed, in some accounts, focusing on "perceptual speed deficits," learning disabilities are virtually *defined* in terms of how they affect the pace at which the student performs complex tasks: the notion is that students with LDs engage in slow or limited automatization of the basic subskills underlying academic performance.[11] The purported failure to automatize skills is believed to result in inefficient processing, and expending an "inordinate amount of attention on skills that normal cohorts perform with little mental effort . . . [i]nadequate automization is purported to interfere with many academic tasks requiring higher order cognition (e.g. reading)."[12]

Other students labeled as having learning disabilities may be aided by other kinds of accommodations (for example, allowing students to take oral rather than written exams, allowing students to tape record or dictate answers, allowing a reader for students with reading difficulties or providing recorded exam questions, assigning an assistant to make sure the student understands both the questions and the directions, or providing a private exam room for the student to minimize distraction).[13] Students with "memory deficits"—"difficulty remembering problems, retaining numerical information such as multiplication tables, dates, etc., difficulty remembering rote facts" in the words of Stanford University's Disability Resource Center—might find it atypically difficult to take closed-book exams.[14]

At the same time, it is important to remember that students with learning disabilities might well improve their relative test scores if the exams themselves were changed. The dyslexic student might do better still (relative to his classmates) on a short-answer exam that demanded little ability to absorb complex factual patterns gleaned from written narratives; the student with memory deficits might do best on an exam that called on knowledge of fewer rules, but more depth in analyzing arguments for and against a certain rule.

Many law teachers, though, would surely resist making certain changes, believing that forcing them to make the alterations would be to compel them to not test skills they valued. Students with "reasoning deficit" perhaps provide the most stark example of how problematic the case for accommodation can be. Stanford students are described by the university's Disability Resource Center as suffering from a learning disability when they suffer from what is called "Reasoning Deficit," defined as "(a) trouble thinking in an orderly logical way, (b) difficulty prioritizing and sequencing tasks, and (c) difficulty applying learned skills to a new task."[15] Presumably, the best sort of exam for a student with a "reasoning deficit"—one that blunted the impact of his disability—would be to ask him to answer a number of distinct, familiar questions rather than asking him to apply diverse rules, some more germane than others, to a complex fact situation he has never before encountered. It is an understatement to note that law teachers will be loath to give him such an exam.

Moreover, it is important to recall the most critical general conceptual point: those students not classified as having learning disabilities or as having any sort of disability perform differently from one another on tests, for reasons that could obviously be redescribed in terms of "deficits," "disabilities," or "handicaps." Some students sort out relevant facts from irrelevant ones better than others; some students organize responses better than others; some have better mastery of formal rules; some understand microeconomics on exams which seem to call for microeconomic knowledge; some process ethnographic skills which others lack. Some students are good at math, others are not. (The difficulty of cleanly distinguishing the learning disabled from such poor performers can be seen when one realizes that a student whom we have just described as "not good at math" might well be described by the Disability Resource Center at Stanford as suffering from "Dyscalculia," a specific learning disability, if he has "the ability to do concrete arithmetic problems but not be able to understand abstract theory" or if he cannot "remember from study session to study session the solution to a problem.")[16]

Test givers assume, perhaps unself-critically, that they are valuing skills that are socially significant and relevant. If exams are at least partly "speeded"—that is to say, most students would improve their raw scores on the exam if given more time—it is presumably because the test givers believe that responding rapidly is a genuine virtue. If exams call on people to have command over a number of formal rules, it is because the examiners believe that having instant access to such rules is a strength. If exams require microeconomic knowledge, or the capacity to deal with numbers, it is because examiners think students who manifest these skills are better manipulators of the material they see as relevant and significant.

At times, of course, examiners discover that the "typical" exam format poses an irrelevant barrier that might literally preclude a student from being able to demonstrate any of the skills the examiner values which the student possesses. Alternatively, but more significantly in terms of students with learning disabilities, the test may give her *inadequate* opportunity to demonstrate those skills the examiner actually values.

Thus the normatively easiest, core cases for accommodation on tests are cases like the following: a law student is blind and asks either to take a Braille version of the exam or to use a reader, rather than to take the exam under "standard" (statistically commonplace) conditions (that is, being handed a piece of paper she won't be able to read). This case is easy because (a) the examiner does not view being able to read hard copy as especially virtuous, compared with being read to or reading Braille. (In fact, she may well believe that the student is more virtuous for being able to integrate a question in the absence of visual reading skills, believing it more difficult to do so.) (b) Moreover, the blind student will have literally *no* opportunity to manifest the range of virtues the examiner values (for example, microeconomic knowledge, memory of formal rules, capacity to sort through complex material) if she must take the "typical," nonaccommodated test. Finally, the case is made even easier because (c) nondisabled students would not be aided by the accommodation the disabled student proposes: a sighted student would obviously prefer to read the hard copy of the exam herself than have a Braille copy or a reader. The exam has not, in any sense, been made "easier" by the accommodation, but rather "different"; the accommodated student has simply been given the same chance to reach her peak raw score as the nonaccommodated student.

The dyslexic student seeking extra time, in contrast, cannot cleanly rely upon any of these three core arguments for extra time relied upon by the blind student. The examiner may well value the ability to work quickly, believing it to be an intrinsic virtue (good lawyers should sort through issues quickly) or predictive of other virtues (those who analyze well analyze quickly). Thus the exam might be "speeded" for non-LD students. Law students certainly experience their exams as speeded, and though there may be little hard evidence that any subgroup of non-LD students (or LD students for that matter) would get better grades if given extra time on law exams, there is plenty of evidence, which we will discuss, that many exams are in fact speeded for most or all test takers. If the exams are generally speeded, though, then there are only two possibilities: either the exam is speeded inadvertently and the examiner does not in fact view speed as virtuous, or it is speeded deliberately. If the latter, in the test maker's mind, the LD student's inability to perform at the same speed as non-LD students is a genuine failing (just as innumeracy, ethnographic obtuseness, or a lack of understanding of microeconomics are each viewed as flaws). Moreover, the student with an LD will not be entirely precluded from manifesting all of his skills if given the nonaccommodated exam: the standard exam does not pose an insuperable barrier to demonstrating at least some skills. Finally, if law school exams are generally "speeded" (even if inadvertently), giving the student with a learning disability more time is giving him something that other students would benefit from; it is giving him an easier exam, not just a different one.

Assuming students are correct when they perceive that their law school exams are speeded, and (far less obviously) that the faculty's choice to speed them is deliberate, the LD student's claim must be more complex. He may claim that while "speed" may indeed be *a* virtue, it ought not so dominate his test-taking experience that he is given *inadequate* opportunity to manifest other important virtues. What should examiners do if they believe speed is *a* virtue, but they worry that a student with a learning disability taking a nonaccommodated exam will display mostly his slowness, and not have enough chance to show his other skills?

Examiners might have two quite distinct goals. In one view, they might want to give the student with a learning disability enough time so that he was exactly as rushed as the "statistically average" student taking the nonaccommodated exam. Alternatively, they might want to rush the LD student more than the average student, "punishing" her some for her slowness, but not so much that she had "inadequate" opportunity to demonstrate her other scholastic virtues. Examiners who value speed highly will believe that the appropriate degree of rushing is high—that is, that the student with a learning disability should be substantially penalized because she works considerably more slowly than the average student does—while those who believe speed a minor virtue, but who worry that the student with an LD lacking adequate time will demonstrate few of his equally or more significant virtues, will give more time.[17]

Advocates for accommodating LD students on exams have far too facilely avoided these difficult questions and fallen back, instead, on a poorly defended web of suppositions. First, they claim that there is overwhelming empirical evidence that non-LD students do not significantly benefit from accommodations. This proposition serves two distinct rhetorical roles: it directly counters the inevitable contention that an accommodated exam is easier rather than different. It also bolsters the claim that examiners do not in fact consider speed a virtue; the "fact" that extra time would not significantly help such non-LD students, though, "proves" they are not tested for speediness, as they would be if examiners valued it. Second, advocates for students with learning disabilities far too facilely claim that even if exams are generally speeded, they are either not deliberately speeded or are deliberately speeded only because faculties have not adequately considered the case for the proposition that speed should be irrelevant. The incapacity of LD students to perform better on nonaccommodated tests is not attributable to flaws that examiners (either do or should) care about. Finally, some advocates accept that the inability to perform well on nonaccommodated exams might indeed bespeak flaws, but that these flaws must be ignored to ensure that schools are adequately open to a class of people (the disabled) suffering from social exclusion and "discrimination." Each of these suppositions, however, proves quite problematic when subjected to close scrutiny.

The empirical basis for the argument that LD students alone

would be significantly aided by increased time is remarkably thin. Runyan and Smith, the leading academic advocates in the law school context for accommodating LD students' requests for extra time on tests, are typical in their confident assertion that LD students alone will be significantly helped by these accommodations (their attitude was mirrored by other members of the special education advocacy community whom we interviewed). In an article in the *Journal of Legal Education* urging accommodation of LD law students[18] Runyan and Smith state:

> Many instructors and university professors believe, despite research to the contrary, that allowing learning disabled students extra time is unfair to nondisabled students . . . [but] studies suggest that non-learning disabled students can perform up to their capability under timed testing conditions and have little room for improvement. Students with learning disabilities, however, cannot perform up to their capabilities under timed conditions. They do show considerable improvement when allowed extra time.[19]

The authors' claim is extremely problematic: they cite only one (highly flawed) published study in support of their assertion, and ignore, rather than criticize, a substantial body of research less favorable to their position. Moreover, even if the limited research they rely upon actually demonstrated that LD students alone are aided by extra time on the particular exams the researchers studied, it is far from clear that Runyan and Smith should so confidently generalize from these findings: it is surely possible that some exams are speeded only for LD pupils, while others are speeded for some or all non-LD pupils as well.

The published study they rely upon—Runyan's own[20]—contains a serious methodological flaw that renders its validity questionable. Two groups of students, LD (reading and attention deficits) and non-LD, were given the Nelson-Denny Reading Comprehension and Reading Rate Test. All students were told to work quickly, reading "normally, as they would in a test situation," until they were told to stop; they were not told how much time they would have to complete the exam. At the end of twenty minutes, the students were instructed to mark where they were on the exam, and hand it in if they had answered all the questions. Those who had not finished were allowed to continue until told to stop, but told not to go back and change answers; they were in fact allowed to complete the exam during the second time allotment. The results indicated, not surprisingly, that while most of the non-LD students completed the exam within the first twenty minutes, the LD students did not; correlatively, the scores of the non-LD students at the twenty-minute mark (the "timed" conditions) were significantly higher. The comparative scores of the two groups on the *completed* exam (the "untimed" conditions), in contrast, were not significantly different, nor was there a significant difference between the scores of the non-LD students under "timed" conditions and LD students under "untimed" conditions.

The experimental design was such that one cannot ascertain whether non-LD students would be aided by extra time on the reading comprehension test, since non-LD students never took the exam using as much time as learning disabled students typically used, nor were the students with LDs forced to try to maximize their score on the exam in as little time as the non-LD pupils typically took to finish. Indeed, the non-LD students may have been unwittingly punished for demonstrating their skill at completing the test quickly in a speeded situation. They may have sacrificed care for speed; if they had received the extra time that the LD students received, they might have spent more time on each question and thus improved their scores. All we can learn from the experiment is that LD subjects read more slowly than non-LD subjects (a trait that virtually defines the distinction between the two groups), and therefore will take longer to finish a reading comprehension task if asked to work toward completion at their "normal" exam pace. A more conventional two-by-two research design, in which both LD and non-LD subjects took speeded and unspeeded versions of the same exam, would better tell us whether non-LD students would benefit if given as much time to complete the exam as accommodated LD students are given.[21]

We present these findings in detail to emphasize the incongruity between the bold conclusion that non-LD students would receive no significant benefit from more time on exams and the decidedly more modest claim the empirical studies appear to justify. Moreover, even if Runyan and Smith could establish that giving extra time to all students eliminates or substantially limits performance disparities between LD students and non-LD students on certain exams, it is not clear that their finding would be generalizable to all types of exams. Thus advocates must eventually convince us that a fair exam is one that is not speeded for anyone and that LD students' performance rises relative to non-LD students' performance on such fair exams. For now, though, LD advocates make do with a simpler empirical claim: that is, that non-LD students simply never significantly benefit from more time.

To make this point, they rely on a very small sample of experiments from which they draw misleading conclusions, while at the same time ignoring decades of research finding that students perform better in a variety of test settings when given more time. A 1960 article by Morrison[22] makes reference to 150 studies in which experimenters distinguished between speed and power tests, references which assume that added time can improve students' raw scores on some subclass of tests.

It is conceivable that Runyan and Smith believe that all the measured improvement in student scores on tests that had been historically deemed speeded occurred among the (undiagnosed) LD students in the groups. They never explicitly make such a claim, however, nor could they plausibly do so, given the fact that there is no evidence in these studies that gains are particularly concentrated among the small subset of the experimental subjects that might plausibly have learning disabilities. There is a large number of studies finding that students from all demographic groups are helped equally by being granted extra time, though of course those with LDs within each demographic group may be uniquely aided.[23] Recent studies by Miller, Mitchell, and Van Audsall indicate that there may be one very significant demographic distinction in "speeding": girls may respond systematically more slowly than boys do on multiple choice exams, and it may be this distinction that accounts for gender bias on the SAT.[24] The researchers found that when the SAT's normal rule of 30 minutes per section was relaxed for high school algebra and precalculus students taking the SAT math exam, girls' scores increased markedly while boys' did not, substantially narrowing, though not eliminating, the gender gap. Lower proportions of girls than boys are both classified as LD and receive testing accommodations—in 1993, College Board Profiles indicate that while only 51 percent of students describing themselves as disabled are male, 63 percent of those receiving nonstandard administrations are male.[25] This evidence further suggests, though it does not prove, that there are classes of non-LD pupils who would systematically benefit from untimed tests.

More persuasively, however, a number of studies that Runyan and Smith ignore have addressed the precise question that concerns us: whether added time helps LD students considerably more than it helps non-LD students and whether it helps non-LD students at all. Some of the studies support Runyan's predisposition that students with LDs are helped *more* by time extensions, though none finds that non-LD students' scores are not also substantially helped. Thus, for instance, Centra, studying the SAT, found a substantial difference in the scores of all students given untimed versions of the test, but found that score improvements were more pronounced for the handicapped students.[26] This is consistent with Ragosta and Wendler's finding that it takes handicapped students roughly one and one half to two times as long as nonhandicapped students to complete as much of the exam as the nonhandicapped typically complete. It is vital to note, however, that Ragosta and Wendler find that even nonhandicapped students typically complete less than two-thirds of the test items, so that they too would be aided considerably by more time.[27]

It is critical to recall that even if students with LDs are helped more than non-LD students by accommodation, the fact that the non-LD would be helped significantly makes the case for accommodation problematic in a number of ways. Furthermore, this fact puts vastly increased stress on diagnosis and accurate labeling: if extra time were unhelpful to non-LD students, we would not have to worry (a) that we had inaccurately labeled some non-LD students as having an LD since we'd be giving them no genuine benefit by doing so or (b) that we were creating (perverse) incentives for students to invest time and resources into being diagnosed as having LDs, since they would know that this would improve their test scores.

Even more striking, some studies find that there is no difference at all between the improvements in the scores that LD (and other handicapped) students achieve when exam periods are lengthened and the improvements that non-LD students experience. The policy implications of this finding are profound. It implies that not only are accommodated students with LDs receiving a benefit that others would likewise enjoy, but also they are receiving a benefit that bears no functional relationship at all to their disability, since the extra time helps them precisely as it would help the nondisabled. Munger and Loyd, in a substantial study of LD and non-LD fifth graders taking the Iowa Tests of Basic Skills (ITBS), found that both nonhandicapped and handicapped students increase their mean scores by 0.1 grade level if given the test under untimed conditions; that the handicapped and nonhandicapped group each completed statistically indistinguishable numbers of items taking the timed version of the test and, similarly, could not be discriminated from one another on the basis of their capacity to complete 90 percent of the test items.[28]

Thus the case seems very weak that exam accommodations give students with LDs nothing that would be of substantial benefit to the non-LD student. The corollary conceptual assumption that tests are clearly intended to be nonspeeded, as they purportedly already are for the bulk of students, is also unconvincing. It is a more open empirical question whether LD students are helped substantially *more* by extra time than non-LD students, though our judgment is that the weight of the evidence favors that proposition. To the degree that the corollary of that empirical finding is the assertion that tests are unduly speeded for LD students, and that the faculty must decide how much they are willing to penalize a student for slow responsiveness, the conceptual debate remains open. Nonetheless, most advocates for accommodating pupils with LDs have tended to rely heavily on the proposition that accommodation is a nonconflictual issue.

SUBSTANTIVE THEORIES OF VIRTUE

Given the dubious empirical support for the claim that extra time would be of little use to nondisabled students, we suspect that many who advocate extra time for learning disabled students would ultimately tend to embrace one of two less fact-sensitive theories. They might, first, adopt a revisionist substantive theory of virtue—a theory in which none of the ways in which LD students are deemed disabled affects them along dimensions that really matter, even if they matter in current exam practice. The alternative argument is that the cost of penalizing LD students for lacking certain virtues that are legitimately admired in non-LD students is too high, that it will lead to an illegitimate level of discrimination or social exclusion of a class. Even if speed is a genuinely socially valuable trait, rewarding it will result in the exclusion of a protected group from normatively adequate levels of public participation.

The skills LD students lack are not genuine virtues Untangling this theory a bit may expose how difficult it would be to sustain: the claim is, essentially, that learning disabilities, by definition, affect only functions that have been wrongly treated as significant by the dominant non-LD culture, but affect no functions that are genuinely significant. While numeracy or microeconomic reasoning may be virtues, speed is not.

This argument might at first appear to invoke some explicit alternative substantive theory of virtue (for example, a theory that excellence as a student consists of virtues A, B, and C—each of which the students with LDs typically possess—but not D, E, and F—which they typically lack). Not only have advocates failed to articulate the bases for this alternative substantive theory of academic excellence, but it seems unreasonable. It is unlikely that any reasonable theory of academic excellence could be constructed which viewed all of the flaws that are characterized as learning disabilities as irrelevant to assessments of academic excellence, even if it could, conceivably, eliminate speedy responsiveness to tests from the standard list of virtues.

Students at Stanford may be classified as suffering from learning disabilities when they have any of the following difficulties (among others):

> Dyslexia (Reading): Difficulty with any task in which reading is an essential component . . .
> Dyscalculia (Math): Difficulty with calculations; difficulty with rapid processing of math facts.
> Attention Deficits: Difficulty concentrating for long periods of time; easily distracted; difficulty organizing work and budgeting time; problems staying at a desk or task for long periods of time . . .
> Memory deficits: Difficulty remembering problems retaining [*sic*] numerical information such as multiplication tables, dates, etc.; difficulty remembering rote facts.
> Reasoning deficit: Trouble thinking in an orderly logical way; difficulty prioritizing and sequencing tasks; difficulty applying learned skill to a new task.

If the *opposite* of these traits cannot constitute academic virtue, it is not easy to imagine what can, unless virtue is wholly based on effort rather than on performance. But a refusal to grade performance is grounded in the position that no one "merits" reward for ability, a position that the school surely disavowed when it chose to grade exams, an anonymous product.[29] For such institutions, virtue is clearly significantly performance-based.

It may well be, though, that accommodation advocates embrace a somewhat different view, one in which a student's virtue is whatever results from some combination of her IQ and her effort. Any barriers to performance that do not result from deficits in "intelligence" or "application" are illegitimate. We discussed some of the complexities of diagnostic practice in Chapters 2, 3, and 4, but let us reiterate that one way we classify students as learning disabled is by identifying students whose performance is significantly lower than we would expect looking only at IQ scores.

While accommodation advocates tend not to draw attention to their proclivity to deify something like "pure intelligence," this is precisely what they appear to do. One ordinarily can detect IQ snobbery as the primary basis for "moral" claims on behalf of the learning disabled only when advocates are at their most informal. Thus Judge Gallet, in his address on the special needs of the LD lawyer to the Buffalo Law School, talks of his own disability:

> My teachers figured I was lazy. You know when you are in school they set you up in groups, the rabbits, the eagles . . . I was always in the turtles. But I could function as a turtle because I was bright enough, *so I could keep up with all those people who had IQs of about seventy-nine.*
>
> *When I was in the first grade, I got the highest mark in my class on an IQ test.*[30]

The ethical basis for this theory of virtue is unclear. Even if one embraced a theory that we discussed (and rejected) in Chapter 6—that society is especially obligated to try to ensure that all students *develop* skills congruent with the expectations we derive from their IQ tests—there appears no good reason to believe that students who have *not* developed such skills must be rewarded as if they had, by ignoring the deficits we have been unable to correct, unless we believe that the remaining deficits are in fact insignificant. The idea that one's "IQ" is one's basic defining virtue—and that it is somehow "more real" or more telling a description of some "true self" than one's inability to read or to pay attention—would seem persuasive only to those who have fetishized the IQ score for other reasons.

The IQ test, historically, has signified the essential self to those looking to differentiate the worthiness of distinct social groups (races, classes).[31] Thus the idea that tests fail to reward virtue if they fail to reward high IQ would seem to be especially attractive to those loath to treat any members of the social groups that traditionally score well on the IQ test as incapable in the "same ways" as members of socially subordinated groups are.

Speedy responsiveness is over-rewarded   Alternatively, and far more persuasively in our view, accommodation advocates may argue that examiners have simply not adequately considered what virtues they wish to reward. First, and most obviously, examiners may have failed to reflect on what skills they consider virtuous. Thus an accommodation advocate may care less about whether speed is actually a virtue than about whether examiners really believe it is. Second, and less obviously, an accommodation advocate may simply mean to draw attention to the possibility that examiners have failed to scrutinize their assumptions about the range of capabilities in the student population. If examiners focused their attention on the students' actual range of capabilities to respond quickly, including the less visible population of students with LDs who deviate significantly from the statistical norm, examiners might no longer so greatly emphasize speedy responsiveness on exams.

Advocates of accommodation typically envision that more self-conscious examiners will recognize, at a minimum, that they have inadvertently posed barriers that preclude LD students from demonstrating genuine virtues, thus resulting in far more extreme differentiation than intended. But examiners may well come to believe, instead, that differentiating students in terms of the speed with which they can respond *is* a poor idea, but only as long as one is considering students in the "statistically normal" range of speediness. They might then decide that students with LDs are so slow to respond that they should be penalized for their slowness.

Our more general point is that we are not sure precisely what would happen if examiners became more self-conscious about what they consider praiseworthy virtues. To the extent, though, that accommodation advocates simply press for heightened self-consciousness both about general conceptions of merit and about measuring merit in the presence of difference, it is hard to disapprove.

In this alternative view, then, the complaints of students with learning disabilities simply give "mainstream" examiners an opportunity to revisit a general question about what traits they value. The result of the inquiry should, perhaps, be that tests are no longer speeded for *any* students (universally mandatory take-home examinations might be one solution) because the examiners come to recognize that they don't want to judge the merit of students based on distinctions in their capacity to respond rapidly. If speed is not a virtue, it is best not to speed exams for any students, rather than to grant LD pupils alone more time. To give extra time only to students with learning disabilities would both raise fairness concerns for non-LD test takers and put undue pressure on a very imprecise diagnostic system: we give an advantage to those called LD, and not to those with undetected or unlabeled but underlyingly similar problems.[32]

Indeed, the affirmative case for speeded exams in the educational psychology literature is, in our view, strikingly weak. Conceptually, it seems to us that those advocating speeded exams must make one of three claims.

First, the weakest claim (albeit the claim that is far and away most commonly made in the testing literature) is that exams are appropriately time-limited simply because it is administratively convenient to devote less time to exams.[33] As long as time limitations do not change the relative scores students would receive on a pure power (non-time-limited, content-focused) test, it is obviously preferable to devote less time to testing.[34] To justify devoting less time to exams, one must believe either (a) that it is reasonably costly to administer longer exams, primarily because students forgo something significant if they spend more time on exams (in law school, however, where exams are generally given only once a semester, it is unlikely that one could make a serious claim that fully unspeeded exams would cut into "instruction time," broadly construed, or that proctoring costs would be substantially higher if exams were unspeeded), or (b) that students' relative scores would be unaffected by eliminating time pressure, so that (even trivial) time savings are essentially costless.

There are certainly studies that suggest that the rank correlations between untimed and timed scores on particular tests are quite high, at least as long as we ignore whatever differences might be caused by the presence of students with learning disabilities whose grades are probably improved atypically if we reduce time pressure. As far back as 1950, Mollenkopf found extremely high correlations between scores on speeded and untimed versions of the same exam.[35] Similarly, the afore-mentioned Centra study indicated that *within* the handicapped group of SAT test takers, correlations between the timed and untimed versions of the test were extremely high (.76 for the verbal section and .85 for the math section).[36] But it is difficult to be sanguine that for any particular test, time pressure has no impact on the rank ordering of students, even if there is some subclass of tests for which this is true.

Thus defenders of test-speededness might be more persuasive if they could make some other compelling claim for the appropriateness of time limitations. Defenders might argue that while speedy responsiveness is not inherently a virtue, it is the best surrogate for some other virtue that *is* useful to performing socially valued tasks which is not otherwise readily measured on exams. Alternatively, of course, the examiners may claim that the sort of speedy responsiveness that time-pressured tests reward is itself a useful skill.[37]

With respect to the first of these two alternative claims, there is very little research to suggest that time-limited tests better correlate with performance on subsequent real world tasks than scores on untimed tests. However, a number of older studies cited in what is itself a rather old study (1964) by Kendall did make precisely that claim. "Several studies indicated that *increasing* the time limit beyond a certain point for a fixed amount of material resulted in *decreasing* validity."[38] Not only is the empirical evidence for the general point rather scant, but there also seems to be little theoretical support for the claim that time-pressured exams measure an otherwise unmeasurable virtue, separate from speed, that in fact proves important in performance, at least for non-LD students.

There is, though, substantial evidence that the predictive validity of the SAT test declines for the handicapped students who receive accommodations: special administration SAT tests overpredict students' grades at college by a substantial amount. While students with LDs who take standard administrations of the SAT receive FYAs (first-year grade point averages) in college that are only .05 standard deviations lower than the grades ordinarily predicted from those SAT scores, learning disabled students who take the accommodated exam receive SAT scores that overpredict first-year college grades by .33 standard deviations. The problem of overprediction is most dramatic among the accommodated students who do well on the SAT; accommodated LD students predicted to receive high grades in college perform .53 standard deviations worse in their first year of college than one would expect, looking only at their SATs.[39] Overprediction is not, however, a serious concern for other accommodated handicapped pupils: hearing impaired students, in fact, do .26 standard deviations better than would be predicted looking at their accommodated SAT scores, while accommodated visually disabled students do just .05 standard deviations worse (and nonaccommodated ones do .15 SD better).[40]

There are two distinct interpretations of this sort of overprediction. In one view, college grades for the students who received accommodations on standardized tests are too low simply because the colleges themselves fail to accommodate appropriately on *their* exams. In that view, the accommodated predictor (the test score) fails to correlate as well with the criterion (grades) only because the criterion fails to measure what it ought to measure: true academic achievement in college. This view, while plausible, is somewhat hard to square with the relative accuracy of predictions for physically disabled students who are accommodated on the SAT, in the absence of proof that colleges more frequently accommodate the physically disabled more appropriately.

In the other view, the speed deficits manifest on the nonaccommodated exam correlate with academic deficits that are not otherwise captured by a "power" exam. For example, students with learning disabilities may answer slowly because they have cognitive deficits that result in their having difficulty managing time demands at college, which ultimately leaves them unable to cope successfully with the workload. That particular cognitive deficit, though, might not be otherwise measured on an untimed power test of academic achievement, directed at high school students. Students with learning disabilities may prove incapable of learning complex material as rapidly as post–high school students must, even if they have been able to master the core aptitudes the SAT tests for.[41]

It would naturally be helpful if test designers looked at the relationship between both accommodated and nonaccommodated administrations of the SAT and performance in college on untimed

tasks (courses that demand term papers, for instance), but such research has not been undertaken, for understandable reasons. (One
would have to be able to read each school's transcript knowing
what was demanded in each course, and problems of noncompara-
bility of grades across courses, doubtless severe in any case, would
be exacerbated when one compared students' grades in a small
number of classes.) There is some very scant evidence, though, that
students with LDs do better in settings not dominated by exams:
Braun, Ragosta, and Kaplan found that the performance of LD students accommodated on the GRE correctly predicts their graduate
school performance. However, the authors could locate only nineteen LD students who took an accommodated GRE between 1981
and 1984 who were now at one of the 339 graduate schools that responded to their survey.[42] In fact, though, the low proportion of college students with learning disabilities who even take the GRE at all
may imply that students with learning disabilities are not doing especially well in graduate-like (non-exam-dominated) work.

With respect to the "pure" virtue of speed, it seems likely that
were law faculties to address the issue directly, there would be dis-
agreements. Runyan and Smith are far too hasty in claiming that
"speed of performance . . . is not necessarily central to the actual
practice of law. [Lawyers] are rarely required in practice to write
everything they know about a topic in two or three hours."[43] True
enough, but hardly dispositive: some, though not all, lawyers are
frequently asked to write a great deal about topics given very short
turnaround times; some, though not all, must respond on their feet
to questions asked by judges or determine almost instantaneously
whether opposing attorneys have asked objectionable questions.
Some, though not all, work in settings where they can readily adjust hourly billing rates downward to reflect that they need more
time than their colleagues to perform the same task; some work in
settings in which they are expected to produce such a large quantity of work that it is not realistically possible for them to expand
work hours to accomplish all that their colleagues do.

PURE ANTIDISCRIMINATION CLAIMS

Misreading Griggs   The final claim made by accommodation advocates—that examiners ought not to be entitled to enforce any conception of merit that results in the uneven distribution of social

benefits by social group (and where students with learning disabilities are classified as a social group)[44]—rests upon a highly controversial view of the appropriate dictates of antidiscrimination law, and applies this controversial vision in a tenuous fashion. Alternatively, accommodation advocates may be seeking, without careful justification, to apply what is in fact a quite general egalitarian principle only to the disabled subgroup: the view that no substantive outcomes can turn on factors, such as a disability, out of the actor's control.

In essence, the advocates of accommodation here are embracing only the first part of the "Griggs" test that has long been used to identify illicit employment discrimination,[45] a test which presumptively precludes employment practices with adverse impact on protected groups. This first aspect of *Griggs* precludes the uneven distribution of a desired good, whether jobs, pay, or promotion in the Title VII context, or high grades in ours, among distinctive social groups.

But advocates have not defended their (implicit) decision to ignore its second aspect—which *permits* such uneven distribution of rewards as long as it is justified by differences in performance. As the Supreme Court found in *Watson v. Fort Worth Bank and Trust*, a screening device may have adverse impact—that is, exclude a disproportionate number of Title VII–protected applicants—as long as it screens out workers who would, if hired, lower company performance.[46] The language in the 1991 Civil Rights Restoration Act is arguably ambiguous on this point: given that the revised act states that the defendant prevails once the plaintiff has shown disparate impact only if "the challenged practice is job related for the position in question and consistent with business necessity,"[47] it is possible to argue either that Congress meant that a test that is job related is *therefore* consistent with business necessity or that the two requirements are independent and conjunctive. The few courts that have interpreted the 1991 act have continued to follow the *Watson* analysis:[48] thus even if the excluded workers could have performed competently, without endangering others, the test is adequately "necessary" so long as it selects a higher-quality work force.[49]

It is, of course, possible to argue that Title VII ought to be revised still further so as to forbid group inequality altogether while permitting individual inequality within groups, but no one could seriously claim that it has ever been so interpreted by the courts or Congress. Even those on the political left who laud *Griggs* for mandating group equality do so on the factual supposition that no group differences in relevant performance will ever be found. Freeman, for instance, argues that *"Griggs* demanded what many knew would be an impossible standard of justification, *since written tests are part of a closed world where all they correlate with is each other."*[50] Setting aside whether Freeman is right or wrong to think that educational credentials and test performance bear no relationship to job performance, our point is that even Freeman concedes that the authors of *Griggs* believe that intergroup inequality of rewards is morally and legally justified under certain factual conditions, conditions which he happens to believe will never obtain.[51]

Sophisticated commentators on the political right who attack *Griggs* for mandating group equality also recognize that the case does not formally mandate equal outcomes. They do, however, believe that as a practical matter, employer efforts to validate practices that disproportionately exclude members of protected groups will be too expensive to undertake so that employers will *opt* for quotas or that EEOC bureaucrats and judges will be *unduly* skeptical of claims that performance is in fact different among distinct groups, so that quotas will be enforced.[52]

Of course, if antidiscrimination law demands only that inequalities of reward reflect relevant distinctions between individuals (even if members of protected groups are disproportionately rewarded less), the "group" of learning disabled pupils is not at all clearly the victim of "discrimination" if it receives systematically lower test scores (the academic equivalent, we continue to assume, of lower pay) as long as the test scores are "merited."

Even if we did alter practice so as to demand equal outcomes for historically "victimized" social groups, though not demanding cross-the-board equality among individuals, we must still determine the degree to which the learning disabled constitute a social group in the relevant senses. We should obviously not define "social groups" in such a way that we've created a paradoxical set of legal commands: we cannot really simultaneously permit inequality of individuals and demand equality of groups if we define as a social group whose rewards must be equalized with those who perform better all those individuals whose performance is atypically poor. Thus, to make any intelligible group rights claim, the learning disabled must form a social group that can be identified on some other basis than their poor performance on nonaccommodated tests.

It is difficult to ascertain what other strong sources of group identity accommodation advocates might claim the LD really have. Typically, when assessing whether a group has a politically meaningful identity as a group, we ask whether members have been subject to aversive prejudice based on common visible characteristics; whether members are victimized by negative false stereotypes; whether the group has unique subcultural traits that must be nurtured; whether the people who we believe constitute the group have atypically interdependent utility functions.

It may well be true that physically disabled people have historically been subject to significant levels of aversive prejudice, based in part on their visible differences from the nondisabled population. But it is not at all clear that all disabled people have been subject to such aversive prejudice against those who appear different; identifying a person with a learning disability requires a team of educational experts. It is far more plausible that the learning disabled require antidiscrimination protection because they are, like the disabled more generally, victims of inaccurate stereotyping (socially common misconceptions of their actual capacities and deficits).

But the form of stereotyping is hardly similar to the form we have long recognized (and sought to counteract) in regard to, say, race or gender (or socially visible physical disability). When we consider ordinary stereotypes, we believe the stereotyper identifies a socially salient fact about the object of discrimination—say, his ethnicity, her gender—and then assumes that the object will have certain traits, for example, poor on-the-job performance, proclivity for violence, or absenteeism or job discontinuity. The purportedly "parallel" process here is that the stereotyper identifies a socially salient fact—the student performs poorly—and assumes he has certain traits, a proclivity for ongoing poor performance. But the parallels between the stereotypers is rather rough: the "traditional" stereotyper makes inferences about conduct based on status, while the "LD stereotyper" remains wholly unaware of status, and simply assumes (wrongly, we will concede solely for argument's sake) that future conduct typically mimics past conduct. The antidiscrimination norm hardly seems designed to eliminate all false beliefs: if the "LD stereotyper's" inference process were more like "X is a handicapped person; most handicapped people cannot do well in school; therefore, I surmise X won't do well either," then it would appear more plausible to characterize him as engaging in the sort of stereotyping that antidiscrimination doctrine has been concerned with. But the supposed stereotyper in this context is misled precisely because he is utterly blind to the person's disability: it is (according to accommodation advocates) the unseen handicap that makes the ordinary inference process (poor performers keep performing poorly) inappropriate in this case.

Moreover, unlike racial or ethnic groups, the learning disabled have no apparent cultural history, even if it is as least plausible that they share a number of experiences (frustration with one's incapacity to perform tasks that appear as though they ought to be manageable; shame at the disability and pride at overcoming it; anger at being treated as "stupid"). It is certainly rhetorically attractive given the current political climate in educational settings to invoke such favorable imagery of group identity: thus, for instance, in the introductory remarks to Judge Gallet's speech on his own learning disabilities to the Buffalo Law School, the learning disabled are indeed applauded as a source of cultural diversity.[53] But it seems unlikely that policymakers seeking to preserve ethnic diversity would have any genuine reason to fear that the LD "subculture" will dissolve if its members are not rewarded to retain their unique subcultural characteristics, as promoters of multiculturalism might legitimately fear that subordinated subcultures will face undue assimilationist pressures if their members generally get fewer rewards when they manifest the characteristics most typical of their groups.[54]

Alternatively, if one seeks greater levels of group equality because the consumption functions of people within recognized social groups are atypically interdependent—so that, for instance, each African-American gains from another African-American's material progress or is harmed by the poor status of other members of her community[55]—then the group-rights oriented accommodationist would have to argue that LD students form such an interdependent community. But there are reasons to suspect that communities emerge over substantial historical periods: those with learning disabilities are members of a multiplicity of far more salient communities (ethnic and religious, political, and so on), and they projected no group identity whatsoever until roughly thirty years ago. While it is surely the case that people may identify strongly with a multiplicity of identity groups, it appears to be the case that the learning disabled constitute a group largely in relationship to a very particular set of political demands, thus constituting what would usually be thought of as an "interest group" rather than an identity group.[56]

Misreading the significance of immutability Accommodation advocates might also argue that the true normative basis of mainstream antidiscrimination law is that no one ought to be penalized for any trait over which she has no control. Thus, in this view, the problem with sexism or racism is that each is a practice that puts people at a disadvantage on the basis of traits they do not choose (their race or gender). Thus, for instance, the Supreme Court, in *Plyer v. Doe*, notes that it is legitimate to punish illegal aliens but not their children, since only the former control their status;[57] in *Frontiero v. Richardson*, the court explicitly states that burdens are unjustified when associated with immutable traits.[58]

What is terribly problematic for accommodationists relying on this version of the antidiscrimination principle is that its proponents concede that social status *may* justly be significantly determined by factors outside people's control. They may well believe that market productivity is heavily influenced by immutable genetic and environmental factors, but that, nonetheless, market productivity differentials justify distinctions in rewards.

Thus, it appears, advocates of this variant of the antidiscrimination principle are actually less concerned with the impermissibility of distinguishing between individuals on the basis of immutable traits than with rewarding or condemning irrelevant traits:[59] what is especially problematic is to judge people on what they see as inconsequential bases (race, gender, sexual orientation). In his classic essay "The Idea of Equality," Bernard Williams notes that even overt racists feel bound in this culture to defend decisions to disadvantage nonwhites by arguing that they are lacking certain virtues (even if the claims are false), that it is simply not a defense to say that they ought to be disadvantaged solely by virtue of their immutable identity.[60] Thus, though it is certainly especially troublesome when victims of the irrational judgment are unable to avoid it, the basis of the conventional antidiscrimination claim is the fact that the judgment irrationally ignores some real virtue of the victims.

The immutability of the trait serves largely to trigger the suspicion that the decision might be based on irrelevant factors. Those who ask us to attend to immutability may well typically believe that one of the reasons that unchosen traits are usually irrational and irrelevant bases for judgment are that such traits are typically not behaviors, and that we ought to judge behavior rather than status. As a matter of constitutional law, criminal statutes may not punish people for their status: criminal punishment is reserved for proscribed *conduct*.[61] But the reach of the principle is limited: even factually inexorable concomitants of a status may be criminally punished (using drugs rather than being addicted to drugs, for instance).[62]

The problem the accommodationists will have in insisting that people with learning disabilities cannot be "punished" for their unchosen disability is that when we judge an exam, we judge its quality, impersonally; its quality may well be a function of traits over which the examinee had no control, but we do not permit ourselves to judge the examinee. Perhaps we presume (unduly wishfully) that she has at least some substantial capacity to alter her performance; more likely, we simply are far less committed to judging unchosen traits to be irrelevant than it might at first appear.

Most important, though it may well be the case that students with LDs are genetically or environmentally predisposed to do poorly on nonaccommodated exams, any argument that their "disability" is more determined than the inability to do well on exams that non-LD students might have would be very difficult to sustain. Once more, if we are assuming, for argument's sake at this point, that speedy responsiveness is a genuine virtue, just as an insightful response would be, there is no coherent approach to this version of the antidiscrimination norm which precludes "punishing" the LD student that wouldn't preclude "punishing" the noninsightful student, that wouldn't demand tailoring an exam so that distinctions in "insight" were also rendered inconsequential. There are, of course, debates on whether IQ tests measure anything real and debates on whether IQ is highly heritable, at least within, if not across, cultural groups.[63] Suffice it to say that the evidence that learning disabilities are immutable physical conditions is surely not obviously stronger than the case that "test-taking intelligence" more generally is.

FINAL THOUGHTS ON MERIT-BASED CLAIMS

If the law faculty's goal is simply to reward merit, it is most persuasive to argue that the faculty ought to give LD students extra time if and only if the faculty believes either (a) that speedy responsiveness is not a virtue worthy of reward or (b) that students with learning disabilities are unable to demonstrate significant virtues because their exam performance is dominated by a single failure, the failure to work quickly, which is only, in the faculty's view, one of a number of useful and praiseworthy skills. It seems unpersuasive, however, to argue that the accommodation should be made because the faculty has *already* shown it believes speed is irrelevant by ensuring that mainstream students face no meaningful performance constraints that would be ameliorated by extra time. Arguments that speed is not in fact a virtue may well be based on the questionable belief that the only academic virtues are (a) a sort of general "intelligence" measured by IQ tests and (b) effort or (c) an as yet unarticulated set of relevant academic gifts that excludes speed (as well, perhaps, as other traits that students with LDs typically lack).

If, though, the faculty comes to believe that speed is not virtuous, it would probably be better to make all exams unspeeded than to give extra time for those diagnosed as having LDs. A system that makes speed irrelevant only for a subset of students will be perceived as unfair by those still forced to take speeded exams, and it will put enormous pressure on diagnostic placement as well.

Similarly, arguments that the faculty cannot justly differentiate the rewards for the LD "social group" from the rewards for other social groups, while it is allowed to differentiate rewards "within" social groups, are unpersuasive. Existing antidiscrimination norms clearly allow differences in group outcomes grounded in genuine performance distinctions, and it is unlikely that any normatively coherent antidiscrimination principle could be constructed which would simultaneously demand full-blown group equality while permitting intragroup inequality.[64] Furthermore, even if antidiscrimination norms, rather than other distributive norms, pushed us toward equalizing group outcomes, which we do not believe they do, it is not obvious that people with LDs would constitute the sort of social group whose rewards had to be equalized with other groups. Finally, no "antidiscrimination" principle resting on the idea that inequalities cannot be permitted when those relatively disadvantaged suffer from traits over which they have no control is compatible with the intragroup inequality we have generally permitted. Immutability is an issue in antidiscrimination law predominantly because immutable traits are generally thought to be immaterial.

Grades as incentives

An alternative explanation for why the faculty gives out rewards (relatively high grades) is that, rather than seeking to reward merit, it wants to encourage better academic performance.[65] Under this view, an advocate of accommodating students with LDs might argue that these students tend to "give up" because they are discouraged by their low grades, and that accommodating them on tests would improve their performance by giving them the sense that it is worthwhile to study.

An incentives-focused faculty is trying to change the trade-off between, say, studying and loafing by increasing the relevant return to studying, just as a legislature assessing what income tax rate to apply doubtless believes it is trying to ensure that workers not substitute too much leisure for labor by ensuring that there are sufficient selfishly appropriable returns to labor.[66]

In standard public finance theory, determining the impact of taxation would require the legislature to consider taxpayers' trade-offs between work and leisure depending on their relative price (the "substitution effect"). (The substitution effect works as follows: taxpayers make trade-offs between work and leisure depending on their relative price. The "price" of leisure is its opportunity cost, that is, how much income will be forgone if the taxpayer chooses leisure. As the return to work rises, either because market productivity rises or workers retain more of their market earnings because income tax rates fall, taxpayers will typically "consume" less leisure, since it will have become more expensive in terms of forgone income. Demand for leisure, like demand for most consumption goods, declines with increases in price.) The legislator will also have to consider the change in demand for goods as income changes (the "income effect"). (An income effect works as follows: demand for most goods, including leisure, rises as income rises. As the return to work rises, for example, because income tax rates on labor income fall, the taxpayer becomes richer and would thus choose to consume more leisure, thus working less, all else equal. The income effect may be explained in a second, quite distinct way as well, which will prove more useful in considering the accommodation problem: to the extent that the worker/taxpayer has some post-tax income target, she will reduce her work hours when she can meet that target working fewer hours, as she will, of course, be able to do if the tax rate drops.) Once we recognize that higher grades serve as the selfish "reward" for the relevant labor (studying), just as material goods serve as the relevant reward for labor in the ordinary public finance discussion, we will soon realize that the case for accommodationism will be difficult to make cleanly.

A faculty that decides to accommodate LD students is essentially changing the expected return to studying for *both* LD and non-LD students. Assuming the accommodation is effective, grades for LD students at any level of "talent" and level of studying will be higher; given our ongoing supposition that grades are either explicitly curved or that students understand their grades only as positional, relative goods, accommodationism *also* means that grades for non-LD students will *decline*, given any level of academic talent and studying.

One would presume that the prospect of an increase (decrease) in grades would simultaneously have positive (negative) "substitution" effects and negative (positive) "income" effects. The substitution effect in the testing context would presumably work as follows: if an examinee with a learning disability were deciding whether to study for an additional hour, rather than engage in leisure activity, his willingness to study would increase as the amount by which studying would improve his grades increased. If the improvement in grades from studying for an accommodated exam would be higher than it would be for a nonaccommodated exam, the relative price of leisure activities would rise in terms of forgone grades, and the demand for leisure would therefore fall. Note that the fact that accommodated grades are higher than nonaccommodated grades does *not* guarantee that the amount by which studying improves grades (the *marginal* return to studying) will increase in the accommodated regime. It is plausible that accommodation acts like a lump sum transfer to all students with learning disabilities, which has no impact on the return to studying: accommodation might simply give each student with a learning disability his old grade plus some fixed increment, but the amount by which the grade will change in response to a particular amount of studying might remain the same. If this is true, there will be no substitution effect and we will observe *only* the income effect when we accommodate (which leads to *declining* study levels).

Yet it is conceivable that accommodating *does* increase the marginal return to work. This may result from the student's simply being able to demonstrate only on an accommodated exam any of the material she has learned while studying. It might also result from some alteration in the social meaning of the returns to studying, even assuming the raw score improvement produced by studying is identical in the two regimes. For example, a ten-point raw score improvement that results from additional studying for an accommodated exam may change the student's grade from "B" to "A," whereas the same ten-point improvement from studying for a nonaccommodated test might change the grade from "D" to "C" in a world where both "C" and "D" grades are below some "hurdle point" (whether the hurdle point is the lowest grade needed to gain any valuable external rewards or self-esteem): thus the movement in raw scores is motivationally relevant only in the former case.

The income effect, though, would of course work in the opposite direction. Once an examinee is accommodated, he can get his same old grade working *less* than he formerly did. If the old grade were his "target," he would not need to work as hard to achieve it. One point that is critical to recall is that at the same time, non-LD students would face the opposite set of incentives under the new regime, since their grades will fall: the relative price of nonstudying leisure activities could fall, since each additional hour of studying might have a less favorable impact on relative grades. (Once more, this is not inevitably true: while *grades* for the non-LD will surely fall, it is conceivable that the return to each incremental bit of effort might remain the same.) In contrast, if the non-LD students tried to achieve the "target" grades they once achieved before students with LDs competed with them more successfully, the decrease in their grades caused by accommodationism would presumably force them to study more.

Accommodation will only unambiguously increase work effort for the group of LD and non-LD students as a whole under a very strained set of assumptions. Essentially, we must assume that non-LD students' incentives are dominated by income effects (so that they work harder once their relative grades decline at their old work levels) while the LD students' incentives are dominated by substitution effects (so that they work harder when their relative grades increase at each work level). Alternatively, we can believe that only students with LDs face genuine substitution effects (that is, that we can alter the return to incremental work by accommodating while at the same time not change the incremental return to work for the non-LD, whose aggregate grades will fall by some fixed amount, owing to the equivalent of a nonavoidable lump sum head tax on being non-LD).

One *can* construct a plausible story to bolster this position: for instance, one could assert that students with LDs have been too "discouraged" to bother to work while non-LD students are more accustomed to and invested in success and will therefore work hard to retain their traditional privileges. (This will give us substitution effects dominating LD pupils' performance and income effects dominating the non-LDs'.) Alternatively, we could argue that the learning disabled will *know* that they cannot reach some "hurdle" level, no matter what effort they expend, unless accommodated, so that accommodation changes the return to work, while the non-LD know that they always do better if they study more, even if the degree of advantage is limited by eliminating their "automatic" domination of their LD classmates. (This will give us *marginal* substitution impacts *only* for the LD.)

But, of course, one can construct such reasonably plausible "just so" quasi-empirical stories for *any* position. One could imagine that students with LDs have low expectations and will thus work little once given accommodations that give them enough of an advantage to insure "adequate" grades; at the same time, non-LD students will believe that effort is no longer rewarded, once accommodations are put into effect. They may believe that the school district is now committed to rigging results so as to achieve (some level of) substantive equality no matter what, and decide that they will do no better, or worse for that matter, if they work little. Presumably they will feel that they will do no worse since the accommodations for poor students will be pegged so as to make them appear to do only as well as the more successful students are doing.

The point of this discussion is not to suggest that we can identify the most plausible among numerous versions of how accommodationism would shift the incentive structure that students with and without learning disabilities currently face. Our point, instead, is to illustrate that it is too easy to assert simply that accommodating students with LDs will make them work harder because they no longer will be discouraged from trying. Incentives arguments are far less determinate than that.

Summary and conclusions

In our view, the law faculty's decision on whether to accommodate should be dominated by its conception of whether doing so would serve to reward merit. Even if the faculty believes, as a matter of abstract principle, that it would like to use grades to maximize the effort of the student body as a whole (or to help employers pick the most capable students), it is unlikely that the faculty will have the sort of empirical information needed even to make very rough guesses to fulfill these goals. We have little idea how either non-LD or LD students will respond to the changing relative grades they will receive if we accommodate the LD. Thus the faculty needn't even consider whether to depart from its usual normative practice—in which high performance is rewarded regardless of whether it's based on effort or talent and in which we would view it as odd to penalize a student simply because she would work anyway, or to reward one more because he's atypically likely to shirk unless we do. The faculty should assume, as well, that its duties to obey norms against discrimination will be met if it is adequately self-critical in assessing its merit criteria; antidiscrimination law not only does not require *equal* group outcomes, it does not demand that any redistributive claims made by particular groups trump the interests of other distributive claimants.

Accommodationism will better serve to reward merit if the faculty decides, in the alternative, that LD students' deficits (for example, the inability to respond rapidly) are not genuine academic flaws (or do not correlate with otherwise unmeasurable academic flaws) or, more plausibly, that LD students are *unduly* penalized for what amount to genuine flaws, because given an inadequate opportunity to manifest virtues. No practical program of testing accommodation will appear fully fair to non-LD students, though, as long as non-LD students would benefit from the same accommodations the LD are offered. As long as exams remain at least somewhat speeded, for instance, giving extra time to learning disabled students will pose genuine equity problems.

Current law does not, in our view, significantly restrain the faculty from making these sorts of appropriate judgments: it is, if anything, too lenient to faculties, which are presumed (without much reason) to have considered testing practices as carefully as they have considered curricula. "Commonsensical" (in our view, largely inertial) judgments by faculties that "speed counts," or that it somehow *must* correlate with some otherwise unmeasured skill should, in our view, be given rather little deference.

At the same time, activist judicial efforts to redesign tests to mask genuine differences caused by disabilities are a genuine danger as well. We are dubious whether courts can, institutionally, force increased self-critical reflection without moving toward a set of illegitimate substantive presumptions about the injustice of inegalitarian outcomes. (If we demand that faculties reward only virtues that predict "better" adult performance, it may well be that nothing that is tested—whether it is speed, knowledge of rules, graceful writing style, issue spotting ability—can be shown, with real precision, to predict something as amorphous as adult success. Both the predictors—the purported academic virtues—and the criteria—whether viewed as adult outcomes or "true success as a student"—are too vaguely specified to expect significant correlations.) Presumptions and burdens of production may be everything in this area (as in so many areas in which courts force agencies or private institutions to build a record before they take action they are nominally free to take). Neither opponents of speeded exams (whether speeded exams generally or speeded exams in particular fields) nor their proponents may be able to offer much hard, convincing data about the relationship between speed and "life" performance or speed and "analytical power" or speed and "serious studying." Given that, the party who must prove his point satisfactorily may invariably lose.

EIGHT

Ideology and Entitlement

The salient aspects of the current legal regime—presumptive claims to costly services, testing accommodation, and substantial discipline immunity—might be seen, analytically and ideologically, as consistent and resonant with two radically distinct sets of political presuppositions.[1]

On the one hand, existing policy toward students with learning disabilities draws heavily on a long-standing theme in conservative conceptions of the appropriate boundaries of the welfare state—that we are duty bound to treat the "deserving" poor considerably more favorably than the "undeserving" poor.[2] Children with learning disabilities are, in this view, entitled to egalitarian interventions that other poor performers are not: their grades are (at least mildly) inflated, their claims for incremental social resources (largely) met, their immunity to the discipline system (partly) granted because they are subsumed in a morally favored category of those who fare poorly in the absence of self-conscious egalitarian interventions, the category of people with disabilities. They have become the moral equivalent, in nonlibertarian conservative thought, of the unfortunate, utterly blameless blind man, implicitly contrasted with the undeserving, "parasitic" never-married "welfare mother." It is surely the case that conservative support for programs that benefit the disabled, rather than other needy constituencies, has been high over the past two decades: federal legislative support for the disabled intensified during an era of pronounced welfare state retrenchment.[3] It is an interesting task, but not our task, to explore both why certain groups are deemed deserving by conservative moralists and whether traditional arguments for differentiating the claims of the worthy and unworthy poor were invoked in differentiating the claims of pupils with LDs and others seeking expanded levels of federal support.

At the same time, policy toward those with LDs draws at least as heavily on what we will call "left-wing multiculturalism," and it is this ideological influence we will examine in detail. From a social policy perspective, this is a political/ideological movement that attempts to defend egalitarian interventions largely on two bases.[4] First, it claims that existing patterns and levels of inequality of reward are problematic mainly because they are based on irrational and biased mischaracterization of the productive ability of the members of oppressed subgroups. Second, it appears to limit its normative egalitarian claims to individuals falling within cognizable groups, rather than extending it to individuals lacking such affiliation.

Both of these cornerstones of the "left multiculturalist" position are problematic. The first element slights what ought to be, in our view, compelling *moral* claims of need and equally compelling calls for increased solidarity among citizens with different productive potentials. Instead the chief critique of existing inequality is grounded in an unpersuasive positivist description of irrationality rather than normative moralism. The claim is that (even? especially?) capitalist institutions frequently treat differences among individuals, especially when these differences are pronounced among more-or-less loosely defined "groups," including those with learning disabilities, as relevant to successful performance of socially meaningful tasks when they are not. Those atop cultural hierarchies (white, straight, able-bodied males) control the firms that make hiring, promotion, and pay decisions, and they impose false, self-serving ideas about requisite job performance.[5] The basic problem those with learning disabilities face, in this view, is the irrational overvaluation of the skills they cannot acquire by people who happen to have those skills.[6]

The tendency of left multiculturalist theory to locate distributive claims in group membership is similarly troubling. Distributive claims based on need, for instance, are hard to articulate unless the "needy" can be (re)defined as a "group": left multiculturalists thus often try to redefine the "needy" as victims of "classism" (the irrational devaluation of the contributions of a group of people on the basis of socioeconomic status/style).[7] The coherent *normative* basis of LD students' claims for resources may well be, when scrutinized, that they are a readily identifiable subset of pupils who would especially benefit from more help. But the broader "group" of "students who can particularly benefit from the infusion of incremental educational resources"—poor learners who are not identified as learning disabled—cannot make typical left multiculturalist claims to resources, simply because they have no obvious cultural commonality. Pupils with learning disabilities alone are *entitled* because they alone have been constructed as a politically plausible oppressed group, a subclass (albeit one of recent social—and legal—construction) of a larger oppressed group, people with disabilities, who are surely victims of both aversive prejudice and stereotyping.

"Left multiculturalism"

We attempt in this section to describe in more detail both the general legal-political manifestations of left multiculturalism and its more specific ideological impact on policy toward the learning disabled. This requires first understanding, in some detail, the relationship among different political conceptions of the appropriate role of the state in combating "discrimination." Such conceptions are grounded both in competing notions of what illicit "discrimination" really is and on distinct beliefs about the capacity of the state to correct unwanted social practices. In our view, it is not surprising to find a wide political spectrum of opinions about the appropriate state role, or to find that the spectrum of views corresponds quite closely to the "left-right" political spectrum historically observed on standard economistic issues.

ECONOMISTIC POLITICAL THEORY

The traditional, economistic political spectrum can perhaps most readily be understood as the set of competing theories about the desirability of market allocations of goods and market distributions of economic wherewithal.

Those on the political right divided, historically, into two camps. On the one hand, traditional (nineteenth-century) liberals[8] (associated in the law school world with Chicago School law and economics) believed that both the distribution of income and the allocation of goods that resulted from spontaneous exchanges among legally unconstrained adults with different tastes and different endowments to satisfy one another's preferences were optimal and just. Self-conscious political action (especially by those with state authority) to constrain free choices (for example, on the basis of paternalistic motives or the belief that exchanges in which clear force or fraud were absent were nonetheless often likely to be tainted by subtler coercion or cognitive manipulation) was especially dangerous. Redistribution from those favorably endowed to satisfy market demands to those less able to do so was also problematic. Some derived this antiredistributive position from a libertarian, entitlement-centered perspective, which emphasized natural ownership rights and "freedom" to trade and contract.[9] Others derived fairly parallel policy prescriptions from a more openly utilitarian outlook, emphasizing the disincentive effects of redistributive measures[10] and our incapacity to discern "utility-enhancing" choices for others.[11]

Others on the political right (Burkeans, broadly construed) saw at least some conflict between market morality and the need to maintain traditional hierarchy, believing that, at least at the margin, traditional authority ought to be bolstered even at the cost of sacrificing the absolute primacy of unfettered market exchange. Reasonably strong redistributive obligations could grow out of traditional privilege or the need to mollify and pacify those who might otherwise feel politically dispossessed.[12] Free choice might govern the exchange of "routine" commodities, but liberty must be curtailed to ensure that antisocial, destructive wants were properly channeled or sublimated[13] (thus, for instance, for such conservatives, fixed-status marriage would dominate contractual partnership between cohabitants; prostitution and private consumption of pornography could be banned).

Political "centrists" historically tended to be more wary than the right-wing "traditional liberals" of numerous non-self-correcting market failures that precluded "free choosers" from reaching optimal positions. While still firmly antipaternalistic, at least when announcing self-conscious, general ideological views,[14] they were far more prone to see ubiquitous market failures:[15] misinformed choices,[16] public goods problems,[17] goods misallocated because of unaccounted-for externalities,[18] non-cost-justified monopolies that both misallocated and misdistributed,[19] and undue "macroeconomic" cyclicity that precluded labor markets from clearing and thus prevented the disadvantaged from working their way out of poverty, even given a reasonable level of skill and willingness to work.[20] Their distributive views were prone to be "pragmatic egalitarian": that is to say, they had no "principled" opposition to self-conscious redistribution. Quite to the contrary, they were prone, presumptively, to prefer greater levels of equality to lesser levels. Nonetheless, they believed that the "utilitarian" limits on redistribution were, while less extreme than the conservative utilitarians imagined, still far from trivial.[21]

Those on the political left typically were considerably more prone to be wary of "free choices." They perceived many preferences as, at best, "adaptive" to existing social practices (for example, people learn to value commodity acquisition over meaningful work when meaningful work is rarely provided)[22] and, at worst, coerced by those with social power (as working-class racism was thought to be largely engineered by capitalists seeking to rule the working class through "divide and conquer" tactics).[23] Although most leftists believed it would be unjust if even genuine differentials in productivity had pronounced material consequences,[24] they frequently argued that existing distributional patterns were largely a function not so much of differential productive endowments as differences in power. The hierarchical division of labor, for instance, was not primarily technologically determined, but instead dictated by the needs of those atop hierarchies to render themselves indispensable coordinators of laborers.[25]

CONTEMPORARY RIGHT AND CENTRIST CONCEPTIONS OF ANTIDISCRIMINATION LAW

The political parallels in competing conceptions of antidiscrimination law and policy are remarkably strong. In illustrating this point, we draw primarily on examples from the area of employment discrimination law, where a good deal of modern antidiscrimination theory has developed. We will subsequently analogize to the context of educational accommodations for pupils labeled learning disabled.

The parallels between antidiscrimination law and economistic political thought have largely been suppressed, in significant part because the field is dominated by various centrist theories which radically *separate* "economistic" distributional issues from "rights-oriented" antidiscrimination issues. In these various (right, mainstream, and liberal) centrist conceptions, to which we will return, antidiscrimination law operates *prior* to redistributive efforts, both temporally and conceptually. In the mainstream centrist view, antidiscrimination law demands only that each person receive what she would receive in a "perfected" impersonal market, her "objective" factor share (marginal product).[26] But once antidiscrimination law does its (limited) job—to rid the world of the animus, false stereotyping, and perhaps rational statistical discrimination as well that block members of subordinated groups from receiving "marginal product" payments—we move on to a distinct redistributive realm.

In this realm of redistribution, all sorts of claims may be made. These include claims based on group rights (including claims to reparations)[27] and claims based on the desirability of encouraging cultural diversity by "overrewarding" (in market terms) activities in which members of distinct subordinated groups might more typically engage. However, centrists generally appear most comfortable entertaining redistributive claims based either (a) on the supposition that aggregate social welfare would increase if those with low incomes had access to funds that richer citizens initially controlled or that such poorer citizens have just claims on such resources,[28] (b) on the desire to minimize unequal opportunity by minimizing, while not eliminating, the environmental differences faced by children,[29] (c) on the perceived need to reward the "meritorious,"[30] or (d) (especially in constitutional law circles) on the aspiration to make the capacity for political participation more nearly universal among individuals (and perhaps even equal).[31]

Libertarian views of appropriate antidiscrimination policy are not really "in play" in American politics at this point, though they were decidedly part of expressed opposition to the 1964 Civil Rights Act (along with states' rights arguments).[32] Even Richard Epstein, the most prominent legal academic libertarian, does not treat the 1964 Civil Rights Act as an impermissible taking of the (common law) right of owners of public accommodations to exclude unwanted patrons, though the omission to do so appears wholly tactical, rather than principled,[33] and Epstein certainly does treat Title VII as illegitimate (if not constitutionally suspect) except to the degree it helped dismantle formal state *bans* on integrating workplaces.[34] Nonetheless, it is fairly clear what the libertarian position on antidiscrimination has been: it is impermissible for the state to compel contracts between parties when all parties do not choose to contract voluntarily. Thus ordering an employer to hire or retain someone he would not choose to hire is impermissible, even if his refusal to do so is motivated entirely by racist animus, as is requiring the owners of "public" accommodations to serve or deal with anyone they do not choose to.[35]

At the same time, libertarians emphasize that the state must not forbid voluntary contracts from being made; thus the role of antidiscrimination law and policy is solely to ensure that the state does not mandate racist and sexist practices. Descriptively, libertarians are prone to believe that discrimination (by race or gender) will survive only when the state mandates it; market pressures to maximize profits, they believe, will typically preclude entrepreneurs from acting on racist or sexist animus. Nor can those acting on false stereotypes survive as entities any better than entities laboring under any other sort of significant misinformation about the availability of "resources" or workers. As long as existing or potential competitors have profit opportunities created by their understanding that, say, African-American and women workers are more capable than bigots wrongly believe them to be, the bigots will be at a distinct, and ultimately fatal, competitive disadvantage.[36]

Burkean social conservatives are somewhat more prone to distance themselves from both the libertarian tolerance for overt expressions of bigotry and the centrist's obsessive Enlightenment "rationalism." It is clear that social conservatives needn't tolerate overt racist or sexist language or direct slights (as libertarians do) as protected exercises of personal liberty. Conceptually, it is obvious that anyone (including the rare libertarian who doesn't make the familiar mistake of reifying common law entitlements as the unique set of "natural rights") *could* choose to treat such dignitary offenses as torts (parallel to the intentional infliction of emotional distress).[37] It is also clear that Burkeans might be predisposed to do so, both in the name of protecting civility against barbarian impulses, and, more powerfully, to protect against the risk of social disintegration (alienation and "separatism" by minority group members). Racist "acts"—refusal to hire out of animus, refusal to provide public accommodations—are proscribed, in this view, dominantly because of their implicit speech content.[38]

At the same time, the centrists' Enlightenment hyperrationalism—in which the state *demands* impersonal, market-rational treatment of all job applicants and would-be customers, insisting that they be judged only as, respectively, productive assets and sources of spending—goes much too far for these social conservatives. *Griggs*,[39] the centerpiece of centrist Enlightenment social engineering, demands that employers use only technically validated screening devices (diplomas, tests, and so on) in selecting employees. An employer, says *Griggs*, ought to be concerned only with his workers' output and cannot exclude minority group members if they are as productive as members of unprotected groups. This is so even though they may lack virtues the social conservative values, so long as these qualities do not correlate, systematically, with on-the-job performance. But the social conservative might be prone to think that even unvalidated tests of, say, reading skills, or Bloomian "cultural literacy," or school diplomas were all legitimate bases of privilege (hiring preference) because they are themselves signs of legitimate (relative) cultural authority and must be rewarded, both for intrinsic reasons and to encourage their preservation. (In a similar fashion, perhaps, recruitment through word of mouth, even though it could clearly disadvantage those now outside the world of privilege, might be legitimate for social conservatives since it bolsters stable communities.)

In fact, though, neither of these conservative positions on antidiscrimination law has much influence in American political life today. Instead, the chief politically viable conservative attack on the hyperrationalism of *Griggs* is pragmatic rather than "principled": the pragmatic "right centrist" opponents of the decision concede that the mainstream centrists are correct in their aspirations. It is indeed unjust if blacks and women do not receive rewards commensurate with their productivity, but the right centrists profoundly doubt the capacity of the state either to recognize or to correct genuine entrepreneurial irrationality. The problem with demanding that, say, tests or diplomas be validated—*proven* to correlate with on-the-job productivity—is twofold. First, the demand for validation overstates the observational skills of technocrats (the industrial psychologists asked to measure performance) and bureaucrats (the judges and EEOC hearing officers asked to decide whether those excluded in fact systematically perform worse on the job). Second, the demand for validation understates the rationality of entrepreneurs, who have powerful selfish material reasons to discard screening devices that exclude workers who could in fact do the work as well as those "screened in."[40]

Since the basic theme of "government failure," coupled with greater, if incomplete, faith in the self-correcting power of markets is *the* basic conceit of right centrist thought outside the domain of antidiscrimination law,[41] it ought not be surprising that it will dominate some ideological understandings of appropriate antidiscrimination policy. Still, one must recall that the right centrists do not believe markets wipe out all social problems. They are more prone than libertarians, who oppose civil rights law far more thoroughgoingly, to believe that discrimination based on animus or commonplace stereotypes can persist even in competitive markets. Thus, like the Burkean conservatives, they are certainly willing to proscribe expressions of animus and, perhaps to a lesser degree, decisions grounded in false stereotypes. But the motivation is different: they are not so much guarding against the social disintegration that might result from the toleration of racist "torts" as attempting to ensure "market rationality."

As an institutional matter, judges (or hearing officers) can, in this right centrist view, only make reasonable factual findings about hostile and (to a slightly lesser extent) stereotyped decisions, for example by "checking" the reactions of a landlord or employer to discrete individuals, one from the protected and one from the unprotected group,[42] identical along all legally relevant dimensions,[43] or by looking at paper trails of bigoted remarks. They are not, though, capable of judging the macro-rationality of a process applied evenly to members of all groups.

Mainstream centrism normatively idealizes what it expects can in fact occur with the prodding of appropriate legal intervention: each member of a protected group must be treated as she would be in a thoroughgoingly rational, impersonal market, that is, as a source of funds to a seller and, to an employer, as a factor of production paid her marginal product.[44]

This result need not occur spontaneously, even in competitive markets,[45] for a number of reasons. First, of course, an individual employer or seller may choose to indulge his animus:[46] owners of public accommodations and employers may be willing to sacrifice financial opportunities to avoid or injure members of protected groups. Alternatively, there may be animus on the part of customers: an unbigoted profit-maximizing employer might refuse to hire those against whom his customers is prejudiced. Some progressive commentators believe that the unambivalent and unambiguous refusal of courts to allow employers to raise customer preference defenses indicates that Title VII is unconcerned with enforcing the mainstream centrist version of "economic rationality." This argument appears unavailing to us: the courts are simply refusing to allow the employers to act as agents of the customers' economic irrationality. A customer is, conceptually, the worker's true employer in the sense that she is the source of the funds that provides the employee's pay: the (formal) employer merely acts as the customer's agent. Similarly, reliance on false stereotypes may preclude market-rational treatment: many owners simply do not realize that members of protected groups provide profit opportunities because of widespread social misimpressions of their qualities.[47] If false stereotypes are socially commonplace, particularly among those with the economic power to make hiring decisions, the capacity of markets to wipe out those acting on "wrong" beliefs diminishes.[48]

Similarly, if firms follow irrational customs whose impact adversely affects protected groups' members, the groups' members will not be treated market-rationally. Mainstream centrists are predisposed to believe that in addition to the most familiar sorts of "stereotypes" about groups of people (for example, "women only work till they have kids," "Jews are avaricious," and so on), there is a narrow category of equally untrue "customary" beliefs about the universal dictates of work organization that don't arise out of such group prejudice (for example, "people with high school diplomas do better work than those without on all jobs," "police officers must always have a great deal of upper body strength") but adversely affect members of subordinated groups. Recognizing the possibility that "custom" is irrational without regard to "prejudice" is almost surely the most politically radical aspect of *Griggs*. It echoes the leftists' more general accusation that markets may not eliminate wrong-headed beliefs about productive imperatives, but rather that those who command market institutions more typically overvalue "customary" practices that reward the conventionally culturally valued traits associated with higher levels of current social status.

The mainstream centrist accounts of entrepreneurial irrationalism are somewhat muted, though. Descriptively, the centrist view seems to be wary only of employers' demands for credentials, not their depictions of "good work" on the job. In terms of institutional competence concerns, the mainstream centrist position demands that judges or EEOC hearing officers interrogate only the form of customary prejudice that is simplest to evaluate: they simply demand proof of statistical correlation between the entrance criterion and job performance,[49] but measures of job performance remain defined by the employer. The centrists do not demand that the courts ascertain whether each organizational decision that puts protected group members at a disadvantage is adequately cost-effective to be sustained.[50]

Furthermore, the mainstream centrist position is that markets may simply not have the opportunity to function, even in the absence of state-mandated bigotry, the libertarians' bête noir, because there may be local, collective, nongovernmental pressures (ranging from violence to ostracism to implicit or explicit boycotts) to maintain the segregated caste system.[51]

Finally, if firms engage in rational statistical discrimination,[52] individual group members whose productivity is higher than that of most members of the group will be underpaid, though the impact on the group's compensation is more ambiguous.[53] If acting on generalizations is cheaper for an employer than gathering more particularized knowledge, it is economically rational for the employer to treat all group members as if they had the traits of typical group members. Members of protected groups who themselves don't possess unwanted traits commonplace in the group will lack opportunities, though.

It is clear that mainstream centrists seek to proscribe irrational business conduct (animus, false stereotypes, unvalidated predictors based on false suppositions about job requirements). It is likewise apparent that mainstream centrists seek to eliminate the most direct forms of statistical discrimination: for example, the refusal to administer strength tests to women when strength is a legitimate job requirement on the ground that most women are too weak to pass them and hence high administrative costs will be incurred in giving strength tests to all women when that will generate relatively few hires.[54] It bears emphasis, though, that the case for proscribing rational statistical discrimination is distinct from the cases against animus and stereotyping; instead of banning practices that ultimately waste resources (because they result in failures to consummate trades that would actually benefit all parties if made), it demands interventions that, at least in the short run, may increase net social expenditures. There is a twofold centrist case against permitting statistical discrimination, though: first, it is possible that such discrimination leads protected group members to underinvest in human capital acquisition (knowing that employers won't recognize that they have skills that are superior to most members of their ascriptive group even if they develop them).[55] Second, one might believe that individuals in protected groups, if not all citizens generally, are entitled to meritocratic treatment, even when more social resources must be expended identifying merit than are saved by ensuring that individuals are employed at as productive a position as they are capable of filling.[56]

The belief among more liberal centrists that firms ought not be permitted to engage in rational statistical discrimination is buttressed by a more general *distributive* conviction that antidiscrimination law mandates that persons be rewarded commensurate with their gross output, rather than their net output (that is, output net of the costs associated with hiring or employing them).[57] The case for rewarding gross rather than net output might well be strongest when input cost differentials between employees result essentially from distinct screening costs, that is, when the costs of identifying that Worker A is as productive as Worker B are higher for Worker A. As we noted, this may be true in part because we believe that it unduly discourages people from developing productive skills if they will be unable to demonstrate them. But it is clear that many liberal centrists believe that workers must be paid in accord with

gross, not net, output, even when no claim could be made that social output will ultimately increase if they are so entitled. Thus the
Americans with Disabilities Act, the clearest legal exemplar of this
viewpoint, mandates that employers pay the costs of accommodating workers with disabilities without reducing their wages to account for the incremental costs of accommodation.[58] In the absence
of such intervention, a profit-maximizing employer (or, for that
matter, a central planner concerned only with reducing goods' production costs), when confronted with a worker requiring accommodations, would substitute an equally skilled worker who required no incremental accommodation costs for one who did.

This liberal centrist belief, when unpacked, is almost surely partly
parasitic on the traditional conservative tendency we touched upon
earlier to distinguish the deserving and undeserving recipients of redistributive largesse. Thus, in the liberal centrist view, a blind lawyer
cannot justly be economically penalized for his blindness (by having
to pay his own assistant or reader, or having the firm dock his pay to
reflect the costs of hiring such an assistant). This view is difficult to
reconcile with the equally characteristic liberal centrist belief that it is
perfectly fair that that same lawyer is paid far more than that same assistant because he was born with (or educated to have) the capacity to
handle the typical legal arguments he is required to make. One seemingly best maintains this cluster of convictions by treating the
lawyer's disability as morally neutral or ennobling, and treating the
assistant as affirmatively morally blameworthy (*unwilling* to develop
his cognitive capacity) or unworthy (because *cognitive* inability, unlike disability, is a shameful mark).

While liberal centrists reject the mainstream centrist notion that
members of subordinated groups can justly demand no more than
"market rational" treatment, they also seek to maintain distance
from the more radical left assertion that the "worth" of persons is
purely "politically" determined, by the decisions of those with social power, rather than market measured, by the impersonal demands of consumers. The gross value added is still determined by
the impersonal valuation of the goods the worker (helps to) produce: thus, the valuation of the blind lawyers' memos and briefs is
a function in the liberal centrist view not of political/moralistic valuation of the worthiness or respectability of the work but of self-interested demand by the products' purchasers.

At the same time, the liberal centrist stance is that members of subordinated groups ought not to be rewarded less highly than workers *currently* more productive than they are so long as the gap in productivity could be overcome by relatively simple, inexpensive shifts in the organization of the workplace. The liberal centrists, in this regard, view practices as illicitly "dynamically discriminatory" whenever easily avoided "static" distinctions in net output ground pay differentials. Thus, in this view, women guards might appear to be legitimately excluded form serving as guards at all-male prisons *unless* the court orders the prison authority to redesign work shifts so that not all guards must perform invasive strip searches (an order designed to eliminate what the court sees as "dynamic" discrimination).[59]

"LEFT MULTICULTURALIST" ANTIDISCRIMINATION THEORY

Those on the ideological left go a significant step further than the liberal centrists in their desire to break the nexus between net value added and social rewards. As we have noted, left multiculturalism makes an egalitarian descriptive claim: that members of dominant social groups (defined by race, gender, physical ability, and sexual preference) control social institutions and misjudge the relative economic contributions of "outsiders" and members of their own group.[60] Thus, in this view, a self-conscious egalitarian intervention (mandating equal pay for those workers who entrepreneurs wrongly believe are differentially capable) will not have the adverse economic consequences that conventional centrist economists fear. Labor will not be misallocated; there will not be layoffs of those who must now receive higher nominal pay if hired at all; firms won't engage in covert and costly evasions of antidiscrimination regulations against nondiscriminatory hiring to avoid taking on employees who they believe will create net losses.[61]

In addition, though, left multiculturalism makes a strong, residual egalitarian normative claim—that even if there are real productivity differences between social groups, these differences ought to be without material consequences.[62] Even if women separate less readily from their children as a result of biological destiny or undominated choice (rather than illegitimate coercion and character-forming social pressure)[63] and even if this inability to separate compromises market productivity, it cannot justify lower pay.

As illustrated above, the liberal centrist use of antidiscrimination norms to squelch market tendencies to reward in accord with net, rather than gross, output is concretized and "legalized" largely in regard to people with physical disabilities, though, to a lesser degree, left liberal proposals to facilitate women's ability to work productively by adding (concededly) costly child-care facilities that (by hypothesis) benefit women more than their male co-workers would resonate in the same tradition. Left multiculturalism has developed the argument for erasing the material consequences of real group differences in productivity largely in relationship to gender differences. This is true, most likely, because of political discomfort on the multiculturalist left with the possibility that groups defined in other ways—by, say, sexual orientation, ethnicity, or "handicap"—are "disabled" (or less productive) rather than "differently abled" (equally, but differently productive) in performing market tasks.[64] The resistance to the rhetorical use of the term "handicap," and more recently "disability," rather than "different ability" seems to reflect this profound difficulty in confronting the possibility of differential market productivity between groups outside the gender context.

In the context of gender, it is reasonable to argue that even if women are less productive than men in performing "market work," they are "hypercapable" in performing equally significant work in the historically demonetized sectors. Given this reasonable supposition, it is plausible to argue, first, that "overcompensating" women for their market work simply makes up for the morally indefensible nonmonetization and devaluation of their socially crucial nonmarket work (from child rearing to caring for extended family to nurturance of social relationships to community service). More critically, though, the recognition that the nonmarket work which has been dominated by women has been devalued permits left multiculturalists to acknowledge (or even embrace) group differences, while, for other groups, the "distinct" social contributions of the oppressed subgroup, even if just as real, are not so readily socially identified and accepted.

The residual left multiculturalist position—the normative claim that even if real productivity differences do exist between groups, they should not have any material impact—*must* ultimately ground left multiculturalist distributive politics because the argument that oppressed groups' genuine contributions are misassessed because the empowered groups make valuation decisions, when scrutinized, almost surely fails. If "overcompensating" women in the traditional labor market were really an attempt to compensate women for performing (undervalued) household-based tasks, we would compensate those who performed household tasks equally (at least as long as they were equally productive in these tasks). To give higher compensation for household work to women who would have earned proportionately more in the market had they not labored at home—for example, to compensate an attorney who stays at home more highly than her secretary who stays at home, as we would do if we demanded that each woman's employer continue to pay her ordinary wages while she took extended maternity leave—would surely be problematic if our goal were to ensure appropriate respect for household work. The fact is that this is not a "rectification" principle that actually attempts to equalize pay for equal productive output by accounting fully for traditionally public and traditionally private output. Rather, it is an attempt to break the pay-product nexus entirely, at least when the nexus results in certain defined social groups being worse off than others.

If the left multiculturalist position really pressed us to reward true productivity, it would force us to ensure that some women achieve the social status the most successful men achieve by paying the "best mothers" salaries commensurate with, say, salaries paid high-priced lawyers and executives. But proposals to do so would serve largely to underscore the awkwardness of proposals to monetize the traditionally demonetized sectors. In this sense, the left multiculturalist position is even more difficult to administer, and conceptually more "state-ist" than the liberal centrist position that disdains market rationality to the extent that it demands that pay scales reflect gross, not net value added. The valuation of household labor, for instance, in this case, is entirely politicized, entirely a function of centralized group decision making on "moral merit," while the gross value added by the protected employee is judged in an impersonal market, in terms of the willingness of the purchasers of the producer's output to pay for that output. Confronted with these difficulties, left multiculturalists more commonly propose not to establish pay scales for historically unpaid domestic labor, but instead simply to ensure that places throughout the social hierarchy are more evenly allocated by group. If males receive a statistically disproportionate share of workplace privilege, there should be a presumption that it reflects discrimination which must be remediated. The difficulty with making this presumption is that the connection between either group or individual oppression, on the one hand, and nonrandom representation in the "pay elite," on the other, is not clearly explicated.

How, for example, can it be considered less moral for a less "productive" *group* to be paid less than a more productive *group* unless it is equally immoral to pay less productive individuals within a particular group less than more productive ones within the same group? Alternatively, why are policies designed to reduce inequality among groups less difficult to administer than programs designed to reduce inequality between individuals?

We have already dealt at length with these issues in our discussion in Chapter 7 of the "antidiscrimination" claims for accommodating learning disabled pupils on exams, and there we concluded that there do not seem to us to be any wholly satisfactory answers. It is not that group consciousness cannot be justified in any way: it *can* readily be justified by, among other things, the fact that group members have atypically interdependent utility functions, that group members in historically disadvantaged communities require "role models," that social integration depends on some measure of group equality, and that members of groups that have been historically stigmatized require substantive improvements in economic outcomes not simply to increase their access to consumption goods but to signal that they are no longer held in disrepute by the dominant, mainstream culture.[65] We must recognize the degree to which individuals derive their identity in significant part from groups, which are not simple voluntary associations of presocial individuals but constitutive of individuality; as a result, high levels of group inequality will have negative impacts on individuals that unpatterned inequality would not.[66]

Individual equality claims may focus, unduly exclusively, on material deprivation—on the distribution of material goods—while much suffering may be experienced not so much as a longing for goods as some combination of a sense of powerlessness and suppressed self-esteem. But powerlessness and suppressed self-esteem may be dominantly experienced by individuals as members of groups, groups that lack social power and groups that are subject to widespread social devaluation. Rectifying those problems may well require more attention to ensuring group participation in decision making and group access to meaning-giving cultural institutions, as well as attention to ensuring across-group representation in socially validated roles.

But none of these observations about the importance of accounting for "group" outcomes in assessing a distributive policy gives rise to anything as powerful as "group entitlement" trumping claims. In our view, they should give rise to something far more akin to contingent social engineering rules of thumb that *one*, among many, desideratum in designing social programs addressing the distribution of resources is that we reduce intergroup hierarchies.

Even more troublesome in our view, the left multiculturalist position fails to confront adequately what seems to us the vitally important fact that the interventions required to mute group inequality are no less problematic than the interventions required by traditional socialists to mute "capitalist" inequality (the "devaluation" of those individuals, however socially identified, who are less market productive). Firms required to pay some employees more than market wages surely won't inevitably go out of business doing so (as conservative alarmists often claim): they will simply face a tax that they will, to some extent, pay, and to some extent, expend resources to evade (such a tax is easier to evade than an income tax since it can be ducked by refusing to hire protected workers or inducing those one must hire to quit). To the degree the tax is paid, it will have some adverse effects on productive incentives: the extent of these adverse incentives is a matter of empirical debate.[67] But the key fact is that this tax will have no more or fewer problems than radically redistributive social democratic taxes or the implicit taxes levied in controlled economies which mute permitted pay differentials. One cannot evade the responsibility to defend (or discard) certain sorts of centralized economic planning by renaming it antidiscrimination law.

While recognizing the burdens of defending the interventionist state, we must recall that even the most humane, legally developed capitalist economies may be radically underinclusive and impersonal, though, and the more laissez-faire versions are far worse. It is not enough to know, for instance, that markets will, left to their own devices, do a good job of putting pressure on people to leave communities to follow shifting job opportunities without ascertaining whether the mobility-based gains in productivity really outweigh the losses in social continuity. The latest round of neoconservative arguments that spontaneous private charity would attend to most genuine need if the state withdrew from the "welfare business" seems almost willfully perverse.[68] Many people have complicated problems, and their problems are rarely self-contained: whether or not these problems might best be handled by close-knit small communities in which personalized oversight of troubled people is really plausible, we don't live in a world in which everyone can reasonably find himself in a tight-knit community. If the options are an imperfect "social work" state and a world filled with anomic, homeless labor market cast-offs, we'll eagerly opt for inefficiently bloated, poorly managed social work budgets. Capitalism remains a system filled with injustices, to individuals and to groups. But if the multiculturalists are to persuade those on the left generally to move away from a focus on this injustice to a focus on productive inefficiency, they have a very tough task.

ANTIDISCRIMINATION CLAIMS ON BEHALF OF THE LEARNING DISABLED

Naturally, the learning disabilities advocacy movement has not had to address these sorts of labor market issues explicitly. Advocates for students with learning disabilities are far more inclined to concentrate on the distribution of educational opportunity than the distribution of social rewards.[69] The claim that students in one group—students with LDs—are more worthy than non-LD students of receiving educational inputs that might help either group reach its potential is not easily shown to follow from the precepts of left multiculturalist antidiscrimination theory, but we think the connections are profoundly important. It is most illuminating, we believe, to look first at how this argument fares under the alternative conceptions of discrimination law that we have set out.

Full-blown libertarians typically deny the propriety of tax-funded education altogether, while acknowledging that differences in the status of children are somewhat problematic for libertarian theory generally.[70] Differentiated children's status is, of course, justified in libertarian theory as derivative of adults' (for example, parents') rights to dispose of their own just holdings as they see fit (and, correlatively, to refuse "coercive" demands to share with children with whom they do not freely choose to share).[71] But the political viability of libertarianism leans rather heavily on the commonplace instinct that rewards should be based on socially valued efforts, rather than on "ontological" claims to have "needs" or "wants" satisfied.[72] In this light, justifications for inequality among equally unproductive children are less socially resonant than justifications for adult inequality.

Libertarian-influenced legal scholars rely not only on the stricter natural rights–based position that the issue of the relative priority of students' claims for public resources simply never arises since *no* student can legitimately claim public resources. Many "quasi-libertarians" (especially those inside the law schools)[73] emphasize as well the need to act "as if" there is a natural rights framework in order to avoid rent-seeking by organized groups seeking unfair shares of state resources. In terms of "antidiscrimination" policy and the learning disabled student, this "quasi-libertarian" position is that the state simply ought not to leave open the possibility that it might distinguish among the claims of different students. The state ought not to grant distinct privileges to distinct students, valuing some claims more than others or tempting citizens to devote their resources to making successful claims at the "public trough." This viewpoint would seem to mandate what we called "democratic equality" in Chapter 6: federal antidiscrimination law might best simply bar local officials from refusing to grant pupils with learning disabilities resources that are available to other students (because of the majority's aversive prejudice to students with learning disabilities or because parents of children with LDs fail to mobilize adequately as an "interest group"), but it should also preclude students with LDs from making claims others cannot. The state cannot grant white children privileges it denies African-Americans: illegitimate "racism" is simply the capture of the regulatory state by socially dominant groups to immunize themselves from market competition by "outsiders" or to capture undue subsidies for themselves as a result of majority status. Illegitimate prejudice against people with disabilities (including those with LDs) is, in a parallel fashion, nothing more or less than the attempt by the "able-bodied" to preclude the "disabled" from receiving subsidies made available to the socially dominant, majority group.

A Burkean social conservative would likely show initial sympathy for the "quasi-libertarian" position that precludes exclusion of any subgroup from the full range of available public benefits. The underlying motivation might differ, though: we suspect the Burkean would be more concerned than the quasi-libertarian that "favoritism" in social spending would compromise both social solidarity and the republican virtues of rulers. At the same time, we suspect Burkean conservatism more explicitly seeks to nurture the autonomy of local political institutions and "authoritative figures" (school boards, principals), institutions central to a stable social order, than would quasi-libertarianism, which is more willing to use central rights-creating authorities (preferably courts) to block even local majoritarian exercises in state favoritism.[74] Thus we suspect that a Burkean would be prone to show considerable deference to diverse local political decisions, unsure whether local authorities *are* unjustly dismissing the interests of "politically disfavored" outsiders in making the resource allocation judgments that advocates for pupils with LDs decry, or simply making distinct educational policy judgments about whether learning disabilities are "real" or "effectively treatable" or whether students with LDs indeed have uniquely untapped potential.

A centrist, we imagine, would demand only that each student with a learning disability receive the resources she is entitled to in a "political market" allocating educational resources "fairly," that is, receiving inputs she would be expected to receive were she not a member of a group facing either aversive prejudice or false stereotypes. A right centrist, like a Burkean, would doubtless despair that "centralized activists" (in Congress, in special education institutes, in the courts) have any more capacity than locally elected bodies to distinguish a false stereotype about various students' potential from a proper educational judgment that certain disabilities are at least as recalcitrant as "general" academic problems or social disadvantage.

A mainstream centrist, worried about the possibility that local legislative judgments are clouded either by "first degree prejudice" (discounting the welfare of the "outsider" group) or by unduly readily accepted false stereotypes about outsiders,[75] should be (but does not seem to be) as prone to worry that local boards will *over-value* claims made by students with LDs as that they will under-value them. If we are wondering whether a certain group of poor-achieving students will be politically disadvantaged in the battle for incremental funds, it is not clear to us why we would believe that pupils with learning disabilities—who are a more random set of poor achievers in class and race terms than poor achievers more generally—will fare worse than their classmates. Unless a main-stream centrist believes the highly contestable proposition that students with LDs are victims of more general stereotypes about the incapacity of people with disabilities, in essence because they've got the word "disabled" as part of their label, he will not conclude that they need protection against especially poor local judgment about their ability to benefit from aid. We are dubious that most main-stream centrists would, on reflection, accept the proposition that educators properly estimate the potential of all students they label "unintelligent" while uniquely underestimating the talents of students with LDs.

The movement advocating special protections for students with LDs to ensure that their rights against discrimination not be violated draws relatively heavily on two aspects of the "liberal centrist" viewpoint on what the antidiscrimination principle entails. Most significantly, it draws upon the systematic tendency of left centrists to ignore the moral salience of "input costs" in evaluating distributive claims.

One can translate the claim of strong opponents of both test accommodation *and* increased resource inputs for the subgroup of students with learning disabilities as saying that those with LDs are not in fact as gifted as their proponents claim, because what it means to be gifted is not simply to be able to do work well when accommodated, whether on testing or with special tutoring, but to be able to do well when given "typical" inputs. In the "traditional" view, Student A does not have the same reading potential as Student B just because, with more effort, we can help him achieve as high a score on a reading comprehension test: A and B would have equal "talent" or "potential" only if they developed the same way given the same opportunities. Thus, in this view, even if we accepted the controversial empirical assumption made by the LD advocacy movement that learning disabled pupils are uniquely capable of benefiting from intervention, it does not clearly follow that the school has breached an obligation to help each student meet her potential by failing to undertake unusual interventions. Potential is nothing more than realized output given certain inputs, just as productivity is net, not gross productivity. A worker is "better" than another worker if she produces more output given equal inputs; she is not better if she produces more output only when given dramatically greater inputs.

As we have noted, the basic liberal centrist claim in the labor market context is that differential input costs are irrelevant, at least as long as members of socially salient groups will be harmed if employers account for differential input costs. To treat workers equally (without illicit discrimination) is to ensure that their pay is in proportion to their ability to produce, without regard to the special inputs necessary to enable members of protected groups to produce equal amounts. In the context of framing policy toward pupils with LDs, we might well be seeing a parallel claim. To treat students equally is to permit each subgroup to reach as high a proportion of their potential as other students reach without regard to the relative costs of students meeting this proportion of potential, at least as long as the inputs provided to one group are of little or no benefit to those not so favored.

This of course meets a second aspect of the general liberal centrist program: the demand to eliminate "dynamic discrimination" (illicit treatment of people in accord with current, but not potential output). It does so, especially, if one defines "potential output" in "gross" rather than "net" output terms.

Ultimately, though, we suspect that existing LD policy draws even more heavily on left multiculturalism than liberal centrism, largely because we doubt that there is adequately widespread belief in the factual proposition that students with LDs are uniquely *aided* by interventions, rather than uniquely *entitled* to them. The "dictates" of left multiculturalist views of antidiscrimination law in this area are not obvious, but we will attempt to trace what we believe they might most plausibly be.

First, and foremost, the belief that the claims of pupils with learning disabilities must have significant priority over the claims of other pupils in order to protect them against discrimination draws on the left multiculturalists' tendency to reject "needs-based" or solidarity-based claims. Thus children are not entitled to potential-maximizing resource infusions because the expenditures will make them function better as adults, or because they will not function above some minimalist baseline without the spending, but instead because they have been denied these resource infusions as a result of animus or irrational stereotypes. In this view, advocates for children with learning disabilities would not seek "charity," or tell us that the children will suffer unless we help them. The task, instead, would be to expose the bigotry of society, to expose our unwillingness to see the true human potential of children with learning disabilities because they are "different."[76] More important, because the claims to resources are not grounded in assertions of community or claims of need, they are not seen to compete with the claims made by others who believe they'd live happier, more productive lives if given incremental educational resources.

To make such "solidaristic" claims that the polity ought to alleviate suffering that we are capable of alleviating is to commit, albeit inadvertently, the paramount sin in left multiculturalist thought. Left multiculturalism most studiously avoids any hint of "blaming the victim,"[77] not in the traditional moral sense (in which we might hold a "victim" morally accountable if she chose to do something morally iniquitous), but in a descriptive sense (in which we believe we can best understand the victim's problems by looking at *her* traits, rather than the traits of those who evaluate her or "treat" her in a particular way).

Second, left multiculturalism, distancing itself from both the class obsession of socialism and the "equal opportunity" obsession of liberal individualism, is prone to contend that irrationality arises from the hegemonic judgments made by those in privileged ascriptive groups. Given this predisposition, advocates for students with LDs, influenced by left multiculturalism more generally, tend to overlook the possibility that educators are no less likely to misjudge the true potential of a whole range of their poor students—whether their "stupid" students, their "antsy" students, or their "verbally inarticulate" students—than they are likely to misjudge the potential of their students with LDs.

The problem with this approach is not just the "internal" one that we have so frequently mentioned—even if we assume "society" is generally more prone to devalue the competence and potential of people with disabilities, are learning disabilities really like other disabilities in this regard?—but a deeper moral one. The duties to students with learning disabilities really ought not to depend, in any way, on educators' *misperceiving* how hard or easy it is to change their performance levels. If the duties arose solely in response to the problem of bigoted misperception, they ought to disappear when the misperception clears up. Thus if all educators learned, through years of implementing IDEA, that these children's achievement improved markedly if, but only if, they received substantially more resources than their non-LD classmates receive, then the duty to provide accommodations would end, since the problem of misperception would be solved.

Surely, the real task of the advocate for pupils with learning disabilities is to persuade us that once the accommodation-dependent potential of students with LDs is recognized, we have the further moral obligation to actually make the additional expenditures. If we think the resource claims of students with LDs should defeat the administrators' potential argument, "we know perfectly well that they can do better if we spend much more educating them but we are unwilling to do so," it is because we believe as a policy matter that the incremental resources are well spent, not because the failure to spend bespeaks either ignorance of the abilities of children with LDs or dismissal of their interests.

Strong advocates for the primacy of obligations to pupils with LDs ultimately draw on some of the most contestable aspects of left multiculturalist employment law theory. For example, left multiculturalism tends to posit that centralized state actors can cleanly distinguish the ignorant prejudices of local dispersed powers (employers in the job context, local school boards and teachers in the LD one) from facts. But just as the claim that employers' bias systematically blinds them to the potential productivity improvements that radically restructured workplaces might bring is dubious in the employment context, the hard evidence for the proposition that local educators radically underestimate the positive impact of remedial efforts aimed at pupils with LDs (particularly relative to other competing interventions) turns out to be very slim. There is plenty of reason to believe that correctly diagnosed students with learning disabilities benefit rather little from special educational efforts.

In addition, left multiculturalism assumes that ignorant prejudices beset historically oppressed groups, but not individuals within the privileged mainstream: thus white working-class males are not subject to irrational devaluation of competence; students without labeled disabilities have no more "potential" than local administrators systematically attribute to them. While we are wholly sympathetic to the claim that racism and sexism are unique and strong systemic sources of irrationality, the parallel claim, in this context, that there is a great deal of group-based irrational devaluation of people with learning disabilities, is quite contestable.

Racist and sexist devaluation occurs in contexts in which decision makers make decisions about performance and potential knowing the ontological traits of the objects of their judgment; the same sort of devaluation could reasonably be said to occur when school officials or employers judge the capacity of students or workers with discernible physical disabilities. But the supposedly "bigoted" administrator judging the potential of a student with an LD may not even know he is dealing with such a student. He does not misperceive potential because he undervalues people with disabilities; on the contrary he does so for the very reason that he does *not* see that he is dealing with a disability. He is not averse to the individual because of his condition, nor does he move too hastily from recognition of a condition to ultimate judgment. The most plausible accusation, instead, is that he moves from a generally salient fact—the student's test scores are poor—to what is claimed to be a wrong conclusion—students with low achievement scores will persistently achieve poorly. But even if this conclusion is wrong, it would seem to be "bigoted" not against students with LDs, but against "poor test performers," whom the school officials falsely stereotype, or discriminate against statistically. "Poor achievers" is the group about whom the officials have (supposedly wrong) opinions: they make no suppositions about the (visually indistinguishable) subgroup who have learning disabilities. Yet IDEA does not direct itself at protecting *all* poor students by mandating that districts develop IEPs for *all* such students to ensure that generalizations about their future capabilities be carefully tested. Unless IDEA's advocates are willing to make the strong supposition that we can correct false stereotypes about poor test performers simply by ensuring that students with LDs are precipitated out from that group, which *should* otherwise be treated as essentially homogenous, IDEA is not, in any discernible way, even designed to correct false stereotypes.

Third, and most important perhaps, the strongest advocates for legal protection of students with LDs draw on the left multiculturalist rhetorical manipulation of the mainstream centrist conception of antidiscrimination law to "legalize" their claims, just as left multiculturalism does in the labor market context. This is most significant in the employment law context when we think of "cost defenses," which can be seen as attempts to "balance" the interest in eradicating "discrimination" with interests in pursuing other social projects.

In the mainstream centrist view, reflected in decisional law, it is fairly clear that employers cannot raise "cost defenses" once they have been found to discriminate. As we have noted, employers cannot act as agents of their customers' animus, for instance, so that the fact that profits might decrease if a company hires African-American salesmen that a large group of customers won't as readily purchase from is of no legal moment.[78] Similarly, an employer might have designed a plant assuming it would never hire women: the fact that it is somewhat costly to remodel to account for the required presence of women will not be a defense.[79] The slogan, "the cost of remedying discrimination is no bar to relief"[80] is a socially plausible slogan when one's *definition* of discrimination is as narrow as the centrist's definition: social resources must be expended to ensure that members of protected groups receive privileges commensurate with market product. Once more, the key rhetorical point is that if one's conception of antidiscrimination law is so narrow, legal claims arising under that body of law are *prior* to more general distributive claims. First, we perfect the market, then "policy" claimants (arguing need, arguing subsidization of merit goods, such as subcultural preservation perhaps) tax some of the now-justly earned funds and expend them appropriately.

Left multiculturalism "uses" that same "cost is no defense" slogan in a context when it is far less socially plausible, drawing on the rhetorical power of the centrist usage, but without being willing to adopt the whole centrist program. One can interpret an employer's unwillingness to pay an unproductive protected group member what she pays a more productive unprotected worker as simply "raising a cost defense": that is, it is true that it will indeed be costly for her to overpay the protected group worker, and that, from her selfish "defendant in this particular lawsuit" vantage point, that additional cost is in fact her primary concern. But the mainstream centrist would simply not accept the proposition that an employer in this case is raising a prohibited cost defense: rather, the centrist would surely argue that there is no discrimination against someone simply because she is paid according to productivity.

The left multiculturalist view blurs the "two stages" of public policy that the centrist so cleanly separates. A centrist is likely to believe one cannot consider making trade-offs between "Stage I" market purification goals and "Stage II" social redistributive goals, but that once we are into "Stage II," various redistributive goals may compete with one another. The left multiculturalist is more likely to argue that the failure to do what the centrist calls "redistribution"—which she calls either "overcoming misevaluation of the contributions of the socially marginalized" or "ensuring that genuine differences have no material consequences"—is discrimination and hence must be remedied without regard to competing uses of the funds expended to remedy it.

In the context of determining the appropriate scope for IDEA, this battle plays out in a structurally similar fashion. Centrists must ultimately be most prone to argue that pupils with LDs, in this culture, are simply making "policy" claims (claims that they are more worthy recipients of incremental resources than others), rather than genuine antidiscrimination claims (claims that their interests have been slighted because their interests are systematically undervalued by state administrators or their interests misunderstood because of stereotypes about their capacities). If they are making such policy claims, though, their claims ought not to be so heavily "legalized," treated as having substantial aspects of "rights" claims, capable of trumping competing resource claims. (In practical terms, districts could compare the benefits of expending funds on students with LDs generally, as well as on particular LD students, with the benefits of other spending plans.)

"Left multiculturalist"-influenced advocates for those with learning disabilities are prone to believe, once more, that pupils with LDs, a victimized group, are subject not to legitimate (even if wrong-headed) educational policy, whether that policy is democratic egalitarian, openly utilitarian, or corrective of prior resource disparities, but to discrimination. The definition of discrimination is even less clear in this context than in the employment context where the *administrative*, if not the conceptual left multiculturalist, definition of discrimination is quite clear: any program with statistically adverse impact (unequal distribution of benefits to groups) is so strongly presumptively illicit that, for all intents and purposes, it cannot be defended.

In the IDEA context, the claim is a bit different, though it is animated by something of the same concern: if students with LDs don't end up performing as well as non-LD students in school, the schools must surely be duty bound to do much *more*, since acceptance by the local districts of anything shy of that end-point demonstrates an ongoing refusal to accommodate difference. The unstated supposition is that if differences were truly accommodated, performance gaps would end, just as the unstated supposition in the labor market context is that group inequality would be eradicated but for the persistence of intolerance of difference. As a discriminated-against group, pupils with LDs are then entitled, absolutely, to order that districts take all steps to end "discrimination" against them: what this has come to mean, practically, is that each student is entitled to the "standard" special ed regimen of treatment for her learning disability.

It is crucial to recall that the left multiculturalist–influenced advocate for pupils with learning disabilities is not attacking what "centrists" would call discrimination, though the remedial requirement is largely premised on the supposition that such discrimination exists. It is not enough for the district to show that it has done far more to bring students with LDs closer to their "potential" than it has done for other students, nor is it enough to show that its policies manifest full awareness of and sensitivity to the importance of and the special needs of the "class" of pupils with LDs. In the left multiculturalist view, the district cannot argue that the advocates for increased spending on learning disabled students have simply lost a fair pluralist battle over resource allocation, just as the employer cannot argue that "socially undervalued" women should take their case for socialized monetization of household tasks or subsidization of market-undervalued child-rearing tasks either to a policymaking legislature or to a court seeking to correct legislative sexism, rather than inventing a new and unworkable concept of market sexism.

Summary and conclusions

Students with learning disabilities receive incremental material benefits (resources, testing accommodation, and partial discipline immunity) that other students might well benefit from. It is possible that they do so in significant part because conservatives, believing this particular subgroup of troubled pupils more "deserving" than other students, have not resisted relatively expansive support for them. More interestingly, though, their claims appear frequently to trump those of other pupils who might benefit from similar interventions because the failure to give these benefits is deemed to arise from a form of discrimination.

The idea that students with learning disabilities do not get all the benefits they seek because they are victims of discrimination is dependent upon a certain vision of what discrimination means. In the traditional mainstream centrist view of the antidiscrimination norm in the labor market context, we demand no more than that employers treat protected group members impersonally, as factors of production, unaffected by false stereotypes or animus: demand for treatment *more* favorable than that may be legitimate, but is thought to raise distinct redistributive claims. In the parallel political context, the antidiscrimination norm forbids undervaluing the interests of a protected group (animus), misevaluating the impact of alternative policies upon the group, or framing a policy that makes sense only given particular misconceptions of the group's qualities (stereotypes), but, once more, no treatment more favorable than that is owed as a matter of right.

Advocates for pupils with LDs cannot readily rely on this traditional centrist conception of discrimination, though, if they are to argue that students with learning disabilities must be protected against discrimination. Instead, they must draw on aspects of both liberal centrist and left multiculturalist accounts of what the antidiscrimination norm entails.

Liberal centrism departs from mainstream centrism in demanding first, that people receive market rewards not solely in terms of current productivity but in terms of the potential they would, over time, manifest under more ideal conditions (that is, it demands the state correct "dynamic discrimination") and, second, that they receive rewards commensurate with "gross" (accommodated), not "net" (unaccommodated), output when differences in input costs are a function of group membership. Advocates for pupils with LDs argue, in parallel fashion, that we are duty bound to ensure that students with learning disabilities end up just like students without them if they are capable (dynamically) with resource infusions (gross, not net output) of performing like their non-LD classmates, and that to refuse to give such infusions is to discriminate since it will result in disparate outcomes that are unjust given equality of "gross" potential.

Left multiculturalism emphasizes the degree to which institutions most typically discriminate by misperceiving the skills and strengths of members of nondominant groups: "difference" is transformed into "incapacity" by the failure of the dominant institutions to appreciate and accommodate alternative styles of work in the employment setting, and of learning in the school setting. In this view, people with LDs, unlike other competing claimants, are victims of discrimination because their learning styles are systematically denigrated in the absence of federal protection. Moreover, left multiculturalism posits that groups can make distributive claims that individuals simply cannot: that group equality is the presumed goal of antidiscrimination law (in part because group inequality would result only from illegitimate undervaluation of subordinated groups' contributions) even though individual equality (within groups) is not so mandated. If one believes, then, that students with LDs form a social group, while competing claimants do not, then LD students may be uniquely entitled to interventions that mute, even if they are incapable of eliminating, distinctions in the social rewards enjoyed by them and "mainstream" students.

The chief difficulties with the second claim are that the "redistributive" taxes needed to ensure group equality will prove at least as problematic in implementation as more traditional egalitarian social democratic taxes and that the argument overemphasizes the unique significance of attaining group equality, compared with other redistributive goals. In our view, though, it is the first multiculturalist claim that most drives advocates for learning disabled pupils in seeking extra resources. The main difficulty with this first left multiculturalist view is that it turns our attention away from moralistic claims of need toward highly contestable claims that local actors (in markets and politics) are systematically far less rational than rights-creating centralized intervenors.

Pedagogic policy must ultimately come to dominate our treatment of students with LDs: if, say, speeded tests are outright pointless (or, more modestly, simply misassess skill levels for some class of students), then we should abandon them. If there are particular gains to certain expensive educational interventions that accrue to some, but not all, students, let those students receive the appropriate interventions.[81]

The very first time we interviewed a campus advocate for students with disabilities, she declared, with great confidence, that "treatment of the learning disabled is a civil rights matter." As long as that statement remains broadly socially plausible, it will remain quite hard to fashion good educational policy in this area. Many perfectly just claims—as well as any number of claims that are either intrinsically unworthy or must be balanced against competing concerns—are *not* civil rights claims, and claims to ensure that more students reach their educational potential, as well as claims that tests should measure genuine skills, or that students not be disciplined when there are viable options that better serve their interests while protecting the interests of students around them, are among them. It will always be tempting to "jump the queue" by claiming that one's distributive interests take priority over the interests of another group: claim hopping on the (ideological) backs of instances of genuine victimization by racism, sexism, able-ism, and cultural stigmatization threatens the real battles against social caste at the same time that it threatens chaotic and irrational distributive politics.

Appendix / Notes / Index

APPENDIX

Interview Methodology

For our survey and in-depth interviews, we targeted special education directors rather than other actors in the special education bureaucracy, schools, or private sector. We did so in the belief that local directors were in the best position to answer our combination of quantitative and qualitative questions about district policy, general demographic data, and diagnostic data. Although we loosely refer to these informants as "directors," "administrators," or "coordinators," the formal title of these actors in fact differed from state to state. The persons we targeted, though, were invariably the senior administrators in charge of special education for their particular school districts (though in some cases, they oversaw more than one district). Directors of special education typically have an advanced degree in education (in several cases a doctorate) with a specialization in special education. They are typically responsible for, or at least have final authority over, hiring and supervising special education personnel; making special education curricular decisions for the district in consultation with the district special education teachers, psychologists, and others; dealing directly with the parents of special education pupils, especially in the context of due process complaints and procedures; overseeing funding decisions at the local level; and dealing with and reporting to their state departments of special education.

All interviewees were informed that their names and the names of their districts would remain undisclosed, but that we would identify the state in which the district was located and some of the district's demographic features. Thus when we quote from interviews in the text, we typically give only the state and socioeconomic status (SES) of the district of the informant, though, if relevant, we might also provide information about the district's racial composition, level of urbanization, and so forth. To the extent possible, we relied on census data rather than self-reporting for statistical and demographic information about the districts in which we conducted interviews.

For the in-depth interviews, we spoke with a total of fourteen special education directors: three in New York, three in California, four in Mississippi, and four in Louisiana. Six of the interviewees were male and eight were female. We selected districts from urban, suburban, and rural regions, and across a range of racial compositions and median incomes, but without matching them from state to state along these dimensions. We give approximate figures only for median household income; educational attainment (proportion of population twenty-five or older with a bachelor's degree or postgraduate degree); and racial composition in order to preserve the anonymity of our informants. The approximate figures are:

Louisiana

District 1: $18,500; 10%; 65% white (almost all nonwhites are African-American).
District 2: $23,500; 27%; 70% white (nonwhites largely African-American; substantial number of Asian-Americans).
District 3: $35,000; 24%; 88% white (almost all nonwhites are African-Americans).
District 4: $18,500; 17%; 81% white (nonwhites largely African-American; substantial number of Asian-Americans).

Mississippi

District 1: $25,000; 16%; 74% white (almost all nonwhites are African-American).
District 2: $15,500; 27%; 43% white (almost all nonwhites are African-American).
District 3: $12,500; 13%; 35% white (almost all nonwhites are African-American).
District 4: $12,000; 12%; 24% white (almost all nonwhites are African-American).

New York

District 1: $47,000; 19%; 91% white (nonwhites rather evenly divided among Asian-Americans, Latinos, and African-Americans).
District 2: $75,000; 52%; 89% white (nonwhites are predominantly Asian-Americans).

California

District 1: $53,500; 28%; 87% white (nonwhites predominantly Latino and Asian-American).
Two SELPAs with a wide range of district demographic characteristics within the covered area.

The in-depth interviews lasted between two and four hours. Ten of the fourteen were tape-recorded and later transcribed, first by a third party and then by the interviewer. Poor sound quality made it difficult to transcribe some of the tapes, and passages in which precise wording was unclear appear in brackets in the text. (On several occasions, bracketed material summarizes a longer, though audible, portion of the tape.) We encouraged informants to tell us anecdotes and stress issues important to them, thus allowing them to stray from the formal agenda. Each informant was also asked to complete a questionnaire using data collected in the district for state and federal reporting purposes, although not all of the informants ultimately completed the questionnaire.

We are cautious in interpreting the interview and survey data for some rather obvious reasons. Self-reports may be inaccurate, and our interpretations of what are often complex, partly internally contradictory and inexact accounts of district practice may be imperfectly reliable. It is not enough to recognize the difficulty of transforming impressionistic evidence into data, and the extent to which the personal experiences and perspectives of the informants influenced the "facts" presented to us in their responses to questions and their narratives. One must remember also that there may well be a substantial gap between a special education coordinator's knowledge of practice within her district and the actual behavior in the schools, as well as wide variations in practice within the same district. Moreover, district special education coordinators are clearly not disinterested parties and are unlikely to represent a consistently neutral viewpoint; they have a stake in presenting district practices in a light more favorable than reflects reality, they may exaggerate problems that interfere with their ability to carry out their administrative function smoothly, and so on. Finally, our own errors and biases may have led us to assess inaccurately the type, degree, and meaning of variability in practices described to us.

LD Diagnostic Methods Phone Survey Questions

Name of district or county:
Name/title of contact:

I. *Basic Question: Necessity and Sufficiency of Discrepancy*
   Yes or no: IQ-achievement discrepancy score testing is used in your district or county.
   IF NO GO TO QUESTION 1
   IF YES GO TO QUESTION 2
1. IQ discrepancy scores are not used in your district/county because
   A. you use non-IQ based discrepancy score or nondiscrepancy methods for diagnosing LDs.
   B. you deemphasize the distinction between LD and non-LD based performance problems in implementing special services.
2. (In the subpopulation that does receive IQ-achievement discrepancy tests,) a *high* IQ discrepancy score is
   A. necessary for LD diagnosis.
   B. not necessary for LD diagnosis.
      IF A: Which is more true?

    i. high IQ discrepancy score virtually guarantees LD diagnosis (sufficient).

    ii. high IQ discrepancy score does not guarantee LD diagnosis (not sufficient).

IF B: Which is most true?

    i. Not only is a high IQ discrepancy score not necessary for LD diagnosis, but it's not even very important.

IF i: Even though you do not rely heavily on IQ discrepancy scores for internally determining placements, do you find that you are more likely to point to the absence of an IQ discrepancy when rejecting a parent's claim for services? (Are there any other particular instances in which the IQ discrepancy score is especially useful?)

    ii. Though a high IQ discrepancy score is not necessary for LD diagnosis, it is useful as a consideration along with several other, equally important factors.

IF ii: A student who does have a high IQ discrepancy will

    a. nevertheless almost always be diagnosed as LD (sufficient).

    b. sometimes not be diagnosed as LD (not sufficient). [If so, why?]

    iii. Though a high IQ discrepancy score is not necessary for LD diagnosis, it is the single most important factor in making your determination: without a high IQ discrepancy score, other factors must be compelling before a student will be diagnosed as LD.

IF iii: A student who does have a high IQ discrepancy will

    a. nevertheless almost always be diagnosed as LD (sufficient).

    b. sometimes not be diagnosed as LD (not sufficient). [If so, why?]

II. *Other Questions*

1. How many students are in your district?
2. What proportion are disabled?
3. Of the disabled, what proportion are LD?
4. Of the LD, what proportion are male?
5. If a student is a very high achiever (top third of class), but she nevertheless has an LD (as measured either by IQ discrepancy or other measures), will you give her an IEP?
6. How many of the nonphysically disabled or mentally retarded kids (LD, SED, BD) are in special day classes (nonmainstreamed)?
7. How many of the physically disabled are mainstreamed?
8. What proportion of the nonmainstreamed kids have behavioral as well as learning problems?
9. How many instances can you recall in the last two years in which an administrator has recommended the suspension for more than ten days or expulsion of a student, but the recommendation was overturned either within the district or by a hearings officer or court because the student's conduct was considered to be a manifestation of his disability?
10. How often did this occur when the student's disability was an LD?

Notes

1. Introduction

1. In Chapter 3, we detail how we arrived at this estimate. We also address the more complex question of the degree to which local districts bear these costs *because* of federal mandates, a question that might prove especially significant if Congress chooses to limit further the degree to which the federal government can impose unfunded mandates on state and local entities.
2. PL 89-313 (1965) amending PL 81-874.
3. For a more detailed treatment of the legislative and decisional backdrop of federal special education law, see Marvin Lazerson, "The Origins of Special Education" in *Special Education Policies: Their History, Implementation and Finance* 15 (J. Chambers and W. Hartman eds., 1983); David Neal and David Kirp, "The Allure of Legalization Reconsidered: The Case of Special Education," 48 *Law and Contemporary Problems* 63 (1985); Comment, "The Least Restrictive Environment Section of the Education for All Handicapped Children Act of 1975: A Legislative History and an Analysis," 13 *Gonzaga Law Review* 717 (1978).
4. PL 89-750 (1966).
5. PL 91-230 (1970).
6. 343 F. Supp. 279 (E.D. Pa. 1972).
7. Id. at 302.
8. 348 F. Supp. 866 (D.D.C. 1972).
9. Id. at 878.
10. Id.
11. PL 101-476 (effective October 1, 1990), 20 U.S.C.A. 1400–1485 (1996).
12. PL 93-112 (1973); 29 U.S.C.A. 701–796 (1996).
13. Accompanying regulations were finalized in 1978, attempting to detail

more precisely what constitutes illicit discrimination. See 34 C.F.R. 104 (1995).

14. We discuss in Chapter 3 whether federal statutes impose "unfunded mandates" in the area of special education. Formally speaking, IDEA does not: no state acting as a simple rational economic calculator would elect to be governed by IDEA unless federal fiscal contributions covered the marginal cost of complying with the statute's demands. Formally speaking, Section 504 does impose unfunded mandates. One must comply with its special education requirements (which may in fact be interpreted to track the IDEA requirements quite precisely) as long as one receives any federal funds, and it is obviously not economically rational to turn down all federal funds to avoid special education mandates.

15. 347 U.S. 483 (1954).

16. See Gerald Coles, *The Learning Mystique: A Critical Look at "Learning Disabilities"* 194–196 (1987).

17. See Lazerson, "The Origins of Special Education" at 41.

18. See Coles, *Learning Mystique* at 190–193 (LD advocacy movement arose when upwardly mobile parents feared that their poor-performing children would not realize the "promise" of untroubled middle class life); James Carrier, *Learning Disability: Social Class and the Construction of Inequality in American Education* 98–101 (1986) (middle-class parents associated mental retardation with the underclass, associated LD label with new scientific/technological explanations of school failure); Christine Sleeter, "Learning Disabilities: The Social Construction of a Special Education Category," 53 *Exceptional Children* 46, 47–48 (1986) (the use of organic causality and an IQ-based method to distinguish LD children from other classes of poor performers initially permitted white middle-class parents to preserve special benefits for their children).

19. See Carrier, *Learning Disability* at 2; Donald Hammill, "A Brief Look at the Learning Disabilities Movement in the United States," 26 *Journal of Learning Disabilities* 295 (1993).

20. It is a closer question in our view whether claims for testing accommodation can profitably be understood, at least in significant part, as valid antidiscrimination claims. We discuss, in Chapter 7, the possibility that members of dominant groups overvalue the academic skills that members of disabled might more typically lack, without reflecting on the narrowness of their perspective.

21. Some may be called disabled because it permits a district to remove them from mainstream classes. In this regard, we look in Chapter 4 at the possibility that African-Americans are overdiagnosed as disabled to permit districts to remove them from white-dominated mainstream classroom settings. Others may be called disabled because their parents aggressively seek more resources, testing accommodations, or supplementary income for which they were historically eligible when they cared for a "disabled" child. We return to these issues in Chapter 4 as well.

22. We note briefly as well the relationship between our discussion of the

ethics of distributing grades to the issue of the ethics of distributing discipline (particularly "long" suspensions and expulsions). Just as good grades are a reward for meritorious performance and poor grades a form of "punishment" for poor performance, so might "discipline" profitably be viewed as punishment for bad behavior. Whether we should refrain from disciplining students whose bad behavior is thought to arise from labeled disabilities, rather than from either "willful malice" or, more significantly, *unlabeled* (or unidentified) causes seems, ultimately, to raise the same basic issues that we raise in discussing grades: *if* we punish, can we defend immunizing some subset of students from judgmental metrics because we medicalize our conception of their particular form of misbehavior?

23. See Jerry L. Mashaw, "Against First Principles," 31 *San Diego Law Review* 211 (1994).

24. IDEA itself was approved by a voice vote in both the House and Senate (49 Cong. Q.W. 2630); more interestingly, its predecessor statute, the Education for All Handicapped Children Act, was passed 375 to 44 in the House (33 Cong. Q.W. 1669) and 83 to 10 in the Senate. Generally, legislation protective of those with disabilities has engendered little controversy, even when employers are mandated to take affirmative, costly accommodating steps: thus, the Americans with Disabilities Act carried the House by a 403–20 vote and the Senate by 76–8.

25. See Jack Tweedie, "The Politics of Legalization in Special Education Reform" in *Special Education Policies: Their History, Implementation and Finance* 48–73 (J. Chambers and W. Hartman, eds. 1983).

26. Opponents of the "therapeutic state" frequently argue that service providers, not recipients, drive legislative program formation. See, e.g., George Stigler, "Director's Law of Public Income Redistribution," 13 *Journal of Law and Economics* 1 (1970).

27. For a discussion emphasizing the disappointment of upwardly mobile parents fearing that the postwar promise of untroubled middle class might not be attainable for their academically troubled children, see Coles, *Learning Mystique* at 190–197.

28. See Carrier, *Learning Disability* at 89–104; Lazerson, "The Origins of Special Education" at 40–41.

29. See Sleeter, "The Social Construction of a Special Education Category," at 48.

30. See Coles, *Learning Mystique* at 197; John Lawrence Miller, "Apocalypse or Renaissance or Something in Between? Toward a Realistic Appraisal of *The Learning Mystique*," 23 *Journal of Learning Disabilities* 86, 87–88 (1990) (emphasizing a social shift in the 1960s away from "judgmental" analysis—that children were "lazy"—into sociological/medical imagery—that they were "troubled"). But see also Scott Sigmon, *Radical Analysis of Special Education: Focus on Historical Development and Learning Disabilities* 65–82 (1987) (arguing that labeling low-achieving or "difficult" children—particularly children from low-income or minority communities—as learning disabled has served to further marginalize them by identifying them as psychologically

and biologically "defective," and reflects ongoing class struggle).
31. See, e.g., Gerald Erchak and Richard Rosenfeld, "Learning Disabilities, Dyslexia, and the Medicalization of the Classroom," in *Images of Issues: Typifying Contemporary Social Problems* 79–97 (Joel Best ed., 1989). See also, more generally, Philip Elliot, *The Sociology of the Professions* (1972).
32. See, e.g., Martin Kotler, "The Individuals with Disabilities Education Act: A Parent's Perspective and Proposal for Change," 27 *University of Michigan Journal of Law Reform* 331 (1994).
33. See, e.g., David Engel, "Law, Culture, and Children with Disabilities: Educational Rights and the Construction of Difference," 1991 *Duke Law Journal* 166; Joel Handler, *The Conditions of Discretion: Autonomy, Community, Bureaucracy* (1986); Susan Silbey, "Patrick Davis: 'To Bring Out the Best . . . To Undo a Little Pain,'" in *Special Education Mediation* in *When Talk Works: Profiles of Mediators* 61–103 (D. Kolb ed., 1994).
34. Neal and Kirp, "The Allure of Legalization Reconsidered"; William Clune and Mark Van Pelt, "A Political Method of Evaluating the Education for All Handicapped Children Act of 1975 and The Several Gaps of Gap Analysis," 48 *Law and Contemporary Problems* 7 (1985).

2. Technical Controversies

1. PL 101-476 (effective October 1, 1990), 20 U.S.C.A. 1400–1485.
2. 20 U.S.C.A. 1401(a)(15) (Supp. 1996).
3. See 34 C.F.R. 104.35(c), 34 C.F.R. 300.533(a)(1), 34 C.F.R. 300.541 (1995).
4. 34 C.F.R. 300.541(b) (1995).
5. Not all district diagnosticians pay heed to the exclusionary clause instructing special educators to withhold special education services if a student's discrepancy results from socioeconomic disadvantage. See J. Harris, B. Gray, J. Davis, E. Zaremba, and A. Argulewicz, "The Exclusionary Clause and the Disadvantaged: Do We Try to Comply with the Law?" 21 *Journal of Learning Disabilities* 581 (1988) (37.5 percent of surveyed school psychologists purposely ignored the command and of those who formally heeded it, they applied it on average to only 2.3 of 69 potential LD cases per year).
6. In the mid-1980s, a quarter of the states still used an IQ cut-off. See George McNutt, "The Status of Learning Disabilities in the States: Consensus or Controversy," 19 *Journal of Learning Disabilities* 12, 14 (1986).
7. William Frankenberger and Kathryn Fronzaglio, "A Review of States' Criteria and Procedures for Identifying Children with Learning Disabilities," 24 *Journal of Learning Disabilities* 495, 497 (1991).
8. Thomas Cone and Lonny Wilson, "Quantifying a Severe Discrepancy: A Critical Analysis," 4 *Learning Disability Quarterly* 359, 360–362 (1981).
9. Frankenberger and Fronzaglio, "A Review of States' Criteria" at 499.
10. Not all state regulations direct that districts translate achievement test scores into standardized—or scaled—distribution terms, and instead frequently direct districts to measure achievement in grade-equivalent terms. Doing so, of course, makes achievement measurement mathematically in-

tractable, in the sense that it is not clear how much "greater" grade four, month nine, achievement is than grade three, month five, achievement unless the scores are scaled.

11. It is questionable whether *any* cut-off discrepancy score method serves to distinguish pupils in a meaningful way. A traditional argument, associated with Rutter and Yule in support of the view that dyslexia is a discrete syndrome, is that when one graphs the gap between students' reading achievement and IQ, there is a "hump" at the lower end of the curve. See Michael Rutter and William Yule, "The Concept of Specific Reading Retardation," 16 *Journal of Child Psychology and Psychiatry and Allied Disciplines* 181 (1975). The "hump," according to this traditional view, could only be explained by the existence of a separate class of individuals with a discrete disorder or impairment.

But skeptics, most prominently Shaywitz and colleagues, make two important linked counterarguments. See S. Shaywitz, M. Escobar, B. Shaywitz, J. Fletcher, and R. Makuch, "Evidence That Dyslexia May Represent the Lower Tail of a Normal Probability Distribution of Reading Ability," 326 *New England Journal of Medicine* 145 (1992). First, they claim that there is no such hump, that is, that there are as many students with reading achievement scores 1.5 SD above IQ as below, and attribute the "hump" that Rutter and Yule found to a methodological artifact (the reading test that they administered was one that discriminated only among poor readers, thus imposing a ceiling on "high" reading scores that would skew the distribution to produce the appearance of a hump at the lower end). Id. at 148. For similar arguments, see A. van Der Wissel and F. E. Zegers, "Reading Retardation Revisited," 3 *British Journal of Developmental Psychology* 3, 4–6 (1985); D. Share, R. McGee, D. McKenzie, S. Williams, and P. Silva, "Further Evidence Relating to the Distinction between Specific Reading Retardation and General Reading Backwardness," 5 *British Journal of Developmental Psychology* 35, 36–39 (1987). Second, and more interesting, they argue that there are no more students with disparities than one would expect by chance given the correlation levels between intelligence and reading in the general population.

The skeptics' data can be interpreted in two ways, though, and the significance of their empirical findings differs radically depending on which interpretation one adopts. In one view, the true population correlation between IQ and reading achievement test scores is higher than the measured correlation of .68 (it might even be as high as 1), but measured correlation is suppressed because one or both tests are, to some extent, unreliable (or what psychometricians call "attenuated") measures of the things they purport to measure. To the degree that IQ tests measure IQ unreliably and to the degree that reading achievement tests measure reading achievement unreliably as well, the true correlation between the two tests will be suppressed. (An analogy might help. If we tried to correlate SAT scores with college grades and some students' transcripts were so illegible that one could only guess at their grades, the measured correlation between SATs and grades would be suppressed below the true correlation. There would be no reason to expect SATs to correlate with the grades we simply guessed at on the illegible transcript.)

If the observed correlation of .68, properly corrected for attenuation, approximated 1.0, the "dyslexia" we think we observe in an "uncorrected" world is totally artifactual, a simple measurement error. The number of supposed "dyslexics" is simply the number of people with a 1.5 SD score gap that we'd expect, given test unreliability. There would be no reason to believe that there were any pupils whose true reading achievement was significantly below true "intelligence" and, correlatively, no reason to believe there were any barriers to reading other than a lack of "general cognitive ability."

One might interpret their data, however, as they themselves do, in a manner far less undermining of the position that learning disabilities exist as a distinct phenomenon. The true population correlation between IQ and achievement, each of which might be accurately measured, might indeed be .68. "Intelligence" (the "attribute" measured by the IQ test) might be an important, but not the exclusive, determinant of reading ability. (An analogy might help once again. We may measure an athlete's capacity to lift weights quite accurately, and also measure just how far she throws a javelin, but recognize that while weightlifting strength is *a* critical determinant of javelin-throwing success, differences in "technique" matter as well. Similarly, "dyslexics" may lack the equivalent of javelin-throwing technique—in these authors' view, something like "phonological capacity"—but they do so in just the same fashion that unexpectedly good readers—the "hyperlexics" who Shaywitz et al. believe are as common as "dyslexics"—possess "technique.")

In this second view, "dyslexia" does not really disappear as a real disorder. It would simply be the name for the *marked* absence of non-intelligence-related reading capacity. The absence of this capacity is on a continuum, however. Thus dyslexia would resemble diseases (like hypertension, unlike cancer) without a clear bright-line diagnostic border.

12. In 1990–91, seven states demanded a 1.5 SD gap between IQ and achievement scores, four demanded more, and eight demanded less. The variation among states appears to be accounted for in part by decisions about the appropriate cap on the LD population.

13. See Esther Sinclair and Joyce Axelson, "Learning Disability Discrepancy Formulas: Similarities and Differences among Them," 1 *Learning Disabilities Research* 112 (1986).

14. For a confirming study, see S. Epps, J. Ysseldyke, and B. Algozzine, "An Analysis of the Conceptual Framework Underlying Definitions of Learning Disabilities," 23 *Journal of School Psychology* 133 (1985) (noting serious classification distinctions when fourteen different procedures for identifying the LD are applied to a sample of forty-eight school-identified LD children and ninety-six non-LD children).

15. Frankenberger and Fronzaglio, "A Review of States' Criteria" at 499–500.

16. For fuller discussions, see Cecil Reynolds, "Critical Measurement Issues in Learning Disabilities," 18 *Journal of Special Education* 451 (1984–85), and Cone and Wilson, "Quantifying a Severe Discrepancy."

17. One "technical" way to accomplish this task is to call a child's scores discrepant when the difference between the scores is greater than the (relevant number) of standard deviations times the square root of [one minus the correlation between the two tests squared, corrected for the unreliability of the tests]. See Cone and Wilson, "Quantifying a Severe Discrepancy" at 365.

18. See Patricia Bowers, Richard Steffy, and Ellen Tate, "Comparison of the Effects of IQ Control Methods on Memory and Naming Speed Predictors of Reading Disability," 23 *Reading Research Quarterly* 304 (1988); J. Fletcher, K. A. Espy, D. Francis, K. Davidson, B. Rourke, and S. Shaywitz, "Comparisons of Cut-off and Regression-based Definitions of Reading Disabilities," 22 *Journal of Learning Disabilities* 334 (1989).

19. See W. White, M. Smith, and S. Wigle, "An Examination of Variability in Identification of Learning Disabled Students According to Selected Discrepancy Formulas over a Three Year Period," Kansas State University ERIC No. ED257235 11–12 (1984).

20. See, e.g., Michael Thomson, "Assessing the Intelligence of Dyslexic Children," 35 *Bulletin of the British Psychological Society* 94 (1982); Linda Siegel and Roberta Heaven, "Categorization of Learning Disabilities," in *Handbook of Cognitive, Social, and Neuropsychological Aspects of Learning Disabilities* vol. I, 95 (ed. Stephen J. Ceci, 1986).

21. See Gary Hessler, "Educational Issues Surrounding Severe Discrepancy," 3 *Learning Disabilities Research* 43 (1987).

22. See, e.g., Albert Harris and Edward Sipay, *How To Increase Reading Ability* 65–66 (9th ed. 1985).

23. See especially Linda Siegel, "IQ Is Irrelevant to the Definition of Learning Disabilities," 22 *Journal of Learning Disabilities* 469, 471 (1989); Alan Kahmi, "Response to 'Historical Perspective': A Developmental Language Perspective," 25 *Journal of Learning Disabilities* 48, 49 (1992) (emphasizing suppression of IQ by "dyslexic" traits).

24. See Keith Stanovich, "Discrepancy Definitions of Reading Disability: Has Intelligence Led Us Astray?," 26 *Reading Research Quarterly* 7, 21 (1991); Herbert Walberg and Shiow-Ling Tsai, "Matthew Effects in Education," 20 *American Education Research Journal* 359 (1983).

25. See, e.g., Siegel, "IQ Is Irrelevant" at 477.

26. Stanovich, "Discrepancy Definitions" at 19–21.

27. While critics of the "looseness" of LD diagnostic practice have frequently highlighted discrepancies in diagnostic rates across states, they have infrequently noted that there is no less divergence in rates of "hard disability" diagnosis by states, though there is likewise no strong a priori reason to believe population prevalences of physical disabilities vary geographically either. If, though, one sums the percentage of children labeled hearing impaired, orthopedically impaired, visually impaired, and deaf-blind by state

in 1989, the mean is .227, the standard deviation .064; thus the SD is roughly 28 percent of the mean in the case of physical disabilities generally thought to be uncontroversially diagnosed while it is only 22 percent in the case of LD. We discuss variation in diagnostic rates in more detail in Chapter 4: the basic finding, though, is that one can explain variation in LD rates far better than one can explain variations in "hard disability" rates on the basis of social, political, and demographic factors that are not obviously relevant to disease prevalence. See also Gillian Lester and Mark Kelman, "State Disparities in the Identification and Placement of Students with Learning Disabilities," *Journal of Learning Disabilities* (Nov./Dec. 1997).

28. For brief articles reviewing developments in cognitive science and learning disabilities, see Wayne Hresko and D. Kim Reid, "Five Faces of Cognition: Theoretical Influences on Approaches to Learning Disabilities," 4 *Learning Disabilities Quarterly* 238 (1981) and Bernice Y. L. Wong, "On Cognitive Process-Based Instruction: An Introduction," 25 *Journal of Learning Disabilities* 150 (1992).

29. Samuel A. Kirk and Winnifred D. Kirk, *Psycholinguistic Learning Disabilities: Diagnosis and Remediation* (1971); S. Kirk, J. McCarthy, and W. Kirk, *Illinois Test of Psycholinguistic Abilities* (1968). Another important figure in the field was Marianne Frostig. See, e.g., Marianne Frostig and David Horne, *Frostig Program for the Development of Visual Perception: Teacher's Guide* (rev. ed. 1971).

30. Reviews of the history of psychological processing models can be found in Kenneth Kavale and Steven Forness, *The Science of Learning Disabilities* 69–72 (1985); and Bernice Wong, "Problems and Issues in the Definition of Learning Disabilities," in *Psychological and Educational Perspectives on Learning Disabilities* 1, 10–11 (Joseph Torgeson and Bernice Wong eds., 1986).

31. For a review, see Diana Brewster Clark, *Dyslexia: Theory and Practice of Remedial Instruction* 17–39 (1988).

32. B. Shaywitz, J. Fletcher, J. Holahan, and S. Shaywitz, "Discrepancy Compared to Low Achievement Definitions of Reading Disability: Results from the Connecticut Longitudinal Study," 25 *Journal of Learning Disabilities* 639 (1992).

33. Siegel, "IQ Is Irrelevant."

34. Maggie Bruck, "The Word Recognition and Spelling of Dyslexic Children," 23 *Reading Research Quarterly* 51 (1988).

35. R. Olson, B. Wise, E. Conners, and J. Rack, "Organization, Heritability, and Remediation of Component Word Recognition and Language Skills in Disabled Readers," in *Reading and Its Development: Component Skills Approaches* 261, 263–288 (Thomas Carr and Betty Ann Levy eds., 1990).

36. Stanovich, "Discrepancy Score Definitions" at 15.

37. Evidence of widespread interest in the subject was manifest by the early 1990s, with the publication of special issues of major journals devoted to strategies instruction (11 *Remedial and Special Education* 7–53 [1990]; 25 *Journal of Learning Disabilities* 150–177, 211–257 [1992]) as well as article an-

thologies, e.g., *Strategy Assessment and Instruction for Students with Learning Disabilities: From Theory to Practice* (L. J. Meltzer ed., 1993), and treatises, e.g., Bill R. Gearheart and Carol J. Gearheart, *Learning Disabilities: Educational Strategies* 130–138 (5th ed. 1989).

38. Bernice Y. L. Wong, "The Relevance of Metacognition to Learning Disabilities," in *Learning about Learning Disabilities* 231, 233–234 (B. Wong ed., 1991).

39. See, e.g., P. R. Pintrich, E. M. Anderman, and C. Klobucar, "Intraindividual Differences in Motivation and Cognition in Students with and without Learning Disabilities," 27 *Journal of Learning Disabilities* 360 (1994); H. L. Swanson, L. Christie, and R. J. Rubadeau, "The Relationship between Metacognition and Analogical Reasoning in Mentally Retarded, Learning Disabled, Average, and Gifted Children," 8 *Learning Disabilities Research and Practice* 70 (1993); and Wong, "The Relevance of Metacognition" at 235–237, 239–240, 243–246 for a review.

40. J. Kirby and A. Ashman, "Planning Skills and Mathematics Achievement: Implications Regarding Learning Disability," 11 *Learning Disability Quarterly* 211 (1988); Elizabeth Short, "Cognitive, Metacognitive, Motivational, and Affective Differences among Normally Achieving, Learning-Disabled, and Developmentally Handicapped Students: How Much Do They Affect School Achievement?" 21 *Journal of Clinical Child Psychology* 229, 234 (1992); Maureen O'Neill and Virginia Douglas, "Study Strategies and Story Recall in Attention Deficit Disorder and Reading Disability," 19 *Journal of Abnormal Child Psychology* 671 (1991).

41. Swanson, Christie, and Rubadeau, "The Relationship between Metacognition and Analogical Reasoning."

42. Bernice Wong and Roderick Wong, "Study Behavior as a Function of Metacognitive Knowledge about Critical Task Variables: An Investigation of Above Average, Average, and Learning Disabled Readers," 1 *Learning Disabilities Research* 101 (1986).

43. Keith Stanovich, "Cognitive Processes and the Reading Problems of Learning-Disabled Children: Evaluating the Assumption of Specificity," in *Psychological and Educational Perspectives in Learning Disabilities* 87, 112 (J. K. Torgesen and B. Y. L. Wong eds., 1986); Keith Stanovich, "Explaining the Differences between Dyslexic and the Garden-Variety Poor Reader: The Phonological-Core Variable-Difference Model," 21 *Journal of Learning Disabilities* 590, 601 (1988).

44. See Wong, "The Relevance of Metacognition" at 241–242.

45. See, e.g., Michael Pressley, "Can Learning Disabled Children Become Good Information Processors?: How Can We Find Out?" in *Subtypes of Learning Disabilities: Theoretical Perspectives and Research* 137 (L. Feagans, E. Short, and L. Meltzer eds., 1991); Short, "Cognitive, Metacognitive, Motivational, and Affective Differences." Also, Pintrich et al. examined the interaction between cognition, motivation, and metacognition in LD and non-LD children, and found that distinct clusters formed that do not precisely match the LD/non-LD groupings. One cluster, dominated by non-LD children,

contained subjects with high levels of comprehension, metacognition, and motivation; another cluster, dominated by LD children, contained subjects with low comprehension and metacognition but high motivation. A third cluster, though, contained a mixture of LD and non-LD students: subjects with average comprehension, metacognition, and attributional style, but low motivation. P. Pintrich et al., "Intraindividual Differences" at 368.

46. See, generally, E. Dooling, "Cognitive Disorders in Children," 5 *Current Opinions in Pediatrics* 675 (1993); Kenneth Kavale and Steven Forness, *The Science of Learning Disabilities* 62–69 (1985); J. Lerner, *Learning Disabilities: Theories, Diagnosis, and Teaching Strategies* 215–243 (6th ed. 1993); Gerald Wallace and James McLoughlin, *Learning Disabilities: Concepts and Characteristics* 39–57 (1988).

47. For reviews, see Bruce Pennington, "The Genetics of Dyslexia," 31 *Journal of Child Psychology and Psychiatry and Allied Disciplines* 193 (1990); Shelly Smith and Bruce Pennington, "Genetic Influences" in *Handbook of Learning Disabilities* vol. I, 49 (K. Kavale, S. Forness, and M. Bender eds., 1987); J. Stevenson, "Genetics" in *Learning Disabilities: Nature, Theory, and Treatment* 327 (N. Thingh and I. Beale eds., 1992).

48. See, generally, Robert Johnson, "Neurological Assessment" in *Handbook of Learning Disabilities* vol. I, 303 (K. Kavale, S. Forness, and M. Bender eds., 1987).

49. J. M. Fletcher, D. Francis, B. Rourke, S. Shaywitz, and B. Shaywitz, "The Validity of Discrepancy-Based Definitions of Reading Disabilities," 25 *Journal of Learning Disabilities* 555 (1992).

50. For reviews of the literature, see vol. 682, *Annals of the New York Academy of Sciences* (1993) (special issue on neurological basis of dyslexia); K. Anderson, C. Brown, and P. Tallal, "Developmental Language Disorders: Evidence for a Basic Processing Deficit," 6 *Current Opinion in Neurology and Neurosurgery* 98 (1993); D. Lynn Flowers, "Brain Basis for Dyslexia: A Summary of Work in Progress," 26 *Journal of Learning Disabilities* 575 (1993); A. Galaburda, "Neurology of Developmental Dyslexia," 5 *Current Opinion in Neurology and Neurosurgery* 71 (1992).

51. While federal law formally excludes from the category of learning disabilities any learning problems caused by "environmental" disadvantage, it is almost surely the case that Congress intended to exclude "discrepant" students whose *educational* environment was unfavorable, not ones whose physical environment *caused* entrenched physical changes in functioning.

52. J. Ysseldyke, B. Algozzine, and S. Epps, "A Logical and Empirical Analysis of Current Practices in Classifying Students as Handicapped," 50 *Exceptional Children* 160 (1983).

53. L. Shepard, M. Smith, and C. Vojir, "Characteristics of Pupils Identified as Learning Disabled," 20 *American Educational Research Journal* 309, 328 (1983).

54. Bob Algozzine and James Ysseldyke, "Special Education Services for Normal Children: Better Safe than Sorry?" 48 *Exceptional Children* 238, 241 (1981). A small sample study by Ross, in 1990, reaches similar conclusions.

Twenty-six school psychologists were sent profiles of two students who did not in fact have significant test-score disparities, though the psychologists would have to manipulate the raw data themselves to determine the significance of the disparities. The correct answer—that the disparities were "not significantly different"—was chosen by only 11.5 percent of the respondents. Roslyn Ross, "Consistency among School Psychologists in Evaluating Discrepancy Scores: A Preliminary Study," 13 *Learning Disability Quarterly* 209 (1990).

55. E. Scott Heubner, "The Effects of Type of Referral Information and Test Data on Psychoeducational Decisions," 16 *School Psychology Review* 382 (1987); E. Scott Heubner, "Errors in Decision-Making: A Comparison of School Psychologists' Interpretations of Grade Equivalents, Percentiles, and Deviation IQs," 18 *School Psychology Review* 51 (1989); E. Scott Heubner and Jack Cummings, "The Impact of Sociocultural Background and Assessment Data upon School Psychologists' Decisions," 23 *Journal of School Psychology* 157 (1985); Jack Cummings, E. Scott Huebner, and James McLeskey, "Psychoeducational Decision-Making: Reason for Referral vs. Test Data," 1 *Professional School Psychology* 249 (1986).

56. Under certain plausible views of how we ought to allocate educational resources that we detail in Chapter 6, we ought to allocate resources so that the return to incremental resources is maximized. Under that view, the justification for placing LD pupils' claims to incremental resources ahead of other pupils' claims is that they will benefit far more dramatically from resource infusions.

57. Those who argue that learning disabled students are uniquely educable will surely criticize studies showing that interventions are ineffectual by pointing out that some of the pupils studied who fail to show progress are surely mislabeled as having learning disabilities. But to do more than sound a note of caution, they would have to argue that the genuinely LD subset in the group did *better* than the non-LD subgroup, rather than that the groups were nondifferentiable (because no one made much progress) or that the non-LD pupils actually did better. Moreover, if we are assessing, as we do in Chapter 6, the justification for federal law demanding that districts spend more on pupils identified as having learning disabilities, it is simply not helpful to note that they could get more educational bang for the buck if they would spend incremental resources on some "genuine" LD class that they do not in fact locate.

58. See, e.g., Thomas Scruggs, "Commentary: Foundations of Intervention Research" in *Intervention Research in Learning Disabilities* 66, 73 (T. Scruggs and B. Wong eds., 1990).

59. The view that LDs are socially constructed does not reject a biologistic etiology of the disability. One need not reject material realism to focus on social construction. Thus in the conception we find most congenial, dyslexia would be "socially constructed" even if it turned out that all dyslexic children had a genetically encoded brain anomaly, because the social meaning of the physical syndrome would be significant unto itself.

Those with relevant political power—members of Congress, special education bureaucrats, teachers, parents, and others—have created a category of people who can best be defined not in terms of their ineluctable physical condition, but as those people for whom political actors believe they can make a particularly compelling case for entitlement to special benefits. "Left" social constructionists are prone to believe that "disabilities" are constructed wholly by the socially empowered able-bodied. In this view, the able-bodied create social environments in which those with *different* skills, the *"dis*abled," have difficulties functioning in a personally satisfactory fashion. Dyslexia is socially constructed in the sense that a certain group of people is rendered unable to read in school, given particular educational practices, or unable to function adequately in the workplace, given undue reliance on conventional literacy. Dyslexia in this view is a function of the social power of those who learn to read differently than dyslexics.

There is nothing inherent in "social constructionism," though, that necessitates this "left" world view (in which disadvantage is needlessly constructed from difference by the socially dominant). A right-wing theorist seeking to expose "rent-seeking" in our society, rather than needless inequality, might just as readily tell a social constructionist story. Out of the world of bad readers, a group of entitlement-mongers, seeking an undue proportion of the school budget, aware of the relatively high level of sympathy for "disability" compared with "intellectual inability," constructs an account of their reading deficits that best bolsters their claims to fiscal largesse. Dyslexia is indeed just another learning style, just as the left social constructionists note. It is constructed as a disability, rather than just another cognitive style teachers must deal with, not by the "mainstream" nondisabled population but by resource-seeking parents of dyslexics.

3. The Federal Regulatory Framework

1. 29 U.S.C. 794 (1995). Accompanying regulations were finalized in 1980. 34 C.F.R. 104 (1995).
2. PL 101-476 (effective October 1, 1990), 20 U.S.C.A. 1400–1485 (1995). IDEA made only modest substantive revisions in the 1975 Education of All Handicapped Children Act.
3. Unlike §504, IDEA covers only persons aged three to twenty-one, in public preschool, elementary, secondary, or adult public education, who need special education or related services.
4. 29 U.S.C. 706(8)(B) (1995).
5. 34 C.F.R. 104.3(j)(2)(i)(B) (1995).
6. See, e.g., Sanders v. Marquette Public Schools, 561 F. Supp. 1361, 1368 (W.D. Mich. 1983) ("Louise is evidently a member of the class that Congress intended to reach by means of the Rehabilitation Act; she has been determined to have learning disabilities, such that she may be considered 'handicapped' within the meaning of the Act"). The Office of Civil

Rights (OCR), the administrative body charged with overseeing compliance with Section 504, had once recognized the possibility that an LD student might *not* be covered by the Act, at least as long as she succeeded in regular education. (The OCR's position, apparently, was that a student with a "C" average succeeded in regular education.) In Sch. Dist. of the City of Saginaw, 352 EHLR 412 (1987), the OCR followed this policy by upholding a district's decision to withhold services from an LD student with a 3.5 GPA.

7. See, e.g., Hessler v. State Bd. of Educ. of Maryland, 700 F.2d 134, 135 (4th Cir. 1983) and David H. v. Spring Branch Independent Sch. Dist., 569 F. Supp. 1324, 1326 (S.D. Texas 1983).

8. 761 F. Supp. 838, 852 (D. Mass. 1988).

9. For instance, until specific congressional legislation excluded them, students who abused drugs or alcohol were deemed to be protected under §504. Even today, students with Attention Deficit Disorder (ADD) (also known as Attention Deficit Hyperactivity Disorder, or ADHD) appear to have clearer claims to protection under the Rehabilitation Act than they have under IDEA. Students with ADD may be covered under IDEA (as "other health impaired," severely emotionally disturbed, or LD), but many districts have resisted characterizing them as such. The Office of Civil Rights appears considerably more willing to identify children with ADD as disabled, so many parents of children believed to suffer from ADD initiate §504 proceedings: in 1992–93, roughly half of the complaints to the Department of Education's Office of Civil Rights in California were efforts by parents of ADD children to force districts to accommodate their child in some fashion.

10. S. Rep. No. 890, 95th Cong. 2d Sess. 39 (1978).

11. 34 C.F.R. 104.1 (1995).

12. This latter conception is embodied in the Americans with Disabilities Act, which largely supplants the Rehabilitation Act on issues of employment and public accommodations though not education.

13. See 34 C.F.R. 104, Appendix A, analysis of Subpart D (1995).

14. See 20 U.S.C. 1401 (20) (1995); 34 C.F.R. 300.340–300.350 (1995).

15. See, e.g., B.G. by F.G. v. Cranford Bd. of Educ., 702 F. Supp. 1140 (D.N.J. 1988), supplemented 702 F. Supp. 1158, aff'd 882 F.2d 510 (1988).

16. See, e.g., McNair v. Cardimone, 676 F. Supp. 1361 (S.D. Ohio, 1987), aff'd sub nom. McNair v. Oak Hills Local Sch. Dist., 872 F.2d 153 (6th Cir. 1989).

17. Disabled students should be educated with persons who are not disabled "to the maximum extent appropriate to the needs of the handicapped person." 34 C.F.R. 104.34(a) (1995).

18. 34 C.F.R. 300.550 (1995). See also B. P. Tucker and B. A. Goldstein, *Legal Rights of Persons with Disabilities: An Analysis of Federal Law* 13:8 (1991).

19. 20 U.S.C. 1412(5)(B); 1414(a)(1)(C)(iv) (1995); 34 C.F.R. 300.550–556 (1995).

20. 34 C.F.R. 104.35, 300.530 (1995). See also *David H.,* 569 F. Supp. 1324 at 1336.

21. 34 C.F.R. 104.36 (1995).

22. 20 U.S.C. 1415 (1995); 34 C.F.R. 300.500–514 (1995).

23. 20 U.S.C. 1415(b)(1)(A) (1995); 34 C.F.R. 300.502–503 (1995).

24. 20 U.S.C. 1415(b)(1)(C), 1415(b)(1)(D) (1995); 34 C.F.R. 300.504–505 (1995).

25. 20 U.S.C. 1415(b)(2) (1995); 34 C.F.R. 506–507 (1995).

26. 20 U.S.C. 1415(d) (1995); 34 C.F.R. 300.508 (1995).

27. 20 U.S.C. 1415(c), 1415(e)(1), 1415(e)(2) (1995); 34 C.F.R. 300.509–511 (1995).

28. 20 U.S.C. 1415(e)(3)(A) (1995); 34 C.F.R. 300.513 (1995).

29. 20 U.S.C. 1415(e)(4)(B) (1995); 34 C.F.R. 515 (1995).

30. 20 U.S.C. 1411 (a)(5)(A) (1995). States are provided funds according to the following formula. The maximum each state receives in federal funds is equal to: "[The number of handicapped children aged 3–5 who are receiving special education and related services (if the state has appropriate preschool programming in place) plus the number of children aged 6–21 receiving special education and related services] multiplied by 40 percent of the national average per pupil special education spending in public elementary and secondary schools for the previous fiscal year." 20 U.S.C. 1411(a)(1)(A), 1411(a)(1)(B). The number of pupils is measured as of December 1 of the preceding fiscal year; average per pupil spending includes local and state spending on both services and administration. If Congress fails to appropriate sufficient funds to cover the results of this calculation, the grant to each state is reduced accordingly. 20 U.S.C. 1411 (g)(1). Concerns that federal contributions were too frequently directed to administrative support, rather than classroom instruction, led to some 1997 reforms of IDEA. For an account of the reforms, prior to their finalization, see "House Passes Bill for Disabled that Adds Education Resource," *New York Times,* May 14, 1997, A1.

31. The Congress that drafted the revenue-sharing plan clearly did worry that states might be tempted to overclassify "ordinary" students as mildly disabled (particularly LD) to gain more federal funds while obliging themselves only to provide "cheap" services, a worry that might have been more reasonable if Congress had ultimately appropriated funds to cover a higher proportion of special education costs. Thus the initial proposed statute forbade districts from counting more than one-sixth of handicapped children as LD. Moreover, if more than 2 percent of the school population were called LD, states would gain no more funds than if only 2 percent of the pupils had been so labeled. However, this proposed revenue limitation was struck out the day the actual revenue-sharing regulations became effective.

32. See, e.g., Yaris v. Special Sch. Dist. of St. Louis Cty., 558 F. Supp. 545, 559 (E.D. Mo.) (1983), aff'd 728 F.2d 1055 (8th Cir. 1984).

33. A local educational agency receives funds bearing the same ratio to the total federal allocation that the number of eligible children aged three to twenty-one receiving special education in that LEA or intermediate unit bears to the number of children receiving special education statewide. 20 U.S.C. 1411(d) (1995).

34. Hearings on the reauthorization of IDEA in 1994 highlighted a controversy in the state funding formulas: many states (e.g., New York) provide more funds for pulled-out students than for students included in mainstream

classes, even when the aides needed to mainstream pupils are as expensive as pull-out classes. Proponents of increasing inclusion levels rightly charge that there ought not to be purely fiscal incentives to pull children out.

35. 20 U.S.C. 1413(a)(10) (1995).

36. One must recognize, as well, that local educational agencies receive not just federal funds but earmarked *state* funds designed to finance some portion of special education expenditures. In 1986–87, states reported that they had spent $9.8 billion on special education and related services while the LEAs had expended $6.3 billion. But the state/local mix varies radically by jurisdiction; in California, for instance, the state contributed nearly five times as much as the localities (though by 1990–91, localities were funding more than a quarter of total special education spending, *including* the federal contribution); meanwhile, in neighboring Oregon, the localities expended more than four times the state contribution. (See *Thirteenth Annual Report to Congress on the Implementation of the Individuals with Disabilities Education Act*, A-209 [1991], and J. Beales, *Special Education: Expenditures and Obligations*, p. 12 [1993].)

37. 20 U.S.C. 2701(a)(2)(A) (1995).

38. 20 U.S.C. 2701(a)(1) and 2701(a)(1)(2) (1988).

39. General Accounting Office, *Congressional Action Needed to Improve Chapter One Handicapped Program* 20–21 (1989).

40. Id. at 27.

41. An additional $140 million was appropriated though Chapter One grants to State Operated Programs for those with disabilities; an additional $320 million was appropriated through grants to preschool programs for those with disabilities; and $170 million was granted through the Part H programs for very young preschoolers. See *Fifteenth Annual Report to Congress on the Implementation of the Individuals with Disabilities Education Act*, A-240 (1993).

42. *Fifteenth Annual Report*, A-240 (1993).

43. State and local governments reported spending $16 billion in 1986–87 on the roughly 4.4 million three- to twenty-one-year-old pupils receiving special education at that time, above and beyond the costs of regular education for that number of children. See *Thirteenth Annual Report*, p. A-210. We "inflate" the $16 billion figure to $26.8 billion to account for both the changes in the special education population, which grew from 4.42 million in 1986–87 to 4.99 million in 1991–92 (*Fifteenth Annual Report*, p. 3, Table 1.1), a change of 12.9 percent, and the general 48.3 percent inflation in non–special education elementary and secondary educational expenditures per pupil during the period. The growth in general education spending was from $145 billion spent on 35.3 million students, approximately $4,100 per pupil, to $225 billion spent on 37 million students (approximately $6,080 per pupil). See *Digest of Educational Statistics*, Table 34 (1993), for total educational expenditures, from which we subtracted special education spending. This estimate of cost/pupil growth is undoubtedly conservative, since special education cost/pupil growth appears more rapid

than general education cost/pupil growth: in Los Angeles, for instance, between 1981–82 and 1991–92, per pupil instructional expenditures rose 47 percent for special education students compared with 24 percent for general education pupils. See Beales, *Special Education: Expenditures and Obligations* 15.

44. *Fifteenth Annual Report*, p. 5.

45. The study we used is D. Lewis, R. Bruininks, and M. Thurlow, "Cost Analysis for District-Level Special Education Planning, Budgeting, and Administrating," 14 *Journal of Education Finance* 466 (1989). The study both measures incremental costs in a sensible way, looking carefully at the use of personnel, equipment, and facilities, and examines the use of these resources by different classes of disabled students.

46. Here is the procedure we followed: LD incremental costs are deemed to be the base or 1, and other costs are listed in relationship to LD costs. The ratio of LD incremental costs to non-LD incremental costs is therefore the ratio of the LD costs/pupil (1) multiplied by the proportion of disabled students classified as LD (.5) to the sum of the costs/pupil of all the other disability categories multiplied by the costs/pupil for these other categories. Speech-impaired students make up 22.2 percent of the population, and costs/pupil are 0.6 (60 percent of the costs of the LD); mentally retarded pupils make up 12.3 percent of the disabled population, and costs/pupil are 2.0 (200 percent of the costs of the LD); seriously emotionally disturbed children are 8.9 percent of the disabled population, and costs are 5.9; it is more difficult to sum up the costs of the other 6.5 percent, but it would appear using a ratio of 2.5 would be a good approximation. Thus the ratio of LD costs to non-LD costs is 0.5 to 1.07; LD costs thus make up 0.5/1.57 of the $28 billion incremental expenditures. Given the "roughness" of all these procedures, it would probably be appropriate to estimate that incremental costs for the LD are between $9 and $10 billion.

47. A number of reasons for the initial decision to resist implementation are discussed in S. Stils and P. Wirth, "Public Law 94-142 and New Mexico: Historical Context and Perceived Impact on SH Programming in Rural Districts," paper presented at the annual conference of the Association of Persons with Severe Handicaps (Chicago, November 9, 1984) at 10–11.

48. 495 F. Supp. 391 (D. New Mexico, 1980).

49. 678 F.2d 847 (10th Cir. 1982).

50. 34 C.F.R. 104.35; 34 C.F.R. 300.530 (1995).

51. 34 C.F.R. 104.35(c); 34 C.F.R. 300.533(a)(1) (1995).

52. 34 C.F.R. 300.541 (1995).

53. 34 C.F.R. 300.541(b)(1995).

54. 20 U.S.C. 1412(5)(C) (1995).

55. 34 C.F.R. 104.35 (1995).

56. 34 C.F.R. 300.540(a) (1995).

57. 34 C.F.R. 300.542 (1995).

58. See 34 C.F.R. 104.35(b)(2) (1995), interpreting §504, and 34 C.F.R. 300.532(a) (1995), interpreting IDEA.

59. 34 C.F.R. 104.35(b)(3) (1995).
60. 34 C.F.R. §300.7(b)(54) (1995).
61. Furthermore, to the extent that African-Americans are disproportionately represented in the class of pupils that is "socially disadvantaged," the underdiagnosis problem will be exacerbated because the statute, strictly construed, forbids districts from diagnosing a student as LD whose discrepancy between achievement and potential can be attributed to social disadvantage.
62. 793 F.2d 969 (9th Cir. 1984).
63. At times, minority children (and their parents) do not challenge the diagnostic tests or procedures, but assert instead that any system that groups pupils by ability (even conceding, arguendo, perhaps, that "ability" is accurately measured by the test) impermissibly racially segregates if it results in disparate placements of African-American students in certain classes. This view is buttressed by the decision in Castaneda v. Pickard, 648 F.2d 989 (5th Cir. 1981) ("ability grouping" is unconstitutional in those districts that have not yet attained "unitary status," i.e., satisfied past court desegregation orders so that the court determines that it has "eliminated the vestiges of prior segregation"). It is undermined, though, by cases such as Georgia State Conference of Branches of NAACP v. Georgia, 775 F.2d 1403 (11th Cir. 1985) (a district that has not achieved unitary status can nonetheless use ability grouping so long as it demonstrates either that black ability isn't currently suppressed as a result of the effects of the prior educational deprivations inherent in the segregated system or that ability grouping will better remedy current ability disparities than a non–ability grouped system.)
64. Similarly, in 1979, the Pennsylvania state court ruled, in Levy v. Commonwealth Dep't. of Educ., 399 A.2d 159 (Pa. 1979), that local districts could not use the IQ test, standing alone, to determine that a child is mentally retarded.

    In contrast, in PASE v. Hannon, 506 F. Supp. 831 (N.D. Il. 1980), the court, after examining each item on the standardized intelligence tests given to minority children, held that while a few of the items were indeed culturally biased, too few of the items were culturally biased to have caused learning disabled plaintiffs to be misdiagnosed as mentally retarded. The court reasoned that IDEA's predecessor statute "does not require that any [single] procedure, standing alone, be affirmatively shown to be free of bias," but only that the diagnostic process, looked at as a whole, did not misdiagnose minority pupils. Id. at 878. The court simultaneously rejected the plaintiffs' claim that the diagnostic decisions were made primarily on the basis of IQ scores because of the "hypnotic effect" of the scores on the evaluation team's determinations, noting that low IQ scores did not always lead to EMR placement, and that the fact that the two were correlated was to be expected since one should "expect [a mentally retarded child] to have difficulty with an I.Q. test." Id. at 880.
65. Crawford v. Honig, 37 F.3d 485, 488 (9th Cir. 1995).
66. There are some significant patterns in the handful of cases, though. In U.S.

v. Yonkers Bd. of Educ., 635 F. Supp. 1538 (S.D.N.Y. 1986) the court held that if a limited English proficiency student scores below the statewide reference point on the English language proficiency test and is referred to the school's committee on the handicapped for possible special education, the student must be assessed for language dominance to determine what language should be used when further assessment tools are employed. Id. at 1549. The court further held that the child must be assessed by diagnosticians proficient in the child's native language, and, if unavailable, then a translator must be provided; that nonverbal assessment instruments be used as well as verbal ones; and that a native language representative must assist the parent and student in all aspects of evaluation, diagnosis, and due process procedures. Id. at 1549–1550.

Letters of finding (LOFs) from the Office of Civil Rights are also directed at minimizing overinclusion of limited English proficiency students in special education classes. For a summary of these LOFs, see Perry Zirkel, "SPED/LEP: Special Education for Limited English Proficiency Students," 69 *Education Law Reporter* 181 (1991). See also 34 C.F.R. §300.505(b)(2) (1995).

67. See 557 F. Supp. 1230 (E.D.N.Y. 1983). The remedial opinion ordered that parents be informed not just of their rights to protest unwanted special education placements, but of their rights to seek such placements; ordered the establishment of an outreach office about the special education programs; forced the district to open bilingual resource rooms and to report on their services for bilingual special ed students.

68. 458 U.S. 176 (1982).

69. Id. at 188–89 (emphasis added).

70. Id. at 192.

71. For discussions of current law, see, for instance, Leslie Collins and Perry Zirkel, "To What Extent, If Any, May Cost Be a Factor in Special Education Cases?" 71 *Education Law Reporter* 11 (1992).

72. "[T]o require . . . the furnishing of every special service necessary to maximize each handicapped child's potential is, we think, further than Congress intended to go." *Rowley* at 199.

73. 930 F.2d 942, 948 (1st Cir. 1991). See also Lewis v. Sch. Bd. of Loudon Cty., 808 F. Supp. 523, 526–527 (E.D. Va. 1992) (rejecting as inconsistent with *Rowley*'s rejection of a potential-maximizing standard those methods which determine a child's placement by comparing two or more proposed programs and picking the best one); Knight v. District of Columbia, 877 F.2d 1025, 1030 (D.C. Cir. 1989) (same).

74. Clevenger v. Oak Ridge Sch. Bd., 744 F.2d 514, 517 (6th Cir. 1984) (". . . cost considerations are . . . relevant when choosing between several options, all of which offer an 'appropriate' education"); *Hessler*, 700 F.2d 134; Bales v. Clark, 523 F. Supp. 1366 (E.D. Va. 1981). Federal courts will not, however, order a school district to implement a cost-savings plan. See In re Smith, 926 F. 2d 1027 (11th Cir. 1991) (reversing on mandamus a district court judge's order that a school district provide the least expensive adequate alternative IEP to a pupil with a disability).

75. See Fisher v. District of Columbia, 828 F. Supp. 87, 89 n. 7 (D.D.C. 1993) ("In fact, the IDEA recognizes that a school district can initiate a change of placement when it believes that a child's placement is inappropriate . . . Cost considerations are a permissible reason for a school district to seek such a change"). See also Abrahamson v. Hershman, 701 F.2d 223, 228 (1st. Cir. 1983) (allowing district to place child in a cheaper community group home, rather than a residential school, if the group home would meet the child's need for a structured environment and thus provide comparable educational benefits).

76. Swift v. Rapides Parish Public Sch. Sys., 812 F. Supp. 666, 669–672 (W.D. La. 1993). See also Age v. Bullitt Cty. Public Sch., 673 F.2d 141, 143 n. 5 (6th Cir. 1982) (affirming the district court opinion which noted but refused to resolve "dispute among the experts").

77. See, e.g., N.H. Rev. Stat. Ann. §186-C:16-b II and VI (1995) (providing that any action to recover costs of a unilateral special education placement must be commenced within 90 days of the placement, and that where no reasonable opportunity has been given to the school district to develop an IEP, reimbursement may not be sought for any costs incurred until the school district is given such an opportunity). See also Vt. Stat. Ann, tit. 16, §2957(b) and §2957(e) (1994) (same). Similarly, Vt. Stat. Ann. Tit. 16, §§2958(a)–(e) (1994) requires schools to notify the state residential placement review team when residential placement is being considered, so that the state team may then "advise school districts on alternatives to residential placement" and "assist [them] in locating cost effective . . . residential facilities where necessary." Naturally, this may be motivated by a substantive desire to mainstream more pupils as well as a desire to avoid more expensive placements, but the fiscal motivation appears clearer in the New Hampshire regulations, which require state review of any residential placement for which the total cost of placement exceeds ten times the estimated state average expenditure per pupil. See N.H. Rev. Stat. Ann. §§186-C:7 IV (1995).

78. *Rowley* at 198. This point is echoed in Oberti v. Board of Educ. of Clementon Sch. Dist. (Oberti II) in which the court notes: "We emphasize that the Act does *not* require states to offer *the same* educational experience to a child with disabilities as is generally provided for nondisabled children." 995 F.2d 1204, 1217 (3d Cir. 1993).

79. As we discuss at length in Chapter 6, one can readily argue that students get the same opportunity under quite conflicting circumstances. For instance, some would argue students receive the same opportunity if given the same resources by the state directly, or by the state *and* their home combined; others would argue they don't get the same opportunity unless outcomes are equal; still others would argue that they get the same opportunity only if the marginal resources devoted to each child yield equivalent improvements in academic performance.

80. *Rowley* at 201–202 n. 23.

81. See, e.g., San Antonio Independent Sch. Dist. v. Rodriguez, 411 U.S. 1 (1973); McInnis v. Shapiro, 293 F. Supp. 327 (N.D. Ill. 1968), aff'd. sub nom.;

McInnis v. Ogilvie, 394 U.S. 322 (1969).

82. *Rowley* at 199–200.

83. Id. at 193, n. 15, quoting the following passage from Mills v. Bd. of Educ. of District of Columbia, 348 F. Supp. 866, 876 (D.D.C. 1972): "If sufficient funds are not available to finance all of the services and programs that are needed and desirable in the system then the available funds must be expended equitably in such a manner that no child is entirely excluded from a publicly supported education consistent with his needs and ability to benefit therefrom. The inadequacies of [the school system] certainly cannot be permitted to bear more heavily on the 'exceptional' or handicapped child than on the normal child."

84. *Rowley* at 204.

85. See, e.g., Straube v. Florida Union Free Sch. Dist., 801 F. Supp. 1164, 1177 (S.D.N.Y. 1992). See also JSK v. Hendry Cty. Sch. Bd., 941 F.2d 1563, 1572 (11th Cir. 1991) (students must benefit more than "a trifle," but noted that "we disagree [that the child must receive a 'meaningful' educational benefit] to the extent that 'meaningful' means anything more than 'some' or 'adequate' educational benefit").

86. See Phipps v. New Hanover Cty. Bd. of Educ., 551 F. Supp. 732, 734–735 (E.D.N.C. 1982); Garrity v. Gallen, 522 F. Supp. 171, 240 (D.N.H. 1981); *Yaris*, 558 F. Supp. 545 at 556–567.

87. See Fuhrmann v. East Hanover Bd. of Educ., 993 F.2d 1031, 1039 (3d Cir. 1993).

88. See *Fuhrmann* at 1040 ("The measure and adequacy of an IEP can only be determined as of the time it is offered to the student . . . Neither the statute nor reason countenance 'Monday Morning Quarterbacking' in evaluating the appropriateness of a child's placement"); Roland M. v. Concord Sch. Committee, 910 F.2d 983, 992 (1st Cir. 1990).

89. See In re Conklin, 946 F.2d 306, 315–316 (4th Cir. 1991).

90. It is important to recognize that individual students seeking *very* expensive services—usually more severely disabled students—may find it difficult to win their claims. At the same time, one must still recognize that services which are not markedly expensive *per individual,* but which may eat up a high share of a district's budget, may well be mandated by statute. In a sense, one may be blinded to the degree to which students with learning disabilities *as a class* make essentially cost-unqualified claims by the fact that students making even more expensive individual demands may, in the context of litigation, fail to prevail in that litigation.

91. Crawford v. Pittman, 708 F.2d 1028, 1035 (5th Cir. 1983) (after noting evidence that some disabled children regress so much during the traditional summer vacation that "their overall progress for the year [is brought] to a virtual standstill," the court held that "rigid rules like the 180-day limitation violate not only the Act's procedural command that each child receive individual consideration but also its substantive requirements that each child receive some benefit"). See also *Yaris*, 558 F. Supp. at 545, 559; Battle v. Commonwealth of Pennsylvania, 629 F.2d 269, 280 (3d Cir. 1980).

92. *Fisher*, 828 F. Supp. at 90.

93. See *Straube*, 801 F. Supp. at 1178–1179.

94. See Florence Cty. Sch. Dist. Four v. Carter, 510 U.S. 7 (1993).

95. Mich. Stat. Ann. §15.41751 (1995).

96. 674 F. Supp. 1296 (W.D. Mich. 1987).

97. Id. at 1305.

98. Ann. Laws of Mass. Gen. L. Ch. 71B, §2 (1995).

99. Roland M. v. Concord Sch. Comm., 910 F.2d 983, at 992 (1st Cir. 1990). See also Geis v. Bd. of Educ. of Parsippany-Troy Hills 774 F.2d 575, 583 (3d Cir. 1985) (court interprets pre–1989 New Jersey statute, since revised, demanding that districts provide disabled children with education "according to how the pupil can best achieve success in learning" to demand not that the district ensure the "best" education but only "what is feasible or reasonably cost-effective").

100. See, e.g., Barnett v. Fairfax Cty. Sch. Bd., 927 F.2d 146 (4th Cir. 1991) (court upholds a local district's refusal to ensure that the school closest to a deaf child could instruct the child with "cued speech," one of the three distinct types of programs for teaching the hearing impaired available in the district, reasoning that even if the child would improve his performance going to the closest school, the district was not obliged to maximize the student's performance). For similar holdings, see Dep't. of Educ., State of Hawaii v. Katherine D., 727 F.2d 809, 813 (9th Cir. 1983); Doe v. Anrig, 692 F.2d 800, 806–807 (1st Cir. 1982).

101. 950 F.2d 688 (11th Cir. 1991).

102. Id. at 697 (emphasis added).

103. See Bd. of Educ., Sacramento City Unified Sch. Dist. v. Holland, 786 F. Supp. 874 (E.D.CA. 1992), aff'd. sub. nom. Sacramento City Unified Sch. Dist. Bd. of Educ. v. Rachel H., 14 F.3d 1298 (9th Cir. 1994), cert. den. 512 U.S. 1207 (1994). It is difficult to imagine how *any* program for the plaintiff herself would really interfere with general educational programs in a city the size of Sacramento, even the one costing $109,000 per year that the district rather unconvincingly claims this pupil's mainstreamed program would cost. But the court does *not* ask whether the cost of placing all children requiring the sorts of aides the plaintiff requires in regular classroom will affect other children in the district. Quite to the contrary, the District Court goes out of its way to note that the district should not count the $80,000 costs of required sensitivity training for all the teachers in the plaintiff's school since the training would benefit other handicapped children as well. Id. at 883.

104. See, e.g., Roncker on Behalf of Roncker v. Walter, 700 F.2d 1058, 1063 (6th Cir. 1983); *Age,* 673 F.2d 141 at 145.

105. 874 F.2d 1036 (5th Cir. 1989).

106. Id. at 1049.

107. Id. at 1033.

108. Id. at 1051.

109. Despite the fact that the record in the case shows no evidence that there

were other disabled children in the plaintiff's prekindergarten class, the court, doubtless fearing that it will appear insensitive to the disabled, notes at one point: "If a regular instructor must devote all of her time to one handicapped child . . . she will be focusing her attention on one child to the detriment of her entire class, including, perhaps, other, equally deserving, handicapped children who also may require extra attention." Id. at 1048–1049.

110. 34 C.F.R. 300.552, Comment (emphasis added).

111. Thus, in Greer v. City of Rome City Sch. Dist., 950 F.2d 688, 697 (11th Cir. 1991), the court emphasizes how skeptical it is that a teacher will be unduly distracted at least so long as a district is mindful of "its obligation to consider supplemental aids and services that could accommodate a handicapped child's need for additional attention."

112. 995 F.2d 1204 (3d Cir. 1993).

113. It is also an empirical question, though the courts do not ordinarily acknowledge it as such, whether "exposing" nondisabled students to disruptive disabled students increases what the New Jersey District Court judge in Bonadonna v. Cooperman, 619 F. Supp. 401, 418 (D.N.J. 1980) called "compassion, understanding, and patience" for those who are "different and less fortunate."

114. Compare, e.g., Ariella Lehrer, "The Effects of Mainstreaming on Stereotypic Conceptions of the Handicapped," 77 *Journal of Educational Research* 94 (1983) (mainstreaming resulted in nondisabled children reacting less stereotypically to a story about a disabled child), and J. York, T. Vandercook, C. MacDonald, C. Heise-Neff, and E. Caughey, "Feedback about Integrating Middle-School Students with Severe Disabilities in General Education Classes," 58 *Exceptional Children* 244, 256 (1992) (only 5.52 percent of 181 surveyed nondisabled children believed that general integration of moderately to profoundly mentally retarded children was not a good idea) with Amatzia Weisel, "Contact with Mainstreamed Disabled Children and Attitudes towards Disability: A Multidimensional Analysis," 8 *Educational Psychology* 161 (1988) (presence of disabled students in mainstream classroom does not cause intensive emotional reaction in nondisabled students, and may be associated with more negative attitudes toward disabled students).

115. I. Hollowood, C. Salisbury, B. Rainforth, and M. Palombro, "Use of Instructional Time in Classrooms Serving Students with and without Severe Disabilities," 61 *Exceptional Children* 242 (1994) (presence in the classroom of a child with a severe disability has no significant effect on the level of task engagement of students without disabilities, and loss of instructional time was typically attributable to factors other than the presence of the disabled children); S. Odom, M. Deklyen, and J. Jenkins, "Integrating Handicapped and Nonhandicapped Preschoolers: Developmental Impact on Nonhandicapped Children," 51 *Exceptional Children* 41 (1984) (integration of handicapped children with various types of disability had no significant effect on nondisabled preschoolers' performance on developmental scales).

116. 484 U.S. 305 (1988).
117. Id. at 328–329.
118. Id. at 328.
119. For a fuller discussion of discipline law, see Gail Sorenson, "Update on Legal Issues in Special Education Discipline," 81 *Education Law Reporter* 399 (1993); Eric Hartwig and Gary Ruesch, *Discipline in the School* 153–165, 202–227, 412–417 (1994).
120. Compare S-1 v. Turlington, 635 F.2d 342, 348 (5th Cir. 1981) (mandating continued educational services to an expelled or long-term suspended student) and Kaelin v. Grubbs, 682 F.2d 595, 602 (6th Cir. 1982) (same) with Doe by Gonzales v. Maher, 793 F.2d 1470, 1482 (9th Cir. 1986) (child can be denied educational services if he is properly expelled, because the child's misbehavior is properly determined not to be a manifestation of his disability). Note that the U.S. Department of Education attempted to deny IDEA funding (more than $50 million) to the state of Virginia in 1994, because it disapproved a regulation in Virginia's state plan stating, "[i]f there is no causal connection [between a child's misconduct and his or her disability] and if the child was appropriately placed at the time of the misconduct, the child may be disciplined the same as a non-handi- capped child." The Department of Education claimed that the state was required to provide education to all disabled students, regardless of their behavior. The Fourth Circuit Court of Appeals, though, granted Virginia an interlocutory injunction pending the outcome of an administrative hearing on the merits of the matter. Virginia Dep't. of Education v. Riley, 23 F.3d 80 (4th Cir. 1994).
121. Sch. Bd. Prince William Cty. of Virginia v. Malone, 762 F.2d 1210 (4th Cir. 1986). Another federal court rejected this notion in dicta, however, stating that one could dismiss a (hypothetical) LD student's claim that he dealt drugs as a result of the negative impact of his disability on his self-esteem and his need to seek peer approval. See *Doe v. Maher*, 793 F.2d at 1480, n. 8.
122. See 1995 California Assembly Bill No. 1290, §5477616 Cal. Regular Session 1995–96 (requiring expulsion for at least one year of students possessing a firearm and establishing a fine for superintendents or principals who knowingly violate the requirement). It is obviously not at all clear that a state would be permitted to interpret such a law to allow expulsion of pupils protected by federal law.
123. Early on, courts sometimes seemed to see this. See, e.g., Frederick L. v. Thomas, 408 F. Supp. 832, 835 (E.D. Pa. 1976) (holding that expulsion is inappropriate before it has been determined that the child is appropri- ately placed); Stuart v. Nappi, 443 F. Supp. 1235, 1243 (D. Ct. 1978) (inap- propriate placement may cause disruptive behavior). But by the late 1980s, the Office of Civil Rights speaks of "manifestation determination" hearings, in which it details procedures to ascertain "whether misbehav- ior is caused by a child's handicapping condition." See Memorandum to OCR Senior Staff from William L. Smith, Acting Assistant Secretary for Civil Rights, 11/13/89, 16 EHLR 491.

124. Courts have not yet ruled on the interesting question of "calibration" or balance. If the court determines that a test is legitimately "speeded" because the institution legitimately considers speedy responsiveness a virtue to be tested, but the court believes that speeded tests "unduly" interfere with the disabled pupil's ability to manifest other virtues, it might order "compromise" solutions (permitting some extra time, but less than the student would most desire). Thus far, however, schools have either been forced to abandon a curricular demand or test format mode or been allowed to retain it; there are, as far as we have been able to ascertain, no judicial orders for calibrated modification.

125. 34 C.F.R. §104.42(b)(2) (1995).

126. 34 C.F.R. §104.42(d) (1995).

127. 34 C.F.R. §104.44(a) (1995).

128. See, e.g., Southeastern Community College v. Davis, 442 U.S. 397, 409–410 (1979) (school needn't eliminate clinical phase of program for a hearing impaired nursing student, because that would result in a "fundamental alteration in the nature of the program"); Alexander v. Choate, 469 U.S. 287, 300 (1985).

129. 932 F.2d 19 (1st Cir. 1991).

130. Id. at 26.

131. 976 F.2d 791, 794 (1st Cir. 1992), cert. denied, 113 S. Ct. 1845 (1993).

132. Id. at 795.

133. Courts are generally deferential to academic judgments when students seek curriculum modification (or waiver of substantive portions of tests). Thus, rather typically, in Doherty v. Southern College of Optometry, 862 F.2d 570 (6th Cir. 1988), cert. den. 493 U.S. 810 (1989), the court rejected the claim of a visually-neurologically impaired plaintiff to be exempted from the requirement to develop and demonstrate proficiency in the use of certain optical instruments, despite plaintiff's undisputed evidence that many optometrists don't use the particular instruments, given the school's counterclaim that their use is becoming more widespread and significant.

  Some courts, though, have shown a willingness to contest even the substantive, curricular judgments of university and college administrators. A state court judge in Texas has ordered the school's journalism school to exempt a dyscalculic student from a math test requirement, refusing to defer to the school's judgment that math proficiency was significant for journalists. See Andrea D. Greene, "Math Disabled Student Wins Right to Take Courses," Houston Chronicle, January 29, 1994 at A2.

  Clearly, too, if the school's judgment that a disabled student may not succeed is based on factors that are otherwise impermissible under antidiscrimination law—for instance, the potential aversion of clients or customers to dealing with a disabled service provider—the court will not credit them. See, e.g., Pushkin v. Regents of University of Colorado, 658 F.2d 1372 (10th Cir. 1981) (school cannot reject a doctor suffering from multiple sclerosis from its residency program on the ground that patients might react adversely to him).

134. See 34 C.F.R. §104.44(c) (1995); Brookhart v. Illinois State Bd. of Educ., 697

F.2d 179, 184 (7th Cir. 1983) ("an otherwise qualified student who is unable to disclose the degree of learning he actually possesses because of the test format or environment would be the object of discrimination solely on the basis of handicap").

135. 34 C.F.R. §104.44(c) (1995).

136. 932 F.2d at 30 (Breyer, C. J., dissenting).

137. It is not clear whether the EEOC means to say "the" skill rather than "a" skill: if it means to say "the," the implication is that all tests must be "purified" in the sense that, at least for disabled applicants, a written test may test only reading capacity while other substantive skills must be tested in ways with which the reading disabilities will not interfere. It is unclear to us whether this interpretation, if correct, represents sensible practice; the employer (or school) might be most interested in reading comprehension in a particular context, and thus reasonably seeks to test a mixture of skills.

138. 56 Fed. Reg. 35732 (1991).

139. 29 U.S.C. §1630.10 (1995).

4. Local Practice I: Diagnosis and Placement

1. See, e.g., Cecil Reynolds, "Critical Measurement Issues in Learning Disabilities," 18 *Journal of Special Education* 451, 455 (1984) ("the tremendous disparities in measurement models adopted in the various states . . . and the varying levels of expertise with which the models have been implemented are obvious, major factors contributing to the difference in the proportion of children served as LD"). See also Cecil Mercer, *Students with Learning Disabilities* 48 (2d ed. 1983); Barbara Keogh, "Future of the LD Field: Research and Practice," 19 *Journal of Learning Disabilities* 455 (1986).

2. There is no strong reason, a priori, to believe that true prevalence rates are the same across jurisdictions. First, the "physical" characteristics of an immobile population may well vary (e.g., if there were more alcohol abusers in jurisdiction A than B and parental alcohol abuse is associated with LD, we would not expect LD rates to be the same in the two settings). Second, we would expect populations to sort geographically to some extent. Thus if state A had better special education programs than state B, one would expect more pupils eligible for special ed to move there.

3. See *Thirteenth Annual Report to Congress on the Implementation of the Individuals with Disabilities Education Act* Table AA23 (1991). For a fuller discussion, see Gillian Lester and Mark Kelman, "State Disparities in the Diagnosis and Placement of Pupils with Learning Disabilities," *Journal of Learning Disabilities* (Nov./Dec. 1997). See also D. Hallahan, C. Kelley, and D. Bell, "A Comparison of Prevalence Rate Variability from State to State for Each of the Categories of Special Education," 17 *Remedial and Special Education* 8–14 (March/April 1986) (noting that variability of LD diagnosis was not especially pronounced).

4. There was a substantial national decline in the number of pupils diagnosed as educable mentally retarded from 1977 through the 1980s. In some districts, the refusal to use stigmatic diagnoses is near absolute. Thus in one New York district that we studied, only 2 of 500 disabled children are labeled EMR, though the district's special education coordinator's perception was that "many, many more are treated just as EMR kids were historically." State *labeling* practices are by no means random. We ran regression equations in which the dependent variable is the ratio of the total LD population to the sum of the EMR and LD population; the independent variables were thirteen distinct measures of the sociopolitical characteristics of a state. The adjusted R^2 was substantial (.38). For a fuller description of the methodology of the study on which this subsection is based, see Lester and Kelman, "State Disparities."

5. The independent variables we measured here were the average pay levels (a measure of how well-off median voters in school elections would likely be); the state's poverty rate; the proportion of the state's population that has received a bachelor's degree (a surrogate for high levels of educational expectations); the serious crime rate (which we thought might be a surrogate for in-school violence); the proportion of the population that is African-American; metropolitanization; per capita state government expenditures compared with per capita income (a measure of the size of the public compared with the private sector); a measure of the relationship between teachers' salaries and average pay (designed to capture the state's concern with education and/or the power of educational providers); the proportion of low birth weight babies in the jurisdiction (which we surmised might correlate with the prevalence of underlying physical disability); the abortion rate (a quite imperfect measure of "social liberalism"); and the Democratic/Republican split in the 1988 presidential election (a measure of political conservatism).

6. For a more detailed account, see Lester and Kelman, "State Disparities."

7. Nationally, the median household income in 1989 was $30,058, and 20.3 percent of adults aged twenty-five or over had a bachelor's degree or more. In one of these towns, the median income was roughly $55,000 and approximately 65 percent of those over twenty-five had a bachelor's degree or more; in the other, median income was approximately $75,000 and roughly 52 percent had a bachelor's degree or more. (We will give approximate figures only to preserve the anonymity of our informants.)

8. The median family income in one was reasonably high (more than $53,000 a year), but only 28 percent had bachelor's degrees or more (compared with 23.4 percent in the state generally). The other administrator oversaw a SELPA (Special Education Local Planning Agency, a cooperative arrangement created by districts to handle special education concerns) in which socioeconomic status varied across districts, but he described middle-class districts within his SELPA as following the pattern we allude to in the text.

9. There is a substantial disparity between the school district boundaries and the relevant census boundaries, and therefore we cannot ascertain median

income or educational attainment levels in the school district. The SELPA coordinator said the school population was more than three-quarters African-American and the free lunch population far in excess of any other district within his SELPA.

10. Federal census data reporting a range of conventional indicators of socioeconomic status (e.g., family income, education level) for cities and towns do not precisely correspond with the location of school districts; school districts are often outside of, or contain only a portion of, the cities and towns used for the census. Therefore, we were unable to rely on a range of conventional census-based indicators of SES (e.g., family income, education level). We therefore limited our basis for selecting districts to one indicator of SES, the rates of four-year college attendance by graduates from the previous year's class. We obtained this data from individual districts (collected for state reporting purposes).

11. See Christine Sleeter, "Learning Disabilities: The Social Construction of a Special Education Category," 53 *Exceptional Children* 46, 49 (1986).

12. Sleeter, "Social Construction" at 50. See also David Franks, "Ethnic and Social Status Characteristics of Children in EMR and LD Classes," 37 *Exceptional Children* 537 (1971) (students labeled LD were 96.8 percent white, and class status was considerably higher than for parents of children labeled EMR).

13. James Tucker, "Ethnic Proportions in Classes for the Learning Disabled: Issues in Nonbiased Assessment," 14 *Journal of Special Education* 93 (1980).

14. Pamela Wright and Rafaela Santa Cruz, "Ethnic Composition of Special Education Programs in California," 6 *Learning Disability Quarterly* 387 (1983).

15. Increasing numbers of black students may have been designated learning disabled over time as more districts shifted to diagnostic techniques that were more inclusive of lower-IQ pupils, given that IQ and IQ-like test scores of African-Americans are suppressed, averaging one standard deviation below mean IQ scores for white Americans. It is, though, a very complex and unanswered question how many African-American pupils have been diagnosed under each sort of system at different times in the past three decades.

A study by McLeskey and colleagues showed how sensitive racial identification rates are to alternative labeling methods. Sampling 218 white and 132 African-American students tested by a school psychologist to determine eligibility for learning disabilities services, the researchers found that blacks were substantially less likely to be eligible if the LD definition included a cut-off (a demand that students be of "normal or near-normal intelligence") since 41 percent of the blacks (as compared with only 16 percent of the whites) fell below the cut-off. Moreover, the use of standard score discrepancy tests produced a far lower proportion of eligible African-Americans than did the regression score method (39.4 versus 23.6 percent for reading; 28 versus 16.7 percent for math), though among whites, the two methods generated the same proportion of LD-labeled pupils. (Recall from Chapter 2 that the regression score method controls for the fact that students with above- and below-average IQ scores ought not to be expected to score as well, or as poorly, on reading tests as they have scored on the IQ given the tendency of test scores to regress toward the mean.) See J. McLeskey, N. L. Waldron, and S. A. Wornhoff, "Factors Influencing the Identification of Black and White Students with Learning Disabilities," 23 *Journal of Learning Disabilities* 362 (1990).

Even groups with the same discrepancy scores might be differentially diagnosed as LD if districts pay heed to the formal requirement that students whose performance shortfalls result from environmental disadvantage are not to be dubbed LD. (Such students are disproportionately students of color, as well as, almost definitionally, lower-class students.) It is not clear that this formal qualification has ever affected actual practice enough to have a discernable demographic impact, nor is it clear that the use of the exclusionary clause has declined over time in a manner that would result in increasing levels of diagnosis for students of color.

16. The contradictory studies are summarized in McLeskey, Waldron, and Wornhoff, "Factors Influencing."

17. Latino underrepresentation might be at least partially explained by the difficulty of diagnosing some disabilities in students who have limited English proficiency. Some students placed in ESL settings might have underlying but undiagnosed disabilities. It is also plausible that native-born and/or immigrant Latinos put less pressure on school officials to provide special services for their children; in the case of undocumented immigrants, one might hypothesize that parents are especially unaggressive in asserting rights to public officials.

18. *Fourteenth Annual Report to Congress on the Implementation of the Individuals with Disabilities Education Act*, pp. 15–16 (1992).

19. Even if districts collected class, gender, and ethnic data by gross placement type, one still wouldn't know *fully* whether, say, black males were disproportionately separated from "mainstreamed" students, since settings described, for instance, as "resource rooms" encompass a rather wide array of mainstreaming practices. Thus in one Mississippi district, an administrator told us that students are "considered resource if they're taking one [mainstreamed] academic and one non-academic course . . . Almost everybody can go in for handwriting and something else. A lot of them are considered resource though they may be in the special ed room most of the time." In a Louisiana district, students spend as much as 180 minutes (half) a day (or as little as 30) in the resource room. Those spending 180 minutes a day may well have little contact with regular ed classmates in academic subjects. The difficulty of speculating about the real nature of nominally distinct "settings" can be gleaned from this comment by the administrator of a California SELPA: "Since *Larry P. v. Riles* [the case that barred IQ testing to place black students in EMR classes], we've seen a shift from high concentrations of blacks in EMR to other dead-end settings, but we don't know what those [settings] are yet."

20. See Derrick Bell, "The Supreme Court 1984 Term: Foreword: The Civil Rights Chronicles," 99 *Harvard Law Review* 4, 47, 67, 68, 83 n. 121 (1985). For other discussions of racial (and socioeconomic) "tipping points," see, e.g., Anthony Downs, *Opening Up the Suburbs* 68–73 (1973); Bruce Ackerman, "Integration for Subsidized Housing and the Question of Racial Occupancy Controls," 26 *Stanford Law Review* 245, 251–266 (1974).

21. It is vital to recall how dead-ended the special day classes generally are. In this SELPA, it was reported that only 10 percent of pupils placed in special day classes make it back to an RSP placement (and *none* to fully mainstreamed classes). By contrast, we were told that a quarter of RSP students return to fully mainstreamed classes, and even those who don't are frequently able to complete a traditional academic degree. In New York City, where nearly two-thirds of special education pupils are placed in segregated settings (compared with roughly one-third nationwide), only 5 percent of special ed pupils return to general education classes; fewer than 5 percent of special needs students graduate on time and less than a quarter graduate from high school at all according to March 10, 1994, congressional testimony by Diana Autin of Advocates for Children of New York.

22. *San Francisco Chronicle,* "Respect Differences: Teachers Learn Ethnic Sensitivity" by Diane Curtis, December 11, 1992, pp. A1, A19.

23. California Department of Education, *Special Education Student Data Report* April 1, 1994, Form ST-470 Compilation, "Enrollment by Ethnicity, LEP, and MR." New York City appears to have a similar pattern. According to March 10, 1994, testimony by Diana Autin of Advocates for Children of New York before the House Committee on Education and Labor, the New York City public school student population is 73 percent African-American and Latino, but children of these ethnicities make up 84 percent of the self-contained class population. White students, 20 percent of the total school population, received 37 percent of the "related services" delivered in mainstream settings. It is not clear whether these patterns are prevalent across the country: in our own interviews, we received a mixture of responses (and a paucity of hard data) when we asked administrators about the relationship between race and class on the one hand and placement on the other.

24. Mary Wagner et al., *The Transition Experience of Young People with Disabilities: A Summary of Findings from the National Longitudinal Transition Study of Special Education Students* ch. 1—p. 3 (SRI, Dec. 1993).

25. Prior to the enactment of EAHCA, there is no good systematic data about placements, so it is necessary to note progress made in mainstreaming since the late 1970s. Unfortunately, the data from the late 1970s is not strictly comparable with the data collected now, so one is making some inexact comparisons. However, it appears that in 1978–79, 39,800 orthopedically impaired students were in separate classes, separate schools, or other nonmainstreamed environments (59 percent of the orthopedically impaired student population); by 1992–93, that number had declined to 23,700

(44.9 percent of that population). Similarly, the number of visually impaired students in separate classes, separate schools, and other nonmainstreamed environments dropped from 13,500 (41.3 percent of the visually impaired population) to 7,900 (33.6 percent of the visually impaired population). The data are more strictly comparable if one compares the mid-1980s figures with the 1992–93 figures; these too show a substantial ongoing increase in mainstreaming. In 1984–85, 20,100 orthopedically impaired students were educated in regular classes and resource rooms (38.8 percent of the total) while 29,100 were in such settings in 1992–93 (55.1 percent of the total); 17,700 of the visually impaired were educated in regular classes of resource rooms in 1985–86 (62.1 percent of the total of visually impaired students), compared with 15,700 in 1992–93 (66.4 percent of the total). See the *Third, Ninth,* and *Seventeenth Annual Reports to Congress on the Implementation of IDEA.*

26. The *proportion* of LD students served in separate classes or separate schools seemingly rose a great deal (given data comparability limits, this is not completely clear) from 1978–79 to 1992–93 (from 17.5 to 21.3 percent). The absolute numbers, of course, exploded given the dramatic increase in the number of children labeled LD: the number of nonmainstreamed pupils diagnosed as learning disabled grew from 227,000 to 500,000 (an increase of 273,000). This increase cannot be a function simply of relabeling EMR pupils as LD, although it is in some significant part a function of that phenomenon. The number of EMR pupils in separate classes and schools dropped from 567,000 to 347,000 (a decrease of only 220,000).

   The same phenomenon occurs in regard to SED pupils. In 1992–93, 212,000 were schooled outside of regular classes and resource rooms, while only 202,000 were in 1984–85, despite the fact that there was a slight decline in the *percentage* placed in such settings (53.7 percent in 1992–93 versus 54.0 percent in 1984–85).

27. Metropolitanization was also highly significantly associated with non-mainstreamed placements ($p < .01$): a possible explanation for this is that scale economies in metropolitan districts permit more ready use of self-contained classes. That self-contained classes may be more prevalent when states can afford them is reflected as well in the fact that higher average pay rates significantly positively affect the proportion of LD students in self-contained classes ($p < .05$). Self-contained classes for LD students are also positively correlated with higher poverty rates ($p < .06$). Interestingly, the serious crime rate in the state is significantly negatively associated with the proportion of LD students in self-contained classes ($p < .01$), just as it is significantly negatively associated with the proportion of the state's six- to twenty-one-year-old resident population consisting of either EMR or LD children in restrictive settings. (The adjusted R^2 for *that* variable is also high, .56, and once more the presence of more blacks in the state's population significantly affects the rate: $p < .01$). We speculate, cautiously, that the impact of crime on placing pupils in self-contained classes might be as follows: in high-crime states,

there may be so much school violence that districts can't realistically hope to use special ed placements to remove a significant portion of disruptive students from regular classes. In the less violent states, though, special ed is a more realistic tool for isolation of the (smaller) proportion of pupils feared to be violent, so a higher portion of the school population may be pulled out.

28. J. Rosenbaum, M. Kulieke, and L. Rubinowitz, "White Suburban Schools' Responses to Low-Income Black Children: Sources of Successes and Problems," 20 *Urban Review* 28, 33 (1988).

29. It is interesting to note that there appeared to be more organized parental political opposition to special ed by the parents of regular ed students in this district than in any other we visited. When asked if parents of regular ed children ever complained about "paired classrooms," the district administrator replied, "Most definitely. They always are here," adding that parents are well organized in their opposition to the policy, appearing at school board meetings and "being very verbal in the community." She perceives that most of the protesters are white, college educated, and financially well-off. She expressed dismay at these parents' desire to separate their offspring from the children with LDs, and speculated that it might stem at least in part from the fact that many such children are "from a low socioeconomic group. He may be from a single-parent home. He may be an Afro-American child . . . differing from my child." She told us also that "mainstreaming" is less of an issue for the (similarly relatively rich, white) parents of high school students, because the high schools are more internally segregated in any case "because their curriculum is so differentiated . . . Your real bright kids will go to AP English. They'll go into history, calculus, trigonometry . . . And your LD students, they're taking general education things."

30. We do not mean to imply that the programs are perfect substitutes for one another. While Chapter One aides may provide many of the same services as a special education aide brought into the classroom to implement a special education pupil's IEP, the special education student will, first, almost certainly receive more focused attention since, as one Mississippi administrator noted, "[with special education], you're going to get a lower student-teacher ratio." Moreover, IDEA children may be able to proceed toward graduation with modified curricular expectations written into their IEPs (including, for example, immunity from taking generally mandatory grade-level achievement tests) while Chapter One pupils unable to keep up with "grade-appropriate" expectations will frequently be retained. In the opinion of that same Mississippi administrator, the fact that regular education Chapter One pupils end up being forced to interact socially with much younger children because they cannot make academic progress is one of the real weaknesses of Chapter One since "self-esteem and age appropriateness is important . . . we need to get [a pupil] into junior high school because he's fourteen."

31. *Fourteenth Annual Report*, p. 11.

32. Michael Rutter and William Yule, "The Concept of Specific Reading Retardation," 16 *Journal of Child Psychology and Psychiatry* 181, 186 (1975).
33. This is the perspective embodied in, for example, Sharon Morgan, "The Learning Disabilities Population: Why More Boys than Girls? A Hot Area for Research," 8 *Journal of Clinical Child Psychology* 211 (1979).
34. S. Shaywitz, B. Shaywitz, J. Fletcher, and M. Escobar, "Prevalence of Reading Disability in Boys and Girls: Results of the Connecticut Longitudinal Study," 264 (8) *Journal of the American Medical Association* 998 (1990).
35. See Mary Buchanan and Joan Wolf, "A Comprehensive Study of Learning Disabled Adults," 19 *Journal of Learning Disabilities* 34 (1986); David Ryckman, "Sex Differences in a Sample of Learning Disabled Children," 4 *Learning Disability Quarterly* 48 (1981).
36. See Susan Vogel, "Gender Differences in Intelligence, Language, Visual-Motor Abilities, and Academic Achievement in Students with Learning Disabilities: A Review of the Literature," 23 *Journal of Learning Disabilities* 44, 47 (1990), citing an unpublished work, J. Chapman, "Social-emotional Characteristics, Teacher Expectations, and Academic Performance of LD Children: A Longitudinal Study" (October 1986).
37. See Susan Vogel, "Gender Differences" at 46, citing J. Downing, "How Society Creates Reading Disability," 77 *Elementary School Journal* 275 (1977); J. Finnucci and B. Childs, "Are There Really More Dyslexic Boys than Girls?" in *Sex Differences in Dyslexia* (A. Ansara, N. Geschwind, A. Galaburda, M. Albert, and N. Gartrell eds., 1981).
38. See, e.g., Lawrence Eno and Paula Woehlke, "Diagnostic Differences between Educationally Handicapped and Learning Disabled Students," 17 *Psychology in the Schools* 469 (1980) (females with LDs spell better); R. Younes, B. Rossner, and G. Webb, "Neuroimmaturity of Learning-Disabled Children: A Controlled Study," 25 *Developmental Medicine and Child Neurology* 574 (1983) (females with LDs write and spell better).
39. See G. Leinhardt, A. Seewald, and N. Zigmond, "Sex and Race Differences in Learning Disabilities Classrooms," 74 *Journal of Educational Psychology* 835 (1982) (discrepancies between performance and expectations based on chronological age).
40. See, e.g., Harvey Clarizio and S. E. Phillips, "Sex Bias in the Diagnosis of Learning Disabled Students," 23 *Psychology in the Schools* 44 (1986).
41. P. Mirkin, D. Marston, and S. Deno, "Direct and Repeated Measurement of Academic Skills: An Alternative to Traditional Screening, Referral, and Identification of Learning Disabled Students" (Report No. IRLD-RR-75, ERIC Document Reproduction Service No. ED 224 191, 1982). See also Nadine Lambert and Jonathan Sandoval, "The Prevalence of Learning Disabilities in a Sample of Children Considered Hyperactive," 8 *Journal of Abnormal Child Psychology* 33 (1980) (43.4 percent of hyperactive boys and 37.5 percent of hyperactive girls exhibited substantial discrepancies between achievement and IQ; LD prevalence rates were close among boys and girls in the control group).

42. Vogel, "Gender Differences" at 48.
43. See C. Berry, S. Shaywitz, and B. Shaywitz, "Girls with Attention Deficit Disorder: A Silent Minority? A Report on Behavioral and Cognitive Characteristics," 76 *Pediatrics* 801 (1985).
44. Practice differs by district: in one New York district we visited, such a committee would consist of the principal, the child's classroom teacher, and special ed personnel (e.g., a school psychologist, a speech/language therapist, a reading specialist, a physical education person trained in dealing with motor problems); in a California district with a similar demographic profile, student study teams (made up of the principal, classroom teacher, parent volunteers, and perhaps a special ed teacher) meet weekly throughout the school year to discuss students' needs, including the need to assess for IDEA eligibility. As of mid-1997 it appears that Congress will reform the IDEA to require that classroom teachers serve on such committees. See "House Passes Bill for Disabled That Adds Education Resources," *New York Times,* May 24, 1997, A1.
45. See 34 C.F.R. 300.504(b)(1)(i) (1995); see also Caroll v. Capalbo, 563 F. Supp 1053, 1058 (DC RI 1983) (noting as well that while the parent needn't consent to reevaluations, she may contest any change in placement that results from reevaluations).
46. We were never given detailed information on what the district did to ensure that recalcitrant parents would consent to work-ups for disruptive children. Testifying before a March 1994 congressional subcommittee addressing the reauthorization of IDEA, though, Diana Autin stated that principals obtained consent in New York City by threatening to refer parents who withheld consent to the Child Welfare Administration, deeming the refusal a form of "educational neglect."
47. Some parents may resist not special education services, but certain stigmatic labels. Middle-class parents in one Louisiana parish frequently resist not services but "severe" (stigmatic) classifications. ("They want LD rather than autistic, OHI [other health impaired] rather than SED.") A California administrator noted that it had recently become fashionable for upper middle-class parents of children who might otherwise be called EMR to demand that districts have them diagnosed "autistic spectrum" children.

    Thus administrators often reported that parents are generally more willing to have their child "worked up" when he is suspected of having a learning disability than if he is suspected by school officials of being seriously emotionally disturbed. A New York administrator noted, "Parents resist the stigmatic labels, especially emotionally disturbed, a lot. In the last five years, though, resistance to the LD label has declined."
48. Judith Singer and John Butler, "The Education for All Handicapped Children Act: Schools as Agents of Social Reform," 57 *Harvard Educational Review* 125, 141–142 (1987).
49. The queue was partly deliberately created. The principal believed that testing was unduly expensive and that it was preferable to offer services with-

out labeling to many of the students who might be "eligible" for testing in some legal sense.

50. One New York administrator informed us that some parents and pupils also believe—whether correctly or not—that colleges may affirmatively seek LD students, either out of an affirmative policy to increase student diversity by admitting more disabled pupils or because they believe admitting such students will decrease their vulnerability to legal allegations that they discriminate against the disabled.

51. W. Willingham, M. Ragosta, R. Elliot Bennett, H. Braun, D. Rock, and D. Powers, *Testing Handicapped People* 54 (1988).

52. The special education coordinator of the district claims, as did the special education coordinator in another district in which middle- and high-SES parents also go to the same hospital, that testing psychologists at the hospital have never, to the best of his knowledge, failed to find at least one learning disability in a child brought in for paid assessment, but it was unclear whether the claims were hyperbolic and/or inadequately informed, given the distaste with which both of these special educators viewed the practice of seeking outside diagnosis. Distaste for private diagnosticians runs high among public special educators. One Mississippi administrator put it particularly colorfully, referring to a local psychologist who frequently diagnosed students seeking extra time for the SATs or ACTs as ADD or LD. "Dr. [X is] a big wonderful man here in the city who charges you $800 and [he'll] tell you you are a flower if you want it right that day. [X] will do this if you give him $800." She did note, though, that the district will accommodate all the students he recommends be accommodated rather than spend money on a hearing to fight parental requests.

53. It is not completely clear why parents seek IDEA identification in order to gain test accommodations. The Educational Testing Service (ETS), which administers the SAT, does not require that a child be IDEA-labeled to grant requests for testing accommodation: the pupil may also base claims for accommodation on two signed documents from private health professionals. The 1991–92 brochure, "Information for Students with Special Needs," notes that an IEP is neither a necessary nor a sufficient condition for receiving a nonstandard test. (See Marjorie Ragosta and Cathy Wendler, *Eligibility Issues and Comparable Time Limits for Disabled and Nondisabled SAT Examinees,* 8–9, College Board Report 92-5, ETS RR No. 92-35.) Internal studies within the ETS of eligibility practices, however, seem to assume that LD students with a current IEP who request accommodation will almost certainly receive it and that those receiving testing accommodations in high school are likely to, while those who once had an IEP but don't now, as well as those who never had an IEP, are far less likely to receive requested accommodations. (Ragosta and Wendler, *Eligibility Issues* 10–11.)

54. The changes were embodied in §211 of PL 104-193 (1996), amending 42 U.S.C. 1382c(a)(3). For a good, accessible journalistic account of the changes, see "Rule Changes for Disabled Kids, Some Will Lose Federal Benefits," *Times-Picayune,* December 22, 1996, p. A22.

55. Administrators voiced some concern about students "faking" disabilities. A Louisiana administrator told the following story: "[I]n the one case I'm thinking of, the parent of the child told the child not to perform [on the assessment test], so the child could qualify [for services and SSI]. But the child told the [special ed] coordinator of the test, so that blew the whole test out of the water." One administrator of a poor rural Mississippi district, though she did not perceive that there were a high number of diagnostic requests from parents generally in her district, did tell the following story. A little girl was performing terribly on an assessment test, running around the classroom where it was being administered: asked why, she responded, "Well, because my Mommy says I don't get any Christmas [presents] if I don't fail the test."

The possibility that "coaching," or the feigning of (especially mental) disability, occurs has indeed concerned some legislators and policymakers prior to the 1996 reforms restricting SSI eligibility for families with less severely disabled children. This may have been an emblematic issue in the criticism of the SSI program for children.

5. Local Practice II: Resource Management and Discipline

1. Also among students classified as LD, though, are students who historically would have been labeled educably mentally retarded but who are now (technically mis)classified as having learning disabilities. We would not expect all such students to be served in mainstreamed settings.
2. Data come from *Fourteenth Annual Report to Congress on the Implementation of the Individuals with Disabilities Education Act* 25 (U.S. Dep't. of Education, 1992).
3. While we did not interview in any districts in which *all* students within the district were mainstreamed, it is important to recognize that such districts exist. We believe such districts typically "farm out" some (small) number of pupils to special classes in nearby districts (usually at astronomical per pupil costs), but they do not maintain their own special day classes. (One of the New York districts we visited receives four pupils from a district nearby which maintains no special day classes.) Usually, we suspect, districts do this primarily for ideological reasons—expressed opposition to pulling students out of regular classes. One surmises, though, that there might be scale economy reasons as well, at least in some smaller suburban or rural districts where it is cheaper to send a small number of students out of the district than to establish special day classes.
4. While it seems clear that there is considerable overlap between LD and conduct disorders, the overlap is not absolute and the causal relationship is not certain. See, e.g., Lorian Baker and Dennis Cantwell, "The Association between Emotional/Behavioral Disorders and Learning Disorders in Children with Speech/Language Disorders," 6 *Advances in Learning and Behavioral Disabilities* 27 (K. Gedow ed., 1990).
5. This conflict is discussed in Bruce Meredith and Julie Underwood,

"Irreconcilable Differences? Defining the Rising Conflict between Regular and Special Education," 24 *Journal of Law and Education* 195 (1995).

6. Whether or not this administrator is correct in his prediction, there is some evidence of local political conflicts over mainstreaming of children whom the school district alleges to be disruptive. For instance, the *Los Angles Times* reported in 1994 on a group of parents in Ocean View, California, who collectively mobilized to oppose the court-ordered mainstreaming of a five-year-old child the district had accused of biting teachers, throwing desks, and hitting and spitting at other students. Twelve of the pupil's thirty classmates boycotted class when the pupil returned (and twenty-one parents of pupils in other classes kept their children out in solidarity with the parents of children in the child's class), and three dozen demonstrated outside the classroom against his inclusion (there were a half-dozen counterdemonstrators as well). See Jaime Abdo, "Boy's Return to O.C. School Sparks Protests," *Los Angeles Times* (Orange County edition), June 10, 1994, pt. A, p. 1, col. 4.

7. Meredith and Underwood, "Irreconcilable Differences" at 213–223.

8. The issue of how to provide services to "soft disability" students is much less complex at the junior high and high school level, since all pupils' days are divided into "periods" anyway. Disabled students simply spend some periods getting special education services, and others in mainstreamed classes.

9. The administrator might or might not have recognized that if one administers two imperfectly correlated tests often enough, one will eventually likely find a substantial discrepancy between the scores on the tests purely as a matter of chance. She certainly did recognize, though, that she was actively seeking to serve pupils who were not the primary intended beneficiaries of the IDEA regime.

10. Levels of "need" in high SES districts may be low enough that IDEA-induced pressure enables special educators to encompass all the educationally needy students. In districts where needs are more massive, though, IDEA pupils are far more prone to compete with nondisabled pupils for remedial aid. In such districts, it is far more likely that there are large numbers of children who are not only educationally needy, but could be classified as LD using discrepancy-based measures, if there were pressures to do so (and the money to accommodate the pressures). Thus in one quite poor Mississippi district, in which 70 percent of the students are served under Chapter One (as a result of some combination of area poverty and widespread low academic achievement), the special education coordinator noted: "We could find twice as many [LD pupils] as we have if . . . we had the personnel to serve them, and we just kept on testing them . . . Over half of [the Chapter One] pupils . . . when you're talking about an IQ of 70, 75, and they're achieving in the 60s and 50s, sure that's LD [in discrepancy terms]."

11. The law is in some flux as of mid-1997. It appears that the 1997 revisions of IDEA will permit disabled students to be suspended from school for up to

45 days if they bring weapons onto campus, but that they will not be subject to earlier federal legislation that arguably *mandated* one-year suspensions for those bringing weapons to school. For a discussion, see "House
Passes Bill That Adds Education Resources for the Disabled," *New York
Times,* May 14, 1997 at A17.

12. Interestingly, the administrator believed that all students who asked for
such a hearing were diagnosed as eligible for special education, and the expulsion recommendation was subsequently withdrawn. Our belief, consistent with this, is that the legal power to expel remains relatively freely
available to districts only because students and guardians are unaware of
the possibility of seeking diagnosis prior to severe discipline. We would be
surprised if a significant proportion of students who commit offenses for
which they could be expelled would fail to be classifiable as SED, given that
the behavior itself would almost surely demonstrate the emotional disturbance, particularly if it were not a completely isolated incident.

13. We were especially interested in how schools dealt with sexual harassment
and sexual violence by (generally emotionally disturbed) disabled pupils,
since the issue would pit two "civil rights" constituencies against each
other—those committed to protecting female students from a gender-
specific hostile educational environment and those committed to protecting the disabled from suffering adverse consequences that (at least arguably) result from their disabilities. In our interviews, though, we saw
little evidence that the districts paid much attention to (or perceived the existence of) sexual violence (which probably occurs largely off-campus) or
sexual harassment (which occurs on-site) so that we never really got to see
whether there was a clash between constituencies, or how the clash was resolved.

14. Although none of our informants reported using the following strategy, it
appears theoretically highly plausible to us that some districts skeptical of
federal limits adopt the position that they will pressure manifestation committees to find that misconduct is unconnected to the child's disability until
the child's parent or guardian fights the recommendation of discipline, at
which time the district will cave in without a fight if the offense is less serious.

The question of whether a district's disciplinary recommendations will
be challenged seems very sensitive to the local parental/legal culture. In
one very high SES, highly legally sophisticated California community, for
instance, the district decided not to try to suspend for a longer than ten-day
term a mildly speech impaired student who had carried a weapon to
school. Administrators believed that it would cost at least $50,000 to defend
against an inevitable lawsuit alleging that the student's behavior arose
from the impaired self-esteem that was a manifestation of his moderate
speech defect.

15. Once the issue had been raised to us, we asked all eleven special educators
we subsequently interviewed about it. Only one administrator (in
Louisiana) seemed unconcerned. She noted that she had little fear of §504

since children accommodated by it were served through general education and would not compromise her budget.

16. This fear does not appear completely rational. First, the federal government provides less than 10 percent of the marginal costs of educating special ed pupils identified under IDEA, in any case, and state decisions about whether to reimburse districts for §504-related costs, while perhaps fixed in the short run, are not dictated by federal law. Second, many districts are at or near their reimbursement population caps so that the district receives no marginal funds when additional special education students are identified, even if identified under IDEA. Third, if a student is identified in the first instance through §504, he could be given an IEP the next fiscal year, so that the district will bear uncompensated costs for one year only.

17. Meredith and Underwood, "Irreconcilable Differences" at 209–213 (emphasizing similar fears of §504 expansion among regular educators).

18. One can make a strong case that the statute was designed, above all, to forbid fiscal considerations, raised by the nondisabled community, from interfering with the education of those who are both expensive to educate and socially "outsiders." Ironically, while we have "medicalized" our conception of two groups not nearly so clearly "disabled"—those who behave badly (often interpreted "medically" as those with an emotional disturbance) and those who are poor students (often conceptualized as learning disabled), we seem to continue to resist "treating" those who are most clearly medically disabled. It may well be right that some entity other than school districts should bear some of these high costs, though it's not clear what good it would do anyone (other than a particular school bureaucrat with a fixed budget) to shift these costs: they will (and should) be borne in any case. (That is obviously the case with a §504-eligible student requiring catheterization; it is more controversial, in the sense of rationing medical care, whether resources should be spent trying to get a brain-dead child to be able to communicate minimally when it is very unlikely he will prove able to do so.) It is far more disputable whether the extra costs of "treatment" should be borne *at all* for the more controversially "disabled" (the LD or the SED).

19. The educators (incorrectly, we believe) interpret §504 to permit a parent who refuses special ed testing or designation nonetheless to insist that the school not discriminate against his child on account of his handicap, and that it manifest this nondiscrimination policy by providing remedial and accommodating services. But the belief that the school cannot simply say that proffered IDEA services meet antidiscrimination obligations is not so clearly incorrect, and the risk that the "served" population would explode if parents could seek special services without stigmatic labeling is, in our view, quite realistic.

6. Extra Resources for the Classroom Teacher

1. For arguments that the schools ought to devote a far higher proportion of available resources to "gifted" children, see, e.g., Carol Tomlinson-Keasy,

"Developing Our Intellectual Resources for the 21st Century: Educating the Gifted," 82 *Journal of Educational Psychology* 399 (1990); Bruce Mitchell and William Williams, "Education of the Gifted and Talented in the World Community," 68(7) *Phi Delta Kappan* 531 (1987). For an argument that even the existing levels of programs for "gifted" students are excessive, see Mara Sapon-Shevin, *Playing Favorites: Gifted Education and the Disruption of the Community* (1994).

2. While the teacher might, as a matter of principle, prefer to make individualized inquiries into which students have actually been deprived of home-based educational inputs, he may end up using socioeconomic disadvantage, or even membership in visible "groups" associated with social or economic disadvantage, as a proxy for educational disadvantage. Obviously, these are imperfect proxies because some students will be educationally deprived though not otherwise materially deprived, and some otherwise materially deprived children live in educationally stimulating environments. The teacher might choose to focus all such resources exclusively on those he knows to be socioeconomically disadvantaged or those he knows to be members of groups which are disadvantaged for two distinct, admirable reasons: first, he may want to avoid the administrative costs of making particularized factual determinations about home life (including the possible costs associated with invading family privacy). Second, he may believe that educational success by members of a disadvantaged group (whether the poor or ethnic groups where poverty is more commonplace) always has positive consequences (both for other members of the group and for those more privileged people who might otherwise doubt the capacity of the disadvantaged to succeed). One cannot rule out the possibility, however, that some teachers would focus attention on the socioeconomically disadvantaged, rather than the educationally deprived, for reasons that were less than admirable. The teacher, for instance, might believe that socioeconomically disadvantaged children would benefit little from additional resources, yet funnel resources in their direction as part of a program of legitimating the privilege of those with social power. The goal of the teacher, in this view, would be to remain well defended against the allegation that social stratification is illegitimate by noting that the state has done what it can to rectify inequality by funneling resources to disadvantaged children, but that the children have failed nonetheless, leaving them with no one to blame but themselves.

3. See, for instance, Mary Kennedy, Richard Jung, and Martin Orland, *Poverty, Achievement, and the Distribution of Compensatory Education Services* 119, U.S. Dep't. of Educ. (1986) (the chance that a child will fall behind in school decreases by 4 percent for every additional $1,000 of family income); Amy Butler, "The Effect of Welfare Guarantees on Children's Educational Attainment," 19 *Social Science Research* 175, 192–194 (1990) (increases in AFDC benefit levels are associated with small increases in years of schooling completed); N. Zill, K. Moore, E. Smith, T. Stief, and M. J. Cole, "The Life Circumstances and Development of Children in Welfare Families: A

Profile Based on National Survey Data," 13–15 *Child Trends* (1991) (14 percent of AFDC children have been suspended or expelled from school compared with 7 percent of nonpoor, non-AFDC children; in only 27 percent of families that were nonpoor and with no history of AFDC receipt did children score below the thirtieth percentile on vocabulary tests, while in 60 percent of families that had received AFDC in three or more of the last five years, children scored below that benchmark).

4. See, e.g., Gordon Berlin and Andrew Sum, *Toward a More Perfect Union: Basic Skills, Poor Families, and Our Economic Future* 10–11 (1988) (among twenty- to twenty-three-year-old males, low scores on the Armed Forces Qualification Test were associated with substantially lower earnings; when the lowest and highest quintiles are compared, low-scoring dropouts earned 50 percent less and low-scoring high school graduates earned one-third less).

5. See Ray Rist, "Student Social Class and Teacher Expectations: The Self-Fulfilling Prophecy in Ghetto Education," 40 *Harvard Educational Review* 41 (1970); Jean Anyon, "Elementary Schooling and Distinctions of Social Class," 12 *Interchange* 118 (1981); Gregg Jackson and Cecilia Cosca, "The Inequality of Educational Opportunity in the Southwest: An Observational Study of Ethnically Mixed Classrooms," 11 *American Education Research Journal* 219 (1974).

6. Christopher Jencks, "Whom Must We Treat Equally for Educational Opportunity to Be Equal?" 98 *Ethics* 518 (1988). There is a different, and in our view slightly less clear, version of the same article. See Christopher Jencks, "What Must Be Equal for Opportunity to Be Equal?" in *Equal Opportunity* 47 (Norman Bowie ed., 1988). Our page references will be to the *Ethics* article.

7. Jencks, "Opportunity" at 519, 520.

8. Id. at 519, 521.

9. Id. at 519, 522–525.

10. Id. at 520–522.

11. Id. at 522–523.

12. Id. at 529.

13. Id.

14. Id. at 532.

15. For lucid discussions of the division between private and state action in classical legal thought, see, e.g., Patrick Atiyah, *The Rise and Fall of Freedom of Contract* 226–231 (1979); Elizabeth Mensch, "The History of Mainstream Legal Thought" in *The Politics of Law: A Progressive Critique* 13, 18–21 (David Kairys ed., revised ed. 1990); Duncan Kennedy, "Toward an Historical Understanding of Legal Consciousness: The Case of Classical Legal Thought in America, 1850–1940" in *Research in Law and Sociology* 3 (Steven Spitzer ed., 1980 vol. 3).

16. See Paul Brest, "State Action and Liberal Theory: A Casenote on Flagg Brothers v. Brooks," 130 *University of Pennsylvania Law Review* 1296 (1982); Shelley v. Kraemer, 334 U.S. 1 (1948). The view is most associated with

Robert Hale. See, e.g., Robert Hale, "Force and the State: A Comparison of 'Political' and 'Economic' Compulsion," 35 *Columbia Law Review* 149 (1935); Robert Hale, "Coercion and Distribution in a Supposedly Non-Coercive State," 38 *Political Science Quarterly* 470 (1923). For a full, critical discussion of Hale's views on the matter, see Barbara Fried, *Robert Hale and Progressive Legal Economics* (forthcoming 1997).

17. See Frank Goodman, "Professor Brest on State Action and Liberal Theory, and a Postscript to Professor Stone," 130 *University of Pennsylvania Law Review* 1331, 1337–1341 (1982).

18. See, e.g., Stone v. Graham, 449 U.S. 39 (1980), rehearing denied 449 U.S. 1104 (1981) (barring school from posting Ten Commandments on public classroom walls); Wallace v. Jaffree, 472 U.S. 38 (1985) (invalidating a mandatory "moment of silence for meditation or voluntary prayer" in Alabama public schools). Obviously there are questions regarding when the state is advancing religion through its programs: see, e.g., Zobrest v. Catalina Foothills School District, 509 U.S. 1 (1993) (state can provide aid to physically and learning disabled students whether in public or private schools to accommodate their disability).

19. The state may not even force parents to offer their children a secular education. See Pierce v. Society of Sisters, 268 U.S. 510 (1925) (court invalidates a law barring private schooling) and Wisconsin v. Yoder, 406 U.S. 205 (1972) (immunizing parents from compulsory school attendance laws that violated religious beliefs).

20. For a conservative defense of drawing a sharp line between the monopolistic public sphere and the noncoercive private one, see Robert Ellickson, "Cities and Homeowners Associations," 130 *University of Pennsylvania Law Review* 1519 (1982). For more politically moderate views that still see particular reason to fear the state's power in a variety of contexts, see, e.g., David Luban, "Are Criminal Defenders Different?" 91 *Michigan Law Review* 1729 (state power against criminal defendants is to be feared more than private violence); Benno Schmidt, *Freedom of the Press vs. Public Access* 29 (1976) (appropriate to fear cultural uniformity imposed by the state far more than the cultural uniformity that might be imposed by the selected group of media owners).

21. The notion that state power is captured by private parties who use that power to expropriate the politically powerless in ways they could not without the aid of the state is the chief message of conservative public choice theory. See, e.g., Sam Peltzman, "Toward a More General Theory of Regulation," 19 *Journal of Law and Economics* 211, 213 ("I begin with the presumption that what is basically at stake in the regulatory processes is a transfer of wealth").

22. For an argument that the state's commitment to family autonomy diversity must inevitably preclude a commitment to strong views of equal opportunity, see Jennifer Hochschild, "Race, Class, Power, and Equal Opportunity" in *Equal Opportunity* 75, 98–100 (Norman Bowie ed., 1983). For an argument that the state must define "child neglect" in a limited fashion—a fashion

that excludes child-rearing methods arguably harmful to children except when the breaches of caretaking duty are most egregious—in order to respect family autonomy and cultural pluralism, see Michael Wald, "State Intervention on Behalf of 'Neglected' Children: A Search for Realistic Standards," 27 *Stanford Law Review* 985 (1975).

23. Jencks, "Opportunity" at 523.

24. Id.

25. For a discussion of the ever-available choice between intentionalistic and deterministic discourse in political and legal life, see Mark Kelman, *A Guide to Critical Legal Studies* 86–113 (1987).

26. We also believe Jencks is mistaken to believe that, politically, actors in this culture are invariably wedded to the proposition that the state is more clearly duty-bound to compensate for environmental than genetic disadvantage. IDEA, the dominant statute that we address in this book, is premised on precisely the opposite view: that the state must provide extra resources for the genetically handicapped but not the environmentally disadvantaged.

    Some economists might argue that it is generally preferable to compensate for genetic, rather than environmental, shortfalls since doing so poses fewer moral hazard problems. At the margin, people will more likely deprive their children of educational inputs at home if the school, in essence, "insures" them against bearing the full consequences of that decision by providing resources for those who have lacked resources at home, while broadly speaking, parents are less *able* to alter a child's biological make-up, even if insured against some of the adverse consequences of harming their child biologically (though, note the possibility, e.g., that pregnant women will, according to this sort of "moral hazard" theory, be less likely to abstain from alcohol if schools are obliged to remediate fetal alcohol syndrome). We have deep doubts about the magnitude of these sorts of moral hazard effects, in either case.

27. His task will also be considerably more conceptually and empirically problematic if he seeks to maximize some "softer," difficult-to-measure variable (like social adjustment, creativity, self-esteem) rather than achievement scores. This is true not only because measuring, say, the social adjustment of any individual is problematic, but because it is particularly unlikely that measurement scales will readily permit persuasive summing across persons.

28. For an early utilitarian formulation of this point, see David Hume's comment: "[W]henever we depart from . . . equality, we rob the poor of more satisfaction than we add to the rich, and that the gratification of a frivolous vanity in one individual frequently costs more than bread to many families"; see David Hume, "Justice and Equality" in *Justice and Equality* 70, 75 (Hugo Bedau ed., 1971). For a typical modern-day formulation of the same utilitarian point, see Walter Blum and Harry Kalven, Jr., *The Uneasy Case for Progressive Taxation* 56–63 (1953).

29. Jencks ("Opportunity," p. 530) cites General Social Survey evidence from

the 1970s and 1980s that self-reports of happiness increase as vocabulary test scores increase, and that the increase in self-reported happiness is more pronounced among the bottom half of the test score distribution than the top half. Twenty-six percent of those who scored 2 or 3 on a 10-point scale described themselves as not too happy; 14 percent of those with scores of 4 or 5 described themselves as not too happy; and 10 percent of those with scores of 6 or 7, 8 percent of those with scores of 8 or 9, and 9 percent of those with scores of 10 described themselves in the same way.

30. See Mark Kelman, "Concepts of Discrimination im 'General Ability' Job Testing," 104 *Harvard Law Review* 1157, 1196–1197 (1991).

31. The posited positive utility effects might well be both direct and indirect. The direct effects are, for the utilitarian, quite simple: if, for whatever reason, a disabled person is happy to see another disabled person succeed more than a relatively privileged person is happy to see another relatively privileged person succeed, then the preference-respecting utilitarian should consider that gain. The indirect, "role-modeling" effects may be more significant, though. Success by members of groups less accustomed to success may spur increased efforts (and ultimately achievement, which we have hypothesized is utility-enhancing) by other members of the historically subordinated group.

32. See Frank Michelman, "Property, Utility, and Fairness: Comments on the Ethical Foundations of 'Just Compensation' Law," 80 *Harvard Law Review* 1165 (1967) (courts should order owners to be compensated when the settlement costs—the administrative costs of compensation—are less than the demoralization costs that would be borne by the owner and other citizens if the owner is, in their view, unjustly expropriated or had legitimate expectations of ongoing capacity to enjoy the property interfered with).

33. See Wald, "State Intervention."

34. See John Rawls, *A Theory of Justice* 152 (1971).

35. Id. at 17–22, 136–142.

36. Id. at 150–161. Rawls's argument is not simply a utility-based argument in which there are thought to be especially high utility gains to insuring against the worst outcomes, since, in this view, those choosing principles of justice are not insuring themselves against losses that might actually befall them but against states of affairs that might hypothetically befall them, assuming they were ignorant of their embodied circumstances.

37. See Wald, "State Intervention" at 1004–1007.

38. Jane Beasley Raph, Miriam Goldberg, and A. Harry Passow, *Bright Underachievers: Studies of Scholastic Underachievement among Intellectually Superior High School Students* 8 (1966).

39. Id. at 194 ("the findings raise serious questions about the practice of placing school failures together for remedial purposes, *particularly if such failures consist of a group with good academic potential*") (emphasis added).

40. Pat Green, "This Bright Child," 1 *Journal of Learning Disabilities* 423, 427 (1968).

41. Id. at 424.

42. Id. at 425–426.
43. Ray Barsch, "Perspectives on Learning Disabilities: The Vectors of a New Convergence," 1 *Journal of Learning Disabilities* 4, 12 (1968).
44. Louise Bates Ames, "A Low Intelligence Quotient Often Not Recognized as the Chief Cause of Many Learning Difficulties," 1 *Journal of Learning Disabilities* 735 (1968).
45. Id. at 736, quoting David Wechsler, "The IQ Is an Intelligent Test," *New York Times*, June 26, 1966.
46. For this to be true, of course, non-LD students would have to be at the point in each and every district at which their performance levels were fixed, no matter what level of resources their particular district expended upon them, while LD students would continue to benefit from incremental resources till they finally reached the satiation point (the appropriate accommodation point).
47. According to a 1995 Wharton School study, a 10 percent increase in the average education level of all workers within a company (the equivalent of a little more than one extra year of school) would lead to an 8.8 percent increase in output. (A 10 percent increase in hours worked boosted output by only 5.6 percent and a 10 percent increase in capital stock raised output by only 3.4 percent.) The impact was both greater in magnitude and statistically more significant in the nonmanufacturing sector. See *The Other Shoe: Education's Contribution to the Productivity of Establishments* (1995).
48. It is hardly preposterous to contest the proposition that additional years of schooling increase people's genuine capabilities; some believe that the observed "return" to education reflects either "screening" effects (identifying which of a group of potentially equally productive workers will get to occupy socially desirable positions) or result from the fact that socially privileged people are rewarded with both higher income and extra years of school, although the latter does not cause the former. We might note, in passing, however, that the position that school provides *no* significant genuine human capital seems extreme to us. Angrist and Krueger compared adult earnings of two demographically random groups of high school drop-outs, one of which was forced to stay in school an extra half-year because of mandatory attendance laws that prohibit children from dropping out if they have not reached the age of sixteen by the time the school year begins. Those in the group that remained in school the extra semester earned more as adults than those with less schooling even though they received no extra credential, since they too dropped out before receiving a diploma. (See Joshua Angrist and Alan Krueger, "Does Compulsory School Attendance Affect Schooling and Earnings?" 106 *Quarterly Journal of Economics* 979 [1991].) Our main point, however, is that advocates for the learning disabled will have difficulty adopting the position that schooling is inefficacious for the non-LD alone.
49. James Coleman et al., *Equality of Educational Opportunity*, U.S. Department of Health, Education and Welfare (1966). For a good summary of the main points of the massive report, see James Coleman, "Equal Schools or Equal

Students?" 4 *The Public Interest* 70 (Summer 1966).

50. Eric Hanushek, "The Economics of Schooling: Production and Efficiency in Public Schools," 24 *Journal of Economic Literature* 1141, 1143–1146 (1986).
51. Id. at 1162.
52. See Anita Summers and Barbara Wolfe, "Do Schools Make a Difference?" 67 *American Economic Review* 639, 640 n. 2 (1977).
53. Samuel Bowles and Henry Levin, "The Determinants of Scholastic Achievement—An Appraisal of Some Recent Evidence," 3 *Journal of Human Resources* 3, 8–10 (1968).
54. See, e.g., Hanushek, "Economics of Schooling" at 1156; Glen Cain and Harold Watts, "Problems in Making Policy Inferences from the Coleman Report," 35 *American Sociological Review* 228, 229 (1970).
55. Cain and Watts, "Problems in Making Policy Inferences" at 235–236; Bowles and Levin, "Determinants of Scholastic Achievement" at 15–16.
56. Bowles and Levin, "Determinants of Scholastic Achievement" at 12.
57. Hanusheck, "Economics of Schooling" at 1156–1157; Summers and Wolfe, "Does Schooling Make a Difference?" employs this methodology.
58. See, e.g., Paul Wachtel, "The Effect on Earnings of School and College Investment Expenditures," 58 *Review of Economics and Statistics* 326, 329 (1976) (one SD shift in per pupil expenditures has only a 5 percent effect on earnings for those who stay in school through high school graduation); Christopher Jencks and Marsha Brown, "Effects of High Schools on Their Students," 45 *Harvard Educational Review* 273, 317 (1975) ("Per-student expenditure has a small and statistically insignificant effect on both educational and occupational attainment"). However, see Thomas Ribich and James Murphy, "The Economic Returns to Increased Educational Spending," 10 *Journal of Human Resources* 56 (1975) (increased school expenditures influence lifetime earnings by influencing the amount of time children stay in school).
59. David Card and Alan Krueger, "Does School Quality Matter? Returns to Education and the Characteristics of Public Schools in the United States," 100 *Journal of Political Economy* 1, 11–27 (1992) (for white men born between 1920 and 1949, being educated in states with lower pupil/teacher ratios, longer terms, and higher teacher pay increased the return gained from each additional year of schooling, controlling for parental education and income); David Card and Alan Krueger, "School Quality and Black-White Relative Earnings: A Direct Assessment," 107 *Quarterly Journal of Economics* 151, 169–187 (1992) (southern black workers educated in states with higher cost/higher quality systems had higher earnings). See also Jere Behrman and Nancy Birdsall, "The Quality of Schooling: Quantity Alone Is Misleading," 73 *American Economic Review* 928, 938 (1983) (the estimated internal social rate of return to investment in school quality in Brazil is larger than it is to investment in school quantity, though it does *not* do so by affecting the amount of future schooling children will receive).
60. See Ribich and Murphy, "Economic Returns."
61. This issue arises in school financing controversies all the time: do political

entities that spend equally actually utilize the same amount of resources "per problem" or do some municipalities suffer from what is usually dubbed "municipal overburden" (in which one municipality faces a higher proportion of high-cost problems, either in or out of the school setting). For a discussion of municipal overburden, see, e.g., Betsy Levin, Thomas Muller, and Corazon Sandoval, *The High Cost of Education in Cities: An Analysis of the Purchasing Power of the Educational Dollar* 53–69 (1973).

62. Summers and Wolfe, "Does Schooling Make a Difference?" at 645.

63. Id. at 644.

64. Donald Winkler, "Educational Achievement and School Peer Group Composition," 10 *Journal of Human Resources* 189, 200 (1975). See also Henry Levin, "A Cost-Effectiveness Analysis of Teacher Selection," 5 *Journal of Human Resources* 4 (1970); Eric Hanushek, *Education and Race* 200 (1972) (finding strong relationship between teacher verbal scores and student test scores).

65. Hanushek, "Economics of Schooling" at 1161 (only 6 of 106 studies which included a variable measuring advanced degree attainment found the variable was positively associated with student achievement at a significant level, compared with 5 that found it was significantly associated with negative changes in achievement, and 95 that found it statistically insignificantly related to achievement).

66. See W. Steven Barnett, "Benefit-Cost Analysis of the Perry Pre-School Program and Its Policy Implications," 7 *Educational Evaluation and Policy Analysis* 333 (1985). See also Janet Currie and Duncan Thomas, "Does Head Start Make a Difference?" 85 *American Economic Review* 341 (1995) (finding white pupils who went to Head Start do better on standardized tests than those who attended other preschools and repeat grades less frequently). For general surveys of some of the substantial number of efficacy reviews, see, e.g., Urie Bronfenbrenner, "Is Early Intervention Effective?" in *Handbook of Evaluation Research* vol. 2, 519 (E. Struening and M. Guttentag eds., 1975) and Lois-ellin Datta, "Another Spring and Other Hopes: Some Findings from National Evaluations of Project Head Start," in *Project Head Start: A Legacy of the War on Poverty* 405 (E. Zigler and J. Valentine eds., 1979).

67. See, e.g., Michael Boozer, Alan Krueger, and Shari Wolkon, "Race and School Quality since Brown v. Board of Education," 1992: *Brookings Papers on Economic Activity: Microeconomics* 269, 295–297, 306–313 (computer use in school varies by race and class background of parents and appears to have genuine labor market effects); Marjorie Ragosta, Paul Holland, and Dean Jamison, *Computer-Assisted Instruction and Compensatory Education: The ETS/LAUSD Study* 97, 105, 110, 111 (1982) (exposure of randomly selected students to increased levels of computer instruction from grades two to six improved students' test scores).

68. Henry Levin, Gene Glass, and Gail Meister, "Cost-Effectiveness of Computer-Assisted Instruction," 11 *Evaluation Review* 50, 66 (1987).

69. Mary Boehnlein, "Reading Intervention for High-Risk First-Graders," 44 *Educational Leadership* Mar. 1987 at 32.

70. Nancy Madden, Robert Slavin, Nancy Kowett, and Barbara Livermon, "Restructuring the Urban Elementary School," 46 *Educational Leadership* Feb. 1989 at 14, 18.

71. Robert Slavin and Nancy Madden, "What Works for Students at Risk: A Research Synthesis," 46 *Educational Leadership* Feb. 1989 at 4.

72. One of the special educators whom we interviewed told us that he believed that roughly half of the pupils labeled LD in the district in which he worked were "truly" LD, but that the correctly identified LD population, in his opinion, made little educational progress. "The 25 percent who eventually show significant changes in their ability were probably misdiagnosed."

73. See Deborah Simmons, "Perspectives on Dyslexia: Commentary on Educational Concerns," 25 *Journal of Learning Disabilities* 66, 67 (1992) (citing an unpublished paper by C. Juel that found that 88 percent of fifty-four first graders who read below grade level at the end of first grade continued to do so at the end of fourth grade while 87 percent of readers who read at the average level at the end of first grade continued to do so at the end of the fourth grade).

74. Elizabeth Short, Lynne Feagans, James McKinney, and Mark Appelbaum, "Longitudinal Stability of LD Subtypes Based on Age- and IQ-Achievement Discrepancies," 9 *Learning Disability Quarterly* 214 (1986).

75. Keith E. Stanovich, "Discrepancy Definitions of Reading Disability: Has Intelligence Led Us Astray?" 26 *Reading Research Quarterly* 7 (1991).

76. Id. at 15.

77. Michael Pressley and Joel Levin, "Elaborative Learning Strategies for the Inefficient Learner" in *Handbook of Cognitive, Social, and Neuropsychological Aspects of Learning Disabilities* vol II 175 (S. Ceci ed., 1987).

78. H. Lytton, "Follow-up of an Experiment in Selection for Remedial Education," 37 *British Journal of Educational Psychology* 1, 3, 5 (1967).

79. James McKinney, "Research on the Identification of Learning-Disabled Children: Perspectives on Changes in Educational Policy," in *Research in Learning Disabilities: Issues and Future Directions* 215, 229 (S. Vaughan and C. Bos eds., 1987).

80. See Michael Rutter and William Yule, "The Concept of Specific Reading Retardation," 16 *Journal of Child Psychology and Psychiatry* 181 (1975), and W. Yule, "Differential Prognosis of Reading Backwardness and Specific Reading Retardation," 43 *British Journal of Educational Psychology* 244 (1973).

81. See, e.g., Michele Labuda and J. C. Defries, "Cognitive Abilities in Children with Reading Disabilities and Controls: A Follow-Up Study," 21 *Journal of Learning Disabilities* 562, 564–565 (1988). Stanovich, "Discrepancy Definitions of Reading Disability" at 15.

82. Otfried Spreen, "Adult Outcome of Reading Disorders," in *Reading Disorders: Varieties and Treatments* 473, 483 (R. Malatesha and P. Aaron eds., 1982).

83. See Steven Schonhaut and Paul Satz, "Prognosis for Children with Learning Disabilities" in *Developmental Neuropsychiatry* 542, 543, 550 (Michael Rutter ed., 1983).

84. See Joan Finucci, "Follow-up Studies of Developmental Dyslexia and Other Learning Disabilities," in *Genetics and Learning Disabilities* 97, 116–118 (Shelly Smith ed., 1986).
85. Wade Horn, James O'Donnell, and Lawrence Vitulano, "Long-Term Follow-Up Studies of Learning-Disabled Persons," 16 *Journal of Learning Disabilities* 542, 554 (1983).
86. Id. at 551.
87. Id. at 552.
88. Id. at 547.
89. See Mary Wagner, Ronald D'Amico, Camille Marder, Lynn Newman, and Jose Blackorby, *What Happens Next? Trends in Postschool Outcomes of Youths with Disabilities*, The Second Comprehensive Report from the National Longitudinal Transition Study of Special Education Students (SRI International, Dec. 1992).
90. Id. Table 3-1.
91. See Mary Wagner et al., *What Makes a Difference? Influences on Postschool Outcomes of Youth with Disabilities*, The Third Comprehensive Report from the National Longitudinal Transition Study of Special Education Students, Table 5-1 (SRI International, 1993).
92. Id. at p. 3-13.
93. Id. at p. 3-11.
94. The same could not be said for SED pupils: the 1992 SRI longitudinal study finds that 58 percent of children classified as SED had been arrested within five years of leaving school. See Wagner, *What Happens Next* at 6-32. The arrest rate for SED children who had dropped out of school was 73 percent. (Actually, the arrest rate for LD pupils is less encouraging than the White study cited in the text implies: 30 percent of labeled LD pupils have been arrested within five years of leaving school, compared with less than 20 percent for all other disability categories [id. at 6-35].)
95. See W. White, D. Deshler, J. Schumaker, M. Warner, G. Alley, and F. Clark, "The Effects of Learning Disabilities on Post-School Adjustment," 49 *Journal of Rehabilitation* 46 (Jan./Feb./Mar. 1983). See also Patricia Sitlington and Alan Frank, "Are Adolescents with Learning Disabilities Successfully Crossing the Bridge into Adult Life?" 13 *Learning Disability Quarterly* 97, 102, 108 (1990) (follow-up study of 911 LD pupils one year out of high school found only 54 percent met the following four criteria: (a) employed or "otherwise meaningfully engaged," (b) living independently or with a parent or relative, (c) paying at least a portion of their living expenses, and (d) involved in more than one leisure activity; average wage is $4.39/hour).
96. Wagner et al., *What Happens Next* at Table 4-9.
97. Joan Finucci, Linda Gottfredson, and Barton Childs, "A Follow-Up Study of Dyslexic Boys," 35 *Annals of Dyslexia* 117, 134 (1985).
98. Id. at 118, 125.
99. Id. at 126–127.

100. Id. at 135.
101. See Susan Vogel and Pamela Adelman, "Extrinsic and Intrinsic Factors in Graduation and Academic Failure among LD College Students," 40 *Annals of Dyslexia* 119, 128 (1990).
102. Id. at 127.
103. See *Fourteenth Annual Report to Congress on the Implementation of the Individuals with Disabilities Education Act*, U.S. Department of Education, p. A-48 (1992).
104. See *Digest of Education Statistics 1992*, National Center for Education Statistics, Table 196 (1.3 percent of postsecondary students had a learning disability in 1986); Vogel and Adelman, "Academic Failure among LD College Students" at 120 (stating figure is roughly 1 percent, but noting that it is likely an underestimate given reliance on self-reporting data).
105. See also Wagner et al., *What Happens Next* at pp. 3–11, 3–13 (while 68 percent of general youth population has enrolled in postsecondary schools within five years of leaving school, only 27 percent of the disabled population has, despite proportional enrollment of physically disabled students in postsecondary schools. Even for disabled students who do not drop out of high school, only 37 percent have enrolled in postsecondary school within five years of graduation).
106. *Fourteenth Annual Report*, p. A-156.
107. See "Graduation Rate for Blacks Up: Numbers Steady for Whites, Latinos," *Los Angeles Times*, Nov. 21, 1994, p. A13. The data reported in the text are consistent with data we obtained from our informants in districts we analyzed more closely: for instance, in one almost entirely African-American Mississippi district, only 10% of the children labeled LD graduate with a diploma compared with 90 percent of the non-LD pupils. Only one 1993 graduate labeled LD had gone on to junior college and none to four-year colleges, while roughly half of the school's non-LD pupils went on to either four-year colleges or junior colleges (60 percent of this group had gone to junior colleges). The failure of pupils with LDs to go on to college may be a result of the failure of remediation to bolster skills, or it may be due to the fact that disabled students are needlessly tracked and take only nondiploma, nonacademic courses.
108. For analyses broadly consistent with this view, see, e.g., Scott Sigmon, *Radical Analysis of Special Education* 75–82, 90–97, 101 (1987); Sally Tomlinson, *A Sociology of Special Education* (1982); John Gliedman and William Roth, *The Unexpected Minority: Handicapped Children in America* (1980); Phillip Jones, "Special Education and Socioeconomic Retardation," 19 *Journal for Special Educators* v (1983); Lynn Gelzheiser, "Reducing the Number of Students Identified as Learning Disabled: A Question of Practice, Philosophy, or Policy?" 54 *Exceptional Children* 145 (1987); Alan Gartner and Dorothy Kerzner Lipsky, "New Conceptualizations for Special Education" in *Critical Voices on Special Education: Problems and Progress Concerning the Mildly Handicapped* 175 (Scott Sigmon ed., 1990).

109. Stanovich seems to us to make a parallel point, arguing against the exclusive use of nonverbal intelligence measures when trying to diagnose dyslexics: "It goes largely unnoticed that, when people argue for the greater fairness of nonverbal tests, they in effect jettison the notion of *potential*, at least in its common meaning. They cannot mean the potential for verbal comprehension through print if the dyslexic's decoding deficits were remediated, because this is not what the IQ tests—particularly the performance tests they are recommending—assess. Instead, people who make the "fairness" argument are implicitly asserting that dyslexics could perform much better if society were not organized so much around literacy . . . It . . . makes little sense to adopt a linguistic usage of the term *potential* that requires the assumption that literacy-based technological societies will be totally reconstructed." Stanovich, "Discrepancy Definitions of Reading Disability" at 17.

110. For strong arguments that cultural-economic disadvantage and racism function much as learning disabilities purportedly do—suppressing the realization of underlying potential—see, e.g., Kenneth A. Kavale, "Learning Disability and Cultural-Economic Disadvantage: The Case for a Relationship," 11 *Learning Disability Quarterly* 195 (1988) and Claude Steele, "Race and the Schooling of Black Americans," *Atlantic Monthly*, April 1992 at 68.

111. One of us has expressed the view that making rationing decisions explicit is the main goal of reasonable health reform. See Mark Kelman, "Health Care Rights: Distinct Claims, Distinct Justifications," 3 *Stanford Law and Policy Review* 90 (1991).

7. Accommodation on Law School Exams

1. Warren Willingham, Marjorie Ragosta, Randy Elliot Bennett, Henry Braun, Donald A. Rock, and Donald K. Powers, *Testing Handicapped People* 47–48 (1988).

2. College Entrance Examination Board, *Profile of SAT and Achievement Test Takers* (1987–1993) 7 (indicating the number of students with "disabling conditions").

3. Communication from Educational Testing Service, summary of responses to Question 39, Student Descriptive Questionnaire.

4. Letter from M. Jane Umnas, Committee of Bar Examiners of the State Bar of California, Office of Admissions, March 15, 1994.

5. Obviously, there is a substantial normative debate about whether an educational institution should serve such a sorting function, which does not, on its face, further the development of students' intellectual or moral capacities. But assuming the faculty believes "signaling" to be one of its roles, it would likely seek empirical guidance in deciding whether to accommodate LD students. The faculty might ask itself whether the correlation between student grades (the predictor) and on-the-job performance (the criterion) will rise or fall if LD students are accommodated.

Alternatively, the faculty may believe that the appropriate question is whether LD students' nonaccommodated grades, while as predictive of performance as non-LD students' grades so long as the workplace is nonaccommodating, would predict performance less accurately than accommodated grades in the limited number of workplaces that are themselves more appropriately accommodating.

Ascertaining whether accommodation increases or decreases the correlation between grades and adult performance, regardless of whether the employment setting is itself "adequately accommodating," is monumentally difficult. Not even the best empirical studies can overcome the lack of normative agreement on the criteria we hope our grades will predict—what does success on the job mean? higher income? higher ratings by supervisors? higher ratings by clients? briefs judged excellent by a panel of law clerks?

The truth is that we have very little idea whether grades are significantly predictive of long-term performance for non-LD students. Most of the studies that have attempted to determine the linkage between grades in either college or professional school and some measure of adult success find that there are statistically significant correlations, but that the magnitude of the effects is rather insubstantial. Those with higher grades may be (modestly) more successful as adults for two quite distinct reasons: their high grades may measure virtues that prove important in adult life, or they may permit the individual who receives them to receive opportunities (especially additional educational opportunities) that increase adult success.

Baird's massive review article ("Do Grades and Tests Predict Adult Accomplishment?" 23 *Research in Higher Education* 3 [1985]) reaches typical conclusions. While the correlations between grades and success are modest, they are undoubtedly suppressed because of both predictor range restriction and criterion unreliability. Students coming from a single institution are generally preselected to be rather like one another in ability; we cannot be sure if students with a broader range of academic abilities would not exhibit a broader, and more predictable, range of adult behaviors. As for criterion unreliability, we would not expect grades, or anything else, to measure a random outcome. Frequently, though, criteria in the studies are indeed rather random, e.g., attainment of a particular prize, supervisor ratings by one party on one occasion, and so on.

If the law school chooses to accommodate students with learning disabilities, still another debate might emerge: whether to disclose to employers that the student received such accommodations (as ETS discloses such information to universities). It may choose to do so, letting employers decide whether the speed deficit is significant in their own setting, or it may withhold such information, on the supposition that employers will mistakenly believe it relevant, thus perpetuating the discriminatory exclusion of qualified people.

6. Grades may well be an atypical consumption good in the sense that they might primarily be consumed as "positional" goods. A good grade in this sense is simply a grade better than other pupils' grades, rather than a "level of praise" that can be assessed without regard to its relative meaning. With traditional, dominantly nonpositional consumption goods (like food), we typically assume that people will enjoy the goods whether others enjoy them or not—that is, we assume interdependent consumption satisfaction (e.g., envy) is the exception. It is difficult to imagine, though, that students would experience nominally high grades as a significant benefit if every- one received those grades, at least in the absence of misperception by the students themselves or by outsiders that the students hoped to deceive.

We do not want to overstate this contrast: one aspect of "traditional" con- sumption goods is that consuming them bespeaks their high relative sta- tus. "Better" food may, in part, "taste better," but access to fancy food also symbolizes relative success.

Despite whatever distinctions one might draw between ordinary con- sumption goods and grades, it still seems reasonable to treat grades— within a culture that typically distributes all consumption goods unequally, anyway—as more like material rewards than they are different. We do not give out differential praise in the form of grades simply because it is the only way of praising: it is far more plausible to say that we differentiate "grade rewards" because we typically differentiate rewards more generally.

7. A 1990 review of the literature on LD college students reports finding no empirical studies, in over one hundred articles published over twenty years, of the effectiveness of measures to accommodate the learning dis- abled (either on tests or in education). See J. O. Smith, Charles Hughes, and Judith Osgood, "Cognitive and Academic Performance of College Students with Learning Disabilities: A Synthesis of the Literature," 13 *Learning Disability Quarterly* 66, 77 (Winter 1990).

8. See John Centra, "Handicapped Student Performance on the Scholastic Aptitude Test," 19 *Journal of Learning Disabilities* 324 (1986). An earlier study by Ragosta found a larger gap between the performance of LD stu- dents who sought accommodation and college-bound seniors during the 1979–1983 period: the LD students taking the nonstandard exam did two- thirds of a standard deviation worse on both verbal and math SATs. See Willingham et al., *Testing Handicapped People* at 53.

9. Libertarians, for instance, contend that a distribution should be judged as just or unjust depending solely upon the historical processes by which it arose, rather than the pattern it assumes according to merit, need, or any other end-state criterion. Thus in libertarian terms, any income distribution is just as long as those possessing goods acquired them legitimately. It might conceivably bolster the political acceptability of libertarian distribu- tive principles if the resulting outcome generally matched the distribution meritocrats would favor, but libertarians note that there will surely be le- gitimate departures from any desired end-state, including one favored by meritocrats (e.g., gifts and bequests won't go to the meritorious in any pat-

terned way). But the libertarian argument against generalized meritocracy, whether convincing or not, is simply not germane to the "micro" case we're posing: the school does not pretend to establish a general social pattern of rewards, corresponding to one ideal of merit. It does not use force to ensure that those judged most competent in its own terms reap more social rewards in every setting, but rather it is simply one of many, independent sources of social rewards.

Similarly, those predisposed to think "economistically" are unlikely to believe that distributions ought to correspond to merit (except to the limited extent that a preference-based, hedonic social welfare function might incorporate the positive value that some individuals might happen to place on believing that merit has been rewarded). Most "economistic" commentators believe that normatively desirable distribution occurs in two stages: first, distributive shares are earned in a relatively unfettered market, which is then, in a "second" stage, "corrected" through tax and transfer programs.

In the first and dominant stage, there is little reason to believe, or hope, that merit will inevitably be rewarded. Those who purchase goods—or "entrepreneurs" (effectively acting as agents for these buyers, attempting to procure them goods at the lowest possible cost of production by hiring producers)—simply reward those who are legally privileged to withhold their resources (labor or capital) in order to induce them to provide the goods they seek. Buyers, though, needn't believe that those privileged to withhold the productive resources they desire have any particular virtues, nor that those unable to withhold such resources are less meritorious; payment is solely instrumental to obtaining goods.

Even when the state self-consciously "corrects" market outcomes, it is unlikely that correcting the market's failure to reward the virtuous will, or should, be an especially significant goal. While one function the state might serve is indeed to increase demand for "worthy" causes for which market demand is deemed inadequate—e.g., "high art," education, and so on—there is little reason to believe that those enriched by the state's support for what it sees as merit goods are, as *persons,* more meritorious than those who are well paid because effective private demand rewards them highly.

Moreover, most government transfers directed toward persons are (appropriately) transferred to those deemed needier (for whom income is generally deemed to have higher marginal utility), not to those deemed more virtuous than those who were highly rewarded in the "private market."

Once more, though, the "economistic" critique of the relevance of merit to distribution, whether persuasive or not, turns out to be rather irrelevant to our law exam "micro" case: the school does not give out grades dominantly to obtain (desired) services from the students, but rather does seek, self-consciously, to reward perceived virtue.

10. The two dominant "left" critiques of the moral relevance of merit-based distributive judgments seem also, on careful inspection, largely to drop out of this "micro" debate. Liberal political theorists, most prominently Rawls, have long argued that one cannot recognize merit by looking at manifest

performance, noting that such performance is grounded in nonmerited capabilities (a result of genetic and environmental advantages that the capable actor does not deserve).

More radical commentators are prone to believe that "merit" judgments illegitimately glorify the achievements of those with social power, and that, in a world of reasonable social equality, all forms of behavior would be appreciated as equally meritorious. (The claims on the more radical "multiculturalist" left are somewhat hard to interpret, however, as to whether they imply that the achievements of all social *groups* would be evaluated as equally meritorious or whether the achievements of all *individuals* would be evaluated as equally meritorious.)

But neither of these criticisms tells us whether to accommodate the learning disabled given a system which rewards people differently, depending on their performance on tests, even if it tells us, more generally, that *any* system that provides differential rewards based on test performance fails to reward true merit. The radical left critique may, in ways we will return to, give faculties a certain salutary self-critical pause in trying to ascertain what skills they believe are genuinely significant, but as long as the faculty ultimately chooses to reward some performance as superior, it disclaims the sort of radical skepticism about differentiation that this critique most lucidly supports.

11. See, e.g., D. L. Speece, "Information Processing Subtypes of Learning Disabled Readers," in *Learning Disability Subtyping, Neuropsychological Foundations, Conceptual Models, and Issues in Clinical Differentiation* (S. Hooper and W. G. Willis eds., 1989).

12. See F. Hayes, G. Hynd, and J. Wisenbaker, "Learning Disabled and Normal College Students' Performance on Reaction Time and Speeded Classification Tasks," 78 *Journal of Educational Psychology* 39 (1986). For confirming studies, see P. Ackerman and R. Dykman, "Automatic and Effortful Information Processing Deficits in Children with Learning and Attention Disorders," 2 *Topics in Learning and Learning Disabilities* 12 (1982); Laird S. Cermak, "Information Processing Deficits in Children with Learning Disabilities," 16 *Journal of Learning Disabilities* 599 (1983).

13. For discussions of the range of accommodations that might be offered, see L. C. Brinckerhoff, "Accommodation for College Students with Learning Disabilities: The Law and Its Implementation" in *Tomorrow Is Another Day* (J. Gartner ed., 1985); Pamela Adelman and Debbie Olufs, *Assisting College Students with Learning Disabilities: A Tutor's Manual* 25 (1986).

14. See "Types of Learning Disabilities" in *Final Report of the Policy Group on Programs for Disabled People*, Appendix B (Stanford University, May 1985).

15. Id.

16. Id.

17. As a practical matter, tailoring an exam to meet these theoretical goals seems nearly impossible. We know neither how "rushed" most students feel on exams nor whether differentiation in the subjective experience of "rushing" has any objective effects on relative performance. Nor do we know for any particular student with a learning disability how much or lit-

tle time will make her feel "appropriately rushed," regardless of our definition of "appropriate." When Bennett, Rock, and Kaplan studied the special
administration of the SAT, they found that none of the nine handicapped
groups taking the accommodated version of the test was disadvantaged by
insufficient time, and that, to the contrary, some groups of disabled test takers completed a higher number of items than nondisabled test takers. (See
4 *Special Services in the Schools* 37 [1988].)

There are also, quite clearly, distinctions within the class of students
classified as LD. Among LD students given extra time for the SAT test between 1979 and 1983, 95 percent were able to finish within six hours (a bit
more than double time), but more than half (56 percent) were able to finish
in four hours. (See Willingham et al., *Testing Handicapped People* at 179.)
Thus determining precisely how much extra time a pupil needs (or will
likely use) simply on the basis of his diagnostic category is impossible.

18. M. Kay Runyan and Joseph F. Smith, Jr., "Identifying and Accommodating
Learning Disabled Law School Students," 41 *Journal of Legal Education* 317
(1991).
19. Id. at 328–329.
20. M. Kay Runyan, "The Effect of Extra Time on Reading Comprehension
Scores for University Students with and without Learning Disabilities," 24
Journal of Learning Disabilities 104 (1991).
21. Subsequent to Runyan and Smith's *Journal of Legal Education* article, a
Canadian researcher did indeed prepare a more conventional two-by-two
research study of changes in the performance of LD and non-LD students
on timed and untimed reading comprehension tests. (The University of
Toronto PhD thesis was written by Susan Weaver and entitled "The
Validity of the Use of Extended and Untimed Testing for Postsecondary
Students with Learning Disabilities.") The study seems far more straightforward than Runyan's, though the author's interpretation of her data
seems overstated: thirty-one university students diagnosed with LD and
forty non-LD students took timed and untimed versions of the Nelson-
Denny Reading Test: LD students' scores in untimed conditions improved
in a fashion the author finds dramatic (from the 48th to the 78th percentile
in vocabulary, from the 22nd to 79th percentile in reading comprehension)
while non-LD students improved in a fashion she declares to be "marginal"
(going from the 83rd to 89th percentile in untimed conditions on vocabulary and from the 70th to the 86th percentile on reading comprehension in
untimed conditions). The seemingly small distinctions in percentile gains,
though, belie that fact that in "normalized" standard deviation terms, gains
for the non-LD pupils, while far lower than the gains achieved by the LD
pupils, are actually quite substantial: assuming the test has a normal distribution, non-LD students made a .27 SD gain on the vocabulary test (compared with the .75 SD gain by the LD pupils) and an extremely substantial
.56 SD gain on the comprehension test. (If one looks at the data in in percentile terms, the gains LD pupils made on the vocabulary test appear
nearly double the gains the non-LD pupils made on the reading compre-

hension test, but small percentile gains among people already near the top of a distribution may be far more dramatic than they at first appear: as a result, in more relevant standard deviation normalized terms, the non-LD students' gains on the comprehension test were 87 percent as substantial as the LD students' gains on the vocabulary test.)

22. See E. J. Morrison, "On Test Variance and the Dimensions of the Measurement Situation," 20 *Educational and Psychological Measurement* 231 (1960). See also C. Anne Moreton and H. J. Butcher, "Are Rural Children Handicapped by the Use of Speeded Tests in Selection Procedures?" 33 *British Journal of Educational Psychology* 22 (1963).

23. For instance, Evans and Reilly perennially found (on the reading comprehension sections of the LSAT, the SAT, and the business school admissions exam) that students across groups completed more items and generally scored marginally better when given more time. See Franklin R. Evans and Richard R. Reilly, "A Study of Speededness as a Source of Test Bias," 9 *Journal of Educational Measurement* 123 (1972); Franklin R. Evans and Richard R. Reilly, "A Study of Test Speededness as a Potential Source of Bias in the Quantitative Score of the Admission Test for Graduate Study in Business," 1 *Research in Higher Education* 173 (1973); Richard Reilly and Franklin R. Evans, *The Effects of Test Time Limits on Performance of Culturally Defined Groups* (Educational Testing Service, 1972). It is clear, as well, that the extent of a nonhandicapped student's gain from more time depends upon how speeded the exam is: Evans, notes, for instance, that nonhandicapped students may be hurt significantly by "reduced time" but gain only modestly from extensions, but of course this implies that they would gain significantly from increased time if the "baseline" were the time granted nonhandicapped students in his "reduced time" experiment. See F. R. Evans, *A Study of the Relationships among Speed and Power, Aptitude Test Scores, and Ethnic Identity* (Educational Testing Service Report 80-22, 1980). Wild and Durso also found relatively small but significant gains for an exceptionally large sample of students who took experimental sections of the Graduate Record Exam (GRE) under mildly less time-constrained conditions. Wild and Durso also found that all groups of test takers gained when given added time on the experimental section; though once more the investigators were not specifically studying handicapped versus nonhandicapped students. See C. Wild and R. Durso, *Effects of Increased Test-Taking Time on Test Scores by Ethnic Group, Age, and Sex* (GRE Board Research Report GREB No. 76-6R, Educational Testing Service, 1979). Similarly, Knapp's study indicated that both Anglo and Mexican test takers received higher raw scores on untimed versions of standard intelligence tests, just as Immerman found that an experimental group of Native Americans scored higher on an untimed standardized achievement test than did the control group taking the test under ordinary timed conditions. See Robert R. Knapp, "The Effects of Time Limits on the Intelligence Test Performance of Mexican and American Subjects," 51 *Journal of Educational Psychology* 14 (1960), and Michael A. Immerman, "The Effect of Eliminating Time Restraints on a Standardized Test with American Indian

Adults" (Southwestern Polytechnic Institute 1980, U.S Department of Health, Education and Welfare).

24. See L. D. Miller, C. Mitchell, and M. Van Audsall, "Evaluating Achievement in Mathematics: Exploring the Gender Biases of Timed Testing," 114 *Education* 436 (1994).

25. College Entrance Examination Board, *1993 Profile of SAT and Achievement Test Takers* 7.

26. John A. Centra, "Handicapped Student Performance on the Scholastic Aptitude Test," 19 *Journal of Learning Disabilities* 324 (1986).

27. Marjorie Ragosta and Cathy Wendler, *Eligibility Issues and Comparable Time Limits for Disabled and Non-Disabled SAT Examinees*, College Board Report No. 92-5, Educational Testing Service RR No. 92-35 (1992).

28. Gail Munger and Brenda Loyd, "Effect of Speededness on Test Performance of Handicapped and Nonhandicapped Examinees," 85 *Journal of Educational Research* 53, 56 (1991).

29. We are dealing with institutions that have neither chosen to grade observed behavioral effort nor refused to grade entirely, perhaps relying in part either on the Rawlsian idea that even distinctions in effort are likely to result from factors that people don't deserve or on the notion that it is not feasible to observe distinctions in effort.

30. Jeffry Gallet, "The Judge Who Could Not Tell His Right from His Left and Other Tales of Learning Disabilities," 37 *Buffalo Law Review* 739, 747 (1988). Emphasis added.

31. For discussions of the historical use of IQ tests, particularly to make claims of racial superiority, see, e.g., Stephen J. Gould, *The Mismeasure of Man* 146–233 (1981).

32. Note the parallel problem in the context of discipline (the distribution of punishment, rather than praise): a child with ADD or an LD may complain that the district overvalues pupils' sitting still, or mischaracterizes walking around the classroom as disruptive. In that case, discipline for getting up and walking around is inapt because the behavior is not properly substantively devalued (just as speed, perhaps, oughtn't to be valued). But the response to that recognition should probably be to remove "walking around" from the offense code rather than to immunize ADD children from the reach of the code, both because it is unacceptable to punish reasonable behavior and because immunizing only a subset of a population from a reasonable code puts undue pressure on diagnosticians to identify who belongs in and who should be excluded from the immunized class. What is most difficult, in both the exam-accommodation and the discipline context, is to figure out what to do when one believes one must balance competing concerns: thus speed is a virtue but testing speed unduly penalizes the students with LDs; not staying put is a flaw but it is such a difficult flaw for pupils with ADD to avoid manifesting that they'll inevitably fail if that rule is dispositive of their right to attend regular classes, even when they're obeying other aspects of the discipline code.

33. See, e.g., G. Kerstiens, "A Testimonial on Timed Testing: Developmental

Students and Reading Comprehension Tests" in *Fiftieth Yearbook of the Claremont Reading Conference* 261 (M. Douglass ed., 1986); Thomas Donlon, *An Exploratory Study of the Implications of Test Speededness* (Educational Testing Service, 1980); Alexander G. Wesman, "Some Effects of Speed in Test Use," 20 *Educational and Psychological Measurement* 267 (1960).

34. Lee Cronbach and W. G. Warrington, "Time Test Limits: Estimating their Reliability and Degree of Speeding," 16 *Psychometrika* 167 (1951).

35. William G. Mollenkopf, "An Experimental Study of the Effects on Item-Analysis Data of Changing Item Placement and Test Time Limit," 15 *Psychometrika* 291 (1950).

36. See Centra, "Handicapped Student Performance" at 325.

37. The first claim amounts to the assertion that speed improves criterion validity; the second that it is content-valid. For a discussion of "criterion" and "content" validity, see Mark Kelman, "Concepts of Discrimination in 'General Ability' Job Testing," 104 *Harvard Law Review* 1157, 1171 (1991); Uniform Guidelines on Employee Selection Procedures, 29 C.F.R. §§1607.5(B), 1607.16(D)–(F) (1990).

38. L. M. Kendall, "The Effects of Varying Time Limits on Test Validity," 24 *Educational and Psychological Measurement* 789 (1964) (emphasis in original).

39. Accommodated SAT scores for LD pupils not only overpredict their future college grades, but correlate more poorly with the grades the student has received in high school than SAT scores generally do, once more dramatically overstating the student's performance levels. In Ragosta's study, students with LDs taking nonstandard exams did two-thirds of a standard deviation worse than nondisabled college-bound seniors on the verbal SAT, but their high school GPAs were .9 SD lower. See Willingham et al., *Testing Handicapped People* at 48–49, 53.

40. Id. at 119.

41. It may also be, of course, that colleges appropriately refuse to back off from a substantive contention that rapid responsiveness is itself virtuous—that the ability to integrate material quickly and respond to problems is one of the genuine virtues educated people should be able to manifest.

42. Willingham et al., *Testing Handicapped People* at 127.

43. Runyan and Smith, "Identifying and Accommodating Learning Disabled Law Students" at 329, n. 68.

44. Even if "people with disabilities" generally form a social group, the question of whether the learning disabled do is hardly transparent.

45. Griggs v. Duke Power Co., 401 U.S. 424 (1971).

46. See Watson v. Fort Worth Bank & Trust, 487 U.S. 977, 978–79 (1988) (employers may use a screening device with adverse impact as long as it screens workers in a fashion that improves company performance; even if the excluded workers could have performed tasks competently, without danger to others, the screening device is adequately "necessary" if it selects a higher-quality work force). For a discussion see Kelman, "Concepts of Discrimination" at 1166–1167, n. 24. See also David Strauss, "Discriminatory Intent and the Taming of *Brown*," 56 *University of Chicago Law*

Review 935, 1012–1013 (1989) (noting that practices forbidden under *Griggs* reveal discriminatory intent in the absence of inevitably unavailable "smoking gun" paper records of racial animus or stereotyping, since economically unjustified practices would not survive unless employers were either deliberately or inadvertently racist).

47. §105(a) of the Civil Rights Act of 1991, adding a new subsection (k)(1)(A) to §703 of Title VII.

48. See, e.g., Nash v. City of Jacksonville, 895 F. Supp. 1536 (M.D. Fla. 1995) (city prevails if test helps select "top-notch fire captains").

49. Commentators differ in their interpretations of just how necessary a practice that causes disproportionate impact must be. Some, like Mark Brodin, argue that a practice is not necessary if the company could survive as a viable entity without it and if hiring excluded workers posed no safety problems. (See Mark Brodin, "Costs, Profits and Equal Employment Opportunity," 62 *Notre Dame Law Review* 318, 327–333 [1987].) But this "strict" view of necessity not only misstates existing law, it ultimately makes little normative sense as well. It seems to make the legal permissibility of a company's efforts to improve efficiency turn on an utterly irrelevant factor, i.e., whether it happens to be earning supercompetitive profits and could therefore "survive" a decrease in efficiency. It might be arguable that all entities ought to be forced, legally, to bear some costs to increase levels of out-group inclusion in the economy (parallel to explicit requirements for "reasonable accommodation" in the context of the ADA). But even if Title VII law were reinterpreted to mandate such an implicit "inclusionary tax," there is no obvious reason why the tax should be imposed on some companies and not others if we view it as a rational regulation-imposed cost of doing business. Nor would ordinary proponents of progressive taxation assume that it was appropriate to impose a 100 percent marginal (regulatory) tax rate on all supercompetitive profits.

50. Alan Freeman, "Antidiscrimination Law: The View from 1989," in *The Politics of Law* 121 at 133 (David Kairys ed., revised ed. 1990) (emphasis added).

51. Freeman wrongly implies that no one believes that written test scores correlate with job performance despite the fact that the mainstream position among industrial psychologists is that test scores correlate highly with such performance. See, e.g., the interchange in F. Schmidt, J. Hunter, K. Perlman, and H. R. Hirsh, "Forty Questions about Validity Generalization and Meta-Analysis," 38 *Personnel Psychology* 697 (1987). We believe this view is about as unpersuasive as Freeman's opposing view that the tests are wholly nonpredictive. See Kelman, "Concepts of Discrimination" at 1208–1220. See also Henry M. Levin, "Ability Testing for Job Selection: Are the Economic Claims Justified?" in *Test Policy and the Politics of Opportunity Allocation* 211, 225–227 (Bernard Gifford ed., 1989) (skeptical of claims of high correlations between tests and performance but conceding that there are almost surely modest correlations).

52. See Michael Gold, "Griggs' Folly: An Essay on the Theory, Problems, and Origins of the Adverse Impact Definition of Employment Discrimination

and a Recommendation for Reform," 7 *Industrial Relations Law Journal* 429, 457 (1985); Richard Posner, "The Efficiency and the Efficacy of Title VII," 136 *University of Pennsylvania Law Review* 513, 515 (1987) (government actors are unlikely to recognize an inefficient mode of operation that market factors fail to perceive is inefficient). Even conservative commentators who most frequently attack *Griggs* for mandating group equality occasionally acknowledge that the case does so by shifting the burden of justification onto employers, a burden they despair cannot be met given the expense of test validation and the hostility of courts to meritorious justification claims. See, e.g., Jan Blits and Linda Gottfredson, "Equality or Lasting Inequality?" 27 *Society* 4, 8 (1990).

53. See Professor David Engel's remarks introducing Judge Gallet. Gallett, "The Judge Who Could Not Tell His Right from His Left" at 740.

54. See Kelman, "Concepts of Discrimination" at 1190–1194, and Mari Matsuda, "Voices of America: Accent, Antidiscrimination Law, and a Jurisprudence for the Last Reconstruction," 100 *Yale Law Journal* 1329 (1991) for arguments in favor of subsidizing "diversity."

55. Kelman, "Concepts of Discrimination" at 1241; Lester Thurow, "A Theory of Groups and Economic Redistribution," 9 *Philosophy and Public Affairs* 25, 32 (1979); Paul Brest and Miranda Oshige, "Affirmative Action for Whom?" 47 *Stanford Law Review* 855, 867–872 (1995).

56. It may well be the case that interdependent "communities" grow up faster nowadays and that "interest groups" are more prone to present their fiscal demands as demands on which "group survival" depends; it is a far deeper sociological question than we wish to explore whether such rapidly emerging "communities" ought to be thought of as a problematic symptom of a rent-seeking culture or as legitimate subcultures, albeit groups without much traditional foundation.

57. Plyer v. Doe, 457 U.S. 202, 219 n. 19, 220 (1982).

58. Frontiero v. Richardson, 411 U.S. 677, 686 (1973) (burdens are unjustified when based on immutable traits). In this view, too, it appears critical for lesbians and gays to argue that their status is unchosen in order to be justly protected against discrimination, and a number of legal commentators have so argued. Others have responded that gay and lesbian identity is indeed mutable, and that the case for legal protection of gay and lesbian rights does not rest on immutability. Compare Harris M. Miller II, "Note: An Argument for the Application of Equal Protection Heightened Scrutiny to Classifications Based on Homosexuality," 57 *Southern California Law Review* 797, 817–821 (1984) with Janet E. Halley, "The Politics of the Closet: Towards Equal Protection for Gay, Lesbian, and Bisexual Identity," 36 *UCLA Law Review* 915, 922–923 (1989).

59. See John Hart Ely, *Democracy and Distrust: A Theory of Judicial Review* 150–155 (1980) (the fact that a decision maker chooses to penalize someone for an immutable trait should trigger concern that the decision is made for irrational, irrelevant reasons).

60. Bernard Williams, "The Idea of Equality" in *Philosophy, Politics, and Society*

(second series) 110, 113 (Peter Laslett and W. G. Runciman eds., 1962).

61. See Robinson v. California, 370 U.S. 660, 665–666 (1962).

62. Id. See also Powell v. Texas, 392 U.S. 514 (1968) (inebriated public appearances by chronic alcoholics may be punished; though such appearances might well be nearly unavoidable consequences of essentially immutable traits, the punished behavior is still socially regulable).

63. See, generally, *Handbook of Human Intelligence* (Robert J. Sternberg ed., 1982); Philip E. Vernon, *Intelligence, Heredity, and Environment* (1979); J. W. Berry, "Radical Cultural Relativism and the Concept of Intelligence" in *Culture and Cognition: Readings in Cross-Cultural Psychology* (J. W. Berry and P. R. Dasen eds., 1974).

64. We differentiate at length in Chapter 8 between *rights* to be free from discrimination, which are not "balanced" against competing interests, and redistributive *policies,* in which prudential balancing concerns predominate. To preview the more elaborate argument, we urge that members of subordinated groups have antidiscrimination rights that protect them against "nonmeritocratic" treatment. At the same time, they are surely entitled to make claims to treatment more favorable than that, competing with other redistributive claimants: as redistributive claimants, such social policy interests as the desire to protect group subcultural vitality or the desire to distribute to members of groups when the impact of such redistribution on other group members will be especially salient compete with other non-rights-based social policy interests (e.g., the desire to eradicate need; the desire to maintain appropriate incentives for certain forms of behavior).

65. In this view, the faculty is fundamentally forward-looking and consequentialist rather than backward-regarding and desert-focused. Obviously, the faculty's goal—in this regard—is to encourage effort (which students control), rather than performance per se (which is doubtless partly a function of "talents" that are essentially immutable, at least by the time students reach law school). Nonetheless, it is perfectly plausible that the faculty believes it cannot disentangle the impacts of effort and immutable talent, and must, to encourage effort, reward output, the only observable product of effort.

66. For good discussions of this problem in the context of setting tax rates, see Barry Bosworth, *Tax Incentives and Economic Growth* (1984) and *How Taxes Affect Economic Behavior* (Henry J. Aaron and Joseph A. Pechman eds., 1981).

8. Ideology and Entitlement

1. For a general discussion broadly consistent with our framework, see Deborah Stone, *The Disabled State* (1984).

2. The attempt to differentiate treatment of the "deserving" and "undeserving" poor has been a constant, critical theme in welfare administration, both in the United Kingdom and in the United States. "Liberal" welfare reformers (especially in the United Kingdom) have frequently sought to universalize benefits to avoid stigmatization of recipients who would other-

wise have to "prove" their moral worthiness. Some of the standard historical discussions of the British experience can be found in Derek Fraser, *The Evolution of the British Welfare State* (2d ed. 1984); Maurice Bruce, *The Coming of the Welfare State: A History of Social Policy since the Industrial Revolution* (1968). See also Walter Trattner, *From Poor Law to Welfare State: A History of Social Welfare in America* (1974). For a good, brief history focusing solely on the American experience, see Joel Handler and Ellen Jane Hollingsworth, *The "Deserving Poor": A Study of Welfare Administration* 15–37 (1971). An interesting theoretical account of the stigmatic labeling of the "undeserving" pauper can be found in David Matza and Henry Miller, "Poverty and Disrepute" in *Contemporary Social Problems* 601 (R. Merton and R. Nisbet eds., 4th ed. 1976).

3. In fiscal year 1977, federal grants to the states under IDEA, Part B, were $251.7 million ($72/disabled child); they had risen to $1.543 billion by 1990 ($350/child) and $1.976 billion by the end of the Bush administration in 1992 ($419/child). (In constant 1990 dollars, the change was from $599 million to $1.543 billion to $1.84 billion; the increase between 1977 and 1990 was 157 percent; from 1977 to 1992, 207 percent.) Appropriations per child rose every year during the period. Rand studies indicate that, in real terms, special education expenditures by the states roughly doubled between 1977 and 1989. Moreover, the Rehabilitation Act of 1973 and the successor Americans with Disabilities Act of 1990, each proposed during Republican administrations, expanded both public and private obligations to those with disabilities during this period.

During the same era, Chapter One appropriations (to aid districts with high concentrations of children living in poverty) fluctuated widely, rather than exhibiting the sort of steady growth we see in appropriations under IDEA. In 1992–93 appropriations were, in real terms, only 16.8 percent higher than appropriations in the act's inaugural year (1965–66); appropriations from 1982–83 to 1989–90 were lower, in every year, in real terms, than they were in any year between 1965–66 and 1975–76.

Real poverty relief benefit levels dropped rather sharply as well during the period: in constant dollars, poor families received $5,355 in cash transfers in 1970, while by 1979, the figure had dropped to $4,427, and by 1986, $3,910. AFDC recipients received $19,753 in constant dollar benefits in 1976; by 1989, this figure had dropped (by roughly 19 percent) to $15,952.

It is doubtless the case that these trends can be explained, at least in part, without reference to Congressional or popular attitudes toward "deserving" and "undeserving" would-be recipients of governmental generosity. In each case, one could argue that Congress was most expansive only when it could readily impose an implicit, regulatory tax on private actors or local governments, rather than expend federal funds directly. The enactment of legislation in 1995 barring the Congress from imposing "unfunded mandates" on state and local governments in excess of $50 million without explicitly analyzing the mandated costs reflects the fear that such implicit taxes have been unduly easy to enact.

4. We discuss "multiculturalism" as a theory of distributive justice, but do not attempt to survey the full range of academic commentary on multiculturalism more generally that has emerged in recent years in philosophy, sociology, constitutional law, and other fields. For more comprehensive accounts of multiculturalism as a social movement, see, e.g., *Multiculturalism and the "The Politics of Recognition"* (Amy Gutman ed., 1992); Kenneth Karst, *Belonging to America: Equal Citizenship and the Constitution* (1989); Richard Abel, *Speech and Respect* (1994); Lawrence Foster and Patricia Herzog, *Contemporary Philosophical Perspectives on Pluralism and Multiculturalism: Defending Diversity* (1994); William Connolly, *Identity/Difference: Democratic Negotiations of Political Paradox* (1991).

5. For rather "moderate" statements of this basic view, see, e.g., Lucinda Finley, "Transcending Equality Theory: A Way Out of the Maternity and the Workplace Debate," 86 *Columbia Law Review* 1118 (1986), and Kathryn Abrams, "Gender Discrimination and the Transformation of Workplace Norms," 42 *Vanderbilt Law Review* 1183, 1189–1192 (1989). See also Christine Littleton, "Reconstructing Sexual Equality," 75 *California Law Review* 1279, 1321–1323 (1987); Diana Poole, "On Merit," 1 *Law and Inequality* 155 (1983). For a particularly vivid, nonacademic account of this viewpoint in the context of disabilities, see, e.g., Joseph Shapiro, *No Pity: People with Disabilities Forging a New Civil Rights Movement* 19 (1993). ("Our society automatically underestimates the capabilities of people with disabilities . . . a disability, of itself, is never as disabling as it first seems . . . the only thing that could have kept [a disabled reporter from working] would have been the paternalistic assumptions of his colleagues.")

6. This position is distinct from the more politically moderate claims from the center and center-left, which we will discuss in some detail, that discriminatory stereotyping may result in individuals' being paid less than marginal product, or that current workplace organization needlessly prevents individuals from being able to manifest their true productivity. The left multiculturalists are, in ways we will attempt to describe, far warier of claims that the traits that those with power value are truly valuable traits; they do not simply believe that those with power fail to recognize that "outsiders" possess these virtues as often as they actually do.

7. For an example of this translation of the claims of the "needy" into claims of being victimized by "classism," see Brian Mikulak, "Classism and Equal Opportunity: A Proposal for Affirmative Action in Education Based on Social Class," 33 *Howard Law Journal* 113 (1990). Vicki Been criticizes the supposition that "classism," rather than inadequate income, leads to one particular form of suffering that the poor bear disproportionately (exposure to toxics and other environmental hazards). See Vicki Been, "Locally Undesirable Land Uses in Minority Neighborhoods: Disproportionate Siting or Market Dynamics?" 103 *Yale Law Journal* 1383 (1994).

8. For cogent summaries of such classical liberal views, see Milton Friedman, *Capitalism and Freedom* (1962); Friedrich A. von Hayek, *The Constitution of Liberty* (1960); Ludwig von Mises, *Liberalism: A Socio-Economic Exposition*

(1978). For representatives in the legal academic world of the nineteenth-century liberal perspective, see Richard Epstein, *Takings: Private Property and the Power of Eminent Domain* (1986) and *Forbidden Grounds: The Case against Employment Discrimination Laws* (1992); Bernard Siegan, *Economic Liberties and the Constitution* (1980).

9. For the most persuasive version of the libertarian position, see Robert Nozick, *Anarchy, State, and Utopia* 149–231 (1974). Richard Epstein's *Takings* (1985) is dominated by natural rights language in the early goings, but it departs from it frequently as well in ways that stricter libertarians have noted, disapprovingly. For a discussion, see Mark Kelman, "Taking *Takings* Seriously: An Essay for Centrists," 74 *California Law Review* 1829, 1852–1858 (1986).

10. See, e.g., Edgar Browning and William Johnson, "The Trade-Off between Equality and Efficiency," 92 *Journal of Political Economy* 175 (1984). In the legal academy, this sort of utilitarian antiredistributionism is best articulated by Richard Posner. See, e.g., Richard Posner, *Economic Analysis of Law* 458–474, 499–502 (4th ed. 1992).

11. Antipaternalist utilitarianism in the law schools is commonplace. For instances, see Richard Posner, *Economic Analysis of Law* at 468–469; Richard Epstein, "In Defense of the Contract at Will," 51 *University of Chicago Law Review* 947 (1984). Obviously, it is commonplace outside the law schools as well. See, e.g., Francis Bator, "The Simple Analytics of Welfare Maximization," 47 *American Economic Review* 22, 25–31 (1957); James Buchanan, "What Kind of Redistribution Do We Want?" 35 *Economica* 185 (1968).

12. For an example of such Tory redistributive sentiments, based on the duty of the rich to care for their social inferiors, see, e.g., Anthony Ludovici, *A Defence of Aristocracy: A Text Book for Tories* 44, 79–81, 101–102, 172–174 (1916).

13. See, e.g., Bruce Hafen, "The Constitutional Status of Marriage, Kinship, and Sexual Privacy—Balancing the Individual and Social Interests," 81 *Michigan Law Review* 463 (1983).

14. See, e.g., Melvin Eisenberg, "The Bargain Principle and Its Limits," 95 *Harvard Law Review* 741, 763–778 (1982) (attempting to establish coherent limits in enforcing contracts given this sort of presumptive antipaternalism).

15. Typical within the liberal centrist law school world in its members' belief in ubiquitous market failures are Bruce Ackerman, *Reconstructing American Law* 56–58, 61–63 (1984); Richard Markovits, "The Distributive Impact, Allocative Efficiency, and Overall Desirability of Ideal Housing Codes: Some Theoretical Clarifications," 89 *Harvard Law Review* 1815 (1976).

16. See, e.g., Charles Stuart, "Consumer Protection in Markets with Informationally Weak Buyers," 12 *Bell Journal of Economics* 562 (1981); Michael Spence, "Consumer Misperceptions, Product Failure, and Producer Liability," 44 *Review of Economic Studies* 561 (1977); Dennis Epple

and Artur Raviv, "Product Safety: Liability Rules, Market Structure, and Imperfect Information," 68 *American Economic Review* 80 (1978).

17. See, e.g., Richard Musgrave, *The Theory of Public Finance: A Study in Public Finance* 43–44 (1959).

18. The classic statement was in A. C. Pigou, *The Economics of Welfare* 172–203 (4th ed. 1932). Obsession with unaccounted-for externalities dominated liberal torts scholarship in the postwar period. See, e.g., Fowler V. Harper and Fleming James, *The Law of Torts* (1955 and Supp. 1968). For an analysis of other "liberal" uses of externality analysis, see Duncan Kennedy, "Cost-Benefit Analysis of Entitlement Problems: A Critique," 33 *Stanford Law Review* 387, 398–400 (1981).

19. See, e.g., Ward Bowman, Jr., "Toward Less Monopoly," 101 *University of Pennsylvania Law Review* 577 (1953);

20. Outside the legal academic world, the liberal centrist focus on involuntary unemployment has been pervasive. Typical centrist works in the "broad" Keynesian tradition include James Tobin, "Inflation and Unemployment," 67 *American Economic Review* 1 (1972); Arthur Okun, "Rational-Expectations-with-Misperceptions as a Theory of the Business Cycle," 12 *Journal of Money, Credit, and Banking* 817 (1980); George Akerlof, Andrew Rose, and Janet Yellen, "Job Switching and Job Satisfaction in the U.S. Labor Market," 1988:2 *Brookings Papers on Economic Activity* 495. Few liberal centrist legal academics have paid much attention to the macroeconomy, though. For a discussion of the limited place of "macroeconomics" in the law school, see Mark Kelman, "Could Lawyers Stop Recessions? Speculations on Law and Macroeconomics," 45 *Stanford Law Review* 1215, 1216–1227 (1993).

21. For especially lucid examples of the politically centrist views, see Arthur Okun, *Equality and Efficiency: The Big Trade-Off* (1975); Paul Krugman, *The Age of Diminished Expectations: U.S. Economic Policy in the 1990s* 19–25 (1990).

22. See, e.g., Herbert Gintis, "Consumer Behavior and the Concept of Sovereignty: Explanations of Social Decay," 62 *American Economic Review (Papers and Proceedings)* 261 (1972). Adaptive preferences are noted in the legal literature, in, e.g., Karl Klare, "Workplace Democracy and Market Reconstruction: An Agenda for Legal Reform," 38 *Catholic University Law Review* 1 (1988), and Mark Kelman, "Choice and Utility," 1979 *Wisconsin Law Review* 769.

23. See, e.g., Michael Reich, *Racial Inequality: A Political-Economic Analysis* (1981); David Gordon, Richard Edwards, and Michael Reich, *Segmented Work, Divided Workers: The Historical Transformation of Labor in the United States* 141–143 (1982).

24. Richard Tawney, *Equality* (4th ed. 1952); Allen Buchanan, *Marx and Justice: The Radical Critique of Liberalism* (1982). For examples in the legal academic world, see Sylvia Law, "Economic Justice," in *Our Endangered Rights* (Norman Dorsen ed., 1984); Peter Edelman, "The Next Century of Our Constitution: Rethinking Our Duty to the Poor," 39 *Hastings Law Journal* 1 (1987).

25. See, e.g., Stephen Marglin, "What Do Bosses Do? The Origins and

Functions of Hierarchy in Capitalist Production," *Review of Radical Political Economy*, Summer 1974 at 60; Paul Blumberg, *Industrial Democracy: The Sociology of Participation* (1968).

26. For a fuller discussion of this aspect of centrist antidiscrimination ideology, see Mark Kelman, "Concepts of Discrimination in 'General Ability' Job Testing," 104 *Harvard Law Review* 1157, 1164–1170 (1991). For a particularly clean statement of this traditional centrist view, see R. Marshall, C. Knapp, M. Liggett, and R. Glover, *Employment Discrimination: The Impact of Legal and Administrative Remedies* 1–2 (1978) ("Institutional discrimination occurs when people are accorded different treatment because of attributes that are not associated with productivity.")

27. For good discussions of why groups might make valid claims on social resources as groups, see, e.g., Michael Piore, *Beyond Individualism* (1995); Iris Young, *Justice and the Politics of Difference* (1990); Paul Brest and Miranda Oshige, "Affirmative Action for Whom?" 47 *Stanford Law Review* 855 (1995).

28. For an excellent discussion of welfarist theories of redistribution, see Joseph Bankman and Thomas Griffith, "Social Welfare and the Rate Structure: A New Look at Progressive Taxation," 75 *California Law Review* 1905, 1916–1918, 1946–1955 (1987). The most compelling entitlements-based claims for redistributing to poorer citizens are found in John Rawls, *A Theory of Justice* 54–108, 258–332 (1971). For arguments emphasizing the moral duties of societies to respond to need, and the requirements to reflect carefully on what others in fact do need, see Michael Ignatieff, *The Needs of Strangers* (1984). For an excellent canvas of arguments about why societies might (and might not) be obliged to redistribute, see Robert Goodin, *Reasons for Welfare: The Political Theory of the Welfare State* (1988).

29. For a good discussion of the complex redistributive tasks that must be undertaken to make meaningful opportunity more nearly equal, see Jennifer Hochschild, "Race, Class, Power, and Equal Opportunity" in *Equal Opportunity* (Norman Bowie ed., 1988).

30. See, e.g., Wojciech Sadurski, *Giving Desert Its Due* 116–157 (1985). But see Joel Feinberg, *Doing and Deserving* 88–94 (1970) (discussing substantial limitations on the commonplace instinct that economic income and desert, measured in a wide variety of ways, should be strongly connected).

31. See, e.g., Frank Michelman, "Welfare Rights in a Constitutional Democracy," 1979 *Washington University Law Quarterly* 659.

32. For a discussion of political opposition to the Civil Rights Act of 1964, particularly among southern congressman, see Robert Loevy, *To End All Segregation: The Politics of the Passage of the Civil Rights Act of 1964* 160–161 (1990) ("When the bipartisan civil rights bill came before the Senate in March 1964, [Senator Richard] Russell [D-Georgia] and his Southern colleagues based most of their opposition on the idea that the bill was unconstitutional. The bill represented, they said, an unwarranted invasion by the United States Government of the property rights of those Americans who owned restaurants, motels, and swimming pools and who ought to be allowed to serve whomever they pleased . . . There is a 'natural right to dis-

criminate,' the Southerners concluded . . . [Moreover], the bill . . . would create a 'Federal blackjack' under which U.S. Government officials could come into any community in the country and override the wishes of the local politicians and the local citizenry . . . [G]iving the national government the power to dictate racial policies to the states violated . . . [the] territorial separation of powers and thus was unconstitutional"). For other negative libertarian responses to the bill, see 22 Cong. Q.W. no. 26, 1274, June 26, 1964 (statements by Senators Hickenlooper [R-Iowa] and Ellender [D-Louisiana]: "I am compelled to conclude that the far-reaching authority given to the Attorney General . . . will establish the pattern by law for the erosion of those rights of personal decision and responsibilities essential to a private economy and a free system"; "It is not possible to force one, by law, to associate with another not of his choosing").

33. For a discussion of this point, see Kelman, "Concepts of Discrimination" at 1170.

34. See Epstein, *Forbidden Grounds*.

35. See, e.g., Ellen Frankel-Paul, *Equity and Gender: The Comparable Worth Debate* 120 (1989) ("We ought not forget that in our headlong rush to create a discrimination free society—begun in the early 1960s with the Civil Rights Act . . . liberty is being squelched: liberty in the sense of freedom to associate, to hire whomever one chooses for whatever reason"). See also Epstein, *Forbidden Grounds* at 496–497, 505.

36. See, e.g., Frankel-Paul, *Equity and Gender* at 44; Epstein, *Forbidden Grounds* at 91–115. Note, though, that libertarian theorists would expect that plantwide segregation, though not industrywide segregation, might survive in a competitive environment either if workers preferred to associate with members of their subculture or if members of subgroups preferred certain culturally specific public goods to be provided at their workplace. Epstein, *Forbidden Grounds* at 45–46.

37. But see Richard Epstein, "Standing Firm, on Forbidden Grounds," 31 *San Diego Law Review* 1 (1994) (denying that antidiscrimination law is needed to supplement traditional tort law protections against infliction of emotional distress since the psychological harms that victims of racism describe are not really distinguishable from the harms that majority males would suffer subjected to parallel slights).

38. In this sense, we think legal writers like Charles Lawrence are correct to point out the considerable continuity between "hate speech" codes, on the one hand, and traditional civil rights legislation and the constitutional mandates of Brown v. Board of Education, on the other, at least as conservative Burkeans might best conceive of such policies. See, e.g., Charles Lawrence, "If He Hollers Let Him Go: Regulating Racist Speech on Campus," 1990 *Duke Law Journal* 431, 436.

39. Griggs v. Duke Power Co., 401 U.S. 424 (1971).

40. See Richard Posner, "The Efficiency and the Efficacy of Title VII," 136 *University of Pennsylvania Law Review* 513, 515 (1987) (government actors are unlikely to perceive an efficient mode of operation that market actors

fail to perceive); Lino Graglia, "Title VII of the Civil Rights Act of 1964: From Prohibiting to Requiring Racial Discrimination in Employment," 14 *Harvard Journal of Law and Public Policy* 68, 71–76 (1991) (unjustified practices with adverse impact are indeed problematic but courts should treat traditional employment criteria as presumptively justified); Stephen Coate and Glenn Loury, "Antidiscrimination Enforcement and the Problem of Patronization," 83 *American Economic Review (Papers and Proceedings)* 92 (1993) (while not objecting to rules requiring employers to treat protected workers "neutrally," authors note that use of neutral rules may be difficult to establish to the satisfaction of the court so that firms choose to use bottom line quotas instead).

41. Thus right centrists will note that an ideal zoning law might correct for low-level externalities that would not typically be corrected through high transaction cost negotiations among a multitude of "neighbors" but argue that *actual* zoning law will misfire. The reason, they argue, is because it relies excessively on unavailable technocratic "planning" expertise, or understates the perverse political pressures that lead self-interested voter coalitions to capture the local legislative process and turn it to selfish advantage. At the same time, right centrists are likely to believe that the "market" remedies (nuisance suits, private contractual land-use plans, and, above all, developer-initiated systems of land-use planning for subdivisions whose units will be devalued if "imposed" land-use plans are suboptimal) work far more passably than we might at first imagine. For the classic discussion, see Robert C. Ellickson, "Alternatives to Zoning: Covenants, Nuisance Rules, and Fines as Land Use Controls," 40 *University of Chicago Law Review* 681 (1977).

42. For a good summary of the virtues and problems with "audit pair" studies of discrimination, see James Heckman and Peter Siegelman, "The Urban Institute Audit Studies: Their Methods and Findings" in *Clear and Convincing Evidence: Measurement of Discrimination in America* 165–216 (Michael Fix and Raymond Struyk eds., 1992).

43. Such tests will be more easily performed when sellers of goods and services allegedly discriminate, since buyers have rather few relevant traits (solvency and mistreatment of seller facilities), than when employers allegedly discriminate, since tester pairs of job applicants can never be adequately matched along all relevant dimensions and efforts to match them along some dimensions may (as Heckman and Siegelman have noted) only lead employers to overreact to remaining distinctions that would not generally be salient.

44. For a fuller discussion of this aspect of centrist antidiscrimination ideology, see Kelman, "Concepts of Discrimination" at 1157, 1164–1170.

45. For a careful empirical study demonstrating that blacks and women may pay more for new cars despite competition among dealers, see Ian Ayres and Peter Siegelman, "Race and Gender Discrimination in Bargaining for a New Car," 85 *American Economic Review* 304 (1995).

46. Traditionally, animus was (mis)understood as a desire on the part of the

dominant group for separation or nonassociation. See, e.g., Gary Becker, *The Economics of Discrimination* 14 (2d ed. 1971). For a more plausible conception, focusing on the desire by the socially dominant group to express and fortify its hierarchical position and to injure and stigmatize the victim group, see Richard McAdams, "Cooperation and Conflict: The Economics of Group Status Production and Race Discrimination," 108 *Harvard Law Review* 1003 (1995).

47. For a typical discussion of the prevalence of negative stereotyping, especially in the gender context, see Bernice Lott, "The Devaluation of Women's Competence," 41 *Journal of Social Issues* no. 4 at 43 (1985).

48. These views are consistent with the views we would ascribe to mainstream centrists generally, outside the discrimination context: such centrists are far more likely than those to their political right to emphasize the untoward effects of misinformation on consumer decisions and of nonmonitorable managerial slack and incompetence on firm performance. Centrists are much more prone than political conservatives to believe both in the frequency of persistent cognitive error and its significance.

49. For discussions of validation requirements, see Uniform Guidelines on Employee Selection Procedures, 29 C.F.R. §§1607.5(b), 1607.16(D)–(F) (1990); Mary Green Miner and John Miner, *Employee Selection within the Law* 75–106 (1978).

50. Judicial inquiry into how work might be organized differently and whether organizational goals should shift has been very limited. See Kelman, "Concepts of Discrimination" at 1177–1183, 1187–1190.

51. See James Heckman and John Donohue III, "Continuous versus Episodic Change: The Impact of Civil Rights Policy on the Economic Status of Blacks," 29 *Journal of Economic Literature* 1603, 1614–1617, 1639–1641 (1991); McAdams, "Cooperation and Conflict" at 1003.

52. See Edmund Phelps, "The Statistical Theory of Racism and Sexism," 62 *American Economic Review* 659 (1972).

53. For a good summary of debates over whether statistical discrimination will adversely affect only atypically productive group members or adversely affect the group as a whole, see Dennis Aigner and Glen Cain, "Statistical Theories of Discrimination in Labor Markets," 30 *Industrial and Labor Relations Review* 175 (1977).

54. See, e.g., Weeks v. Southern Bell Tel. & Tel. Co. 408 F.2d 228, 235 n. 5 (5th Cir. 1969) (employers may use statistical rather than individualized screening devices only when "it is impossible or highly impractical to deal with women on an individualized basis").

55. See Stewart Schwab, "Is Statistical Discrimination Efficient?" 76 *American Economic Review* 228 (1986); Shelly Lundberg and Richard Startz, "Private Discrimination and Social Intervention in Competitive Labor Markets," 73 *American Economic Review* 340 (1983).

56. Rational statistical discrimination poses conceptual problems for political centrists for any number of reasons: first, the rational statistical discriminator is engaged in individually rational behavior, assessing probabilities

in a world of costly information, and testing hypotheses until beliefs correspond as closely as possible to reality, given that it is costly to make more precise judgments. This sort of judgment process is just the sort most frequently glorified as the basic underpinning of liberal civil society. At the same time, though, the "object" of such rational statistical discrimination entirely loses her individuality, her capacity to be differentiated on the basis of her true self-created uniqueness; the possibility (or myth) of the self-created individual emerging out of an undifferentiated (status-based) mass is equally central to the ideology of liberal culture, and therein lies the paradox for centrists. Second, centrists cannot resolve questions about whether to focus on discrimination as a wrong perpetrated by morally compromised bigots—in which case the rational statistical discriminator must be *contrasted* with the bigot—or as an injury experienced by members of a historically subordinated community—in which case the injuries of statistical discrimination loom quite large.

Because the opposition to rational statistical discrimination is not based on attacking economic irrationality at the firm level, however, it is not wholly comfortably embraced by mainstream centrism. The mainstream centrist position on statistical discrimination most clearly strains when confronted with practices that do not overtly statistically discriminate on the basis of group membership as such, but which nevertheless preclude disproportionate numbers of capable members of historically oppressed groups from receiving rewards they would receive if it were costless to identify each individual's talents.

Imagine, say, a psychological test that weakly predicts an applicant's proclivity to stay in the work force, which women fail in wildly disproportionate numbers: can the employer refuse to hire all those (men and women alike) who fail the test, knowing it has many false negatives (many who fail would, in fact, stay in the work force) and that such false negatives are concentrated among women? Is such a test any more acceptable than a decision not to hire women if it is known that it is generally true that women are (very marginally) less likely to stay in the work force? In the first instance, the screening is based on a psychological test, while in the second, stereotyping is applied to the group member qua group member, rather than the group member qua test failure. More realistically, can employers use relatively weakly predictive "general ability" job tests, knowing that African-Americans fare far worse on the tests, and that false negatives are therefore disproportionately high among blacks?

57. For a discussion of the belief that people are entitled to be paid in accord with their gross output, rather than their output net of differential costs of employing them (so long as the unusually costly inputs used for one group of workers would not help other groups of workers produce more as well), see Kelman, "Concepts of Discrimination" at 1198–1204.

58. For a Rehabilitation Act case making this holding, which appears obvious (though not as yet specifically litigated) under the ADA as well, see Nelson v. Thornburgh, 567 F. Supp. 369 (E.D. Pa. 1983), aff'd 732 F.2d 146 (3d Cir.

1984), cert. denied 469 U.S. 1188 (1985). In fact, firms need not always pay the incremental costs of accommodation: state agencies or private charities often finance accommodations. Thus, for instance, employers alone funded the full cost of accommodating only fourteen of the initial forty-seven workers placed by Palo Alto's Sensory Aids Foundation. See J. Frierson, *Employer's Guide to the Americans with Disabilities Act* 1001 (1992).

59. For a fuller discussion of "dynamic discrimination," see Kelman, "Concepts of Discrimination" at 1170–1183.

60. See, e.g., Young, *Justice and the Politics of Difference* at 200–206. For an application to the special education context, see, e.g., Harlan Hahn, "The Politics of Special Education," in *Beyond Separate Education: Quality Education for All* 225, 227–228 (D. Lipsky and A. Gartner eds., 1989).

61. The various positions we have thus far reviewed might better be understood by considering alternative reactions to typical academic economists' findings that women are paid some significant chunk less than men who work equal hours, with equal experience, education, and skills.

It is not simply the case that the right centrist predisposition is to accept the lowest numerical estimates of how much variance between male and female wages remains unexplained once one accounts for "measurable" differences in worker quality. More interesting from our vantage point is the right centrist belief that such "unexplained" variance is far more likely to reflect the social scientist/market interventionist's inability to measure true distinctions in worker quality than it is to reflect actual discrimination against women. Thus, for instance, right centrists will typically argue that when women, as a group, have the same "years of schooling" as men, they will have learned fewer (technical, mathematical) skills relevant to job performance.

At the same time, the "multiculturalist left" position is that "wage decomposition" equations that attempt to predict women's and men's earning functions on the basis of measurable quality traits understate true discrimination just as the right centrist belief is that they overstate it. The argument is that many of the factors that statistically correlate with higher wages for both women and men are valued not because they actually increase productivity but because men, with cultural hegemonic power, typically possess them. Thus, for instance, job continuity or availability at all hours may be valued because male career patterns (which permit greater levels of such continuity and availability) are valorized without regard to their actual effect on output.

The liberal centrist view is not only that the existing unexplained gap is a result of the unwarranted static discrimination (grounded in animus and stereotypes) that mainstream centrists agree the state is duty bound to eliminate, but also that levels of gender inequality could be decreased still further if workplaces were reorganized to permit the greater flexibility in the market that women frequently require, given strong social conventions about the division of household labor. Thus the liberal centrist view in this regard is that current arrangements are "dynamically discriminatory," i.e., they do not reward people in accord with the productivity they would manifest under more ideal conditions (assuming, for the moment only, that such "ideal" organizations are not perpetually more costly than current modes of organization). At the same time, the liberal centrist view might well be that women who could produce as much as men if, but only if, given certain *costly* inputs (e.g., on-site day care) are nonetheless entitled to pay based on gross, rather than lower net, output. The liberal centrist view, though, is distinct from the more politically radical position that given current work practices, the typical "male traits" are without genuine productive value (nor do the liberal centrists adopt the multiculturalist "distributive" claim we soon discuss in the text that women deserve rewards from the firm for "socially valuable" activity of little benefit to the firm).

62. See Christine Littleton, "Reconstructing Sexual Equality," 75 *California Law Review* 1279 (1987).

63. For an argument that coercion and illicit character-formation dominate women's experience of the workplace, see Vicki Schultz, "Telling Stories about Women and Work: Judicial Interpretations of Sex Segregation in the Workplace in Title VII Cases Raising the Lack of Interest Argument," 103 *Harvard Law Review* 1749 (1990).

64. Littleton, "Reconstructing Sexual Equality" at 1287–1291.

65. In our view, the last of these factors may well be the most important, especially, though by no means exclusively, in the context of disability rights. For a superb discussion of the degree to which identity groups seek resources to undo historical stigma, see Michael Piore, *Beyond Individualism* 36–44 (1995).

66. Thus "white workers" in deindustrializing cities may focus not exclusively on the loss of convertible commodities (income, housing) but on their inability to influence the decisions that dramatically affect their lives; plant-closing legislation and antigentrification rent control statutes may reflect group-based political mobilization against group powerlessness, rather than loss of goods. Gays proudly reclaiming demeaning labels (Queer Nation, for instance) are not seeking to smooth their access to goods (by, for instance, forbidding economically irrational discrimination which would harm them in material terms), but rather struggling against social marginalization, hostility, and (the risk of) introjected lack of self-respect.

67. Obviously, conservatives are prone to believe that taxes and transfers have dramatic incentives effects, while politically progressive observers typically believe that incentive effects are more muted. One can see this contrast whether one is talking about income taxes on the wealthy, implicit taxes levied through the reduction of welfare benefits, or the choice between market work and benefits receipt when "welfare" eligibility loosens. For high (politically conservative) estimates of negative labor supply effects caused by taxation, see, e.g., Jerry Hausman, "Labor Supply" in *How Taxes Affect Economic Behavior* 27 (Henry Aaron and Joseph Pechman eds., 1981); for a high estimate of the impact of the availabil-

ity of redistributive transfers on work decisions, see Charles Murray, *Losing Ground: American Social Policy, 1950–1980* (1984). For representative liberal responses, see, e.g., Barry Bosworth, *Tax Incentives and Economic Growth* 172–174 (1984); T. MaCurdy, D. Green, and H. Paarsch, "Assessing Empirical Approaches for Analyzing Taxes and Labor Supply," 25 *Journal of Human Resources* 415 (1990); David Ellwood and Lawrence Summers, "Poverty in America: Is Welfare the Answer or the Problem" in *Fighting Poverty: What Works and What Doesn't* 78 (S. Danziger and D. Weinberg eds., 1986).

68. See Epstein, *Takings* at 319–323. See also Russell Roberts, "A Positive Model of Private Charity and Public Transfers," 92 *Journal of Political Economy* 136 (1984).

69. To the degree that the advocacy movement is "outcome egalitarian" at all, it is only in the relatively trivial context of reforming the grading reward structure to dampen the inequalities that would result from ongoing use of unaccommodated exams.

70. See, e.g., Nozick, *Anarchy, State, and Utopia* at 238.

71. Id. at 155–160.

72. Id. at 158–160.

73. See Epstein, *Takings* at 344–346; Richard Epstein, "Toward a Revitalization of the Contract Clause," 51 *University of Chicago Law Review* 703 (1984); "Proceedings of the Conference on Takings of Property and the Constitution," 41 *University of Miami Law Review* 49, 122–123, 177–178 (1986).

74. Compare Epstein's nondeferential attitudes toward state property law decisions that interfere with "natural rights" with the deferential attitudes of the more Burkean Justice Rehnquist, who places a much higher value on the capacity of local institutions (local leadership?) to mediate potential problems of social disorder. Compare, for instance, Justice Rehnquist's opinion in PruneYard Shopping Center v. Robins, 447 U.S. 74 (1980) with Epstein's condemnation of the opinion in *Takings* at 65–66.

75. See John Hart Ely, *Democracy and Distrust: A Theory of Judicial Review* 152–160 (1980).

76. The special educators we interviewed often differed in their beliefs about the degree to which LD children should generally expect to be able to do the same things (educationally and vocationally) as non-LD pupils with similar IQs, aspirations, and cultural advantages. These beliefs would affect, directly or indirectly, their views about the forms of counseling that are appropriate to older pupils. Two broad themes in this regard seemed to emerge in our interviews: some of our informants expressed the view that a learning disability is a genuine handicap that limits what the pupil is likely to be able to do, even in a world that accommodates appropriately to difference. The role of the counselor, in a sense, is (a) to help the pupil identify his strengths and weaknesses, to compensate as well as he can for his weaknesses, but then to "play to his strengths" and (b) to support the pupil's self-esteem by urging him to judge himself favorably

while having a realistic sense that there are things that he does poorly, without disparaging these deficits as meaningless artifacts. One New York administrator told us:

> [We don't counsel much about how to cope in life given the learning problems] though we're concerned with the social and emotional problems that go with the learning disability. Many students are really relieved by the LD diagnosis [because it makes them feel] less stupid and more like they've got a very specific barrier to success which they can work around . . .
>
> The trickiest issue is how to keep people motivated while still making them aware of realistic limits. Their teachers, too often are passive ("they can't do anything, they've got an irremediable barrier") or angry ("they're just lazy and we're coddling them") and they're ignoring that the *effect* of an LD varies tremendously with student effort . . .
>
> We certainly don't tell dyslexics that they might be better off avoiding careers where they'll have to read a lot, but we think we help them realize that, so long as the decision they're making isn't too charged with negative self-esteem issues.

Other special educators expressed the view that the pupil with a learning disability has difficulty performing certain tasks that are traditionally done in a certain way by the non-LD, but that the underlying ends can generally be met through some alternative mechanism. Thus even if the pupil with a learning disability cannot be educated to do something the way his mainstream classmates do, he can virtually always find a substitute that is perfectly satisfactory so long as institutions do not mindlessly force conformity with traditional work modes. A different New York administrator told us: "Junior high and high school are the only time these disabilities should really get in these kids' ways. College students record classes comfortably and don't bother to fail at taking notes; secretaries and computers cover up for them in adult life." Thus, in his district, there is no attempt to urge pupils to adjust their plans to their disability since, in his view, they really don't have to, as long as they are aware of accommodation strategies and their entitlements to accommodations.

77. Images of the horror of blaming the victim abound in left multiculturalist thought in the legal academic world: see, e.g., Robert Mison, "Homophobia in Manslaughter: The Homosexual Advance as Insufficient Provocation," 80 *California Law Review* 133, 170–174 (1992); Anthony Chase, "Toward a Legal Theory of Popular Culture," 1986 *Wisconsin Law Review* 527, 548–552; Timothy Lytton, "Responsibility for Human Suffering: Awareness, Participation, and the Frontiers of Tort Law," 78 *Cornell Law Review* 470, 482–483 (1993).

78. See, e.g., Fernandez v. Wynn Oil Co., 653 F.2d 1273 (9th Cir. 1981).

79. See Arthur Larson and Lee Larson, *Employment Discrimination* vol. 1, §11.02(4) (2d ed. 1996).
80. One of the fullest and best defenses of the viewpoint embodied in the slogan is in Mark Brodin, "Costs, Profits, and Equal Employment Opportunity," 62 *Notre Dame Law Review* 318 (1987).
81. For an excellent argument consistent with the one we are making, in the context of reforming the ADA, see Jerry L. Mashaw, "Against First Principles," 31 *San Diego Law Review* 211 (1994).

Index